D1256904

Problems of the Psychology of Memory

MONOGRAPHS IN PSYCHOLOGY
an International Series

EXPERIMENTAL ABNORMAL PSYCHOLOGY
B. V. Zeigarnik • 1972

FUNDAMENTAL PROPERTIES OF THE HUMAN NERVOUS SYSTEM
V. D. Nebylitsyn • 1972

INNER SPEECH AND THOUGHT
A. N. Sokolov • 1972

PROBLEMS OF THE PSYCHOLOGY OF MEMORY
A. A. Smirnov • 1973

Problems of the Psychology of Memory

A. A. Smirnov
Director, Institute of Psychology
Academy of Pedagogical Sciences, Moscow
Professor of Psychology
Moscow State University and Moscow City Pedagogical Institute

Scientific and Translation Editor
Samuel A. Corson
Professor of Psychiatry and Biophysics
Director, Laboratory of Cerebrovisceral Physiology
The Ohio State University College of Medicine
Columbus, Ohio

Plenum Press • New York-London • 1973

Translation Panel: Justina Epp and Roland G. Dartau
Editorial Assistant: Judy W. Van de Geer

The translation and editing of this book was supported in part by Research Grant LM00635 from the National Library of Medicine, National Institutes of Health.

The British-American Standard Transliteration System has been followed

The original Russian text published by Prosveshchenie Press in Moscow in 1966. This translation is published under an agreement with Mezhdunarodnaya Kniga, the Soviet book export agency.

PROBLEMY PSIKHOLOGII PAMYATI

A. A. Smirnov

ПРОБЛЕМЫ ПСИХОЛОГИИ ПАМЯТИ

А. А. Смирнов

Library of Congress Catalog Card Number 72-83045
ISBN 0-306-30574-7

A Division of Plenum Publishing Corporation
227 West 17th Street, New York, N.Y. 10011

United Kingdom edition published by Plenum Press, London
A Division of Plenum Publishing Company, Ltd.
Davis House (4th Floor), 8 Scrubs Lane, Harlesden, London, NW10 6SE, England

Printed in the United States of America

EDITOR'S PREFACE

Contrary to popular opinion, contemporary psychology in the USSR is far from being monolithic. It is true that the development of Soviet psychology does have characteristic features which distinguish it from the development of Western (and particularly Anglo-American) psychology. Perhaps the most distinguishing features of Soviet psychology are represented by the predominance of the historical-evolutionary approach and the emphasis on integrative physiological mechanisms underlying behavior. The development of Soviet psychological thinking can also be characterized as having been free of the fruitless discussions of mind–body dualism and of dominance by rat-and-pigeon-centered behaviorism.

Soviet psychology had the benefit of a rich inheritance from the Sechenov–Botkin–Pavlov school that laid the foundation for modern psychobiology and biological psychiatry. Unfortunately, the politically engendered omnipresent dogmatism during the Lysenko–Stalin era of obscurantism tended to pervert this rich scientific heritage and hindered the development of a diversity of concepts and methods in the behavioral and biological sciences.

The past two decades have witnessed the development and flourishing of a number of distinct and fruitful approaches in Soviet psychology. In addition to the traditional Pavlovian school of higher nervous activity, one should mention the school developed by D. N. Uznadze in Georgia (theory of set), the system of abnormal neuropsychology or "defectology" developed by A. R. Luriya, the cybernetic and systems approach in psychobiology developed by P. K. Anokhin (the theory of the functional system), the ecophysiological ethology studies by A. D. Slonim, differential psychology developed by B. M. Teplov and V. D. Nebylitsyn, and studies of educational and developmental psychology and memory initiated by P. P. Blonskii and L. S. Vygotskii and developed particularly by A. N. Leont'ev and A. A. Smirnov.

This monograph by Professor Smirnov presents a critical review of the extensive investigations on memory and learning in children, adolescents, and adults conducted by the author and his many students and by other Soviet psychologists. Of particular interest to Western psychologists and educators should be investigations on retroactive inhibition and on comparative studies on involuntary and voluntary memory involving mnemonic devices.

Professor Smirnov is director of the Institute of Psychology of the Academy of Pedagogical Sciences in Moscow and editor of the prestigious Soviet periodical *Problems of Psychology*. He was the president of the organizing committee of the Psychological Society of the USSR.

I wish to take this opportunity to express my appreciation to Professor Ian Gregory, Dean John A. Prior, and Vice President for Medical Affairs Richard L. Meiling for their continuing interest in, and the provision of facilities for, our survey and translation project on "Psychophysiology and Psychosomatic Medicine in the USSR." To my wife and collaborator Elizabeth O'Leary Corson I am greatly indebted for lending her linguistic talents in the translation and editing of the manuscript. I am grateful to David Smith for his meticulous typing and proofreading of the manuscript.

Samuel A. Corson

Department of Psychiatry
The Ohio State University College of Medicine
Columbus, Ohio

AUTHOR'S PREFACE

The book includes publications by the author on problems of the psychology of memory The monograph *The Psychology of Memorization,* originally published in 1948, constitutes the main part of the book. For the present edition, the Introduction of the monograph has been rewritten. Additions have been made to several chapters, primarily to reflect the present status of the subjects discussed. No changes have been made in the experimental part of the monograph.

We have also included in the book the experimental investigation "Conditions for retroactive inhibition," originally published in *Scientific Reports of the State Research Institute of Psychology,* Vol. 1 (1940). The third section, "The interrelation of image and word in the development of memory," is an excerpt from the article "The development of memory" published in 1959 in the two-volume anthology *Psychology in the USSR.* It is a review of investigations of this problem by Soviet psychologists, including experimental investigations carried out under the direction of the author.

The section "On some correlations in the field of memory," published here for the first time, summarizes the results of a study recently conducted (1962–1966) by members of the laboratory headed by the author.

I am deeply grateful to K. P. Mal'tseva for her extensive help in preparing this book for publication. I am also very grateful to N. I. Balasheva for her active part in the work on the book.

A. A. Smirnov

CONTENTS

A. THE PSYCHOLOGY OF MEMORIZATION

THE PSYCHOLOGY OF MEMORIZATION

INTRODUCTION

1. INITIAL PROPOSITIONS

This work presents the results of investigations conducted by the author within the conceptual framework of Soviet psychology. The basic concepts which determined the problem and the orientation of the investigations are:

1. Cognition of reality is inseparably connected with life. The main content of man's life is his activity, and above all, his material, practical, and creative activity. It is activity and not passive contemplation which is the most important source of cognition and which is the criterion of the verity of man's knowledge. He perceives the surrounding world by reacting to it and changing it. The process of perception, its results, and the verification of its correctness also depend on the goals which man sets for himself in his activity, on the problems solved by him, and on the motives for and contents of his activity.

The cognitive processes are not only carried out but are also formed in human activity. "People who develop their material production and material association change along with it their thinking and the products of their thinking" (Marx and Engels, Vol. 3, p. 25).

The interdependence of consciousness and activity is one of the most important concepts of Soviet psychology and is the basis for the study of human psychology. Man's activity itself is understood to have objective reality as its source and determiner. "Man in his practical activity," wrote Lenin, "has before him the objective world, depends on it, and determines his activity by it" (Lenin, Vol. 29, pp. 169–170).

2. Human cognition, while always part of some kind of activity, is in itself a special kind of activity directed by goals, problems, and motives of cognition. It is activity which includes a great variety of mental actions and operations, means and methods of achieving the contemplated cognitive

goals, and quests for the solution to cognitive problems. "The reflection of nature in human thought must not be understood as 'dead,' 'abstract,' without movement, without contradictions, but rather as an eternal process of movement, an emergence of contradictions and their resolution" (Lenin, Vol. 29, p. 177).

In the process of cognition we are always acting, although some of our actions are of an "inner" intellectual nature, not apparent, and only known to ourselves. We are not a passive arena in which events occur or where processes take place which occur "within us" but seemingly "without us." In the process of cognition we ourselves are the acting subjects, deliberately executing various actions and operations and voluntarily choosing them for the achievement of set goals, for the solution of problems before us.

Man is an active worker in the process of cognizing reality and reflecting the objective world, and it is he who is active and not the individual processes of cognition. Cognition does not cognize, neither does thought think nor memory remember and recall—it is always man, a definite personality, that cognizes, thinks, remembers, and recalls. Therefore, to speak about the activity of cognitive processes in the literal sense of the word would mean their hypostasis, their transformation into special "substances," into a reality not dependent on man; it would mean separating them from man and understanding them regardless of what they are in reality.

"Everyone knows," wrote Lenin in criticizing the reactionary positions of Bogdanov, "what human sensation is, but sensation without man, before man, is nonsense, dead abstraction, idealistic vagary. In essence we have before us not the familiar, ordinary human sensations, but some kind of imagined ones, sensations *per se* which belong to no one, divine sensations, just as ordinary human thought became divine for Hegel, once it was separated from man and man's brain" (Lenin, Vol. 18, pp. 238–239).

The psychological process can be considered active only in the sense that in it the activity of a concrete subject, acting man, is revealed and manifest.

3. The preceding statements fully apply to the processes of human memory as an essential component of any cognitive activity. Memory processes, just as all cognitive processes (and even all mental processes) depend on the human activity within which they are executed, its goals and problems, its motives and specific content. At the same time, they themselves can function as a special kind of activity and constitute a special, mnemonic, human activity.

Thus, we have here a wide range of problems among which the following occupy an important place:

a. the dependence of memorizing and of its productivity on the presence or absence in the activity being performed of a special mnemonic problem, that is, the problem of memorizing the object of the activity. This is a problem of the relationship between two fundamental types of remembering: involuntary and voluntary; its solution requires in its turn a variation of the activity in which involuntary remembering takes place.

b. a description of the thought processes which occur for the purpose of remembering, since it is they that are the central component of mnemonic activity.

c. the problem of repetition, the positive role of which is well known, since it was convincingly shown by Pavlov that one of the most important prerequisites for the coupling of neural connections, i.e., for the physiological mechanism of memory, is the repeated pairing of stimuli and, consequently, also of the excitatory processes of stimulation during a certain period of time. This mechanism is the basis of both the "lower," more elementary and not transmitted, types of memory and the "higher," more complex types which are transmitted by thought activity and volitional processes Its "higher" types, the physiologic mechanisms of which are more complex (they are, nevertheless, mechanisms of temporary neural connections) are not separated from its "lower" types as asserted by Bergson (1911), but are executed in conjunction with them and develop from them and on their basis.

Memory mechanisms of the "higher" order by no means cancel out those of the "lower" order, they only complicate and, in a number of cases, alter them. The active and meaningful nature of memory does not exclude, therefore, the role of repetition. However, its essential uniqueness was determined on the "higher levels" of memory. Each repeated perception of what is remembered is, in these cases, a distinct activity and is carried out, not stereotypically and tritely, not in the same manner each time, but with a rather wide variety of executions. The variation of repetitions is a characteristic feature of active and meaningful human activity during memorization. This aspect of the problem of repetition will be examined in this book.

2. MEMORY THEORY IN NON-SOVIET PSYCHOLOGY

The problem of memory has attracted special attention in psychology and has been studied intensively. The number of experimental investigations in this field compares only with that of the study of perceptions and habits, which, incidentally, is closely related to the problem of memory.

However, in the large number of publications on memory the questions pointed out above concerning the dependence of memory processes on activity, the content of these processes themselves as a special kind of activity, and the uniqueness of repetitions at the higher levels of memorization have not received the attention appropriate to their actual significance.

In this context, the present work is not a broad survey and critical analysis of theoretical conceptions and experimental investigations in the field of memory. This problem has been successfully dealt with by Zinchenko in his monograph *Involuntary Memorization* (1961), in which the main theories of memory as well as the many experimental investigations in this field have been subjected to extensive examination and have received a correct theoretical evaluation. In non-Soviet survey literature specially pertaining to problems of memory and learning, in particular in the recently published works by Woodworth and Schlossberg (1954), McGeoch and Irion (1961), Hilgard (1956), and Hovland (1951), these problems have not been examined since they were not the object of study of the literature surveyed.

Here we shall briefly indicate that the above problems chosen for study (with a few exceptions which will be discussed in the course of our investigations) were not studied by other investigators because they did not fall within the scope of their theories.

The first attempts to study memory experimentally were made by representatives of associative psychology: Ebbinghaus (1885, 1912), Müller and Schumann (1893), Müller and Pilzecker (1900), Müller (1911–1915), and many others. This determined the basic direction for the study of memory during the first decades of investigation in this field and, in essence, still characterizes many investigations conducted by non-Soviet psychologists.

Among the representatives of associative psychology there were certain differences of opinion on memory. Some of them introduced seemingly different concepts (Müller, for example, proposed his theory of "complexes"). These differences were not great and of no real significance, since in actuality they did not influence the main direction of the investigations.

The major area of study common to all associationist investigations was the well-known study of the prerequisites for the formation, attenuation, and interaction of associations which are mechanistically understood as purely external, based only on the proximity in time and on the repetition of the connection between the individual elements of what has to be committed to memory.

Since the physiological mechanism of memorization involves establishing the coupling of temporary connections, and this is the formation of associations, the study of the latter is naturally not only completely justified, but also necessary. One cannot deny the significance of many investigations of the associationists which have revealed a number of important principles which also, to a certain extent, hold true when one is committing to memory more complex and qualitatively different material than that used in the majority of earlier investigations (and also many later ones) in the field of memory. Yet, the study of the mechanically formed connections, the almost complete disregard of complex mental activity (especially thought activity during memorization), the investigation of the dependence of memorization on only external conditions and especially on the number and organization of repetitions, the almost exclusive attention to the results of memorization, to quantitative indexes—all this must be considered as an erroneous direction taken by the associative psychology of memory.

The aspect of capacity in memorization as a special type of activity and the dependence of memorization on a larger activity into which it can be incorporated—these problems were not among those studied by the adherents of associative psychology.

It would be incorrect to assert that the associationists completely ignored a qualitative analysis of the processes of memory and were satisfied with only quantitative indexes of effectiveness of memorization and recollection. In a number of investigations one even finds a rather detailed analysis of memorization and reproduction. It is sufficient to mention Müller's three-volume work on memory (1911–1915), which is completely devoted to a qualitative analysis of mnemonic processes. However, the utilization and depth of such an analysis in the investigations of associationists were exceedingly limited due to the conceptual framework iteslf—all efforts in these investigations were directed towards a maximum simplification of activity on the part of the memorizer and towards a standardization and most strict regulation of the whole process of memorization.

In itself, this regulation is imperative in solving many questions and cannot be evaluated negatively. However, to restrict the investigations of memory to only such conditions as deprive the subject of the freedom of action greatly limits the content of mnemonic activity, renders it unrelated to what occurs under real-life conditions.

Thus, it can be said that the characteristics of memory processes revealed by the investigations of the associationists, although of some value, were far from revealing the true wealth of the "natural" mnemonic activity of man. The analysis of the thought processes utilized in memorization and reproduction was most adversely affected since the material presented to the subjects by the associationists usually did not require a thorough conceptual processing in order to be memorized. Those cases in which the subjects were given more complex material to memorize (meaningful texts) and which required a more diversified activity, including thought activity, were a rare exception. Kraemer's investigation (1911) conducted under the guidance of Meumann is almost the only one in which such material was used and where a qualitative analysis of memorization was given.

It is also characteristic of the associationists that instead of making a qualitative analysis of the *processes* of memory as a special kind of activity, one often finds in their works an analysis of the subject matter of reproduction, i.e., *what* was reproduced and not *how* memorization and reproduction were accomplished.

The strong opponents of the associationists, the gestaltists, who categorically deny the basic role of associations and repetition in the formation of memory processes, also failed to study these processes either in relation to the activity of the person who memorizes or as a special, mnemonic activity.

Although the gestaltists' theories differed from those of the associationists, they were no closer to the real questions involved in the study of memory processes. This is illustrated by their concept of memorization as the development of structures (*Gestalten*) and the theory that these structures are complete formations which cannot be reduced to a simple sum of their parts, the parts being properties of the material with which the subject has to deal. The genesis of the structure is organization, moreover "spontaneous," "autochthonous" organization or, more precisely, self-organization, of the material in accordance with the principles of proximity, similarity, "self-sufficiency," "good continuity," and "good form" which operate independently of the subject. The attraction of the parts of the whole to these principles is supposedly inherent, that is, the parts themselves "strive" towards the formation of a structure. These principles are the fundamental basis of structure formation and need no further substantiation or explanation. The comprehension of what is being memorized, as well as the advantage of memorizing meaningful material, is also interpreted from this point of view. Comprehension is also a spontaneous emergence of a structure due to the properties of the material itself; its self-organization, which is more perfect, establishes itself earlier and is more stable than the self-organization of meaningless material. This explains the advantage of meaningful memorization involving the comprehension of subject matter.

For the gestaltists, the active work of the subject, including thinking, is not the basis or the most important condition for memorization. The gestalt principles operate regardless of the subject's activity. He is indeed only the arena in which the actual laws of structure formation themselves are the true actors. Consequently, in regard to the memorizer's activity, the gestaltists and the associationists do not differ in any fundamental way.

Kurt Lewin's theory (1922, 1926) occupies a special place in gestalt psychology. Like the founders of gestalt psychology, Wertheimer (1945), Köhler (1929, 1933). and Koffka (1935), Lewin also proposes the principle of wholeness, or structuralness as a basic tenet. But, whereas the representatives of gestalt psychology always interpret the structure as a definite organization of the content of perceptions, memory, and thinking, Lewin, in developing his theory of actions (especially, voluntary actions), includes in their structure the memorizer also, or more correctly, his needs and intentions.

According to Lewin, there are dynamic interrelations between the subject and his environment, between him and what stimulates and at what his actions are oriented. Lewin considers the subject, his needs and intentions, as well as all external stimuli and objects of his actions, as forces affecting one another. The subject not only acts, but is himself an object of the action of external forces: demands coming to him from the outside, from the objects themselves which induce him to act, direct his actions, and are the objects of his actions. A complete "force field" is formed which varies in accordance with the changes in the state of forces entering into it, and is especially dependent upon the intensity of the needs and intentions of the subject. The character of such a dynamic field has influence on the productivity of the actions themselves, as well as on their resultant effect.

In the field of memory this is manifested in the influence which the force relationships—the tension or discharge in the force field—exert on the productivity of memorization. Characteristic of this is the better recollection of incomplete actions as compared with completed ones (as shown in the widely known investigation of B. V. Zeigarnik [1927]); when an action is incomplete, there remains a greater intensity of need than when an action is completed, resulting in a discharge or diminished need.

Like the concept of psychological processes advanced by Wertheimer, Köhler, and Koffka, the dynamic theory of actions proposed by Lewin ignores the role of the content of the activity itself. The actions of people are examined only in their dynamic, and to a certain extent formal aspect, and are regarded as the result of the interaction of forces in which the internal forces of the subject (needs and intentions) are, in essence, on the same plane as outside forces. The explanatory principle underlying this theory is the intensity of need and motives, the dynamics of action and not its content, not what man *does* and what in itself can determine the intensity of his needs and motives, that is, the condition of the "force field."

Although the gestaltists rejected the main concepts of associative psychology concerning the dependence of mental processes on activity and the significance of these processes as a special type of activity, their position on these questions turned out to be fundamentally similar to those of the associationists. The behaviorist position is even closer to the theories of the associationists.

In spite of some major differences among the behaviorists, their basic approach is the same. Some behaviorists completely deny the existence of consciousness, others contend that it is unfathomable, and still others claim that it does not play an active role in behavior. Although divergent, these positions all lead to the same result, that is, the study of behavior isolated from the qualitative aspect of mental activity.

Watson (1924) takes an extreme position and claims that connections originate mechanically as a result of proximity and frequency of repetitions. More than those of other investigators, his theories approach those of the associationists, and in a certain sense he goes even further, reducing all of mental activity, including thinking, to visible body movements and to visible or hidden speech ("laryngeal") habits. He completely rejects even the possibility of studying states of consciousness, which in his words "can never become the object of truly scientific investigation."

The elucidation of the principles of memory ("verbal acquisitions" according to Watson) is reduced to the exposition of the purely quantitative indexes obtained in the experiments of Ebbinghaus and several other extreme behaviorists. Guthrie (1935, 1940) considers temporal proximity most important in the formation of connections; however, he rejects the paramount role of repetition. According to Guthrie, connections between stimulus and reaction are formed immediately, automatically, after the first reaction to a given stimulus. Repetition becomes necessary only because in subsequent presentations the stimulus can be somewhat different from the original one and, therefore, the original reaction to it may not occur. To avoid this, the given reaction must be established over a certain range of variations of the stimulus and, therefore, repetition is necessary. Such a theory completely eliminates not only the need, but even the possibility of active participation on the part of the subject.

As opposed to Watson and Guthrie and some others, many behaviorists believe that neither proximity nor frequency of repetition of a stimulus are sufficient conditions for the appearance of connections between a given stimulus and reaction. In their opinion, *reinforcement* of the reaction to the stimulus is necessary. This theory is illustrated in Thorndike's (1914, 1931, 1932) law of effect in which he also points out the important role of the association (belonging) of the stimulus and the reaction, without which a connection cannot be formed. A similar opinion is held by such outstanding behaviorists as Hull (1943, 1951, 1952), Skinner (1938, 1940, 1959), and a number of others. Even though in man reinforcement can be manifested in his *being conscious* of the correctness or incorrectness of a given reaction to a presented stimulus, the behaviorists do not regard it as conscious *activity* on the subject's part, in which he chooses and stabilizes the correct reaction himself. The behaviorists, while acknowledging the important role of reinforcement in the formation of connections, do not consider it in this particular capacity. The content aspect of activity that follows the reinforcement is not a subject of investigation and is not utilized to elucidate the "mechanism" of the action of reinforcements.

Tolman (1932), another behaviorist, describes the formation of significant (symbol) structures that encompass the symbol and what it designates, i.e., that which is to be connected and which is a necessary condition of learning. Although he acknowledges the important role of these structures, he does not describe how they are formed, that is, the activity of the subject due to whom they originate. Thus, Tolman's theory, in this respect, has the same shortcomings as those found in gestalt psychology.

It should also be noted that the behaviorists, because of external behavioral isomorphism and other shared characteristics of man and animals, used only animals in their investigations and not human subjects, thereby precluding any study of the learning process that is particular to man.

Freud's (1898) concept of memory is also far removed from the true nature of mnemonic activity. His concept of memory is based on his "pleasure principle," that is, that the pleasure drive is at work in the subconscious. Anything not related to the pleasure drive tends to be expelled from the consciousness and forgotten. The active agent is not man, but rather the emotional coloration of that which affects him, this coloration being due to whether it does or does not conform to the subconscious drive of the ego. There is no special activity of the subject consciously directed toward remembering or recalling, nor is reference made to the dependence of the memory process on man's total experience, since Freud accords the most important role to *unconscious* drives in human behavior.

Freud's hypothesis that one forgets that which is unpleasant was questioned and it inspired a considerable number of investigations on the influence of positive and negative emotions on remembering and retention. However, the results of these numerous investigations were contradictory and provided no clear answer to the problem. This is quite understandable, since memorization depends not only on the emotional coloration of the material being memorized, be it pleasant or unpleasant, but also on its particular content and significance for the individual. In these investigations emotions were evoked by diverse stimuli: words and sentences, colors and odors, facts and events from the personal life of the subject. However, the nature and strength of these stimuli can vary greatly, and, in turn, affect the rate of memorization and its stability. It is especially important to note that all these investigations ignored the effect of the subject's *activity* evoked by a particular emotional coloration of a stimulus, including his mnemonic activity which is specifically used in retention. The influence of emotions was studied also divorced from the activity in which and because of which these emotions originated (aside from its goals, problems, and motives, its specific content and results of actions). The emotions were regarded as acting independently, although in reality they always arise under conditions of some kind of activity, are caused by it, depend on it, and in turn themselves exert an influence on it. All this was ignored in these investigations.

A few psychologists take a somewhat different attitude towards the problem of memory as activity. However, their work, which is not widely known, basically amounts to postulates not supported by extensive factual and experimental data. For example, Janet (1928) viewed memory as an action which is formed in the process of social and historical development—"invented by man during his progress" and "quite different from simple and automatic repetition."

The nature of this action differs at the various stages in the development of memory, but the characteristic common to all of these stages is the struggle with the absence of past experience, since memory, according to Janet, wants to triumph over the absence of the past. At first this is expressed by an expectation that what once was will appear again, and then by the search for it. This gives way to a delayed action or postponement of an action which would be executed upon the appearance of that which is presently absent. The next stages are *commission* and *verbal commission* which also must be executed after a certain time and at the onset of specific conditions. Finally, the last to appear are those manifestations of memory which are social in nature and most characteristic of man: recitation by heart, description, and narration. Janet does not furnish any experimental evidence to support this "structure" of consecutive stages of the development of memory but it indicates his desire to relate the historical development of memory to changes in the nature of human activity in the process of memorization and reproduction. This characteristic distinguishes his theory from those discussed previously.

The theories advanced by Bartlett (1932) and Stern (1930) occupy a special place in the theory of memory. Like Janet, Bartlett emphasizes the socially-conditioned nature of human memory. Memorization and recall are determined by the set of an individual, his interests, other characteristics, and his social group. However, Bartlett incorrectly interprets the true role of these individual sets, implying that recall is simply a constructive justification of an attitude or set of an individual. Thus, recall is not so much a reflection of objective reality as a justification of the individual aspects of the person to whom the sets refer. He states that "to a great extent, human recall under normal conditions is subject to errors" (1932, p. 176) and that "an exact reproduction is an exception and not the rule" (1932, pp. 61 and 93).

According to Stern, the function of recall is to "guarantee an individual his past experience in a form acceptable and essential to him" (Stern, 1930, p. 359). Memory is subservient to our "ego." Stern's theories are similar to those of Nietzsche, who said, " 'I did this,' memory said to me. 'But I could not have done this,' pride told me and was adamant, and memory had to yield to it." Thus, memory does not reflect objective reality but rather distorts it, so as to please an individual's ego, including his pride, vanity, and ambition.

Stern believes that this is especially true in children, whose recollections are often based on a certain "magical reality." He described a "primitive magic" exemplified by the "fantastic fabrications" of children in regard to their past experience (Stern, 1930, p. 376) and goes so far as to say that a young child cannot differentiate between reality and his fabrications. He carries this theory further, stating that this subordination of memory to subjective experience is also, to a great extent, true in adults.

It is evident that this entire concept is extremely idealistic and diverges from fact. Furthermore, Stern's theory fails to differentiate between man's particular individuality and that of plants and animals, thereby reducing its qualitative importance.

Among the experimental investigations on involuntary and voluntary memorizing and their interrelationship, a considerable number of them came close to discussing the problem of the dependence of memory processes on activity. Stern's investigations (1903–1904, 1904–1906) into the reliability of witness testimony were the first studies dealing with involuntary memorizing. These investigations were performed under natural conditions.

Later, various comparative studies of involuntary and voluntary memorization were conducted. Individual differences were examined in both cases. The relationships between reproduction and recognition in both types of memorizing were elucidated, as were differences in the involuntary memorization of meaningful and uncorrelated material. The role of self-instruction, or latent instruction, was investigated extensively. Many other problems were studied.

The majority of such studies have been made in recent years, after the publication of our works (Smirnov, 1945*a*, 1945*b*, 1948) and those of Zinchenko (1939–1964). A summary of these studies will be given when we present the results of our investigations later in this book. Here we will restrict ourselves to a general evaluation of them. Although the investigations present much factual data, they are somewhat limited in scope. Only one characteristic that distinguishes involuntary memorizing from voluntary memorizing, i.e., the presence or absence of a mnemonic task, was varied — not the content and nature of the activity which involved involuntary memorizing. Yet the relationship between the two types of memorization can depend greatly on the degree of this activity and the significance of the material to be remembered. In their investigations, Soviet psychologists have shown the special significance of activity in involuntary memorizing and the diverse and complex relationship between voluntary and involuntary memorization.

3. MEMORY IN RUSSIAN PREREVOLUTIONARY PSYCHOLOGY (I. M. SECHENOV AND K. D. USHINSKII)

In prerevolutionary Russian psychology the two names that are important are K. D. Ushinskii and I. M. Sechenov, psychologists who emphasized the role of activity and intelligence in memorization. Sechenov (1947) ascribed primary importance in the function of memory to a correct "organization of traces" of impressions we receive, to a well-organized "mental habit," in which all that has been perceived in past experience "is distributed not uselessly, but in a definite order, like books in a library." Everything that we learn is stored in the "register of memory" under specific headings (parts belonging to a whole according to similarity of objects and phenomena, etc.). "The greater the number of various relationships, the greater the number of points of contact a given thing has to other objects, the greater is the number of directions in which it is registered in the memory, and *vice versa*" (1947, p. 438). Sechenov calls this process the "processing of raw impressions in a conceptual direction" (1947, p. 357). He describes how this "processing" is carried out "in the recesses of memory, outside of consciousness without any participation of the mind or will "(1947, p. 356). He maintains that a child organizes a "mental habit" and that even a "3–4 year old child knows how to analyze objects, compare them, and draw conclusions about their interrelations" (1947, p. 439). In addition he states that "in the realm of learning, only assimilated and comprehensible material can be reproduced. Exact duplication is secondary in this case and the sense of what has been heard is of primary importance" (1947, p. 447).

Furthermore, in Sechenov's opinion, "the repetition of impressions and the ability to remember them are as closely related as cause and effect."

Sechenov further states: "If mental experience is given the form of what is to be remembered, then in this form it becomes especially clear that *its development is rooted in the repetition of impressions under the greatest possible diversity of conditions of perception, both subjective and objective"* (1947, p. 442).

Repetition, since it is the basis for memorizing, must not be stereotyped and should be varied within quite broad limits.

Similarly, Ushinskii (1950*a*, 1950*b*) affirms the important role of repetition as one of the bases for memorizing. He describes two types of repetition: passive repetition (the subject is passive and perceives again what he perceived earlier) and active repetition (the subject plays an active role and reproduces independently impressions perceived previously). Ushinskii emphasizes the much greater efficiency of active repetition. He also notes the necessity for variation in repetition: "There is no need to repeat in a precise order what has been learned; varied combinations of the same material are more useful" (1950*b*, p. 427).

Ushinskii asserts that remembering "is work and sometimes not easy, and that a child must be trained gradually to do it since the cause of forgetfulness is often laziness to remember the forgotten" (1950*b*, p. 429). He regards the process of memorization as the formation of associations, but in his view associations are by no means based only on proximity (in time and space), but also include logical associations, emotional associations, and quite-special developmental associations.

According to Ushinskii, we make rational associations when "we relate memory traces according to inner logical necessity, as, for example, when we relate a cause to its respective effect, a means to a certain goal, a whole to its *necessary* part, etc." (1950*a*, p. 358). Obviously, rather complex conceptual processes must be used in the formation of such associations.

Ushinskii states that a mechanical association is not transformed into a rational one by simply complicating the mechanical association by increasing the number of paths leading from the initial link of the connection to the final one, but by substituting one basis of connection (for example, the sequence of time or unity of place) for the other—the logical necessity of connection. "Two consecutive phenomena," he says, "the appearance of spring warmth and the appearance of grass, can be related at first as a purely mechanical association of time. This very same mechanical association can be transformed into a rational association by recognizing the cause in the one and the effect in the other" (1950*a*, p. 358).

Ushinskii purports "the basis, the main cause, the chain of associations" in rational associations to be the intellect (reason). The conversion of mechanical associations into rational ones is exceptionally important according to Ushinskii. He says: "The intellectual activity of humans consists of converting mechanical associations in time and place into rational ones, some rational associations into other rational ones, connecting individual rational associations into general ones, and relating the most precise and broad observations and discoveries of science" (1950*a*, p. 361).

These premises also lead Ushinskii to draw practical pedagogical conclusions. He writes, "Of course it is taken for granted that the educator accepts man as an integrated organism and, while enriching the mechanical memory with traces of associations, he at the same time exercises reasoning over these associations and prepares material for the future development of the child" (1950*b*, p. 432). At the same time, Ushinskii emphasizes the importance of the student's independent thinking: "Even if one assumes that the student understands the idea explained to him by the teacher, he will never commit it so firmly to memory as when he himself reasons it out" (1950*b*, p. 422).

Ushinskii assigns an important role to emotional associations, which are based on an emotional attitude towards what enters into the association and play a substantial part in the moral development of personality and in the moral influence of what is remembered. "If what is memorized by children," writes Ushinskii, "does not evoke any feeling, desire, and inclination in them, what has been memorized cannot have any *direct* influence on their morals; but if reading and learning *touch the heart,* then the memory trace will contain a combination of concepts with feelings, desires, and inclinations which will be retained more firmly in the memory. When such a complex *trace* rises to consciousness, it will evoke not only an idea, but also a desire, inclination, and feeling" (1950*a*, p. 400).

Ushinskii also describes a close relationship between remembering and one's inner life: "The less a man has lived an inner life, the less integrated is the network of his memories. In an underdeveloped person, memories are stored in separate disconnected series and groups; in the reflective person who sorts and examines his memories, the material is woven together into a net of meaningful experience, into an overall interpretation of all his experience into a world view" (1950*a*, pp. 388–389).

Associations made during human growth and development play an especially important role in personality development. This is how Ushinskii characterizes them: "Let us assume that a child has committed to memory some verses in a foreign language; consequently, he committed to memory only sounds in their sequence. Consciousness, of course, participated in his memorization. Without participation of attention, the child would not have heard the sounds, without the participation of reason, he would not have perceived their differences and similarities and consequently would not have mastered them in sequence. However, the role of consciousness was passive. Eventually, the nerves master the mechanical habit to pronounce the memorized verses and consciousness participates even less, enabling the child to pronounce the verses while thinking of something else. Let us assume that the child, after some time, learns the language in which the verses are written and translates them literally word for word. He now understands the concept of each word, but not the idea expressed by the series of words. At this point, the less mechanical association of understood words comes to the aid of (is added to) the former mechanical association of sounds. But, through practice, these series of words too become only a mechanism. Let us now assume that the child, as he grows older, understands the thought expressed in the words, but that the thought is so foreign to him that it remains an isolated entity in his mind. This thought, when often repeated, will once more become a mechanism. An unexpected stimulus might evoke the memory, but the idea will die within the child without consequence. Let us finally assume that the child has become a youth and a *question* has matured within him to which the idea enclosed in the verses is the answer, or a feeling has matured for which the memorized verses will be a more complete poetic expression. The grain enclosed in the verses, freed from all its casings, will enter the *spiritual* memory of the youth, not in the form of verses of words, not even in the form of the idea expressed in the words, but in the form of a new *spiritual strength,* so that the youth, not at all thinking about these verses, not even remembering the idea in them, will after mastering them look upon everything with somewhat different eyes, he will feel in a somewhat different manner, will want not quite what he wanted before, in other words, he has developed one step higher" (1950*a*, pp. 363–364).

These concepts proposed before the experimental period in the history of psychology, almost one hundred years ago, were not based on broad experimental material and are of a very general nature. Certainly, some of Sechenov's and Ushinskii's views are antiquated. Some of what Ushinskii proposes is definitely idealistic, as, for example, his theory of a higher type of memory, the spiritual memory. However, as a whole their major theories are to a great extent in harmony with the main concepts of Soviet psychologists and have received further development and experimental corroboration in their investigations.

Having as a basis of their work dialectical materialism, the Marxist–Leninist theory of reflection, Soviet psychologists still find many valuable ideas in the leading representatives of Russian psychology of the period prior to Marx.

4. CONCEPTS OF MEMORY IN SOVIET PSYCHOLOGY (P. P. BLONSKII AND L. S. VYGOTSKII)

The two concepts of memory in Soviet psychology that should be examined are those of P. P. Blonskii and L. S. Vygotskii. Both theories are rooted in the dialectical-materialistic conception of the mind and solve the problem of the development of memory by considering questions of the *development* of mental processes or mental functions to be of primary importance. Both, from their dialectical-materialistic viewpoint, reveal the qualitative uniqueness of memory at its various stages of development. Yet, both develop a different solution to the problem.

In his major work, Blonskii (1935, 1936) describes the successive developmental stages of memory as *motor, affective, image,* and *verbal,* focussing his attention on the last two. This qualitative classification is Blonskii's most important contribution in the field of memory.

According to Blonskii, such classification is necessary in any scientific study of memory; he considers a word such as "association" somewhat ambiguous: "from a certain point of view, anything at all can be called a 'connection' or, by extending common usage, 'association,' but this looks more like word stretching than scientifically valid conclusions" (1964, p. 406). He believes that *what* precisely connects or associates with what, that is, what kind of association is made in a particular instance, must be clearly defined.

In his discussion of "image memory," Blonskii describes those visual image impressions that are easily and clearly remembered. If the image is clear, it is easier to remember. If the emotional coloration of an image impression produces a strong effect, remembering is facilitated. Small, rapidly moving objects contemplated for an extended period of time are also more easily remembered. Furthermore, the state of the subject influences "image memory." Remembering images is easier if the man's conscious level is lower or in a dozing state than when he is wide awake. The absence of muscle tension and the passivity of the subject are also conducive to remembering. Blonskii states that "movement and images are antagonists" (1964, p. 350).

Yet, he notes that the images themselves are mobile, dynamic, and variable. Under pathological conditions where great nervous shock occurs, an image persists over a long period of time, but under normal conditions, the life of an image is usually short. Blonskii points out that in his experiments it was most often of such short duration that his subjects, who were speaking rather slowly, had just enough time to describe the images, almost without pausing.

An image is not a frozen photograph; it usually changes continually. Two basic types of change occur: transformation and reintegration of images.

Blonskii's subjects compared transformation to a multiplication process, describing it in these terms: Some parts of the image fade, others become clear, and the form of the object gradually changes (for instance, the object becomes round or enlarges). Sometimes the position of the object changes (for instance, a vertical position becomes horizontal). As a result of these numerous changes, a new image is formed in which, however, the original image is easily discernible. The image sometimes multiplies into similar ones. This multiplication sometimes creates the impression that the object is moving. In a number of cases, quite fantastic images emerge. Sometimes, however, the image "fades" into darkness, disappears, "the image dies" because of the subject's movements, unpleasant emotions, the appearance of a new stimulus, or the fact that the transformed image is very different from the original one.

Reintegration, the second form of image change, involves restoring an image of a whole object or whole situation from the image of one of its parts. Reintegration is a genuine memory process, while transformation is, according to Blonskii, "that which is commonly known as imagination." Nevertheless, he regards "image memory" as only one form of imagination (1964, p. 356), since by imagination he means "manipulation of images" (1964, p. 367).

Blonskii supposes a relationship to exist between his two forms of image change and *association by similarity and contrast* and *association by contiguity* (time or place). In his opinion, association by similarity and contrast is merely what he defines as a transformation of images. He feels that in order to prevent serious error it is imperative to introduce this concept in place of, or as an elaboration of, the concept of "association" or "connection." He denies the existence of certain stable "concepts" that evoke other similar concepts in the consciousness. He purports that, in reality, association by similarity and contrast involves changing an original image. It is not a case of the connection of various phenomena, but the changing of one phenomenon. Thus, Blonskii considers these particular concepts of associative psychology to be clearly mechanical and metaphysical (1964, p. 362).

According to Blonskii, there is less discrepancy between his concept of reintegration and association by contiguity and, therefore, less chance for confusion in the future. In the case of reintegration one can indeed speak of previously formed connections that are at a given time being restored. But, in Blonskii's opinion, "reintegration" is a more explicit term than "association" or "connection."

In a more detailed description of "image memory," Blonskii, drawing from his own experimental data, states that over a prolonged period of repeated reproduction from memory there is a tendency to *simplify* an image, to *merge* different images, and to *exaggerate* objects or their individual parts. Simplification leads to schematization, that is, an image becomes a schematic image. Merging facilitates generalization of this scheme and the emergence of a general concept. Exaggeration, however, can lead to a certain symbolization, since a particular part of the image is hypertrophied and the emerging image becomes a symbol. In many cases, there is also a fragmentation of images.

Blonskii feels that all these characteristics of images are utilized in creative imagination and poetic fantasy. All poetic composition and the various tropes: metaphor, metonymy, and synecdoche originate from them. Indeed, memory and the imagination overlap. "Reproduction is the point of departure for the work of the imagination," states Blonskii (1964, p. 376).

Blonskii distinguishes between two types of reproduction from memory. The first type is spontaneous remembering in which there is no active participation of consciousness or of the subject. The second type is remembering as a "conscious act and supposes that the subject is aware that he is just reproducing from memory" (1964, p. 376).

The first type of reproduction develops into fantasy in its basic form which originates also without the participation of consciousness and volitional efforts, while the second type develops into creative fantasy, into conscious and intentional poetic creativity.

In his discussion of the relationship between "image memory" and the creative imagination, Blonskii points out that the images that are the "best and clearest are those reproduced of uncommon objects and not those met with on a daily basis" (1964, p. 380). Thus, this limited number of stored uncommon images renders the "image memory" somewhat incomplete.

"Visual memory in itself is of little use as memory," states Blonskii (1964, p. 381), and is much better utilized in the creative imagination. The schematism and "commonness" of some images are advantageous to the memory, but not to imagination. Conversely, the artist's genius lies in knowing how to utilize clear, individual images, in both their *conscious* and *voluntary* reproductions.

According to Blonskii, the same relationship that exists between "image memory" and the imagination exists between verbal memory and thinking. Verbal memory traces its origin back to the time when an individual narrated an incident occurring in the past in the form of an acted-out story. Its verbal expression was supplementary to the actions the narrator performed. This kind of acted-out story is an early example of reproduction from memory. Since at this time in history speech was in one of its earliest stages, the stories were acted out in maximum detail from memory to ensure comprehension.

Later in history, as speech was developed, the roles of action and speech were reversed. Whereas actions were initially accompanied by words, later on words were accompanied by actions. Still later, these actions became only supplementary to speech to give it added expressiveness.

Although it had taken on an altogether verbal quality, this type of memory was still a form of reproduction from memory. This characteristic of verbal memory is, according to Blonskii, generally typical of it. In any case, he closely links one of the types of verbal memory, just because of this characteristic and the highly important role of repetition, with motor habits and regards it as one of their special varieties, as verbal habits which, although they are, of course, not identical with manual habits, are, nevertheless, similar to them since in both cases repetition is the most important condition of memorization.

Blonskii separates verbal memory into several more forms: *narration from reproduced images, verbal reproduction of visual material, and verbal reproduction of verbal material.*

In the case of narration from reproduced images, the verbal transmission of material perceived previously is based on image reproduction. These images emerge neither chronologically nor logically, and the story is disconnected and "skips back and forth." Frequently the narrator describes very minor points in minute detail in an attempt to convey his visual image as clearly and completely as possible. It should also be noted that these accounts are variable. After a comparatively short time, a new variation of the same story is related.

Verbal reproduction of visual material is generally straightforward and unembellished. According to Blonskii's data, such accounts abound with descriptions of actions and with reproduced sentences. Usually they are reports of what was said and done. On the whole, such accounts are short and condensed. They are chronological and describe the same phenomenon in a relatively consistent manner.

Verbal reproduction of visual material often corresponds very little to the original material. Details are omitted, events and structure are simplified, the original material is sometimes transformed into something more familiar, or embellished. This description is reminiscent of Bartlett's qualitative analysis of such changes as so-called serial reproduction. However, Blonskii does not agree with Bartlett's assertion concerning the gradual rationalization of reports which are repeated many times. Blonskii contends that the fantastic nature of the story that Bartlett presented for reproduction made it necessary for the subject to rationalize it.

Since narration from memory is a form of communication between people, it is socially regulated. Blonskii states that "during verbal reproduction of material that has been heard, there is a dual relationship between the narrator and the person from whom he has heard the story and between the narrator and the listener. The first demands a faithful reproduction, while the second, the listener, demands a reproduction that is interesting to him" (1964, p. 425). Thus, the narrator is obligated to render a faithful reproduction and, at the same time, select the most important details from the original story. Blonskii then points out that "such a reproduction already verges on thinking (thought)." However, a more accurate statement of the relationship might be that the boundary between memory and thinking (thought) disappears completely and that memory merges with thinking.

A similar situation occurs in verbal reproduction of visual material. Although the narrator in this case strives for a maximum detailed reproduction, his listeners usually demand only those details interesting and important to them. The question of the interrelationship of memory and thinking thus emerges as a very important problem of psychology.

Blonskii asserts that "the junction of remembering and thinking occurs in the sphere of internal speech." He states that listening "even in phylogenesis was very likely not merely listening but also repetition" (1964, p. 451), which served as the source of subsequent verbal reproduction. While we listen, we memorize the material being heard by means of internal speech (words, sentences, stories, etc.) and consequently the thoughts being expressed are transformed into objects of verbal memory. *Here thinking becomes memory.*

However, the reverse also takes place: *the transformation of memory into thinking*. In this connection, Blonskii discusses memory's role in the *formation of concepts,* a development that passes through *three stages*. In the first stage the concepts are incidental, superficial, and unimportant, and thinking is most closely linked to involuntary attention and the imagination. In the second stage there is an intimate relationship between verbal memory and verbal habits and thinking. The concepts reflect similarities and invariables and are often metaphysical. It is only in the third stage that memory plays no role at all. At this level, the thought processes operate with opposites and contradictions and take on a dialectical nature, completely displacing verbalism and the conservatism of memory. Blonskii describes these particular characteristics of memory as actual obstacles to the thought processes and implies that he no longer considers them to be the only foundation upon which all thinking is built, as had been believed until his time.

Memory also plays an important role in basic reasoning. Elucidation entails rendering the unknown known and requires reliance on memory; therefore, initially, reasoning involves remembering rather than thinking. References to examples, i.e., simple recollections of past incidents, are important in early reasoning (explanations and proofs), particularly in children. Consequently, the memory prepares the ground for its eventual replacement by reasoning, a substitution which occurs only at a specific stage in the development of the memory processes. "An empty head," writes Blonskii, "does not reason: the greater experience and knowledge this head has, the more capable it is of reasoning" (1964, p. 470).

In daily life, a seeming division frequently appears to take place between thought and memory. For example, one does not think about a familiar action or known and comprehensible phenomena, but on the other hand, in a new, unfamiliar, and incomprehensible situation one concentrates one's thoughts. However, this split occurs only in specific cases, i.e., when remembering involves habits and recognition. Otherwise, there is actually an intimate relationship between remembering and thinking. The memory assists the thought processes, and, likewise, thinking exerts a very strong influence on memory. "The thought processes," Blonskii states, "actively participate in the process of remembering; they give meaning to the material being committed to memory, discover and establish connections in it, and act as a check on the accuracy of the memorization" (1964, p. 482). Recall, a process which often involves the restoration of forgotten material with the aid of thinking (1964, p. 486), is a good illustration of the influence of thought over memory. Blonskii analyzes it as an active, voluntary act in another of his works (1940 and 1964).

Blonskii's several postulates are a valuable contribution to the *qualitative analysis* of the mnemonic processes, especially his description of image and verbal memory as higher stages in the development of memory.

Vygotskii's *cultural–historical theory of mental development* is another important contribution in the field of Soviet psychology. According to this theory, modern, civilized human behavior results from two different processes of mental development: the *biological evolution* of animals and their *historical*

development. In phylogenesis these processes develop separately and independently, whereas in ontogenesis they merge and form one single process. Vygotskii states: "A child's cultural development occurs simultaneously with his physical maturation. The physical and the cultural development concur and fuse. Both series of changes interpenetrate and essentially form a single thread of sociobiological personality development" (1960, p. 47).

Historical development, in other words, is cultural development or the development of *higher mental functions*. Man works out symbols during his cultural development which serve to regulate behavior or master a specific kind of behavior. Vygotskii writes: "In the course of his social development, man created and perfected complex systems of psychological connections (relationships) without which neither work nor social activity would be possible. Symbols, i.e., artificial stimuli, are the means for these connections. These artificial stimuli form new conditioned connections in the brain and influence behavior" (1960, p. 113). Symbolization is a new principle for controlling human behavior (1960, p. 120). The invention and use of symbols is characteristic of human cultural development. This is what transforms *directly* occurring mental processes into *indirect* mental activity. Vygotskii states: "The structure of civilized behavior is based on indirect activity, that is, the use of external symbols as a means for the further development of behavior" (1960, p. 201). These symbols become a psychological tool and assist in all mental operations. As a stimulus they help man execute activity (1960, p. 121). Under certain conditions, neutral stimuli can become such stimuli. For example, a person faced with an unsolvable problem incorporates entirely neutral stimuli into his behavior and these stimuli acquire a symbolic function (1960, p. 161).

The use of symbols influences both an individual's behavior and that of others. Symbols first influence others and then become a means for influencing oneself, thus illustrating the general rule, "through others we become ourselves." This statement refers not only to the personality as a whole, but also to each individual function of it (1960, p. 196). According to Vygotskii, every higher mental process first passes through an "external" or "social" stage of development. Subsequently, it is manifested psychologically, becoming *intrapsychological*.

Vygotskii sees the development of the memory, i.e., the appearance of its higher forms, as similar to the development of the higher psychological functions. Memory is essentially active memorization with the help of symbols (1960, p. 120). The first stage in the development of the cultural memory can be compared to the act of "tying a string around one's finger," an action that is sometimes actually performed in some situations. Here, man is employing an artificial stimulus, an object, to influence his remembering as well as his reproduction from memory. Eventually, this artificial stimulus is replaced by a word, a verbal stimulus which plays the same role as a symbol.

How is memorization accomplished through these stimuli? Vygotskii's experiments have shown that in human ontogenetic development this kind of memorization is not achieved immediately, but rather gradually through the transition from the initial, "natural" stage of memory to its higher, refined forms.

In experiments conducted with six–eight-year-olds, each child was given several pictures and told to press a particular button for each picture shown. The children usually made many mistakes when required to respond to each picture, and it was almost impossible for them to remember which button corresponded to a particular picture. In this situation memorization was "natural." In subsequent experiments, in order to facilitate memorization and to establish a relationship between each picture and its corresponding button, the children were offered *external* means. Another set of pictures was introduced, each of which was pasted on a particular botton. Thus, in order to respond appropriately to a given picture, the child had to associate these pictures with the pictures pasted on the corresponding buttons. Such an association was easily made, since each pair of pictures was related by meaning (horse—sleigh, etc). This time the children's responses were accurate.

However, this did not necessarily mean that the children had fully mastered this new form of memorization, i.e., indirect memorization with the aid of pictures. This fact was illustrated when the pictures on the buttons were rearranged and the meaningful relationship between the pictures was disturbed. For example, a picture of a knife was substituted for the picture of the sleigh on the button that corresponded to the picture of the horse. Although the children claimed that they could remember which button was to be pressed, when asked to do it, they could not.

Obviously, the children did not yet appreciate the *nature* of the relationship between the words, i.e., what was helping them to solve the problem before them. They were not yet aware of the necessity of an *internal* relationship between words. With experience, however, the child discovered that one set of pictures made remembering and response to a given picture easier, whereas another set did not. As a result, the child discovers for himself the need for a special kind of association between words.

Next, the child must learn how to arrange the pictures *himself* in such a way that they will help him remember and produce the appropriate response. He now creates associations and remembers them. Vygotskii states that "he organizes the stimuli in order to execute a response" (1960, p. 217). The child begins to understand how one memorizes.

As the experiments are repeated, the child's responses are quicker. Vygotskii suggests that this is due to the fact that the child is no longer using external means (pictures) to respond. His response mechanism has changed: the remembering operation has been internalized. From an external operation achieved by means of stimuli that act indirectly (pictures), memorization becomes an internal reaction which does not require such stimuli.

Thus, Vygotskii's major theories concerning memory and its development are focused on the *qualitative* nature of the memory process during its several stages of development and suggest that it is a special kind of human *activity*.

Vygotskii's postulates were further developed and defined by his close collaborator Leont'ev (1931). As a result of his experimental investigations (methods and major results will be discussed in one of the following chapters), he was able to determine ontogenetic changes in the relation between direct and indirect memorization.

In his investigations of disorders of mnemonic activity in the case of brain damage, Luriya (1962) proceeds from the same concept. As a result of his investigations, substantial differences in the use of indirect memorization in relation to the nature of the damage were revealed. While patients with focal brain damage without general dementia do not differ noticeably from normal subjects in the use of auxiliary semantic devices, in the case of damage to the frontal lobes of the brain one often observes an inability of the patient to recognize and use auxiliary semantic connections as a means of memorization.

Part I: Voluntary and Involuntary Memorization

Chapter 1

VOLUNTARY MEMORIZATION

1. GENERAL CHARACTERISTICS OF VOLUNTARY AND INVOLUNTARY MEMORIZATION

Memorization, being the mnemonic effect of psychological process always taking place during the execution of an activity, is not independent of the characteristics of this activity, but, on the contrary, is very closely determined by them.

Any human activity is characterized primarily by its orientation. It produces not only a particular result but is always aiming at something which can be different from the actual results or the activity. The study of the dependence of memorization on the orientation of activity under the conditions of which it is accomplished is, therefore, a part of the more general problem of the influence of activity on memorization.

In its clearest form the orientation of activity is presented as a *conscious intention* to solve a particular problem: to achieve a particular goal. The presence of this intention characterizes every conscious activity of man. This activity is always the result of some consciously set goal. "In what is given by nature," says Marx, "he (man) [A. S.] also reaches his conscious goal which as a rule determines the method and nature of his actions and to which he must submit his will" (Marx and Engels, p. 189). Being determined by the consciously set goal and conscious intention to reach this goal, human activity in its orientation is, however, dependent not only on conscious intention, but also on unconscious sources of direction. In particular, these are various *sets** which are often completely unperceived.

*The extensively developed theory of set based on vast experimental data has been proposed by Uznadze (1961) and is being successfully developed by his co-workers and students.

Neither conscious intention nor unconscious sets are the primary sources of human activity. The goals man sets for himself and the unconscious direction of his actions are based on the real conditions under which man lives and acts. The true source of human activity is reality.

"In reality, the goals of man," says Lenin, "are engendered by the objective world which is assumed to exist. But it *appears* to man that his goals are from outside of the world and independent of the world ('Freedom')" [Lenin, Vol 29, p. 171].

The most important role in determining human activity, its direction and nature, is played by the social relations of people, which develop differently according to the material conditions of their society. Human activity is socio-historically determined.

The orientation of man's activity is extremely diverse. The study of dependence of memorization on different orientations of activity is a complex task. This is not our purpose here; we want only to describe how one of the types of orientation, the one most characteristic of learning in man, and in particular the *assimilation of knowledge* influences memorization. We have in mind the *mnemonic orientation,* or the orientation to memorize.

If the direct source of the mnemonic orientation is the conscious intention to remember, then memorization is a special type of mental activity, often very complex, and, in essence, *voluntary*. Usually it is contrasted to *involuntary* memorization, which occurs when there is no intended mnemonic task and the activity leading to memorization is directed towards some other goal. When we solve a mathematical problem we do not at all intend to remember the numerical data which are in the problem. Our goal is to *solve* the problem, not to memorize the numbers in it, and yet we do remember them, even if only briefly.

The difference between these types of memorization is quite justified. But it would be incorrect to interpret this difference as absolute. Undoubtedly, a series of transitions, or intermediate forms, exists between voluntary and involuntary memorization. One type is the memorization accomplished not by conscious intention to remember, nor under the influence of a mnemonic problem, but as a result of the presence of a mnemonic set. Such memorization is not voluntary inasmuch as voluntary memorization is intentional, but at the same time it is characterized by a more or less pronounced mnemonic orientation which does not occur in involuntary memorization. Therefore, it cannot be regarded as a relatively incidental mnemonic effect of an activity directed towards another goal—as is characteristic for involuntary memorization. This is undoubtedly one of the transitional forms between voluntary and involuntary memorization.

Some investigators, namely Schellow (1923), Postman and Senders (1946), and also McGeoch and Irion (1961), authors of a review, are all in agreement in their opinion that in involuntary memorization there are usually *mnemonic sets* of a latent nature and that, therefore, there are no special differences between voluntary and involuntary memorization (in the sense of presence of mnemonic orientation). This conclusion is derived from experiments in which memorization was accomplished as the result of simple reading of some text, always connected, in the opinion of these authors, with an orientation, even if unconscious, towards comprehension of what had been read and retaining it in memory.

However, simple reading (without performing any other task demanding attention which would completely eliminate even a latent orientation towards memorization) is not the only type of activity in which involuntary memorization can be accomplished. There are also possible types of activity which are not necessarily connected with an orientation towards retention of objects of actions. Therefore, there is no basis for denying or minimizing the differences between voluntary and involuntary memorization with regard to retention. Even if the involuntary memorization would always include a latent mnemonic set, its effect could not be simply identified precisely—due to its special, latent nature—with the action of an obvious, completely conscious intention arising in a subject memorizing under the influence of a specific instruction, or as the result of some conscious self-instruction.

The mnemonic orientation is most clearly expressed in voluntary memorization. Therefore, a comparison of this type of memorization with involuntary memorization must furnish the most valuable data for the characterization of the effect of mnemonic orientation in its most succinct form. The aim of our experimental investigations was to clarify a number of questions concerning the dependence of memorization on the orientation activity.

The presence of mnemonic orientation is of great importance, first of all, for the *productivity of memorization.* The low productivity of involuntary memorization was noted in a number of publications [Stern (1903–1904, 1904–1906), G. Myers (1913), and others]. It is well known that, all other conditions being equal, voluntary memorization is considerably more effective than involuntary. The intention to remember must be considered one of the most important conditions for the success of memorization. Everyone is well aware of this from personal experience and observations. It has also been well demonstrated in experimental practice. One of the most striking examples of its significance is the case described by the Serbian psychologist Radossawljewitch (1907) and often cited in psychology literature. One of his subjects did not understand the problem before him because he did not know the language of the experimenter well. He was to memorize a small amount of nonsensical material. As the result of his lack of comprehension, memorization of even a small amount of material could not be accomplished in spite of the fact that the material had been read aloud 46 times. However, as soon as the subject understood that he was to memorize, he could reproduce the entire list exactly after only six trials.

The data of the investigations by Poppelreuter (1912), Wohlgemuth (1915), and Mazo (1929) on the effect of the task to memorize show similar results. The task for the subjects was to look at some material with the aim of remembering it and become familiar with analogous material without the requirement to memorize it. In both cases the subjects were subsequently asked to reproduce the trial material. The results of the experiments showed that in the first case memorization was much more productive than in the second case.

Everyone who has conducted experimental investigations of memory is well aware of the poor memorization of trial material by the experimenters. While subjects memorize the material completely and exactly, experimenters reading this material to their subjects reproduce it inadequately despite the fact that the experiments are conducted with several subjects, so that the material is perceived many more times by the experimenter than by each subject.

This was the object of a special study in the investigations of Jenkins (1933) and Alper (1946). The explanation of these observations is that the experimenters are not required to memorize the material.

A considerable effect of mnemonic orientation is also noticed when using the method of paired associations (words or syllables to be memorized are presented in pairs; in recall the first member of a pair is presented and the subject is asked to reproduce the second). It turned out that even when the first word of each pair was stressed the second member was better remembered; under the influence of the demand to recall the second member, its memorization was voluntary, while that of the first member of each pair was involuntary (Meumann, 1912).

In the experiments of Woodworth (1915), conducted under the same conditions, reproduction of the second member of each pair in response to presentation of the first member occurred in 74% of all cases; but the words which were first in each pair were remembered in only 7% of all cases in response to the presentation of the second words of each directly preceding pair. Analogous results were obtained by Thorndike (1931,1932). In his experiments, memorization was not required—material was merely read to the subject. However, the difference in the reproduction of the first and second members of each pair was quite clear. In this case there is an involuntary mnemonic orientation toward one member of the pair and the absence of such orientation toward the other member of the same pair.

In noting the significance of the effect of mnemonic orientation on the productivity of memorization, it must be pointed out that in checking memorization by various methods (*recognition* and *reproduction*), the influence of mnemonic orientation is not the same as is shown by the experimental data of Kirkpatrick (1894), Hollingworth (1913), A. Myers (1914), Bennett (1916), Achilles (1920), Schellow (1923), Postman, Adams and Phillips (1955), and Denny and Greenway (1955). In the processes of *recognition,* the effect of mnemonic orientation is observed to a lesser degree than in the processes of *reproduction.* Sometimes it is not observed at all.

This important difference in the effect of mnemonic orientation in recognition and reproduction by no means weakens the general position which characterizes the mnemonic problem as one of the most important conditions promoting memorization.

It is clear from analysis of the causes of the difference that recognition is a much easier process than reproduction. Its productivity is usually higher than the productivity of reproduction. This is well known from everyday experience and is also clearly shown by experimental data. This advantage of recognition, its relative ease, holds true whether memorization is assigned or not. It is natural that the ease of recognition is sometimes so great (even when memorization has not been assigned), that the presence of this task cannot change the already rather high productivity of recognition. Thus, the small effect of mnemonic orientation in the case of recognition, and sometimes its complete absence, are no basis for limiting the significance of the above-mentioned principle; on the contrary, they rather emphasize the positive effect of mnemonic orientation. It is especially necessary where memorization is accomplished with greater difficulty.

2. TYPES OF MNEMONIC ORIENTATION (TOWARDS ACCURACY, COMPLETENESS, SEQUENCE, OR STABILITY OF MEMORIZATION) AND THEIR EFFECT ON MEMORIZATION

Mnemonic orientation is not something uniform, in that it is always manifested in qualitatively distinct contents.

What characterizes the specific content of the orientation are *the demands which must be satisfied by memorization,* i.e., precisely what must be achieved as the result of memorization. From this point of view, one can speak of an orientation towards a particular quality of memorization represented by a number of basic and most typical problems or sets which change in each individual case and thereby determine the qualitative nature of the orientation of memorization.

What are these problems and sets?

Every mnemonic activity is oriented primarily towards a particular degree of completeness of memorization. In some cases we are faced with the task of memorizing the *whole* content of what affects us *(complete memorization)*. In other cases we aim to memorize only *part* of what we perceive: the gist of a text, individual facts, etc. *(selective memorization)*.

Furthermore, there are differences in the orientation towards *exactness* of memorization which in some cases can refer to the content of what is memorized, in others to the form of its expression. In the latter case, one of the extremes is the task *(or set)* of memorizing a particular material literally, learn it *by heart*. The other extreme is to memorize maximally "in one's own words."

The differences observed in the orientation for memorizing the sequence of what affects us must be specifically distinguished. In some cases we aim at memorizing events, facts, and verbal material in the same sequence in which they were actually presented. In other cases such a task or set is absent and sometimes we more or less consciously aim at the opposite: to change the perceived sequence of the material, make, for example, the verbal material more logical or simply more convenient for memorization.

The next feature characterizing the orientation towards memorization is orientation towards *stability* of memorization. In some cases we strive to memorize the material as stably as possible, and lastingly, in a sense, *"forever."* In other cases memorization is directed towards retaining the material for a *short time,* in particular to retain it only long enough to be able to reproduce it immediately after its perception (*long-term* and *short-term memory*).

A special type of mnemonic orientation is that towards *opportuneness of reproduction,* i.e., to reproduce what is being memorized at a particular time, in a definite situation (to remember, for example, something upon meeting a certain person, upon coming to a certain place, etc.).

It stands to reason that the specific features of each of these facets of orientation towards memorization can be combined in various ways. For example, the orientation towards most complete memorization can be linked either with rote learning, or with memorization in one's own words. The orientation towards maximum accuracy of memorization can be combined with the different degrees of orientation towards stability of retention in memory. Thus, in reality there is an exceptionally great diversity in the content of mnemonic orientation, depending on the demands which must be satisfied by the results of memorization.

How do these types of mnemonic orientation affect memorization itself?

Zankov (1941, 1944) studied this question most thoroughly. In his work, partially based on Dul'nev's investigations (1940) under his direction, his aim was to trace how orientations towards accuracy, completeness, and sequence of reproduction influence memorization.

Let us examine the data characterizing the orientation towards *accuracy* of memorization. One group of subjects was asked to memorize and reproduce the presented story as exactly as possible ("word for word"); the other subjects were told to reproduce it completely but that they could relate the story "in their own words." Naturally, in the first case the number of exactly reproduced words of the text was greater than in the case of the second instruction. It is important, however, that even in the second case it was rather high (about 40%). The author explains this result by saying that "the correct transmission of the content of the text demands its reproduction to a certain extent in words from the original text." In these experiments this was most clearly manifested when the basic content of the sentence was, as the author puts it, spread through the whole sentence and the sentence dealt with objects for which there are specific words; i.e., their number of "substitutes" is very limited.

In contrast, sentences having, as it were, a nucleus concentrated in one small part of the sentence are generally reproduced with a low degree of accuracy (both when subjects are instructed to reproduce exactly and when permitted to relate "in their own words"), but one, nevertheless, observes a certain polarization: the nucleus of the sentence is reproduced exactly, but the remaining parts of the sentence are to a great extent substituted by other words. Sentences the main content of which is spread over the whole sentence but which permit substitution of some words without distorting the meaning (a considerable number of words is, nevertheless, of great significance for the expression of the content in its originality) are reproduced with a high degree of accuracy when the text is memorized with the aim for exact reproduction. On the other hand, there is a low degree of exactness where the subject is permitted to reproduce the text in his own words.

Characteristic of the different types of orientations toward accuracy of memorization (to reproduce "word for word" or "in one's own words") are, furthermore, the number and nature of additions to the text during its reproduction.

In memorization according to the first instruction the number of additions (in relation to the number of reproduced words) is 26%, in memorization according to the second instruction it is 36%. In the first case *single* words are usually added to the sentences in the text, in the second, words which make up new sentences generated during reproduction and not present in the original text. The main part of the additions in the first case occurs from trying to make the reproduced story more understandable to the listener and to connect the separate parts of the story more closely. They add no new content to what was in the presented story. In contrast to this, the majority of sentences added in the second case are a contribution of new content, which are, however, related to separate parts of the story.

These are the results of experiments with adult subjects. What were the results of experiments with schoolchildren of the fourth grade?

In schoolchildren the ratio of the number of accurately reproduced words according to the first instruction to the number of accurately reproduced words according to the second instruction remained the same as for adults. Only the total number of accurately reproduced words diminishes considerably in both cases. The ratio of the number of substitutions and additions to the number of accurately reproduced words is different for the schoolchildren when reproduced according to the first instruction. When reproduction is "in their own words," the relative number of substitutions and additions remains the same for schoolchildren and for adults; but when reproduced according to the first instruction ("word for word"), it is considerably higher than for adults. This leads the author to the conclusion that although the intention to reproduce the story as close to the original as possible has a tendency to increase the accuracy of reproduction in children, this effect is considerably smaller than for adults. *The effect of orientation towards accuracy of reproduction is observed in children to a lesser degree than in adults.* This is the effect of the intention to reproduce more accurately on the *result* of memorization.

How does the presence of the same orientation affect the very *process* of memorization, the *actions* aimed at achieving the most exact memorization?

In order to elucidate this problem, we conducted small series of experiments, since there were no corresponding data in Zankov's work. The subjects were ten adults, some with a secondary, some with a higher, education, and six fourth and eighth graders. The subjects received the same instructions as in Zankov's experiments: to memorize as accurately as possible. However, attention was focused not on the result but on the process of memorization. For this purpose we utilized observation of subjects as well as reports of their self-observation. For comparison, experiments were conducted with ordinary memorization, i.e., without the task of memorizing as accurately as possible. As a result of both experiments certain characteristics of memorization under conditions of orientation towards accuracy of mastering the text became apparent.

The first thing that is noticed by the adults under these conditions is *a considerably greater clarity and accuracy in the perception of each part of the text separately,* while in memorizing without the task "to memorize as exactly as possible" much of the text is inadvertently read very superficially, even if the reading of the text is repeated. In this case only the general content of each part of the text is grasped (at most, of each sentence separately), and only some individual words and expressions, the most important or characteristic ones, reach clear consciousness. In memorization with the orientation towards accuracy, the amount of what reaches clear consciousness and the very level of this comprehension increase considerably. Many words are clearly comprehended which in ordinary memorization do not require this at all. Most often this occurs with words which have no essential significance for the understanding of the main content, but introduce a particular shade or a specific limitation of the meaning. One must assume, therefore, that the presence in the text of a considerable number of such words makes literal memorization very difficult. Such words are not remembered by themselves easily and freely, but demand a special fixation and special effort, i.e., active memorization.

The same must be said about words having a large number of "substitutes" (in particular, synonyms). Under normal conditions the general meaning of these words is remembered easily and freely, but the words themselves are just as easily and freely replaced by others having the same meaning, which naturally is not permissible in exact memorization. Epithets demand the most attention, verbs which do not express concrete actions of the objects demand less, and designations of the objects themselves demand the least attention.

The grammatical form of the words is sometimes clearly perceived (for example, the augmentative or diminutive of a noun, the aspect of a verb), as well as the form of individual expressions (for example, a complete or reduced subordinate clause). Sometimes the sequence of words is perceived, especially when in the interest of style it is deliberate and deviates from the usual sequence.

Let us give as an illustration an excerpt from V. G. Belinskii's article "The Works of Alexander Pushkin," which we presented to our subjects for memorization as exactly as possible (by heart), and note specifically *what* demanded of subjects a more clear comprehension since they could not remember it by itself.

> The laws of the heart, as the laws of reason, are always the same, and that is why man by his nature always was, is, and will be the same. But both reason and heart live, and to live means to develop, move forward: therefore, man cannot feel and think in the same way all his life; his manner of feeling and thinking changes in accordance with the phases of his life: a boy recognizes objects differently and feels differently than a youth; a man in the prime of life is quite different in this respect from a youth, an old man from one in his prime, although all of them feel with the same heart, think according to the same laws of reason.

According to reports of subjects, the following items required special conscious fixation: a) the word *potomu* ("that is why"), since it showed a tendency to be replaced by the word *poetomu* ("therefore"); b) the phrase *po nature* ("by nature"), which stood out as an uncommon synonym for *po prirode;* c) the sequence of words *po nature svoei* ("by his nature") instead of the more common *po svoei nature;* d) the words "was, is, and will be" as imparting an especially significant concept to what is said here about man; e) the sequence of the words "reason" and "heart," which differs in the second sentence from that in the first; f) the sequence of the words *vsyu zhizn' svoyu* ("all his life") instead of the more common *vsyu svoyu zhizn';* g) the word "manner" as giving a special shade to the thought of the author (not simply "feeling," but "manner of feeling"); h) the word *soobrazno* ("in accordance") so as not to replace it by its equivalents *soglasno* or *sootvetstvenno;* i) the archaic form *nezheli* ("than") instead of *chem;* j) "in the prime of life" instead of "mature" or "grown"; k) "differs much" *(mnogo raznitsya)* instead of "differs greatly" *(sil'no raznitsya* or *sil'no otlichaetsya);* l) "in this respect" as limiting the concept.

These reports have been obtained from different subjects since not all these words demanded a special conscious fixation for every subject. Some subjects consciously fixed some words, others distinguished other words. The number of words chosen was also different. But all subjects reported the necessity of a special conscious fixation as necessary for accurate memorization. Again, let us remember that in this case we are dealing with adult subjects.

The second important feature of memorization under conditions of orientation towards accuracy of memorization is the *mental repetition of separate small parts of the text* (sometimes individual words, sometimes parts of sentences). Our observations and the data of self-observation by the subjects showed that even when we suggested memorizing by the complete method, without breaking the text into parts, the subjects could not refrain from attempts to stop immediately after having read a small part of the text (even a separate phrase) and mentally reproduce it, sometimes more than once. "Here we have to cram, otherwise nothing will come of it," is how they usually characterized their memorization. By "cramming" is meant numerous repetitions of separate small parts of the text. In adults this repetition was, however, accompanied by a clearer comprehension of the repeated part of the text. Therefore, the term "cramming," if understood as mechanical repetition of material to be memorized, does not at all apply or, in any case, has a special connotation here.

The third clearly manifested feature of literal memorization is the *considerable role of the motor and especially the speech-motor aspects.* In spite of the fact that all subjects claimed to be of the visual type, all of them resorted to speech-motor aspects to some degree when learning by heart. Sometimes this was manifested simply by slowly reading aloud after first reading the material silently. In other cases they reread parts of the text, evidently the most difficult to memorize. Sometimes the text or parts of it were read in a whisper: sometimes clearly discernible, sometimes perceptible only from the movements of the lips. Often the subjects remarked that although they did not pronounce anything aloud or in a whisper they nevertheless mentally "pronounced" the text or parts of it, performing the necessary but unobservable articulations.

In addition to the speech-motor features, some other kinds of movement were also of assistance to memorization. Sometimes the subjects inclined their heads, sometimes they moved a hand or a foot as if beating time, in some cases their bodies moved.

Sometimes the subjects felt the need to take notes, sometimes they made some note-taking movements with their fingers, in the air or on the table, which, as the subjects indicated, did not represent actual notation, that is, they did not fully correspond to the movements made during writing.

It is characteristic that the subjects themselves often did not notice the involvement of motor aspects in the process of memorization. Only later they realized that some movements had been made. The actual time of these movements often remained quite unnoticed. "I did not notice when I started to read aloud (or in a whisper), I caught myself doing it and was surprised"—such statements were heard repeatedly. The participation of motor aspects was especially apparent during memorization of rhythmic material (poems).

Noting the considerable role of motor aspects in literal memorization, the following often-occurring feature must be pointed out. Stopping at some place in the text, the subjects often closed their eyes or stared into space (sometimes at the ceiling or the wall) or at a particular object, in some cases stopping visible movements, reducing them, for example, changing to a whisper or slight nodding of the head, or slight movements of the hand. Reports of self-observation reveal that in these cases the subjects often tried *to mentally visualize the part of the text to be memorized (internal scanning)*. This was accomplished with various degrees of awareness. Sometimes it was a precise picture of the words, even seeing their arrangement in the text. Sometimes it was some allusion to visual images, rather a knowledge that "here in front of me I place such and such a word," "I project or attach something here which indicates such and such a word." Simultaneously, there is often distinct internal pronunciation of words, sometimes there are auditory images. In some cases the subjects notice a clearer *emotional experience of the word* than is usual in memorization; this is connected with the clearer perception of the meaning of the word. All this indicates the highly diverse, often very complex activity accomplished by adults when they have to accomplish a most exact memorization.

In order to compare these results with what happens in schoolchildren, analogous experiments were conducted using other material with pupils of the fourth and eighth grades, eight pupils from each. Reports of self-observation of these subjects are naturally less reliable and less complete. Nevertheless, some definite data were obtained.

Although one could quite often observe in the pupils, especially the eighth graders, the above-mentioned delay or stopping at certain parts of the text which were accompanied by repeated reiteration of these parts, these delays were, however, not connected (especially in the fourth graders) with so great a concentration on the corresponding part of the text as was observed in the adults.

The rate of pronunciation (aloud or in a whisper) of the repeated words is more rapid than for adults. The manner of pronunciation is less tense, without a specific tinge of "cramming in," i.e., of making real impressions as is often observed in adults. Finally, the reports of self-observation in most cases did not include indications of attempts to comprehend the characteristics of what was repeated, or the pupils often directly denied the existence of such attempts when we asked about them. All this shows that the internal activity of the pupils (especially the younger ones) was less complex and diverse than in adults.

But the outward actions (reading aloud or in a whisper, or various kinds of movement) were in pupils no less distinct, and in fourth graders even more distinct, than in the adults. These outward actions were often mechanical since they were not related to the same degree of inner concentration as was observed in adults. In adults, aside from directly assisting motor memorization, they served to a certain extent as support for better perception of what was being memorized; in the pupils they were sometimes detached from this perception, performing only their own specific function, and were a separate means of memorization.

Yet, it must be noted that the participation of speech-motor factors in the schoolchildren (especially the younger ones) is rather prominent even in ordinary memorization without special orientation towards "word for word" literality. Therefore, the difference in this respect between the two types of memorization (literal and "in one's own words") is smaller in pupils than in adults.

We think that what has been said can serve as a sufficient basis for the explanation that, as shown in the work of Zankov, the orientation towards accuracy of memorization appearing in the form of conscious intention to memorize "word for word" was less effective in pupils as compared with ordinary memorization than the same orientation in adults.

It must be noted that in method our experiments differed considerably from the experiments of Zankov. We had our subjects read the texts, we did not hamper the process of reading and memorization, but allowed the subjects to read and memorize at their convenience. In Zankov's experiments the material was read by the experimenter, which naturally lowered the possibility of extensive and varied activity on the part of the subjects. Therefore it cannot be determined which of the actions oriented towards the achievement of most accurate memorization could have also occurred in Zankov's subjects who were working under conditions which hampered these actions. Nevertheless, in a rudimentary or weakened form, some of them could also occur in his subjects, especially in the adults. Therefore we believe that although the differences we have demonstrated in the *processes* of memorization in adults and pupils perhaps do not fully explain the difference in the *results* of memorization in both groups, they at least indicate the direction in which to look for the explanation of this difference.

Considering that the lesser effectiveness of the intention to remember as exactly as possible is in schoolchildren the result of the specific characteristics of the *process* of memorization, we must, however, emphasize that in itself this fact is not yet sufficient basis for judging whether the weakened effect of orientation in children is limited only to orientation towards accuracy of reproduction or whether it signifies a certain generally weakened influence of the voluntary intention in pupils in comparison with adults (independent of what aspect of memorization this intention is directed at).

To solve this problem we must examine what effect the intention has on the other aspects of memorization and reproduction in pupils as compared with adults or, in other words, to show the influence which is exerted by the other above-mentioned forms of orientation, primarily orientation towards *completeness* of memorization. What characterizes the effect of this type of orientation? For the answer we turn to the same work by Zankov, based in this part also on the investigation of G. M. Dul'nev. This time the method of the experiments consisted of the same story being read with the specific task to reproduce it as completely as possible for the first group of subjects and without this specific task for the second group. Adults and fourth graders were the subjects. As a result of this experiment the following data were obtained, which show the number of reproduced sentences of the story in both cases (Table 1.1).

As can be seen from these data, the difference between reproduction with the task of reproducing as completely as possible and without the task is much higher for adults than for schoolchildren. Thus, *the effect of a special orientation towards completeness of reproduction is less in pupils than in adults.*

This conclusion is confirmed by comparative analysis of the *gaps in reproduction* occurring under both conditions, i.e., the presence and the absence of the intention to remember as completely as possible. In adults, orientation towards completeness of reproduction leads to an equalization of the various parts of the story, i.e., in the presence of such an orientation the increase in forgetting those parts of the story which caused some difficulties in the absence of such orientation (due to their position in the text or for other reasons) is halted. In pupils, this was not observed. A considerable number of them, even with an orientation to complete memorization, con-

TABLE 1.1

Subjects	Percentage of reproduced sentences	
	with task	without task
Adults	12.5	8.7
Pupils	7.6	6.8

tinue to forget some parts of the story which were difficult without this orientation. As the author points out, in adults the intention of remembering as completely as possible has as its result, in addition to an overall increase in the frequency of reproduction of all parts of the story, an especially sharp rise in the reproduction of those parts which are easily omitted in ordinary reproduction; in the pupils, however, this special intention leads to a reproduction of mainly those sentences the objective characteristics of which in themselves are conducive to reproduction. The effect of intention here, too, is less in the pupils than in the adults.

In summing up we have, consequently, the same result as in studying the influence which orientation towards accuracy of reproduction exerts on memorization in adults and pupils. *A weakened effect of orientation is a characteristic feature in pupils and is inherent equally in the orientation towards accuracy and towards completeness of reproduction.*

What is the relation of the differences in the *results* of memorization in pupils and adults found by Zankov (under conditions of orientation towards complete reproduction) to the characteristics of the actual process of memorization in both when it proceeds under the influence of this orientation? Zankov's investigation does not deal with this question and for the answer we turn to our own experiments.

Various types of text were given to our subjects, who were instructed to memorize them as completely as possible. For comparison, material was given for ordinary memorization without specifically explaining this task. Our subjects were 12 adults and 14 schoolchildren, seven of the fourth and seven of the eighth grade.

Observation and the data of their own self-observations have shown that *in adults, reading for memorization directed towards the solution of a task proceeds more slowly than in ordinary memorization,* and this is a result of the more complex inner activity which they are accomplishing at the moment. As with the task of memorizing as exactly as possible, the subjects again try to perceive as fully as possible all that is in the text. But, in the first case they consciously fixed *specific* characteristics of some fractional parts of the text (sentences, words, including even their form), while they now confine themselves to the *meaning* only of what is said (keeping mind the essentials as well as every detail).

This time, too, reading proceeds with interruptions, but they are made less frequently than in memorization with orientation towards accuracy. The subjects stop after reading larger sections of the texts, and these stops are filled not with repeated reiteration of the limited part of the text just read, but with a single recall of a more extensive content read during a longer period of time. Such recollection is accomplished not in the original expressions of the text, but, often, only in hints, when the subjects, in their words, only "estimate" what has been read or "have in mind" a particular part of the content without reproducing it in a developed and strictly formulated pattern.

In contrast to memorization directed towards accuracy of reproduction *the subjects not only fix separate parts of the text* (for the purpose of their multiple repetition), often unrelated with other parts, *but they try in various ways to tie the separate parts of the text as closely together as possible.*

This time the role of motor factors, including the speech-motor factors, diminishes considerably, although they are now in some subjects more pronounced than during ordinary memorization. However, in contrast to the case of orientation towards accuracy of memorization, now even in these subjects the movements are considerably less pronounced than in literal memorization. At the same time they are limited for the most part to indefinite, rudimentary movements (head, hand, or, occasionally speech movements) connected with "inner scanning" of what has been read during the stops in the reading and during self-evaluation as if fixing each separate stage of this scanning. For example, with a light nod of the head or a movement of a finger the subject seemingly notes the appearance in his consciousness of what must be remembered, doing this consecutively as he recalls the individual places in the text.

The outward expression of this "inner scanning" consists of the subject's *closing his eyes, gazing somewhere into space, or staring at some object, evidently hardly perceiving it.*

For the schoolchildren, in the eighth graders the same thing occurred in many cases, although to a lesser degree than in the adults. This may be due to the fact that self-observation in schoolchildren is not reliable. But there are other objective indications: the children stopped their reading and returned to what had already been read less often, and outward expressions of inner "scanning," which is so characteristic for adults, were less frequent and definite. In fourth graders the phenomena observed in the adults were barely detected. Usually the process of memorization, as far as can be judged from the reports of the pupils and data of observation, was merely a repeated reading of the text. The number of readings varied with the subjects and the text. But subsequent self-checking was important for these pupils. This was a *mental retelling* of what had been read, with "peeking" into the text to see what had been left out and to perceive once more what had been forgotten.

Thus, the study of memorization with an orientation towards complete reproduction shows that the pupils, especially the younger ones, just as in the case of exact memorization, exhibit a less complex and less diverse activity than the adults. The task of "remembering as completely as possible" stimulates the adults to actions which under ordinary memorization are either absent entirely or are present only in a weak form. It is therefore quite natural that the difference in productivity of memorization, accomplished in the presence or absence of this task, is less pronounced in schoolchildren than in adults, as shown by the experiments of Zankov.

In saying that the source of lesser influence of special forms of mnemonic orientation noticed in schoolchildren is that the process of memorization itself proceeds under the influence of a particular orientation differently in pupils than in adults, we must, however, note also the following circumstance. It is possible that the orientation towards accuracy and completeness of reproduction may be present in schoolchildren (although in an unrealized form) even under conditions of ordinary memorization, in particular under conditions of schoolwork. Therefore, giving pupils the special assignment to achieve the most accurate and complete memorization possible means a transition from a set unaware but familiar to them to a conscious, active intention and therefore promotes an increase in the productivity of memorization. This increase, however, is far less than in adults, who change to this intention from an almost complete lack or special orientation towards accuracy and completeness of reproduction. Thus, it is quite admissible that the source of the above-mentioned lesser influence exerted by the special forms of mnemonic orientation towards memorization can in fact be in pupils twofold. On the one hand, it may consist of a smaller diversity than in adults and in less complexity of the activity in the schoolchildren when the above-mentioned special tasks are given. On the other hand, it may consist in the fact that these children under ordinary conditions of memorization already have a tendency, although unrealized, towards accuracy and completeness of reproduction. In other words, having received a special task, that of achieving the most complete and accurate reproduction possible, the schoolchild does not do *everything* that the adult does, but even when such a task is not specifically given to him, he nevertheless does something in that direction. Thus, both factors decrease in pupils as it were from both ends the difference between the productivity of memorization observed in adults under the same two conditions.

Among the various types of mnemonic orientation, a special place belongs to that for memorizing material in a definite *sequence*. The influence of this task on the characteristics of reproduction was traced in work by Zankov. In his experiments with adults, the subjects were asked to memorize a number of geometric figures, some of which were similar. In some cases the subjects were asked to reproduce these figures exactly in the same sequence in which they were presented, in others they could be reproduced in any sequence. The results of the experiments showed that the difference in the task had an essential influence on its reproduction. When asked to retain the order in which the figures were given, this sequence was observed in reproduction in the large majority of cases (80% of all transitions from one figure to the other). Its retention was observed not only the first time, but also subsequently, even when the sequential reproduction was asked 12 days after the figures were presented.

Other data were obtained when the subjects were given the opportunity to reproduce the figures freely, that is, in any sequence. In these experiments transitions from one figure to an adjacent one were observed in only 43% of all cases; in the following reproduction this percentage dropped sharply; in the third reproduction (12 days after the figures were presented) it dropped to 17%, and transition to *similar* figures was better than transition to *adjacent* figures.

Of great importance is the fact made apparent by the author in a special series of experiments. It turned out that the retention of the "original" sequence is observed only when the subject is instructed beforehand to reproduce the figures in the same sequence as presented. If the instruction is given after the material has been perceived (in one of the series of experiments the author gave it before the second reproduction), then it no longer has influence on the sequence of reproduction and the subjects are unable to reproduce these figures in the order in which they were presented.

Somewhat different results were obtained from the experiments with schoolchildren. As did the adults, the children maintained the sequence well when asked to beforehand and greatly disrupted it (in 70–72% of all cases) when they were allowed to reproduce the material in any order. However, in contrast to the adults, the sequence in reproduction (when they were asked to maintain it) was retained by them only when immediately reproduced. Reproduction postponed for six days after the figures were given showed a sharp drop in the number of transitions from one figure to an adjacent one. Such transitions were observed not in 70%, but in 28% of all cases.

Of other results obtained by Zankov in his experiments with schoolchildren the following finding must be noted: when the subjects were not given geometrical figures, as was the case in the above-mentioned experiments, but pictures which presented various stages of some event, not in the sequence corresponding to the course of its development, the pupils, when not instructed to remember these pictures precisely in the sequence in which they were presented, observed the sequence still less frequently than during the memorization of figures. Transitions according to adjacency were observed in only 9% of all cases, while in the control experiments (geometrical figures) conducted with the same subjects they were observed in 50% of the cases. Meaningful connections between pictures distributed nonadjacently in the series had a still greater counter-effect against reproduction of pictures in the same sequence in which they were presented for memorization (i.e., out of logical sequence). When, however, asked to reproduce the order in which the pictures were given, there was no longer such a considerable difference between the reproduction of pictures and geometric figures.

These data reveal the considerable influence which the sequence memorization *task* has on the *results*. However, they do not reveal the actual characteristics of the *process* of memorization under these conditions.

In order to solve this problem we conducted special experiments, in some of which the subjects were told that after reading the text they had to reproduce it in a coherent form and in the same sequence in which it had been presented. In the other cases they were told that it was not necessary to reproduce the text in a coherent form; instead they would have to answer questions which would be asked by the experimenter. The subjects were 20 students. Texts on natural sciences were the material for memorization ("On Bacteria" and "On Plankton"). Each of the subjects participated in the experiment twice: asked once to memorize with the aim of coherent reproduction, a second time to answer questions. The text given to one group for coherent reproduction was given to the other for answering questions, and what the first group received for answering questions was given to the second group for coherent reproduction.

The results of the experiments showed that the process of memorization differed depending on which of the tasks the subjects were given. When the subjects had to memorize the content of the text in the same sequence in which it was given and then retell it in a coherent form, many of them noted the following characteristics of memorization under the influence of such a task:

1. a considerably more attentive reading of the text;

2. a special attention to the structure of the material and a clearing up of what main parts this material consists of and how these parts are connected; a brief verbal definition of each part;

3. the attempt not only to observe the order of the exposition, but also to understand what causes a particular sequence in the distribution of the material, to understand the *principles* of its distribution;

4. a mental repetition of headings of the already isolated parts of the text during familiarization with subsequent parts of the material;

5. a mental retelling of the text which usually was absent in the case of memorizing without the intention to remember the sequence of the presentation;

6. an additional reading of the text (as compared to the cases when the

subjects were informed that after memorization of the text they would have to answer questions);

7. less attention to the details of the text (as compared with the cases when memorization for answering questions was required) and a greater fixation of the main points in the text;

8. increased attention to the wording of the text; the attempt to adhere to it.

In pointing out all these characteristics of memorization (caused by the task to memorize the sequence of the material) it must be noted that in each case only some of them occurred in the subjects. In some cases, for example, the attempt to find the structure of the text to be memorized, the principle of disposition of its parts, without any tendency to reproduce the material to oneself, was strongly manifested. In other cases, on the contrary, it was evident that in memorizing the sequence of the text the subject relied not so much on clarifying the inner relationships between the separate parts of the material as on "uttering" to himself or an additional rereading.

Some subjects did not notice any differences between the two cases of memorization, asserting that the process of memorization proceeded the same way whether they were tasked with coherent reproduction or answers to questions. Such reports, however, were in the minority. And when making these statements, the subjects usually noted one of two things: the material which was given to memorize seemed to be easy and the memorization of its sequence presented no difficulty (even when they knew they would have to answer questions), or, when memorizing with the aim of answering questions, they tried to "insure" themselves and memorized the material in order not to fail, should the experimenter suddenly demand of them not only answers to the questions, but also a coherent sequential exposition.

Let us turn to the next type of mnemonic orientation, to the orientation towards *stability* of memorization. Some data on this question are found in the work of the Norwegian psychologist Aall (1913). He notes a twofold relation to what we memorize.

In some cases we attempt to remember something "forever," that is attempt to keep in memory something in order to utilize what has been mastered even after a considerable interval of time. In other cases, on the contrary, we grasp something for a short period and do not care whether it will be retained in memory after this period ends. As an illustration to the second case Aall cites observations from his own experience. When he had to get ready for semester examinations, he would review the pertinent literature the day before, refreshing in his memory all the details of the course which might prove necessary during the examination. It frequently happened that he later had to review the same information, which after one semester was again forgotten. The attention which he allotted to each bit of information renewed in memory was sufficient, they did not present any difficulty for memorization, yet they were not retained in memory since each item was acquired not to achieve general enrichment in knowledge, but only for the needs of the next day, that is, to pass the examination. Beyond this period they lost all significance. The same thing is also shown by this experience of an actor: one time he unexpectedly had to substitute for a colleague and memorize the colleague's role in one day; during the play, he knew the role perfectly, but afterwards everything he had learned was, in his words, "as if wiped off with a sponge" and he had completely forgotten the role.

These personal experiences are corroborated by experimental data. The method of experiments conducted by Aall with schoolchildren consisted of two stories to be memorized several weeks apart. One story was given with a warning that the next day questions would be asked; before reading the other story the children were told to memorize it "forever," that is, so that the teacher when asking several weeks or months later could be convinced that everything had been retained correctly in memory.

After reading the first story the questioning actually occurred after four or eight weeks and on the day for which the questioning was originally scheduled the subjects were told that nothing would come of the experiments and that at some later time experiments would be conducted and other material used. Four or eight weeks later the children were also examined in the second experiment. The results were better in this second experiment, i.e., in memorization with the set for a prolonged period.

Similar experiments were conducted with memorization of objects. This time too, the results of memorization were worse with the set for a short period.

According to Aall, the fact that orientation towards stability of memorization yields good results is based on some kind of "tensions" and "forces" which, he thinks, arise in these cases (their nature, however, is not revealed). The *activity* which is accomplished by the memorizer under the influence of this orientation is passed over without notice. Yet it is legitimate to assume that in memorization for a lengthy time the activity of the memorizing subject is more intensive and the perceived material is comprehended by him more deeply than when something is memorized for a short period.

In recent years special attention has been given to the question of the duration of retention in memory and the role of orientation towards a certain period of retention, mainly in connection with the problems of engineering psychology.

Two types of memory are distinguished: *short-term* and *long-term*. Hypothetically, differences are pointed out between their physiological mechanisms. Functional changes of a temporary nature (change in excitability of nerve cells, the appearance of reverberatory circuits in the brain) are considered a mechanism of short-term memory, the first phase in the formation of traces in the nervous system. Structural changes of a more stable nature (hypothetically: the growth of protoplasmic nerve processes, changes in synaptic endings, changes in properites of the cell membrane, changes in the composition of RNA) are the material basis of long-term memory, the second phase of trace formation (Burešová and Bureš, 1963).

In short-term memory, so-called *operative memory* is especially distinguished as memorization which is accomplished during any kind of activity, has as its object what is needed for its accomplishment, and is designed for only a short period—to the end of the given activity. This is memory which functions only as one of the conditions for the successful achievement of the activity. Upon completion of this activity it is no longer necessary to retain what had been needed. It can (and often must) be forgotten in order not to hinder the following activity. Such is, for example, memorization and retention in memory by the typist of what he is transcribing, in this case only short segments of the text must be retained in memory only until they are typed.

In a number of recent psychology publications on memory and other problems [in the USSR, works by Zhinkin (1958), Zinchenko and Repkina (1964); abroad, investigations of Schwarz (1961), Broadbent (1961, 1962), Brown (1954), and others] special attention is given to operative (immediate) memory; it is the subject of special study or is drawn upon for the explanation of certain psychological phenomena.

It is quite evident that the orientation of the subject in those cases when operative memory is involved is of a specific nature and its effect on memorization (on its productivity and on how it proceeds, that is, what activity is accomplished) demands special study.

3. SOURCES OF MNEMONIC ORIENTATION

We examined the influence which the various types of mnemonic orientation towards quality of memorization exert on memorization (on its productivity and its content as a special kind of activity).

What are the *sources* of these orientations? Their diversity is, of course, very great but one can nevertheless distinguish those of greatest significance.

They include first of all the *goals* of memorization, i.e., precisely *for what purpose* we remember. It is quite evident that here we are faced with an exceptional diversity caused by the fact that the types of activity in which we utilize memorized material are in their turn very diverse.

The schoolchild preparing his homework, the actor studying his role, the telephone operator working at the switchboard and memorizing the telephone number which she must connect, the operator working at a control board and receiving varied information which he must retain until he can execute actions in response to signals received, the scientist fixing in his memory the results of an investigation which he himself has conducted or with which he familiarizes himself by reading the work of another scientist, the speaker or lecturer planning the content of his forthcoming report or lecture, any person with an assignment to be completed at a definite time is directed toward memorization corresponding to the specific nature of the activity which he performs.

The goals of memorization are not the same for every one of them and this determines the difference in content of the mnemonic orientation, and, first of all, the difference in the orientation towards *quality* of memorization, towards *what* must be achieved. What is demanded of the telephone operator who must retain a number given her for a very short time can not at all satisfy the student memorizing historical data or the most important quantitative indexes in the field of economic geography, and what completely satisfies the speaker (memorization of the main content of his intended report) or the scientist (memorization of the main results of the work of another investigator), can not at all satisfy the actor who must achieve a literal memorization of his role.

The completeness, accuracy, stability, and sequence of memorization are each time very specific and depend on what goal is pursued by memorization. The activity accomplished in the process of memorization also varies within wide limits.

A very important role in the realization of the mnemonic orientation towards a specific quality of memorization is played by the demands presented to the memorizer by other people or by himself. Students preparing their lessons are oriented by the demands set by the school and teacher. Their clear comprehension is, therefore, the essential premise for correctly directed memorization. The student must clearly understand not only *what* but also *how* and to *what extent* he must learn the assignment. Yet far from all students have a clear understanding of the demands for memorization set by the school. The school demands from the students a memorization to a considerable degree complete, exact, stable, and sequential. This demand in many cases, especially in younger schoolchildren, is distorted in the mind of the student into the necessity of memorizing literally.

In the lower grades, the material to be memorized is of small volume and compactly written, giving little opportunity to retell it "in one's own words," and the pupils at this age are not yet sufficiently able to tell it "in their own words." This contributes to a considerable extent to literal memorization.

All this often results in a false orientation towards literal memorization which does not correspond to the actual demands of the school and the goals it sets. Such a false orientation becomes sometimes a habit and remains in force at the later stages of education where it greatly differs from what is demanded. In the upper grades because of the greater volume of material and a diversity in significance of content which demand selective memorization, such an habitual false orientation towards complete, literal memorization may become a serious inhibition to absorbing knowledge. It is therefore natural that the elaboration of a correct and precise mnemonic orientation of the students, corresponding to the *actual demands* of the school, is one of the essential tasks for school and teacher.

The *conditions* under which memorization must be accomplished are an important factor in determining orientation towards a specific quality of memorization. Naturally, where, for example, repeated undisturbed perception of the same material is possible the mnemonic orientation may be expressed quite diffferently than when a person is restricted by the conditions of memorization, i.e., is deprived of the opportunity to repeat the material, cannot make its perception clear and distinct, and must perform it in the shortest possible time. Undoubtedly, this can demand a much more clearly expressed and intense orientation than the first case in which such an orientation may not be needed.

One of the bases for orientation towards a particular quality of memorization is the *individual psychological qualities of the personality* of the memorizer. First, one must distinguish the individual characteristics of a person's memory, the *mnemonic* aptitudes expressed by the speed, accuracy, and stability of memorization. Like all aptitudes, they do not uniquely predetermine a person's mnemonic orientation, but undoubtedly have an influence on it, depending on the specific situation in which memorization occurs. Doubtless, too, is the effect of a number of *character traits of the personality* of the memorizer, in particular those which are expressed in the attitude towards the work and demands for quality which must be met. Here acquired *habits* play an important role.

Speaking of the influence of the *attitude* towards the material, it must be emphasized that the *emotional attitude* towards and *interest* in what must be remembered is of great significance. It is still debatable as to what material is easier to memorize (pleasant or unpleasant) and whether the positive or negative emotional tone of the material has any effect on memorization. It is hardly debatable that the orientation towards memorization, the *desire* to memorize a material, and the attitude towards memorization are determined by the emotional effect, the emotional tone of the material. From personal experience everyone knows the desire to memorize what he likes, what evoked a positive emotion. No less important is the influence of the interest which the material evokes from us. It is well known what effort it takes sometimes to compel oneself to memorize boring, uninteresting material and, *vice versa,* how easily orientation towards memorization arises when the material interests us in some respect.

Along with the psychological qualities of the personality, ontogenetic characteristics must be taken into account, which essentially determine the direction towards a particular quality of memorization because they are linked with the abilities acquired in the field of memory, the experience of memorization, the nature of the goals of memorization, and the specific attitude towards what must be achieved as the result of memorization.

The nature of the material to be memorized and, first of all, its *volume,* are an important group of conditions which determine the specific content of the orientation towards memorization. It is natural that a small volume of material stimulates complete and exact memorization to a greater extent than voluminous material. This is explained by the fact that the possibility to achieve full and accurate memorization is less with a large volume of material, and this does not remain without influence on the orientation towards memorization. Where it is more difficult to achieve complete and exact retention in memory the goal to achieve such a memorization is set by the influence of some special considerations. Yet, in memorizing a small volume of material, the orientation towards complete and exact mastery often may arise by itself in the form of a little-recognized set.

The second characteristic of the material which influences the orientation of memorization is its *density* or the number of thoughts and factual data per unit of volume. A concise exposition saturated with factual data predisposes to a full and exact memorization more than an expansive, developed exposition containing a comparatively small number of factual data.

The significance of the individual parts of the material plays an essential role. When material of diverse significance must be memorized, the orientation towards selective memorization, which in one way or another deviates from the "original," develops more readily and sooner.

The orientation towards memorization also differs with *the kind of material* we memorize. Some types of material almost compel a certain orientation. Other types leave greater freedom to the memorizer. By themselves they have only a small effect on the orientation towards memorization. Let us examine some examples.

One type of material which most stimulates a specific orientation towards memorization is terms, titles, formulas, and, to a certain extent, numerical data and the like. This material demands an orientation towards maximum mastery corresponding absolutely to the "original" (in reference to numerical data we made a reservation by saying "to a certain extent" because sometimes in memorizing these data we are satisfied with the mastery of only their scale, i.e., remembering only their order of magnitude).

Similar to this group (in their effect on the orientation of memorization) are definitions, aphorisms, riddles, proverbs, sayings—in general, anything that demands an exact, clear, definite formulation. Where a thought and its verbal expression are so closely connected that even the least deviation from the given formulation changes the sense, naturally, the orientation towards exact memorization is maximally stimulated, and not by some incidental consideration, but precisely by the nature of the material.

With the orientation towards completeness and exactness of memorization, the material can also evoke an orientation towards memorization of the sequence in which it is given. Such material includes, e.g., anything that contains a more or less complex course of reasoning or proof, i.e., material characterized by a strictly logical sequence. In memorizing this material it is necessary to remember also the sequence in which the separate parts are given (various interrelated postulates which are derived from each other). Without this, the mastery of such material loses what is most important, it loses much of its meaning. Hence it is natural that the orientation during memorization of this material must include the tendency to retain not only the parts by themselves, but also their sequence.

Material of a narrative nature, revealing a sequence of facts, actions, or events has a similar, though less pronounced, effect on orientation in memorization.

The *difficulty* of the material plays an important role as the basis of mnemonic orientation. Very easy material (especially material small in volume —which, in its turn, is one of the causes of its facility) evokes the tendency to memorize completely and as exactly as possible. The same is observed, however, in the opposite case, that is, when very difficult material must be memorized. The orientation towards exact memorization can be especially pronounced in these cases. Material of intermediate difficulty permits a wide range of orientations and in these cases the orientation is not unequivocally related to the material.

In stating the considerable influence of the material and its characteristics on the content of mnemonic orientation it must be emphasized that in itself the material does not evoke a strictly defined mnemonic task or set if there is no subjective attitude towards the material which corresponds to a particular orientation.

In this case, *realization* of the nature of the material and its demands upon memorization plays an essential role. In order for a particular material to evoke the appropriate mnemonic orientation it is necessary that in memorizing we understand with what kind of material we are dealing and what problems it poses for memorization.

Naturally adults have the necessary premises for this to a much greater extent than do children. Therefore, the specific effect of various types of material on the orientation of memorization is more pronounced in adults than in children. To children, the nature of the material which determines the characteristics of mnemonic orientation is yet insufficiently apparent. The attitude towards various types of material is not yet sufficiently differentiated. Therefore, the orientation towards memorization bears for them an as yet insufficiently specialized nature.

4. MOTIVES FOR MEMORIZATION AND THEIR INFLUENCE ON ITS PRODUCTIVITY

Of exceptional significance for the characteristics of mnemonic orientation are the *motives for memorization,* i.e., that which prompts us to memorize. In this respect, memorization is naturally no different from any other activity in which the motives prompting its performance or nonperformance are of paramount importance. From everyday experience it is well known how great the differences are in the process of memorization and in what we achieve as its result depending on what prompts us to memorize. While some motives considerably facilitate memorization, and have an exceptionally great effect, others inhibit the work of memory and lower to a great extent the effect of memorization.

Investigations of the role of the motivation for memorization (motives for study in general) were conducted in various directions. Without giving a broad survey and analysis of these works, we will point out some problems which were the object of study.

In a number of investigations the effects of praise and censure on learning were compared. Thus, in the investigation by Hurlock (1925) one group of schoolchildren working on additions consistently received praise in front of the whole class after each exercise, another was reprimanded for the quality of their work, a third did not receive any evaluation. All the groups were first equalized according to their progress and some other indicators. The first group was the most productive, the second was the reprimanded group, while the third which had not received any special motive showed in general a very small educability.

Much attention is given by foreign investigators to the study of the influence of nociceptive stimulation (electric shock). As a result of a number of experiments it was revealed that the use of this stimulus accelerates the exercise not only when it is given for incorrect actions (in experiments on the mastery of motor habits), but also when it is used as indication of correctness of the action, if such a "reverse" informative meaning is told to the subjects beforehand [investigations of Muenzinger (1934*a*, 1934*b*), Bernard and Gilbert (1941), and others].

An object of investigation was, further, the influence of competition on the success of learning. American psychologists compared for this purpose two types of competition: individual competition when two subjects competed against each other (all participants were divided into pairs and competition was, therefore, within each pair) and group competition. In the investigation of Sims (1928) individual competition (in reading speed) was more effective. Analogous results were obtained by Maller (1929).

Generalizations of such results are obviously incorrect, since the effect of the motives studied in these and similar investigations undoubtedly depends completely on the specific sociohistoric conditions of life and upbringing of people in a particular country. The same must be said about correlations of "ego orientation" and "task orientation." In these investigations conducted by American psychologists (Shaw, 1944; Shaw and Spooner, 1945; Alper, 1946, 1948), ego orientation also exerted the stronger influence.

In a number of investigations, the influence of the "degree of encouragement" on the effect of memorization was studied. To this end, for example, Thorndike and Forlano (1933) varied the amount of money given as reward to the subjects in their experiments with "multiple choice" (i.e., from a number of possible actions to select the seemingly correct one). The experiments were conducted with boys 10 to 16 years of age. As a result of the experiments it was established that an increase of the reward for a correct answer (given at random) accelerated learning (selection of an increasing number of correct answers) within certain limits, but afterwards even had a negative effect. Such results can hardly permit any generalization.

Sears (1937) and also Russel and Farber (1948) studied the influence of failure on memorization. In the second of these investigations it was revealed that subjects who had failed in memorization (which was determined during reproduction occurring immediately after memorization) showed at the next check (one week later) better results than the participants of the experiment who had shown good results before. McGeoch (1961) in discussing the results of these investigations correctly points to the close connection between the effect of competition, success, and failure and the level of motivation in the subjects. No less important, however, is the dependence of the effect of motives on the content and character of the *activity* itself in which motives must manifest their impelling strength. In itself a motive does not determine completely either the nature of the activity or its productivity. Moreover, the motives themselves, or rather, the degree of their influence, depend on the actions to which they impel man.

In Soviet psychology literature Istomina (1948*a*) has investigated the effect of motives for activity on memorization under the guidance of Leont'ev. The author wanted to determine how the motives for memorization affect the success of retention.

Two series of experiments were conducted. In one, preschool children were told to repeat a number of words after the experimenter. Memorization was thus accomplished under ordinary experimental conditions. In contrast, in the other series of experiments it was incorporated into the play activity of the children. The children played "store" and in the course of the game one of the children was asked to go to the "store" and "buy" for the "kindergarten" a number of things. These objects were named for the child. The names were approximately the same as were memorized under laboratory conditions. It is quite evident that the memorization motives in the second series of experiments were different. Moreover, they now had a social character since the child had to remember what was demanded from his participation in a group game and that he had to "shop" for the "kindergarten."

The results of the experiments showed that the effect of memorization in the second series was noticeably higher than in the first and this held true for all age groups, as can be clearly seen from Table 1.2.

Different motivations also caused qualitative differences in the behavior of the children during memorization and reproduction in the presence or absence of a goal to memorize and recall the words. From the data obtained, the author notes three types of behavior in the children: characteristic of the first of them is the absence of a goal to memorize and recall the words; for the second, the presence of this goal but without the application of any special mnemonic devices directed toward accomplishing the set goal; for the third, the application of these devices. The data which characterize the distribution of the types of memorization and reproduction depending on motivation have shown that under play conditions the higher (second and third) types of behavior were observed more often than under experimental conditions. Under the influence of some practice, motivation showed its effect on the change in the processes of memorization and recall. The increase in the number of words reproduced as a result of practice which occurred, on the one hand, under conditions of laboratory experiments and on the other in the play activity of the children, is presented in Table 1.3.

From these data it follows that practice under conditions of play activity is much more pronounced than in the laboratory experiment. This difference is especially striking for younger children.

TABLE 1.2

Age of children in years	Mean percentage of reproduced words	
	under experimental conditions	during play
3–4	0.6	1.0
4–5	1.5	3.0
5–6	2.0	3.3
6–7	2.3	3.8

TABLE 1.3

Conditions of the exercise	Increase in the percentage of reproduced words in children		
	4–5 years old	5–6 years old	6–7 years old
In the laboratory	33	66	107
During play	62	87	113

Very characteristic also is the following observation: it turned out that children on whom the laboratory experiments were repeated and then play conducted (which was done to check the effect of practice) had a much smaller increase in productivity of memorization than children whose practice was conducted in the process of play, and the checking of the achieved effect was conducted under laboratory conditions. For four–five-year-old children the increase in practice was in the first case equal to 40%, in the second, 100%; in the five–six-year-old children in the first case, 60%, in the second, 108%; in the six–seven-year-old children, 106% and 127%.

All these data clearly show that when the children had a memorization motive which was clear to them, directly resulting from the nature of their play activity, memorization and recall proceeded with greater success: in the higher indexes of productivity as well as in the higher level of the processes of memory themselves, in their nature, and also in the results of practice.

In her next investigation Istomina (1948*b*) compared memorization in play and practical activity (preparation for an exhibit; in the process of this work each child was asked to memorize a number of objects necessary for the exhibit). For each age group the results of memorization were higher in the second case than in play, namely: in play the three-year-olds reproduced 1 word; the four-year-olds, 3; the five-year-olds, 3.2; the six-year-olds, 3.8; but under conditions of practical activity the corresponding values were: 2.3; 3.5; 4.0; 4.4.

In a more recent work Istomina (1964) studied a different problem, but again various types of activity were utilized in which memorization was carried out, namely: play, work, listening to a story, and learning words (the latter proceeded as it does under ordinary laboratory conditions); the results obtained from laboratory experiments were, again, for all age groups noticeably lower than what was reproduced in all other types of activity; there was little difference in memorization productivity among the other three. Lower values for the laboratory experiments were also obtained in the study of delayed reproduction. The stability of retention of what had been memorized was least in these experiments.

Zinchenko (1945) devoted an investigation to the influence of motives for activity. The experiments consisted of the following: children (preschool and schoolchildren of the second and fifth grades) were asked to find a word that had a definite relation to the word given to them (preschool children were given 10 words, the schoolchildren 15) or to point out either what was concretely connected with the given word ("house—window") or to define the quality of the given object ("house—wooden") or to find a word with the same first letter (this assignment was not given to the preschool children). In some cases the subjects were told that the task was given in order to find out whether they knew how to think correctly (a situation similar to school work), in other cases the experiment was conducted in a play situation (a game of "thinking up words"). After each assignment the words had to be reproduced (those named by the experimenter and those invented by the subjects). For the preschool children, in performing both of the first tasks the best memorization indexes were obtained in play; for the schoolchildren, on the contrary, memorization was better under the influence of school motives.

All these experiments point clearly to the essential role which the motives of activity play in memorization, and that the same motives in different subjects can evoke a completely different response.

Chapter 2

INVOLUNTARY MEMORIZATION

1. THE DEPENDENCE OF INVOLUNTARY MEMORIZATION ON THE ORIENTATION OF ACTIVITY

We have examined the great influence exerted on memorization by mnemonic orientation. The very fact of its presence or absence and also the nature of the mnemonic tasks, their specific content, to a considerable extent determine the productivity as well as the qualitative nature of memorization.

Both, however, depend not only on the mnemonic orientation but also on activity which in itself is not aimed at mnemonic achievements. Its orientation can vary greatly and this cannot fail to influence in some way the results of memorization, what remains in memory as the result of this nonmnemonic activity.

Just how are these results of memorization limited to the nonmnemonic orientation of activity within which an involuntary memorizing is accomplished?

In order to obtain at least some material elucidating this question we conducted the following experiments (Smirnov, 1945*a*). We asked the subjects to recall some facts from their recent past. They had to recall what had been involuntarily memorized. The activity as the result of which the memorization was accomplished, as any activity, was directed towards something definite (moreover, over a rather long time). Our task was to trace the dependence of memorization on this specifically characterized orientation of an activity proceeding under the ordinary conditions of life.

Two series of experiments were conducted with several subjects each. In one case we asked the subjects to recall everything that had occurred to them when they walked from home to the institute where they worked. The questioning was unexpected for the subjects and occurred usually 1.5–2 h after work had begun. The subjects had to give a very detailed account of all they saw, heard, all they did, of what they thought, what they emotionally experienced. They were told that if they did not want to tell something they could limit themselves to a general description of what was in their consciousness or not tell anything, only pointing out how clearly and fully they recalled what they did not want to tell. However, there were no such cases in our experiments: not even once did the subjects remark that they had something which they did not want to tell the experimenter. On the contrary, they were very interested in recalling and telling as much as possible and exerted all effort to do so.

In the second series of experiments the subjects were asked (again, unexpectedly) to recall everything that occurred in the course of a scientific conference at which they had been present a week before the experiments. They had to write a report on the content of a paper that had been read at this conference and the discussions that followed. The subjects in both cases were psychologists experienced in self-observation.

Let us now examine the data. We start with the first experiment. Subject B. remembers from his way to work the following:

> First of all I remember the moment I left the subway. What precisely? I thought that I must quickly take up the necessary position to get out of the subway and walk fast, since I was late. I remember I was in the last car. Therefore, I could not get out quickly and had to go into the crowd. Previously the people leaving the car took up the whole width of the platform. Now, in order to secure a passage for those entering the cars, officials are stationed who turn the public from the edge of the platform. It caught my eye that at each post stood a man for this purpose; otherwise the public would walk at the edge of the platform. [There follows a description of several men standing at the pillars, not letting the passengers to the edge of the platform.] I think I did not look at the clock. The road further is a blank. I remember nothing about it. There is only a hazy recollection from previous trips. I walked to the gates of the university without noticing anything. Don't remember what I thought of. When I entered the gate I noticed someone was hurrying. Who precisely, a man or a woman, I don't remember. More I don't remember.... Now about the first half of the way. I do not remember leaving the house. I remember that when I was leaving the gate I remembered that I did not take along the book of tickets. I thought of how much it would delay me, since there is always a line at the ticket window. Usually I go to the subway station turning into the lane with the streetcar. I turn where the streetcar rushes downward. Every time I look at the streetcar. This time I also walked there and looked at the streetcar cautiously. Coming up to the subway station I saw the booth and thought: are there newspapers? I decided to stand in line if there were some. There were none. I stood at the ticket window. Somebody took a long time. Over his head I thrust my money, walking through very fast. I slowed down at the checker. I noticed that the checker tore the tickets very fast. I heard the train and hurried. I looked at the food stand with a hurried glance. I noticed that the things I needed were not there. I ran to the train. I entered the car. I don't remember the passengers. I went up to the opposite door. I decided to go through the car and stand at the first door. I went

> through. I think I stood between two men. What I thought in the train I do not remember at all. Without a doubt I had some thoughts.

What is characteristic of this story? The first conspicuous thing is that the subject clearly indicates that he does not remember at all what he thought about although he is quite convinced that at a certain point of the way he did think about something. Further, the story contains indications of everything that hindered or could hinder the accomplishment of his being on time for work: the impossibility of slipping quickly through the crowd, the impossibility of using the edge of the platform for this, his forgotten ticket book, the delay in buying his ticket. In the story there are also observations which indirectly assisted in the quickest arrival at the institute: the fast work of the ticket checker, going over from one door to the other for the purpose of shortening the way and speeding up his exit. It is characteristic that the subject remembered relatively well the people standing at the pillars of the platform directing traffic, which prevented the subject from passing the platform quickly, but did not recall any one of the passengers. Of the people on the street he remembered only one man who was hurrying as he did. He remembered the newspaper booth, which is evidently connected with the reflection on whether to buy a paper or not and his doubts in view of the lateness. Thus, the biggest part of what he remembered was in one way or another connected with the main channel of the subject's activity: going from home to the institute without being late. Of all that the subject reproduced only one remembrance did not have reference to the main line of his action. The remembrance of the food stand and the thought in connection with it. Everything else was in the channel of the basic activity and was closely connected with the main motive which determined it: the necessity to come to work on time.

We turn to the second story. The female subject, N., reproduces the following:

> I remember first of all the fateful moment of crossing at the corner of 25 October Street. Now the complex images of today's, yesterday's, and earlier crossings. I must distinguish what was today. Usually there is a crowd there in which one gets confused. It is more difficult than among automobiles. It was about the same today. While you walk to the middle of the street, the automobiles have not yet come up. Therefore the first half of the street you cross calmly. On the second half one has to go somewhat downhill. It seems there were not the usual trucks there. Today there were many turns which had to be made to go around the standing automobiles. Usually after crossing I head towards the bookstore. Today there was no snow and I walked diagonally. I don't remember how I crossed Herzen Street. Very clearly I remember as I entered the small gate of the university (usually I use the large gate, but today an automobile was parked there). The entrance to the small gate was strewn with sand (not as usual). I remember walking up the courtyard. Students were hurrying to their lectures. I noticed that I was not late. A feeling of quiet upstairs. I noticed on Kuibyshev Street the clock had stopped at 5:30. Today I was afraid to be late, and the clock was of no help. What was

> in the background of all this? There were thoughts. But I do not remember where and what thoughts. On 25 October Street I had thoughts about the comedy film and Alexandrov. Before that thoughts of whether it was worth while to write a plan for the study of discipline in school. What did I think about the comedy film? About its plot. Rather, why it was not successful. What did I think of the plan? Whether it is worth thinking about it and working on it. I am not sure it is necessary. It is possible I thought about it while still at home, before I started out. The road along 25 October Street I do not remember. Somewhere along the way my hands became cold. I covered them. I had an unusual suitcase. When I walked along the lane (here I usually think intensively) I thought of something, but remember nothing. Of the passersby I remember a woman near the university. I do not remember faces at all.

It is not difficult to see that in this story the subject notes the fact of forgetting her thoughts, although not completely. It is true, some of them she does remember but she is not sure of even them, whether she had them on her way or before she left the house. But the main part of her story is once again the reproduction of the difficulties in connection with her transportation, i.e., connected with the main channel of activity and the motive which determined it.

The third subject, T., tells the following:

> Leaving the house I knew I had to go by subway since it was late. I turned the corner immediately and walked along the lane to the subway. What did I think about? I don't remember. No recollection has remained. But there is a visual image of this morning, of me walking. I walked slowly. I don't remember the people. I thought: Is it all right to walk slowly? Crossing the street I had to wait, a car came. I stood in a group of people ready to cross, I did not look to the side because my collar was raised. In the middle of the street I again waited for the cars to pass. In front of the subway station was a long line of people waiting for newspapers through which I had to pass. On the subway stairs there is a terrible draft, which lifts everybody's coat flaps strangely. I thought: I probably look strange right now too. I did not buy tickets, but used my last token. By necessity I took the stairs to the right. There were many people. The descent was slow. I found the train standing. Too bad, the doors were closing. I can well see a part of the car with the closed door. I walked along the empty platform. There were two other people who were late. I walked to the end as usual. I came to the place from where the clock can be seen. It was 8:45. I clearly see now the position of the hands. I saw a tall man with a newspaper in his hand. I thought: very likely yesterday's. I remembered the line at the subway. No, it was today's. Saw that the news bulletin from military headquarters was a long one. Here I met G. (last name of acquaintance). He also was interested in the bulletin and walked up to the man reading the paper, who was reading the last page. He showed G. the first page but immediately turned back to the last page. G. tried to look from below. The train came. We entered. How G. entered I don't remember. I let several women with bags pass. I stood at the doors. Close to me two more women were at the corners. One with a bag of groceries, without gloves. I see her hands. I thought: why without gloves? In her hands was a newspaper. Again I remember G. We talked about the bulletin. What happened to him before this I don't remember. In the car I remember our conversation, but I do not remember him. I don't remember where he stood, etc. [There follows an account of the talk with G. about the events at the front.]

> The walk through the station I do not remember at all. I remember crossing the street. I waited a long time for the cars to pass. In the middle of the street I had to stop again. I remember looking at my watch but do not remember what time it was. I felt no hurry at that time. I have forgotten what we talked about on the way to the university. At the university gates I saw B. I remember the snow drifts in the university courtyard and the talk about this year's snow with G.

T.'s story differs greatly from the preceding ones, since on the way he met an acquaintance with whom he continued the rest of the way and with whom he talked almost all the while. But if one compares the first part (before the meeting with G.) with the reports of the other subjects, it is not difficult to notice a similarity. As had the preceding subjects, T. had forgotten what he thought on the way, but well remembered the hindrances and difficulties in transportation as well as other, even trivial, facts connected in one way or other with arriving on time at work. It is characteristic that of two thoughts noted in the story again one was connected with the main aim of the activity ("Is it all right to walk slowly?"). Well reproduced also was everything connected with the continuing interest in the events at the front (remembering the man reading the paper at the subway station, the woman with the paper in the car, the talk with G. about the bulletin of military action at the front).

We turn to the story of the last subject. Sh. describes his way in the following manner:

> Sometimes I walk from home on the boulevard, sometimes on the sidewalk. Today I walked on the sidewalk. I met two acquaintances (I meet them every time). Near the house being remodeled stood a car which had to be bypassed. I crossed to the subway station at a right angle. What was in the subway station? When I descended my glasses fogged. I had to hold on to the rail. There was a crowd at the escalator. A boy was apprehended for attempting to ride without a ticket. On the escalator I felt that my shoe had become untied. I went to a bench. I discovered that the shoelace was broken. I tied it. I found that I had missed the train. To the left, on the bench, sat two women, to the right I do not remember who. A man came up while I was tying my shoe. As soon as I finished I walked to the train. I entered the second-to-last car. I found that there were few people. There were two in front of me. I looked at their faces. The face of one was very strange, very stupid. I thought for a long time what his job is. Both were conversing. One wore a brown hat, the other a black coat and a black hat. At the door when I walked out there stood a man in a fur coat. I did not know if he was getting out or not. Coming out of the car I did not look at the clock. Who was with me on the escalator I do not remember. I glanced at the store counter, seeing what was there. I went up to the apothecary booth. I asked if there was anything for a headache. I don't remember the salesman at all. I bought some shoelaces. At this time another man came up to him in a black coat and a black fur cap. He asked foolishly, "Do you have shoelaces?" although there hung many of them at the vendor's. At the exit doors there was a great crowd. I did not have to wait for cars to pass when I came out. I don't remember crossing the street. I glanced at the window of a bookstore. I remember the book *Chemistry of Defense*. I remember the book because of its peculiar title. Other books I do not remember. When I passed the American Embassy an automobile came out. I saw that

> the cigarette stand was closed. I immediately crossed Herzen Street. Somehow I remember the tram-rails visually. At a distance there was an approaching streetcar. There were no automobiles. Entering the university courtyard I wanted to turn left, but a woman with a child was in the way and I walked on the sidewalk. When I was passing the lecture hall, I met A. At the door of the library I met a man, don't remember who he was.... While walking to the subway station I don't remember what I thought about. When I passed the People's Commissariat of Education Building, I thought I might meet G. (I needed to see him). When I descended the stairs of the subway I took care so as not to stumble. On the escalator I thought of my shoelaces. I was afraid they would get caught in the steps. Of what I thought on the other escalator I don't remember. When I walked along the corridor I thought of buying laces. In crossing Herzen Street I was aware of the ease of crossing. Of what I thought walking along Mokhovaya St. and in the university courtyard I do not remember.

The report of this subject is fuller than that of the others and in this respect his report differs greatly from the other ones. Considerable space is taken in the story by the recollection of the strange, unusual, peculiar (the face of one of the passengers, characterized as stupid, "foolish question" addressed to the vendor, the "peculiar" title of one of the books). The greatest attention is again given to what in some way hindered or could hinder his main task: the transportation, and it was connected with the motive which guided him, (to get to work on time). This subject, too, notes that much of what he thought during considerable segments of time was forgotten completely.

What are the overall results of the first series of experiments? It showed that the subjects' recollections referred much more to what they *did* than to what they *thought*. The content of the thoughts is seldom recalled and very scanty although the fact itself of *thinking* on the way is beyond doubt and they state it repeatedly.

It is characteristic that when thoughts are recalled they are still connected with the *actions* of the subject. They are thoughts in connection with what the subject performs at a given moment, i.e., which in one way or another are related to traveling from home to work, or thoughts of imminent or contemplated actions (N.'s thoughts about her anticipated work; the question arising in Sh. as to whether he would meet the man with whom he had to speak).

Of the same nature are the recollections of what they *perceived* on the way. The subjects in this case recall mainly what was connected with their own movements, that is, with precisely the activity which they were performing. As this is also very important, they usually speak about what confronted them as obstacles in their paths or, on the contrary, about what facilitated their progress.

The presence of certain difficulties or their absence where they could occur, where they were expected, and where they usually are, form the content of a considerable part of the reports of each subject.

The following fact is in full agreement with this. When the subjects recalled something not connected with their progress, their remembrances referred most often to some question that arose, perplexity, surprise, i.e., in essence it was again some peculiar *hindrance* or *delay,* and indicated the existence of some kind of task for perception or comprehension. Such are, for example, the questions: "What's new in the paper?"; "Is such and such a thing in the booth?"; "Is a certain booth open?"; "Why wasn't the comedy successful?"; "What does this man do?" This category also includes the recollection of something strange, incomprehensible, or unusual which did not fit in with an automatically proceeding perception ("the subway passengers' coattails strangely flapping in the wind," "the foolish question as to whether there are shoelaces," "the foolish face of one of the passengers," "the unusual sanded sidewalk in the university courtyard," "the absence of the woman's gloves in spite of the cold," etc.).

What do these findings show? How does one interpret what the subjects each asserted: the difficulty of remembering (in most cases, a complete inability) their thoughts although they were able to remember their actions well enough?

Proceeding from the reports of the subjects it would be quite incorrect to maintain that thoughts in general are recalled with great difficulty and disappear quickly from memory. Such a generalization would be absolutely unjustifiable.

Admittedly, better remembrance of actions than of thoughts may occur. By itself such a situation, which is of great theoretical significance, is possible. The data of our experiment undoubtedly support it, although they need additional and more extensive checking on broad and varied material. But from this it does not follow at all that thoughts in general are poorly remembered. The *relative difficulty* of their memorization (as compared with actions) must not be taken as an *absolute* characteristic of their retention. Our experiments reveal only the former and say nothing about the latter.

How then can the findings of our experiments be explained? This can be answered only when the orientation of the subjects at the moment when they performed the activity which they reported is taken into account.

Toward what were they oriented on the way to work? Toward reaching a goal on time; to get to the institute where they worked, without disturbing the discipline of labor. Such was the task before them, their set, and the motives for their activity. The movement on the street was not simple walking. It was purposeful, under specific conditions, i.e., connected with a definite time, traveling from home to work. This traveling was the *basic* activity which they performed. The subjects did not *think and walk* more or less automatically while thinking but *walked and thought* while walking. This does not mean, of course, that all their attention was concentrated on walking and that all their thoughts revolved only around this. On the contrary, they were full of thoughts, undoubtedly, of different contents, not referring to what they were doing at the moment. But the main thing they did during the period of time which they described was the traveling from home to work and not those processes of thinking of which they had, undoubtedly, quite a number but which were not connected with the *main channel of their activity.*

In what relation to this main channel of activity, i.e., to the main orientation of the subjects, was the content of what was reproduced in these stories?

It is not difficult to see that it coincided with the main channel of activity, to a considerable extent. For the most part, the subjects described what precisely was connected with the main channel of their activity (for a certain segment of time), i.e., with their trip to work. And, *vice versa,* all that was outside of this channel, extraneous to their main orientation at the moment, was dropped from their memory and was not at all reproduced, in spite of considerable efforts to remember all that had occurred. Not being connected with the main orientation of the activity, the thoughts were completely forgotten although the subjects knew very well that they had had them and that the whole time of their traveling from home to work was filled with all kinds of reflections.

Thus, the *most important condition determining remembrance in these experiments was the main channel of activity of the subjects, the main line of their orientation, and those motives by which they were guided in their activity.*

Our experiments showed also the concrete relation of everything that was better remembered to the main channel of activity of the subjects. Best remembered of all was whatever arose as an *obstacle or difficulty* to the activity. This is also a determining factor in remembering everything that did not pertain to the main orientation of the subjects. No matter how insignificant the reproduced material not pertaining to the main activity, however, the subjects remembered best what had been an obstacle or difficulty in the activity. Therefore, the relationship of anything to an activity impeding its execution is, undoubtedly, one of the main conditions determining the effectiveness of remembering. As we saw, it determines the retention of what is connected with the main channel of activity. It serves as a source of remembering what goes beyond the limits of this channel.

We turn to the examination of the second series of experiments. The subjects were asked to remember discussions and the content of a report which they had heard at a scientific conference attended a week before the questioning. We cite the reports of three subjects and then give a general analysis of these accounts.

Female subject Sh. relates:

> M. [name of the speaker] began by writing two difficult examples on the blackboard (Russian and Belorussian words); showed the errors: *Khodyut'*, *Khochut'*, I don't remember exactly (palatalization and ending incorrect). He explained it by the similarity of the two languages. This was the basis of the work. He pointed out that it is similar when memorizing historical, no, geographical material (Kalinin district and another one, I think Moscow district) where everything is the same except one thing. He showed examples of difficulty. This was the basis for the desirability to study the problem of similarity and difference. After this he stated how this problem is substantiated, how Marxism answers the question of similarity and difference. Then he criticized existing theories. He grouped them: those speaking of similarity as a positive and as a negative factor. This principle was not quite sustained. He pointed out that similarity in connection with difference had not been studied by anyone. Proceeding from correct methodological premises, he proved that similarities and differences are inseparable, that in similarity there is difference and in difference, similarity. I liked this point of view. It was not quite clear why he checked the experiments of R. From the history of this problem he gave several names [the subject mentioned several names]. He pointed to R.'s experiments with chess. He told of how he repeated these experiments. The distinguishing feature of his work is its qualitative analysis. As a result of his experiments he found that the perception of the principle, the understanding of the situation, does not evoke a negative effect of similarity. He pointed to the nature of the errors: sometimes mix-up, sometimes forgetfulness. In contrast to this, R. did not give anything but figures. After that he proceeded to his own experiments, giving similar material in prose. He did something else. First the prose. Description from Sholokhov.... Either a thunderstorm or a forest. No, ruts.... Forest. Not a thunderstorm, but a forest. It is spring. Not a thunderstorm, no, a forest or spring. In Turgenev or Sholokhov. He did not cite excerpts. Almost one and the same sentence in both texts: hit the horse with the rein and hit the horse with the whip. The subjects got confused. This raised doubts in one of the opponents. Why must one look at this as a difference and not a similarity? M. answered that this depended on the situation. This was the strongest objection. M.'s answer did not convince me. Then he spoke of the second series. What was it? Botanical material? Historical? Geographical? Very likely historical. I don't remember the second series. Problems? No. Russian language? No. Now the content of the discussions. At first no one wanted to step forward. Why, I don't know. There was an awkward pause. Who broke it? Sh. spoke, and S. did. Not immediately, but towards the end. I remember. R. may have started. He said that M. had pictured the scheme beautifully but conducted the experiments on chess and on artistic material. Maybe he did not say it that way. This will have to be checked in school. One must find a Belorussian school and check the obtained results. R. said also that M. had come very well prepared and this showed in the quality of his work. The work is indisputably valuable, but it was not clear why M. had not begun with spelling. What T. said I do not remember. He may not have spoken. No, he did speak. Clearest are the discussions of Sh., R., and K. K. summarized. D. did not participate. She said maybe a few words. V. also said a few words. About what? He said one had to go to a school. S. said the work was good. D. added that the discussion in the laboratory was useful. S. pointed to some shortcomings. B. spoke. What he said surprised me somewhat. He said that much had yet

to be worked out. K. said that the work was good, exceptionally thorough, elegant, and well-refined, but is it worth spending time on minor problems. It was illogical. Graduate students should very likely be given other topics. He appealed to B. I have, he said, a different system: to give a wide-range problem useful for life. In answering, M. did not say anything new. He said he would go to a school and thanked everybody. He said he would work it out in two months. Relative to K.'s question he said that he will answer it later.

The second subject, T., recalled:

First of all I remember where I sat. Then I saw M. in a blue suit standing in front of the table and often going to the blackboard. At the very beginning of the report Belorussian and Russian words were pointed out. The thoughts expressed by M. I remember. What were the words? Something about "a" and "o," something "tsa" as ending of the infinitive of a verb. I see well the blackboard with two triads of words. Everything comes to vague visual images. During the report I looked at the head of M. I noticed something about it. What, I do not remember. One more example he cited relative to two fields. He pointed out their similarity and difference. Flax, similar or different. Coal as different. Then he talked about his experiments. Very likely he spoke about theoretical premises between the examples and experiments. I don't remember them. What was the problem? Relative to remembering similar material, which similarity helps and which impedes. He spoke of the history of the problem [the subject cites several names]. I thought: why does he not mention the work by S-v. Then he spoke of his own experiments. He read from texts. One was the thunderstorm from "Biryuk" [story by Turgenev]. The thunderstorm, the forest, the hitting of the horse with reins. I remember, they hit with reins and the whip. The ruts changed to bumps. The same was done with something else. With what? Ah, with mushrooms. What was the result of the work? In the similar, the different is remembered and in the different, the similar. Yes! There was a part where dialectics was mentioned. More conclusions I do not remember. *Content of discussion:* Sh. said, why is this similar and this different. All this is relative. Reins and whip. You call it different, but in my opinion it is similar. He said this was not an objection, it was a question. This seemed clever and I remember it. Then S. pointed out that in this laboratory work is conducted on a similar topic. He mentioned his own work. B. said this must be checked on school material. V. spoke earlier about the same thing. R. said everything was good but something else should be done. Yes! He said the center of the work should be in the further development of the views of the founders of Marxism–Leninism. I think he was also for the necessity of continued work on school material. K. said that the work was good and jewelry-like, but that he himself prefers the "broad picture." He asked where the work leads and said he would bring it up when M. defends his thesis, if it weren't pointed out. I don't remember what M. answered. He said to K. that he refuses to think of a "broad picture." I waited for what he would say, what he would think, but he refused to think. More I do not remember.

The third subject, D., said:

The first thing I remember is the structure of the report. First the theoretical part. What theories? M. discussed them critically. The main problem is similarity and difference. How it is resolved philosophically and psychologically. He discussed the experimental material of a number of authors [with uncertainty he recalls several names]. There were no less than five or six authors. The second part was the exposition of the method. The first part of the experiments consisted of checking the older investigations. The method of the work by R. was completely reproduced; in particular, nonsense syllables were utilized. I remember this because he protested against utilization of nonsense syllables and assumed that this series would be evaluated negatively. Then followed stories whose subject matter was biology. Two stories. Here he found deficiencies in the work of the author under discussion. One cannot come to the conclusions drawn by R. One cannot simply decide about similarity or difference. There are stages where the plus changes to minus. He told who were his subjects and how many experiments he conducted. Then he came to the main conclusions. The biology stories were about mushrooms. I don't remember exactly. Yes! He took the seasons from somewhere. One event in the summer, the other in winter. One in the Ukraine. Something connected with seasons. One about a forest, the other about the steppe. Ah! From Turgenev. One about mushrooms, the other a poetic story, a description of nature. From this his biology conclusions. Winter.... About what? One where there is a forest, the other connected with the steppe. Visually I do not at all remember. What is the essence of M.'s conclusions? The error of foreign authors is that they took similarity and difference separately, did not seek unity. In checking R.'s experiments, M. established the role of perceiving the similarity when this similarity is helpful. Catching external similarity hinders. Of help is the similarity attributed to generalization. Even with nonsensical material this was of great significance. He gave an illustration. The second factor: at what stage is this similarity a negative, at what a positive factor. For M. this is a positive factor. He presented the diagram of one author (don't remember whom) and said that basically one can accept this, but the process is not that simple. He did not give as careful an analysis as he did with the experiments with the chess pieces. But mainly they corroborated the other series. He appealed often and well to pedagogical examples. When telling about theory he cited educators (including Ushinskii). The last part consisted in pedagogical conclusions. Yes, he began with teaching (the Russian and Belorussian languages) and finished with it. He pointed out that this was a very important problem for educators. I know these proofs but do not remember precisely which he cited in his report. Now for the content of discussion. Who spoke? Sh. About what? Asked some question. I don't remember. I know one thing. He said that the problem was important. He welcomes its solution from the point of view of dialectical materialism. It is important for psychology. R. What did he say? That M. to no purpose.... That the importance of such work consists not of disproving the bourgeois theorists but of presenting one's own positive theory. He did not assess the work as criticism, and M. considers this to be to his credit. R. said it does not pay to waste time on criticism. A solution must be given from the point of view of dialectical materialism. Something close to it. Who else? I talked. I remember about what. About deadlines. (Somebody asked about it.) I reminded them that there would be a test on school material. Who else? B. He was asked to speak. What did he say? That as a whole the report satisfies him. What he said I don't remember. He sat not far from us, bent over, very excited. He was satisfied that the report went over well. He said something important, but I don't remember what. I think that M. had a certain part not sufficiently developed which is present in the material....Then S. described the state of this problem in the laboratory. By this time I calmed down and when I did calm down I stopped trying to remember, although at that time I had absorbed everything very well. Then K. spoke. Here I became tense again. He said that the work was like fine jewelry, filigree work. For teaching purposes it is possibly of interest, but it does not impress him. There is no wide range in the formulation of the problem, basis for discussion, debates. He is for broad pictures. M. answered K. that K.... Yes. He have no answer to the broad pictures. But this question of K. he answered: how the work gets into practice. M. spoke also about an unpaid bill and that he will think about it. About what? I forgot about what.

What do these reports reveal? Without doubt they all differ. What each subject remembers is not the same. While, for example, subject Sh. relates in detail the first, theoretical, part of the report, T. in reference to the same part says: "Very likely spoke about theoretical premises. Between the examples and the experiments he very likely talked about them. I don't remember them." Only later the subject remembers, and then only one fact in reference to this: "There was a part where he talked about dialectics." In speaking about the history of the problem, subject T. again limits himself to a brief comment: "Told some history of the problem (names a few authors). He did not mention the work by S-v." The subject does not mention anything about the first part of the investigation of the speaker where it deals with the experimental criticism of the conclusions obtained in the work of R.

For all the differences in the testimony of the subjects, their stories have much in common. All subjects remember comparatively well the overall structure of the report, its plan. Well remembered also are the main propositions of the speaker concerning the subjectivity of the contrast between similarity and difference, about their correlation, about the varying influence of the similarity of material on memorization, and about the significance of the realization of similarity. To some extent these propositions are expressed in the stories of each of the subjects. The subjects correctly remember almost all comments during the discussion. As a whole each subject relates, although very briefly and often in fragments, much of what was perceived of the report and the discussion. This must be specially emphasized, since here we see something different as compared with what was obtained in the preceding experiment, where the subjects very skimpily reproduced not only the content of their thoughts but also what they perceived during the time of their walk along the streets. The difference is all the more striking in that for the first series of experiments the reports were given 1.5–2 h after the incidents described, while in this case the stories were told one week after the conference.

How can this difference be explained? Undoubtedly, one of its essential causes must be that in the second experiment everything perceived by the subject was a *logically connected whole*. This pertains primarily to the report, but to a considerable extent also to the discussion which naturally was related to the content of the report. In the first experiment the subjects perceived a great deal on their way to work, not as a single whole but as a series of broken impressions. This undoubtedly played a considerable role as the source of essential differences of remembering in the two cases.

The following also played an important role as a source of differences. In the first experiment the subjects reproduced primarily *specific objects,* moreover objects seen by them for the first time. In the second case there were more or less *general propositions* expressed in the report and closely related to the knowledge and interests of the subjects. Moreover, the speaker referred to them more than once in the course of his report.

Noting the significance of these two factors it must be pointed out, however, that both of them do not exhaust what could be considered a sufficient cause for the differences observed between the stories of the subjects in the first and second series of experiments. Indeed, although it is fully justified that in the first series of experiments there was no connection in the perception of what the subjects saw on the street, one can hardly assume that the thoughts of the subjects on some segment of the way were also unrelated. Even if the goal of these thoughts was not especially long-term, it nevertheless was there. However the subjects could hardly remember them. One cannot explain the difference between the first and second series of experiments only by the relatedness or unrelatedness of what was remembered.

The same must be said in regard to the second difference between the experiments. In the stories of the subjects concerning the report, considerable space was taken up by reproducing the main propositions to which the speaker often returned. Nevertheless, even specific data given by the speaker only once were reproduced just as extensively and this was done in spite of the fact that this time the delay of reproduction was considerably longer. Even under these conditions the subjects remembered comparatively well the examples given by the speaker as illustrations of the practical significance of the investigation. In particular, spelling errors observed during simultaneous study of two languages, Russian and Belorussian, the examples illustrating the difference in the sentences given for memorization ("he hit with the reins" and "he hit with the whip"), and a number of other specific factors were noted.

What has been said prompts us therefore to look for other causes which would explain the difference in the completeness of memorization between the first and second series of experiments. Undoubtedly, differences in the orientation of the subjects must be of importance.

In what respect did the second series of experiments differ from the first? In the first series the subjects were oriented towards getting to work on time, in the second, towards perceiving the report. In the first case the main channel of their activity was their movement on the streets, and a considerable part of all that they perceived or thought was just something extraneous, not at all connected with what was the content of their main activity. Of a different nature was the activity of the subjects in the second series of experiments. In this series it was directed toward getting acquainted with the report, its content, and with the subsequent discussion. In its very essence this was a *cognitive orientation* of activity, and this must play an important, if not decisive, role in explaining the differences observed between the stories of the subjects in the first and second series of experiments. It certainly was one of the most important bases of these differences.

A number of other findings revealed that the orientation of the subjects played an important role not only in the first but also in the second series of experiments. Let us note several of them. Considerable space in subjects' reports was taken up by the reproduction of specific details together with the account of the plan and main propositions of the report. To some extent all subjects remembered examples which the speaker gave as illustrations of the propositions of his report. Opposite cases were also observed, the forgetting of some specific factors which were beyond the scope of the main propositions of the report. None of the subjects could remember sufficiently well the topic, sometimes even the general nature of the texts which were used in the investigation. Subject Sh. for example, in speaking of the texts of the second series of experiments "sorts out in her mind" completely different types of material as possible variants. In speaking of the material of the first series she is again not sure what texts were given; whether from Turgenev or Sholokhov. In fact, works of both were utilized. Subject T. remembers only the thunderstorm from "Briyuk" and something about "mushrooms." Noticeable difficulties in recalling the texts are observed in subject D.: "Something with the seasons of the year, one event in the summer, the other in winter; one in the Ukraine; one in a forest, the other in the steppe." In fact there were no such texts, there were two descriptions of a thunderstorm.

In itself, forgetting some specific factors is, of course, nothing unusual. It must be considered natural and common. It is, however, of interest that the reports of the subjects obtained in the second series of experiments reveal a considerable coincidence in the forgetting of some items and recalling of others, some even of the same nature. Such a coincidence, naturally, poses a question concerning its causes. Why, indeed, did all subjects remember poorly what was used by the speaker as experimental material, but remember well the fact that in the texts presented there were similar sentences about the hitting of the horse with the reins and the whip? Why did they remember the examples cited to illustrate the errors caused by similarity of the material (all subjects clearly remembered that these examples referred to cases of simultaneous learning of the Russian and Belorussian languages)?

Our data do not give a clear answer to this question. But one can assume with considerable certainty that the basis for this coincidence was the *orientation* of the subjects in listening to the report.

What were they directed toward in this case? Undoubtedly, they were to make clear to themselves the gist of the report and, in particular, to learn the method of the investigation. For the method of the work (especially directed toward the study of the influence of similarity on memorization), it was not the subject and general nature of the texts that were significant, but the report on how the similarity of the experimental material was reached, and what specifically this similarity was. This was necessary for an understanding of the method, its characteristics, and for an evaluation of the conclusions obtained; the subject and general nature of the texts were rather immaterial. Thus, the examples which illustrated the similarity of the separate parts of the material corresponded to the main orientation of the subjects, whereas familiarization with the topic and nature of the texts was extraneous to the main line of their activity.

The same thing must be said about the examples used to illustrate the errors caused by the similarity of material (in studying two similar languages). Pointing out these examples at the very beginning of the report made immediately clear the practical significance of the question studied by the speaker as well as the very essence of the investigated problem, and that again corresponded to the main orientation of the subjects during the report.

Indicative of the nature of the role of orientation is also *what* was recalled of the discussion. In analyzing the pertinent evidence it is not difficult to see that all subjects, especially Sh. and D., in telling of the discussion recall most of the evaluation of the report given by the participants. What was the reason? In order to understand this it must be taken into account that the report was a scientific account of a finished dissertation of a graduate student which soon was to be defended. Hence it was natural that, aside from the main, *cognitive* attitude toward the report directed toward revealing the content of the work, some subjects would be oriented toward learning about the *evaluation* of the work. This orientation could be expected to the greatest extent in the subjects Sh. and D. Sh. herself was at this time working on her dissertation on a similar topic, and she very shortly would have to report on her investigation. D. was intimately involved with dissertation work on account of her position as director of graduate studies.

Very characteristic in connection with what has been said is one place in the report of D. In speaking of the remarks made by one of the participants in the discussion (S.) and having difficulty telling what precisely was said by him, she relates the following: "By that time I had quieted down and when calm set in I stopped remembering, although by then I assimilated everything well." In order to understand this it must be taken into account that S.'s opinion of the work of the speaker was already known to D. before the conference and, consequently, could no longer give anything new to the satisfaction of her orientation toward learning about the evaluation of the work during the discussion. The same must be said of the report of B. His opinion was also clear to D. before the report. Therefore, in spite of the exceptional attention with which D. usually listened to all comments of B. and which she also showed this time, she, nevertheless, could not remember this time what B. had said, recalling only that he was satisfied with the report. "He said something essential" she says in connection with B.'s comments, but what precisely he said she is not able to remember. On the other hand, she remembers very well the main position of K.'s comments since at that moment, according to her own account, her tenseness returned again (because she did not know the opinion of K. on the one hand, and because of its importance as the opinion of the director of the institute, on the other). Thus, the connection between memorization and orientation in D. was confirmed by her herself; it must be considered as quite definite. What corresponded to this orientation was better remembered; what was beyond it was reproduced with great difficulty or was not remembered at all.

Thus, the results of the second series of experiments fully confirm the correctness of the general proposition introduced above: *memorization is dependent upon the main line of activity as the result of which memorization is accomplished and on the motives by which this activity is determined.* The material of both experiments makes it possible to consider this proposition as having general significance. *It is one of the most important conditions for the success of involuntary memorization.*

2. THE DEPENDENCE OF INVOLUNTARY MEMORIZATION ON THE CONTENT AND NATURE OF THE ACTIVITY

Orientation is only one of the facets of activity. Other, no less important, facets are the *content and nature* of the activity, i.e., *what* is performed in the process of its accomplishment and *how* the actions entering into this composition are accomplished. It is therefore also justifiable to ask to what extent memorization occurring in any activity also depends on *these* facets and what these relations are.

The possibilities of varying an activity in content and character of performance are limitless. Therefore, the study of the dependence of memorization on these facets of activity is a vast and complex task demanding many investigations. In this section we will only examine the dependence of memorization on one of the peculiarities of activity, the one which relates directly to the problem of activeness of memorization. We have in mind the *activeness* of activity. The study of its influence on memorization is especially important since activeness is the basic and most characteristic feature of any activity. This necessarily follows from its very essence and at the same time varies greatly in degree in specific types of activity.

The same activity can be performed with varying degrees of activeness. Acquisition of knowledge by way of listening to ready-made information can proceed, for example, with various degrees of attention, especially volitional, at various intensities of effort directed toward memorization, toward understanding the material, etc. All these are indexes of the various degrees of activeness revealed by those who acquire knowledge.

Of great interest is therefore the question of how memorization achieved as the result of *active* acts on the part of the subject differ from memorizing material which was not the object of *active* action of the memorizer. This question was studied by the non-Soviet psychologists Claparede (1915), Key (1926), and Mazo (1929). In Soviet psychology this problem has been studied most extensively by Zinchenko (1939).

In Zinchenko's experiments the subjects were given 15 pictures of various objects. In the upper-right-hand corner of each picture were written numbers about 4 cm high. With the exception of three, all pictures were selected in such a manner that they could easily be arranged into groups according to a common content, e.g., pictures with a kerosene burner, a teapot, and a saucepan, or with an apple, a pear, and a raspberry. The subjects were told to arrange the pictures in groups and to separate those that could not be classified. No mnemonic task was given, and nothing was said concerning the numbers on the pictures.

After completing the classification of the pictures, the subjects were, unexpectedly, told to perform a double task: to reproduce from memory the names of *all the objects* on the pictures and to reproduce *all the numbers*. The experiments showed that reproduction of the two differed greatly. While very many objects were reproduced, the numbers were very poorly remembered.

What causes these differences? One could assume that, in general, objects are better remembered than numbers and that this causes the differences mentioned. To check this assumption, Zinchenko conducted another series of experiments in which other subjects were given the same material, but the task was different. The subjects had to lay out the pictures in such a manner that the numbers formed an ascending series. The last three numbers had then to be added and the sum told to the experimenter. After the task was completed the subjects were told, as in the first series, to reproduce all numbers and names of the objects on the pictures. This was again unexpected.

The results of the experiments showed that this time the subjects reproduced the numbers very well and poorly recalled the names of the objects. Thus, the productivity of memorization was this time opposite to that observed in the first series of experiments. This means that the differences in memorizing found in the two series of experiments cannot be explained by differences in the material, but are evoked by other causes.

It would be easiest to assume that the cause is a different degree of attention payed by the subjects to the objects and numbers depending on the task assigned to them.

In the first series, the task of classifying the pictures by the degree of commonality of the objects depicted on them compels one to pay attention to the objects. But the numbers, in spite of their considerable size (4 cm), are outside the field of attention of the subjects. In the second case, the task of arranging the numbers in an ascending order, to sum up the last three numbers, and to remember their sum prompts the subjects to concentrate their attention on the numbers; the objects are perceived without sufficient attention.

The author of the investigation asserts, however, that such an explanation is inadequate. In his opinion one cannot explain the findings by differences in attention. To confirm this, he refers to the following experiments conducted especially to check this assumption.

These experiments consisted of two parts. In the first part the subjects were given two sets of pictures. One was laid out on a table, the other was handed to the subjects. The subjects had to put each picture from the second set on one of the pictures of the first set, covering each with the picture whose object begins with the same letter as the object on a picture of the first set.

In the second part of the experiments (conducted with other subjects) this task was replaced by another: to cover the pictures not by similarity of *names* but by the similarity of the actual *objects* depicted.

No demands to remember the pictures were made in either case, but upon completion of each part of the experiment the subjects were unexpectedly asked to reproduce the names of the objects on the pictures.

In setting up these experiments the author was guided by the following considerations. Both tasks demand intensive attention to what is depicted as well as to the name of the objects. Therefore, if the success of memorizing is determined by the intensity of attention given to what is memorized (even if involuntarily), the mnemonic effect of the performance of both tasks must be the same.

In fact, however, the experiments revealed something different. Memorization of the pictures in the second part of the experiments was better than in the first part. Equality in the degree of attention paid to the names and content of the pictures was not a condition assuring an equal memorization of the material during the performance of two heterogeneous tasks. Memorizing was consequently determined not by attention, but by something else which resulted from the very essence of the task before the subject in both parts of the experiments.

By what was it determined then? The author, in summing up his experiments, says: "An object can be remembered only when it is an object of the activity of the subject and not an object of passive perception evoking only a sensory impression." This explanation is undoubtedly correct but not sufficiently exact. Even in the first part of the experiments a certain activity was required of the subjects. They had to notice the similarity of names and cover the pictures in accordance with the noticed similarity. The essence, consequently, lies not simply in the activeness but in its peculiar form and content.

Comparison with the second part of the experiments reveals just what this activeness must involve. It must be directed toward a *deepened understanding* of the meaning of what is being perceived. Precisely such an activeness was demanded of the subjects in the second part of the experiments. *This* is what distinguished it from what was in the first part, and *this* factor must be considered as a condition for the success of memorizing.

This also explains the results obtained by Zinchenko in his first experiments on the memorization of numbers and pictures. They are also based on a specific activeness, the activeness of an intellectual nature which is characterized by revealing the meaning of the material to be memorized.

The dependence of memorization on the nature of the actions the object of which is the material to be memorized is very clearly revealed in another investigation by Zinchenko (1945). He conducted three series of experiments. In one the subjects (schoolchildren and adults) were told to solve arithmetical problems, after which they were unexpectedly asked to reproduce the numbers which were given during the problem. In the second series problems had to be devised which were to include the numbers given by the experimenter. In the third series it was demanded that they again devise problems, but the numbers were not given this time. In the latter two series the subjects also had to reproduce the numbers in the problems later, but they were not informed of this beforehand. In the first two series the numbers were thus given in ready-made form and played a supporting role in reaching the main goal which confronted the subjects, while in the third series they were devised by the subjects themselves as the result of active thinking.

The results of the experiments showed that the effect of memorization in the last case was approximately twice as great as in the first two cases. Only first graders were the exception; in them a difference in memorizing was observed, but only to a limited degree. The author interprets this as meaning that while for older children and adults the operation with numbers is already an almost automatic intellectual habit (mental "operation"), for the first graders it is still a specific goal-directed action. The results of the investigation show that the effect of memorizing is most closely dependent on the nature of the actions as a result of which involuntary memorization is accomplished. An object of specifically goal-directed *actions* is considerably better remembered than one that serves as an object of quite automatic *operations*.

In the investigation just examined memorization encompassed two kinds of material: on the one hand, material which the subjects themselves devised (under conditions of independent problem solving), and on the other, material presented only as a starting point for the solution of the problem. Both were incorporated into the solution of the intellectual problem, but the functions of each were different. The experiments showed that there is a definite difference between the memorization of what in the process of the solution is perceived as *given,* serving as a *starting point* of the solution and of what is the *unknown* and is the *result* of the solution we find.

This proposition is fully confirmed by our experiments (Smirnov, 1945*b*) conducted by the following method. The subjects were given pairs of sentences selected in such a manner that each of them corresponded to some orthographic rule, for example: "My brother is learning [uchitsya] to speak English" and "one must learn [uchit'sya] to write in short sentences." The words of the sentences which corresponded to the rule were underlined, but the rule itself was not pointed out to the subjects. They had to learn for themselves for which rule each pair of sentences was given and then independently devise another pair of sentences for the same rule. No memorization of either pair of sentences was required, but the next day when the subjects had come for new experiments they were asked to reproduce all the sentences with which they had dealt the day before. Each subject had received eight pairs of sentences corresponding to eight orthographic rules. The subjects were eight students. The experiments were conducted individually.

The results of the experiments disclosed a great difference in memorizing sentences presented to the subjects for recognition of the rule and the sentences *they themselves* had devised. This difference is quantitatively shown in Table 2.1.

The summary data in Table 2.1 are fully confirmed by the results obtained for each subject separately. Not a single subject reproduced fewer sentences composed by himself than sentences presented by the experimenter.

Very important is the following fact: in remembering the sentences given by the experimenter the subjects often could well recall the *rule* to which these sentences applied, but not the *sentences themselves.*

In summarizing, one can consider as established that memorization of material incorporated into active activity as only its starting point and therefore given in a *ready form* is accomplished with less success than memorizing material found *independently* as the result of *active* activity.

But it must be noted that it would be erroneous to explain the better memorization of the material in the latter case by a larger number of its repetitions in the process of the independent performance of a task. In fact,

TABLE 2.1. Results of an Experiment Calling for the Reproduction of 64 Sentence Pairs Each Provided by the Experimenter and Composed by the Subjects

Sentences provided by experimenter				Sentences composed by subjects			
pairs of sentences	individual sentences	total number of sentences	individual words	pairs of sentences	individual sentences	total number of sentences	individual words
2	20	24	23	28	18	74	1

as the data of our investigation show, rather the opposite is observed. The sentences presented by the experimenter were sometimes read many times. This was due, first, to the necessity of making clear the rule for which they were composed, second, to the fact that the subjects used the content of these sentences in devising new ones. Because of this, not only the rule corresponding to these sentences but also the sentences themselves were for a long time retained by the subjects. On the contrary, the sentences composed by the subjects themselves were usually fixed in the consciousness for a short time since immediately after composing them the subjects began with another pair.

The basis for these differences must therefore be seen not in the frequency of the repetition of specific sentences (the correlation of the number of repetitions had to lead to the opposite result), but in the fact that in one case the material which was memorized served as a *means* of reaching the goal and was presented in a ready form, while in the other case it served as a *goal itself,* which was reached as the result of independent active activity of the subjects. Our experiments showed that memorizing in the latter case was considerably more productive than in the first.

The fact that the rules were better reproduced than the sentences also demonstrates the importance of activity. The rules were clarified by the subjects *themselves.*

Essentially the same results were obtained in one of the more recent investigations by Zinchenko. In one of them (1945) the subjects were given 15 words designating common, familiar objects and for each of these words they were told to devise their own word: in some experiments, a word related to the given one by meaning, in others designating a property, state, or action of the object expressed by the given word, in still others, any word beginning with the same letter as the given word. After that the subjects (different ones in different experiments) were told to recall the given and devised words. The experiments were conducted with schoolchildren of the second and fifth grades, with college students, and, in part, with preschool children. Memorizing was characterized by the number of given words reproduced.

The results of reproduction were that all subjects recalled best of all the words for which other words were devised according to meaningful connections, then the words for which designations of properties of the objects were chosen, and, worst of all, the words for which words beginning with the same letter had to be devised. It is quite obvious, notes the author of the investigation, that the devising of words by initial letter differs radically, in the intellectual operations involved, from the first two tasks, and here, undoubtedly, lies the source of differences in the productivity of memorization. Less great, the author points out, but nevertheless noticeable, is the difference between the first two tasks: devising words according to properties is easier than finding words with meaningful connections (in these cases there are many, more stably fixed, associations); less activeness is demanded here of the subjects and this is once more the cause for somewhat lower indexes of memorization obtained in these cases.

In another work by Zinchenko (1956) the subjects (students) were given ten series of four words each. The first word in each series was differently related to the other three: with one, by a cognitive connection (house-building), with the other, by a meaningful connection (house-window), with the third it was not connected at all. In one series of experiments the subjects had to select from these three words the one connected with the first by a cognitive connection; in the other series, connected with the first by a meaningful connection; in the third, not connected with it. Each time this word had to be underlined. At the end of each series (all series were conducted with different subjects) all these words had to be recalled. After this a second reproduction of the same words was demanded, with a difference—this time the experimenter named the first word of each series, facilitating thereby the reproduction of the following words. One week later a delayed reproduction was demanded.

As a result of the experiments it was found that in all cases those words were recalled noticeably more successfully which corresponded to the task put before the subjects, to underline the word of a definite category.

All these experiments quite definitely attest to the correctness of what was pointed out in the exposition of our experiments: the closest dependence of involuntary memorization on the nature of the activity in which it occurs, on the place which the memorized item occupies in the structure of the activity, on the function which it performs in it, and, in particular, on whether it is the *goal* of the activity or only the *means* of its performance.

The works of other Soviet psychologists show the same, in particular the joint work of Leont'ev and Rozanova (1951) and the investigation by Rozanova (1959) conducted after our investigations. In the first of these works the subject was in front of a square screen on which there were 16 cardboard disks (four rows with four disks in each); on each disk was a word of four letters. The words were lighted in turn by a spot of light. For the different series different instructions were given. In the first, the disks were to be removed as indicated by the experimenter's pointer. In the second, all disks bearing words beginning with a certain letter were to be removed. In the third, it was necessary to establish with which letter the largest number of words began.

The results of the experiments showed that the subjects remembered whatever was the object of their active familiarization. Since in the first series of experiments there was no such familiarization at all and the subjects of this series passively carried out the direction of the experimenter who demanded of them the simplest movements, they did not remember anything.

In the second series, they remembered only the starting letter of the words they took off (under the conditions of the experiment all words began with the same letter), but did not remember the words themselves. In the third series only the letters with which the words began were retained (but now these were the initial letters of *all* words and not only the ones removed, since in order to solve the problem the subjects had to examine all the words for this feature). The words themselves in this series were again not retained since the subject's familiarization with these words was not needed this time for the solution of the problem.

In contrast to the second and third series, in the fourth series, in which the subjects had to remove the disks with names of animals, these words were remembered; however, all other words were forgotten. The authors explain this by the absence of reinforcement of connections corresponding to these words.

In the fifth and sixth series the subjects were asked first to determine with what letter the largest number of words on the disks began and then, turning again to the disks, remove those with words beginning with this letter. In these experiments the initial letters of all words were remembered but the words themselves were not, although the subjects could point out the locations of words which began with the letter they had isolated, as in the second series.

In contrast to the fifth and sixth series in which words for each letter were distributed uniformly in all rows, in the seventh series, the words beginning with the most frequently occurring letter were distributed predominantly in the first two rows of the disks, from which the scanning of all words began. This time, the subjects not only did not memorize the words themselves but could not reproduce even the initial letters of the words which were not distributed in the first rows. After so many words beginning with the same letter and situated in the first rows, the subjects no longer familiarized themselves with these words.

In the eighth series the subjects had to remove the disks with words denoting invertebrates; they could reproduce only these words, since only the connections corresponding to these words were reinforced.

In the ninth series disks with names of invertebrates again were to be removed, but this time names of vertebrates were included and these were not to be removed. In these experiments the subjects reproduced the names of all animals, since the solution of the problem demanded of them a more thorough familiarization with all names.

The results of all series are in agreement about the determining role of *orienting actions* performed by the subjects in memorization. Specifically, these are *tentative* actions, familiarization with the material in accordance with the *problem* to be solved. Of essential influence on memorizing also is the fact of *reinforcement* or *nonreinforcement* of specific connections which, again, is connected with the problem confronting the subject and with the orientation as a *result* of the actions.

Finally, the tenth series of experiments, in which one of the words written on the disks was circled and all subjects remembered that word, showed that what evokes an *orienting reflex as a novelty* is well remembered. Proceeding from these last experiments the authors point out that those connections which do not depend on the content of the actions can also be formed and stabilized. However, in all cases the processes of orientation are determining.

Memorizing as found in the above investigation, along with what enters into the content of the action and also what is not the object of the actions, does not mean the same degree of memorizing of both. This is clear from the experiments by Rozanova (1959), which deal with a comparison of the mnemonic effect of the main stimuli entering into the content of the action and of background stimuli which are not the object of the action.

In these experiments the subjects sat in front of a drawing board on which were arranged 15 cards with pictures of various objects (one object per card). The objects were of different colors and at various places on the board. By means of a spot of light of five-second duration the subject could successively view each object. The subjects named the object viewed and the category to which it belonged. After the presentation of all the cards the subjects were unexpectedly asked to name the objects shown and also to point out their color and place on the board (which was beyond the scope of the previously performed actions, and pertained to background components of the situation). This task was performed by the subjects quite satisfactorily. However, this did not mean that the background components of the situation (color and placement of objects) are equivalent in their mnemonic effect to the main components (naming and form of objects). This was clearly shown in other experiments by Rozanova in which one group of subjects had to remember the color of an object and point out its location according to the name of the object. Another group was asked the opposite, i.e., to recall the name of an object by its color or location. In these cases a marked difference was seen between the two groups. The first assignment caused no special difficulties, while the second proved to be almost impossible to accomplish. The mnemonic functions of the main and background stimuli were, consequently, very different. This was confirmed also by the data of the following series, in which one group of subjects had to recall not only the object they saw but also its color, and another group was asked to recall both the object and its location. It turned out that in these cases recall of the objects' colors by the first group and of their locations by the second group did not present any greater difficulties, since these features were no longer background but main components of the situation during memorization.

Experiments by Idashkin (1959) on the study of latent learning show the great significance of orienting activity as an essential condition of memorization.

In one group of his experiments adult subjects had to find for each of the objects shown them a corresponding cutout on a board. The selection of these cutouts posed great difficulties since each object fitted easily into any opening, but without an exact matching of the edges. Memorization was not required, but after all selections the subjects were unexpectedly asked to name all the objects shown. On the whole, recall was quite satisfactory, especially taking into account the additional recalling accomplished by means of showing auxiliary objects. However, in other experiments conducted by Zinchenko's method (cards with pictures to be arranged in a definite order, according to the numbers on these cards) the recall of the perceived objects was quite different: as in Zinchenko's experiments, the numbers were recalled well in this case, but the pictures poorly. Recall of the pictures became noticeably better upon the showing of auxiliary pictures.

On the other hand, the components of material not corresponding to the task are remembered well if they are an object of orientation. This is shown by the experiments of Idashkin in which the subjects were given cards with pictures of various objects and were asked to select pictures of household objects. Although these objects were recalled better than the others, the difference was not great. This is explained by the fact that these other objects also were objects of orientation.

It is characteristic that an effect of orientation was observed even when the subjects were instructed not only to remove some objects but also to memorize them, and not to memorize those objects which were not to be removed. The difference in recall of both in these experiments was somewhat greater than in the preceding ones, but did not increase significantly.

To this same group of investigations belong those by E. V. Shorokhova and M. D. Aleksandrova conducted under the guidance of Anan'ev (1960). Shorokhova studied the recall of the object and means of work performed by students (the construction of a labyrinth for experiments in animal psychology). The most important parts of the construction and the tools most used were best recalled, as well as the content and sequence of the actions themselves. Everything which was of no significance to the activity performed was retained considerably less well. Analogous results were obtained in studying what was recalled after the completion of work under industrial conditions by the students of vocational schools.

In this investigation the influence of attitude towards work on memorization was also studied: with a positive attitude toward accomplishing the assignment 6% of the objects previously perceived were forgotten, with an indifferent attitude 28%, with a negative attitude 56%. Thus, the difference was very great.

In the work by Aleksandrova, the students were given a neutralization experiment involving titration. In checking recall it was found that the neutralization reaction, which was the most meaningful part of the activity (acquiring new knowledge in chemistry), was recalled much better than the titration itself, which was only the means for obtaining neutralization.

Pinskii (1948, 1952, 1954, 1962) also obtained similar results in his investigations. In his experiments the subjects, normal and retarded schoolchildren, were given 45 cards, on each of which was written a letter of the Russian alphabet (nine letters were used in all; each of them on five cards). Using a Morse-code dictionary the subjects were to lay out the cards in three groups according to the number of symbols (1, 2, or 3) by which the letters on the cards were designated. Twice the cards were arranged. Memorization was not assigned beforehand, but after the cards were arranged the subjects were unexpectedly told to lay them out once more, this time from memory. It turned out that the subjects performed this task well, by recalling the number of symbols representing each letter, but they could hardly recall precisely what symbols designated these letters. The cause for this inability to reproduce them was the fact that the object of orientation in the performance of the preceding actions was only the number of symbols and not their nature.

In other experiments by the same author cards with letters of the Russian alphabet were put on squares of a chart with Morse code. Here not only the number of symbols but also their nature had to be taken into account. As a result, the number of correct answers concerning the nature of symbols increased considerably. Thus, all these investigations reveal that the most important condition for involuntary memorization is *action* associated with what must become the object of memorizing.

Chapter 3

THE CORRELATION OF VOLUNTARY AND INVOLUNTARY MEMORIZATION

1. THE DEPENDENCE OF THE CORRELATION OF VOLUNTARY AND INVOLUNTARY MEMORIZATION ON THE NATURE OF THE ACTIVITY

What has been said above points to a clear dependence of memorization on the orientation and nature of the activity in which it is performed. The influence of each of these facets of our activity was examined only individually, without correlation with the effect of the other facets of activity. Yet such a comparison is absolutely necessary, since in specific forms of an activity there are possible various combinations of characteristics of some of its facets. Of greatest significance here is the comparison of memorization occurring under conditions of mnemonic orientation but not included in the solution of any intellectual problems with its opposite: mnemonic orientation is absent, but memorization is accomplished as the result of an active, independent solution to any problem.

The significance of such a comparison is determined by the possibility of elucidating more exactly the theoretically and practically important question concerning the correlation between the two types of memorization (voluntary and involuntary), and the comparative productivity of the two.

Little attention is given in the literature to the study of involuntary memorization. The majority of investigations deals with voluntary memorization. It is characteristic that this type of memorization is the main object of study even by representatives of associative psychology. True, this is explained not by their acknowledgement, in principle, of a special significance of the activeness of memorizing, but by the fact that voluntary memorizing in the form of learning by heart (i.e., repeated perception of the material), opens wide possibilities for the study of the principles of *repetition*. The latter, as is well known, was considered by the long-dominant associative psychology to be the basic, important condition for the formation of associative connections, to which the associationists tried to reduce the essence of memorization.

Noting the preferred study of voluntary memorizing it must, however, be emphasized that the insignificant attention given to involuntary memorizing does not at all correspond to its actual significance. Certainly, the mnemonic effect of psychological processes not directed especially toward memorizing is in a number of cases insignificant. As was pointed out, the presence of mnemonic orientation is one of the most important conditions for the productivity of memorization. Other conditions being equal, voluntary memorizing, as is well known, is much more effective than involuntary. Nevertheless, there is no doubt that much of what we master in life is the result of involuntary memorization. The data of experience are retained in memory often without any effort on our part, without any special task to memorize, and yet they are often retained exceptionally stably, even better than something we try to remember. Undoubtedly, in school much is also memorized by the students involuntarily without any special intention directed toward memorization.

It is not our task to examine all the conditions for the successful involuntary memorization which sometimes make it more productive than voluntary memorization. We limit ourselves to the study of only those conditions which are determined by the *characteristics* of the *activity* resulting in involuntary memorization.

Since involuntary memorization is the result of activity which proceeds without mnemonic orientation, and this in itself can only lower its productivity, it is quite obvious that the condition for effectiveness of this type of memorizing must be sought not in the nature of the *orientation of the activity* but in the characteristics of its other important facets, its *content and nature of performance*. Precisely this determines the significance of the comparison of memorization proceeding under conditions of mnemonic orientation, but without solving any intellectual problems, with memorization accomplished without mnemonic orientation, but as a result of an active, independent solution to a problem.

Non-Soviet psychologists have compared involuntary and voluntary memorization and found a considerable advantage in the latter. But in studying these problems and, more important, in comparing the productivity of both types of memorization no systematic variation in *content* and *nature* has been made. Yet only this makes it possible to solve correctly the problem of their correlation.

In Soviet psychology Zinchenko conducted a study on the correlation between voluntary and involuntary memorizing: at first in work published in 1939 and then in other investigations conducted later. He compared memorizing of material (pictures and numbers) depending on the goal of the subjects' actions. These were the experiments on involuntary memorization. For the purpose of comparison, however, in the same investigation experiments were also conducted with voluntary memorizing (pictures). Moreover, in some of these experiments the subjects were not just asked to memorize the pictures but a means, a mnemonic device, was pointed out which should facilitate memorizing, i.e., the same operation of classifying the pictures by groups which was performed in the experiments with involuntary memorization. In other experiments such means were not pointed out and the subjects could memorize the pictures as they liked. All experiments were conducted with preschool, younger and older schoolchildren, and adults individually or in groups.

The results of experiments using 15 pictures are presented in Table 3.1.

From the table it can be seen that for the preschool children involuntary memorization predominated greatly over both cases of voluntary memorization. For the younger schoolchildren, involuntary memorizing gave higher indexes only in comparison with the case of voluntary memorizing when no mnemonic device was pointed out. For the older schoolchildren and the adults, involuntary memorizing was also more productive, but as compared with voluntary memorizing accompanied by mnemonic devices was *less* productive than in younger schoolchildren.

Thus, common for all groups was the advantage of involuntary memorizing while performing an active activity over voluntary memorizing proceeding without a mnemonic device (first principle). Differences between the groups were observed only in cases of voluntary memorizing when the experimenter pointed out a mnemonic device. The older the subjects, the more sharply rose the productivity of such voluntary memorizing. In preschool children it was less effective than involuntary memorization, for the younger schoolchildren it was already equalized in productivity, for the older ones and adults it was even more productive (second principle).

TABLE 3.1. Results Obtained in the Memorization of 15 Pictures

Types of memorization	Percentage of reproduced pictures		
	preschool children	schoolchildren	adults
Involuntary memorization	10.6	13.2	13.2
Voluntary memorization with mnemonic device	7.4	13.0	14.1
Voluntary memorization without mnemonic device	7.0	10.0	11.5

Both these principles are essential to an understanding of the correlation between voluntary and involuntary memorizing. The first principle shows quite clearly that the absence of mnemonic orientation can not only be compensated for by the *nature* of the activity resulting in memorization, but is overlapped by it. In other words, *the nature of the activity can in some cases be more significant than the mnemonic orientation.* The predominant significance of the nature of the activity can be observed in all age groups. Consequently, here we encounter a broad principle.

Essential also is the second principle found by Zinchenko. It reveals that mnemonic devices have a positive effect only on older schoolchildren and adults. On the younger schoolchildren they have neither a positive nor a negative effect. On preschool children their influence is negative. The preschool children evidently could not utilize as yet the mnemonic device pointed out by the experimenter and they did not apply it even when they were told to *intentionally* use it. Therefore, their memorizing in these cases proved to be less effective than when the same mnemonic device was actually used by them *involuntarily*.

Noting the essential significance of both principles found by Zinchenko, it must be emphasized, however, that in his experiments involuntary memorizing was studied during the performance of only one type of activity, the classification of pictures. Only this activity was proposed to the subjects as a mnemonic device. Naturally, this narrows the significance of the conclusions since the only thing proved is that with an appropriate choice of activity involuntary memorizing *may* have a considerable effect (exceeding even the effect of intentional memorizing which is accomplished under the influence of a mnemonic task). How *extensive* this possibility is, i.e., in precisely what forms of activity, which comprise the basis of involuntary memorizing, it is realized and in what forms it is not, is not shown in Zinchenko's work. Yet, for an understanding of this principle the answer to this question is absolutely necessary.

We have attempted to elucidate this problem at least partially. Experiments conducted for this purpose were constructed on the same principle. The subjects were at first told to perform some kind of activity in which involuntary memorizing was to be accomplished. The task of memorization was thus not assigned, but upon completion of the activity the subjects, unexpectedly, had to recall the material with which they had dealt while performing the activity. After this, analogous material was given for voluntary memorizing in accordance with which the subjects were given the mnemonic task of memorizing the material presented. Then, as in the first case, memorization was checked. In some experiments, along with direct reproduction delayed reproduction also occurred (as in the cases of voluntary and involuntary memorizing).

In the selection of an activity in which involuntary memorizing was to be accomplished, we were guided by the following considerations. We considered it necessary to select the forms of activity so that they differed from each other by the depth of penetration into the meaning of the material. The choice of this criterion was determined by the fact that it undoubtedly can serve as an index of differences in *intellectual activity. The activeness of the activity is its most essential property which in our opinion is necessary to compensate for the absence of mnemonic orientation.*

In selecting various forms of activity we thought it desirable to select them in such a manner that there would be a simultaneously a variation of the material which had to be memorized. In particular, we deemed it necessary to utilize not only separate words but also more meaningful material, whole sentences.

Proceeding from these considerations we chose two groups of experiments, one of which was to study memorization of individual words, the other to investigate the memorization of sentences. The first group consisted of writing words dictated by the experimenter. This served as activity demanding, relatively, the least depth of penetration into the meaning of the material and, consequently, the least intellectual activity. This group also used so-called free association, i.e., the naming by the subject of any word that came to mind in response to a word given by the experimenter. This activity demands greater attention to the meaning of the material, since the subjects answer in these cases not literally with the first random word but with a word which in one way or another is connected by meaning with the word named by the experimenter. However, the degree of penetration into the sense of the word in these cases is as yet insufficient, since, being free in his association, the subject can perceive the meaning of a word from any, e.g., a random, facet and, consequently, reveal a relatively low degree of intellectual activity. Finally, the last activity, also in the same group, consisted in the subjects' finding an idea connected sensibly with what had been named by the experimenter. The accomplishment of this task demands a deeper penetration into the sense of the words (those given by the experimenter as well as those selected by the subjects) and thereby considerably greater intellectual activity.

The second group of experiments for the purpose of studying the memorizing of *sentences* included the performance of two types of activity. In some experiments the subjects were given sentences which they had to read in order to find spelling errors which had been made intentionally. In other experiments the subjects were to evaluate the *sense* of the sentences given, i.e., to indicate whether a sentence was factually correct. For this purpose the subjects were given sentences correct in meaning, i.e., with content corresponding to reality, as well as incorrect ones, not corresponding to reality.

It is quite clear that the activities differed greatly in their depth of penetration into the meaning of the sentences. Understanding the meaning of sentences could occur in performing the first activity, which was fully confirmed later by the subjects. However, the depth of the subjects' understanding of the sentences in these cases was considerably less than that necessary to accomplish the second task given by the experimenter (when the correctness in meaning of the sentences had to be evaluated).

In accordance with the types of activity selected we conducted the five experiments described below.

First experiment (taking dictation). In the first part of the experiment (conducted to find the productivity of *involuntary* memorizing), the subject had to take dictation of 10–15 words (depending on the age of the subjects). In order that the purpose remain unknown, the experimenter said that the experiments were conducted for the purpose of obtaining material to study handwriting. At the end of dictation the sheets with the words were taken away and the subjects were unexpectedly asked to reproduce all the words written, if possible. Immediately thereafter the second part of the experiment was conducted, directed towards the study of the productivity of *voluntary* memorizing. The subjects read the same number of words as in the first part, but with the task of memorizing them as best they could and, after reading, of reproducing them. Thus, this time the subjects were warned about the subsequent check of their memorizing and they were confronted with a mnemonic task. The words in this part of the experiment were different but of the same type in content as well as in construction (in the number of syllables and in stress) as the first ones. Twenty minutes after completion of the second part the subjects reproduced once more both series of words (delayed reproduction). As in further experiments, the subjects were second and fourth graders and college students (ten in each age group). All experiments were conducted individually with each subject. M. F. Smirnova conducted the experiments with schoolchildren. In order to avoid possible influence on the results of the experiments due to differences in the material (the words written under dictation might be easier or more difficult than those which had to be memorized), the method of "crossing over" was used. For this purpose the subjects of each age group were divided into two subgroups of five each. The words which were written by the first subgroup were given to the second for voluntary memorizing, and, *vice versa,* the words memorized by the first subgroup were given to the second to write under dictation.

Second experiment (free associations). In the first part of the experiment words were read to the subjects and they were asked to speak aloud, immediately after hearing each word, any word that came to mind. After this, all the words given by the experimenter had to be reproduced. This the subjects had not expected, since they were not told about it beforehand. In the second part of the experiments analogous words were given for voluntary memorizing (the same number of words). The whole series of words was read by the experimenter with approximately the same speed as the words in the first part of the experiment. The results of memorizing were checked immediately, and after 20 min delayed reproduction of both series of words occurred. As in the first case, the method of "crossing over" was used. The subjects of this experiment did not include any of the participants of the first experiments. This was done to guarantee the subjects' ignorance of the true purpose of the first part of the experiment.

The third experiment (meaningful connections). The method of this experiment was analogous to that of the preceding experiment with the difference that this time in the first part of the experiments, instead of responding with a random word, the task was to respond with a word meaningfully related to the one named by the experimenter. In the experiments with schoolchildren this connection was no further specified, i.e., the subjects could answer with any word similar in meaning to the one given. Moreover, in explaining this task the experimenter purposely cited as examples several pairs of words related by different meaningful connections. In contrast to this, in the experiments with adults a strictly specific connection between the words was demanded: they had to find not just any meaningfully connected word, but a more common, generic term to the word given by the experimenter. This difference in tasks was due to the necessity to equalize them, at least approximately, according to the degree of difficulty for the schoolchildren and the adults. As preliminary experiments had shown, the task of finding the generic term was much more difficult for schoolchildren than for adults. This was clearly shown by the rate of response, their quality, and the number of cases in which the task remained unperformed. On the contrary, the task of answering with any word meaningfully connected with the given one proved to be almost identical with free association for the adults and was very easy for them, which could not at all be said of the schoolchildren. In the free-association experiments the latter usually answered with meaningfully connected words, but when the same *random* meaningful connection was demanded of them by the experimenter, the connection was found with greater difficulty than in the free-association experiments. This was clearly seen by the fact that the time expended by the schoolchildren to find the answers was quite different for the two cases. For the free-association experiments it was considerably less than for the experiments in which the experimenter, although allowing considerable freedom in the choice of the words, demanded nevertheless a meaningful connection with those words named by him.

Fourth experiment (indicating spelling errors). The subjects read six typewritten sentences. In five of them spelling errors were intentionally made.

Each sentence had to be read twice in succession and then the subject had to tell whether there were errors in it and, if so, how many. After this the subjects were unexpectedly asked to reproduce these sentences. In the second part of the experiments, the same number of sentences analogous in length were given, but this time with the task of memorizing and subsequent reproduction. Again, each sentence was read twice and then reproduction of all sentences was asked. For the various subgroups of subjects the sentences given in the first and second part of the experiments were crossed over.

Fifth experiment (evaluation of the meaning of sentences). In the first series of these experiments, 6, and in the second series, 12 sentences were given to be read. Some of the sentences did not correspond to reality. As in the preceding experiment, the subjects read each sentence twice and then noted whether it was correct. After this, they were unexpectedly asked to reproduce what had been read. In the second part of the experiments new sentences were given (6 or 12, as in the first part). This time, after reading each sentence twice the subjects had to try to memorize it as well as possible. After reading all sentences the subjects reproduced them; but in the series of experiments where 12 sentences were used, both immediate and delayed reproduction (24 h after the first experiments) were required. As the experiments had the purpose of stimulating the subjects to reason out the meaning of the sentences, it was not possible to use the same material for the various age groups of subjects (adults and children), since such material would not be of the same degree of difficulty to each age group. Therefore, the content of the sentences was changed.

The numerical indexes obtained are presented in Table 3.2. They characterize the percentage ratio of the material reproduced by *involuntary* memorization to the material reproduced in the same experiment by *voluntary* memorization. The number of reproduced material in the *latter* case is always assumed to be 100%.

TABLE 3.2

		Immediate reproduction			Delayed reproduction		
Experiment No.	Activity during involuntary memorization	second graders	fourth graders	older students	second graders	fourth graders	older students
1	Copying of words	108.6	101.6	83.5	96.1	—	55.1
2	Free associations	100.0	92.7	76.8	—	—	121.1
3	Meaningful connections	128.1	135.9	140.2	129.4	187.1	307.4
4	Spelling evaluation ..	—	—	45.6	—	—	—
5A	Evaluation of meaning (6 sentences)	114.3	109.1	104.4	—	—	—
5B	Evaluation of meaning (12 sentences)	—	—	129.6	—	—	139.7

In examining Table 3.2 one notices immediately that different experiments gave unequal results. In some experiments *involuntary* memorizing was more productive (the indexes are above 100), in other cases *voluntary* memorizing (the indexes are below 100). In some cases, going over from direct reproduction to delayed caused the indexes to increase, in others, to decrease. The same can be noticed when comparing the age groups of the subjects: in some cases the indexes are higher for the older groups, in others, on the contrary, for the younger groups. At first glance it seems that no general principle can be derived from the results obtained. Actually, this is not so.

In order to verify this, let us examine the indexes in the light of our basis for the selection of types of activity. We noted that they were selected in accordance with the difference in depth of penetration into the meaningful content of the material and in the corresponding degree of intellectual activity.

We turn to the *first group* of experiments (the first three experiments). As was said, in these experiments the finding of words meaningfully connected with those named by the experimenter was the activity demanding deeper penetration into the content of the material and greater intellectual activity. What distinguishes the indexes found in the third experiment from those obtained in the other two experiments? As can be seen from Table 3.2, the indexes of the third experiment are higher than all other indexes of the first group of experiments, and they all exceed 100. What does this signify? It means that involuntary memorizing in the third experiment was more productive than in the first two experiments. It was more productive for all subjects in immediate *and* delayed reproduction than was voluntary memorizing.

Thus, of all types of activity which were included in the first group of experiments, the most favorable for involuntary memorizing was the activity demanding the greatest penetration into the content of the material and, consequently, the greatest intellectual activity of the subjects. On the contrary, the forms of activity which did not demand this to the same extent proved to be less favorable for involuntary memorizing.

Further, it can be seen from Table 3.2 that each form of activity (copying of words and free association) gave different results. Judging from the indexes for direct reproduction, the results of these forms of activity differ from what one would assume from their characteristics. We considered copying of words to be an activity demanding less absorption in the content of the material and, consequently, less intellectual activity than free association. Therefore, it could be expected that it would be less favorable for involuntary memorizing. In fact, the opposite was true. The indexes found for the first experiment (direct reproduction) were higher than those of the second experiment. This is explained by the duration of each activity. Free association proceeded rapidly, and this made it possible to equalize the speed in presenting the material during involuntary and voluntary memorizing. Here the time factor did not play a role as the source of the different results noted between the two parts of the experiment. The situation was different in the experiments involving the copying of words. In this case it was not possible to achieve equal speed in presenting the words to be copied and those used in voluntary memorizing. Even for the adults, writing demanded more time. Therefore, each word that was written was retained in the consciousness of the subjects for a longer time than each word that was presented for memorization. The productivity of memorizing in the first part of the experiment should be higher here than when presentation time was equal for both stages. The indexes of the ratio of involuntary to voluntary memorizing should, therefore, rise and could easily exceed the corresponding indexes in the experiments with free association. Thus, the divergence of the obtained results from what could be expected (proceeding from the role of intellectual activity as basis for memorization) does not at all mean that our initial premises are wrong. It only points to the fact that in the experiment with writing under dictation the insufficiency of the effect of intellectual activity was compensated for by the favorable conditions of the time (during which the subjects retained in their consciousness the material in the first part of the experiments).

Writing of words under dictation is connected with a motor activity which is also one of the conditions for successful memorization. All this led to the finding that the correlation of copying the words and free association (according to the indexes of involuntary memorizing) proved to be the reverse of what could be expected by proceeding from their differences in intellectual activity. What did *delayed* reproduction produce?

First of all, the difference between the third experiment and the first two was more pronounced. The indexes found in the third experiment exceed to a great extent the indexes of the first and second experiments. The different degree of influence exerted on the involuntary memorizing by different forms of activity was now more pronounced than in immediate reproduction. How did these differences increase?

On the one hand, they increased by means of a rise of the indexes in the third experiment, especially for the adults. This shows that in delayed reproduction the advantage of involuntary memorizing resulting from an active intellectual activity is more pronounced than in immediate reproduction. In other words, for stable retention, memorizing which is the result of such an activity is especially favorable. The mnemonic effect of such an activity is more stable than the mnemonic effect of an activity which, although directed especially toward memorizing, is not distinguished by high intellectual activity.

The second factor revealing why the differences increased is the decrease in the indexes of the first experiment. This is important in connection with what was said relative to various conditions of the time under which memorizing occurred in this experiment. The longer retention of words being written than of words being read for memorization increased the possibility of memorizing. The data on delayed reproduction show, however, that this influence was only temporary. In delayed reproduction the effect of involuntary memorizing occurring during writing of the words was for all subjects less than what was retained as the result of voluntary memorizing.

It is especially important to take into account the lower indexes of the first experiment in connection with the increase of the index obtained in the second experiment. The increase of the latter this time even exceeded 100. In other words, the stability of retention of what was memorized during free association was greater than during intentional memorizing. This is quite understandable. Free association actually consisted in naming by the subject not the first, random, words but words meaningfully connected with what the experimenter had presented, and this, undoubtedly, demanded a certain intellectual activity. But the presence of the latter, as was already noted, in the transition from immediate reproduction to delayed, entails a rise in the indexes of involuntary memorizing.

What has been said clearly determines why the correlation of the first and second experiments (copying of words and free association) during delayed reproduction is the opposite of that in immediate reproduction. And yet it is clear why it fully coincides here with the assumptions based on the characteristics for each activity given above. The decrease in the positive influence which the duration of writing had on memorizing and the increase (in connection with delayed reproduction) in the positive effect of the intellectual activity during free association are the sources of the changes which occurred in these cases in the correlation of the mnemonic effects during transition from immediate to delayed reproduction.

We turn to the *second group* of experiments, i.e., to the results obtained in the fourth and fifth experiments. First of all let us examine to what extent in these experiments our premise (i.e., that productivity of memorizing is determined by intellectual activity and that this activity can not only compensate for the absence of mnemonic orientation but also can make involuntary memorizing more productive than voluntary) was justified.

An analysis of Table 3.2 shows that the quantitative data of the fourth and fifth experiments differ greatly. In the fourth experiment the productivity of involuntary memorizing (carried out during the checking of spelling in sentences) is below that of voluntary memorizing. The difference is quite significant: the effect of involuntary memorizing is only 45% of what the subject memorized in the presence of a mnemonic task. In other words, the results of involuntary memorizing in this case were less than half as high as the indexes of voluntary memorization. An entirely different picture was obtained in the fifth experiment, in which involuntary memorizing occurred during a sense evaluation of sentences. In this case it gave not lower, but higher indexes than voluntary memorizing.

These quantitative differences fully correspond to the reports of the subjects concerning the various degrees of difficulty with which both tasks (to recall the sentences read for the purpose of checking their spelling and to reproduce the sentences read for the purpose of pointing out whether they were correct in content) were accomplished. In the first case the task, to recall the sentences, caused a state of complete perplexity. At first it even seemed to the subjects that they were not able to recall what they had read. Often they succeeded in recalling only fragments of the sentences. It is characteristic that all these difficulties arose in spite of the fact that during the reading of the sentences and the checking of their spelling the content of the sentences was adequately understood.

The task of recalling the sentences when the subjects had to evaluate their meaning evoked a different state. No confusion or perplexity was observed. The task presented was accepted as quite feasible, not presenting special difficulties. While in the first case some of the subjects in expressing their surprise at the presented task said the experimenter should have warned them about the impending reproduction of the sentences, no such remarks were made now, although the subjects participating in this experiment were not participants of the preceding one and the task, to recall the content of the sentences, was for them also unexpected.

Above, it was pointed out that one of the important differences between the forms of activity in the fourth and fifth experiments was the difference in the degree of intellectual activity with which the depth of understanding of the material is connected. It is quite obvious that the evaluation of the sentences performed from the point of view of spelling can be made with a less-deep understanding of what has been read than the evaluation of the sentences according to meaning. Correlating this with the results of the experiments we get a complete confirmation of the conclusion that *depth of understanding and intellectual activity connected with it are the most important conditions for the productivity of involuntary memorization.* For this reason they are the source of its advantage over voluntary memorizing. Activity demanding considerable intellectual participation for a deepened understanding of the content of the sentences (in the sense evaluation of these sentences) was more favorable for involuntary memorizing and made it possible to obtain higher indexes than those that were obtained under conditions of the effect of a mnemonic task.

Along with this general premise, the results of the fifth experiment also confirmed the conclusion that in delayed reproduction the advantage of involuntary memorizing brought about as the result of active intellectual activity was greater than in reproduction immediately following this activity. In other words, *what the subjects memorized involuntarily in the process of active intellectual participation was retained more stably than what was memorized voluntarily under normal conditions of performing a mnemonic task.*

2. AGE DIFFERENCES IN THE CORRELATION OF VOLUNTARY AND INVOLUNTARY MEMORIZATION

Zinchenko's experiments pointed to the substantial age differences in correlating voluntary and involuntary memorization.

In all but the third of the experiments described above, we observe the same principle: the indexes decrease with age. This means that *in the older subjects the effect of involuntary memorizing decreases relatively,* i.e., if involuntary memorizing is more productive than voluntary this advantage decreases with age and sometimes (as is observed in the first experiment) the correlation even becomes reversed: voluntary memorizing is more productive in the older subjects (students). In those cases in which involuntary memorizing, even in the younger subjects, does not reveal greater productivity than voluntary (as, in particular, in the second experiment), it becomes still less effective with age. Thus, in the younger subjects involuntary memorizing in all cases (except for the third experiment) has a relatively greater effect than in older ones, especially adults. How can this principle be explained?

That for adults the tasks presented (writing words under dictation, answering a given word with another random word, evaluating the meaning of sentences) are easier than for the younger subjects must be considered as its basis. The older the subjects and the higher their general mental development, the less intellectual activity is demanded of them to carry out these activities. And this must entail a lowering of the effectiveness of involuntary memorizing. Thus, the differences between the younger and older subjects are but a specific case of our general principle that the productivity of involuntary memorizing is determined primarily by the degree of intellectual activity necessary to carry out the activity as the result of which memorizing is accomplished. How does one explain the deviation from this principle observed in the result of the third experiment? First of all it should be recalled that, in contrast to the other experiments, the third was not identical for the schoolchildren and adults. The schoolchildren were asked to answer with any word connected in meaning with the one given to them. The adults had to find a generic term. It is clear that the second task is more difficult than the first. That is why we had to refrain from giving it to the children. It may be assumed that this facilitation was too great and exceeded the correction which had to be made for age. Thus, the difference between the data obtained in the third experiment on schoolchildren and adults deviates only outwardly from the general principle. In reality it does not contradict it, but rather confirms it, once more pointing to the fact that with greater intellectual activity the productivity of involuntary memorizing increases.

The data in Table 3.2 reveal one more deviation of the third experiment from the others. The indexes obtained in this experiment increase not only between schoolchildren and adults, but also between second graders and fourth graders, although this time the task given to both was identical. How can one explain this deviation?

Its source lies in the different qualities of performance of the two groups of children. The second graders in responding to the words presented by the experimenter used familiar, trivial, and therefore often only external connections. The fourth graders had a deeper understanding of the task. They tried to answer with words more connected in meaning with those given to them. This demanded a deeper penetration into the content of the words and, consequently, the deviation in the third experiment does not contradict the general principle, but only confirms it.

What is the overall summary of our experiments? We recall that we wanted to find out just how much higher a productivity can be achieved by involuntary memorizing than by voluntary. Our experiments showed that the possible productivity of the former is very great. In any case, if we combine our findings with what had been obtained earlier, in Zinchenko's investigation, it is obvious that the advantage of involuntary memorization over voluntary is not an exception. Under certain conditions it is quite a regular phenomenon.

Our experiments have also shown *what* is needed for such an advantage to occur: deep penetration into the meaning of the material, a *high degree of intellectual activity*. This entails not only a more extensive impression of the material than in voluntary memorizing but also its more stable retention. This was clearly shown from the results of delayed reproduction.

The premise about age differences in the correlation of voluntary and involuntary memorization and that of the dependence of these differences on the nature of the activity performed by the subject is also confirmed in Zinchenko's later work (1961), published after our experiments, in which his first investigation was continued.

In another of Zinchenko's investigations, both types of memorizing were compared in experiments with the memorization of meaningful texts (descriptive, narrative, explanatory) after reading them three times (in some cases without the task of memorizing, but with the assignment of determining the degree of difficulty of one text as compared to another; in other cases the task was to memorize). The subjects were schoolchildren of the second, fourth, sixth, eighth, and tenth grades (the descriptive text was not given to the second graders and the explanatory text was given only in the eighth and tenth grades). This time, in the experiments with the *narrative* texts the difference between involuntary and voluntary memorization (according to the total amount of material reproduced) was insignificant in the second grade. The productivity of involuntary memorization in the fourth grade was 91% of that of voluntary memorization, while in the following grades it was 73%, 68%, and 72%, respectively. In the experiments with memorization of *descriptive* texts, the indexes beginning with the fourth grade were 88%, 77%, 76%, and 77%, respectively, i.e., here too there is a difference between the fourth grade and those that follow, though a smaller one than that encountered in the experiments with narrative texts. All indexes (except for the first) are higher than in memorizing narrative texts. But in the experiments with an *explanatory* text (conducted only in the eighth and tenth grades) still higher indexes for involuntary memorization were obtained: 90% and 94% of those for voluntary memorization. The difficult texts even out the differences between voluntary and involuntary memorization, demanding in the latter case more intellectual activity. All indexes were calculated on the basis of Zinchenko's absolute values.

Along with the experiments in which memorizing was accomplished by simple reading (though repeated three times), Zinchenko conducted experiments in which the subjects, as an aid to performing their task (to determine the degree of difficulty in understanding the text or memorizing it), were given in some experiments an outline of the text for their use, and in others were asked to make an outline themselves. This time the results of the experiment were somewhat different. In the experiments involving the use of a given outline in memorizing a *narrative* text, there was no essential difference for the second graders in what was reproduced in the two types of memorization; but in the higher grades the productivity of involuntary memorization came considerably closer to the productivity of voluntary memorization (as compared to the above-examined experiments, in which only simple reading was involved, without the use of an outline). The respective indexes were this time: 93%, 82%, 92%, 95%, i.e., even in the highest grades involuntary memorization had almost the same effect as voluntary. Similar indexes were obtained in the experiments with *descriptive* texts (again with the use of given outlines), namely, 90%, 82%, 88%, 91%, and, finally, as in the preceding experiments, both types of memorizing were almost the same for the eighth and tenth grades when working with *explanatory* texts: 93% and 98%.

Thus, when memorizing was supported by an outline for the text (even if provided by the experimenter), the difference between involuntary and voluntary memorization was considerably equalized as compared to experiments without outlines. Moreover, the more difficult the texts were for memorizing, the more definitely expressed was this leveling.

In the experiments in which the subjects themselves had to make an outline, in memorizing *narrative* texts almost identical indexes were obtained: 89%, 83%, 85%, 89%. All of them (except those for the fourth grade) proved to be higher than those obtained in the experiments with simple reading of the text (in the fourth grade the respective index was already high). In the experiments with a *descriptive* text the indexes rose again and were: 131%, 103%, 93%, 99%. In other words, this time in the fourth and sixth grades involuntary memorizing gave even better results than voluntary, while in the tenth grade both types of memorizing were almost equal in productivity. Memorization of *explanatory* texts in the eighth and tenth grades gave these results: 111% and 96%, that is, in the eighth grade involuntary memorizing was once again more productive than voluntary, and in the tenth grade they were again almost the same, i.e., a more active participation in which memorizing was included (the independent composition of an outline and not the use of a given one) considerably increased the productivity of involuntary memorizing and in a number of cases made it even more productive than voluntary memorizing.

Such are the indexes of the *quantity* of reproduced material. As for the *quality* of the reproductions, it was found that of 14 indexes, 8 showed an advantage to involuntary memorization, 2 the equality of both forms of memorizing, and only in 4 cases was a higher quality noted in voluntary memorization.

Interesting data are presented by Pinskii (1952) with respect to experiments conducted by him for the purpose of comparing involuntary (unintentional) and voluntary (intentional) memorizing in normal and mentally retarded schoolchildren. In some cases meaningful texts were given, the assignment being to read them and tell whether everything was understandable in the text (involuntary memorizing), in others a memorizing assignment was given.

The results were: intentional memorization in schoolchildren of the public school predominated over unintentional (since the task in the latter case presented no difficulties for the schoolchildren, demanded no significant intellectual activity, which made it impossible to obtain high indexes of memorization). In pupils of the school for retarded children, the advantage of voluntary memorizing was considerably less, due to the greater difficulty for them to accomplish the activity, which had as its result involuntary memorization. For the public-school children the relation of involuntary to voluntary memorizing was 62% for one text and 58% for the other; for the retarded children it was 86% for the first text and 81% for the second.

Indicative also are the data characterizing the differences between the subjects—normal and mentally retarded schoolchildren—observed for each type of memorizing, separately. For voluntary memorization there was a much sharper difference observed between the children than for involuntary memorization. In the two texts the productivity of voluntary memorizing for the mentally retarded schoolchildren was 58% and 66% of that for memorizing the same material by the public-school children; in involuntary memorizing, however, the analogous indexes were considerably higher: 80% and 93%. The source of such a leveling out of the difference between the two categories of children was once more the fact that while for the normal children the simple reading of a text for the purpose of understanding it did not evoke an active thinking activity and this lowered the effectiveness of memorizing, for the mentally retarded children it demanded more-active thinking processes and therefore yielded a relatively higher result. However, another, very probable source for these differences must not be denied—a mentally retarded child's difficulty in voluntarily concentrating on some activity demanding considerable effort (which characterizes the essence of voluntary memorizing, differentiating it to some extent from involuntary memorizing).

In her investigation, Istomina (1964) compared involuntary and voluntary memorization in children. A set of pictures was given to preschool children (ages three to six) which they had to look over (memorization was not assigned) and then a similar set was presented and memorization asked.

In contrast to the data obtained by Zinchenko in his first investigation (1939), the children of all ages gave better results for voluntary than for involuntary memorizing. The basis for this divergence must be seen in the fact that the simple looking over of pictures occurring in Istomina's experiments in involuntary memorization did not evoke the activity which the experiments with voluntary memorizing demanded (in spite of the fact that the time for the perception of each picture was in both cases exactly the same) and which was demanded in involuntary memorizing in Zinchenko's experiments.

The Polish psychologist Szewczuk (1965) studied very thoroughly the correlation of voluntary and involuntary memorizing. His detailed work was published later than ours (first edition, 1954) and takes into account the results of our as well as Zinchenko's investigations.

The experiments were conducted with adults (for the most part students). Types of activity in which memorizing was carried out (in some cases without a mnemonic task, in others with it) were: "trip" of the subjects along the streets for the purpose of making some purchases in the stores, viewing of a short (five minute) popular scientific film about natural science, viewing of a set of photographs in connection with a talk on photography just heard, examining a set of complex colored geometric figures (allegedly, products of children's fantasies), reading of a text (allegedly, for the purpose of getting acquainted with one of the novellas from a newly published book), reading of a number of sentences for the purpose of establishing in them some logical contradictions, reading of a long, involved sentence as an example of the difficulties which such syntactical forms can cause, reading of words written on cards which had to be put in a definite place in a definite manner, and, finally, reading nonsense syllables (allegedly, to determine visual acuity). Each of these actions, as was said, some subjects performed without the task of memorizing, the others with such a task (everything that was on the street; the whole presented material).

For all experiments, voluntary memorizing gave better results than involuntary, but the degree of difference between them was not the same in different experiments. On the basis of the summarized data cited by the author (p. 158 in his book) we calculated the ratio of involuntary to voluntary memorization (Table 3.3).

As can be seen from this table, least significant was the advantage of voluntary over involuntary memorizing in the "shopping" experiments where in neither voluntary nor involuntary memorizing was any particularly active thinking activity demanded (which to some extent equalized the cases). Then follow memorizing a text and memorizing a list of sentences where, on the contrary, in both cases the subjects' goal, although involuntarily, was to understand the text, which again equalized the possibility of memorizing. Maximum lagging of involuntary memorizing is noticed in the experiments with individual words and nonsense syllables which in a situation of involuntary memorizing had only to be read; but their voluntary memorizing needed

TABLE 3.3

Objects of memorization	Absolute indices (in %) involuntary memorization	Absolute indices (in %) voluntary memorization	Relative indices (ratio of involuntary to voluntary memorization, %)
Shopping in city	55	71	77
Film	26	41	63
Photographs	40	58	69
Geometric figures	75	51	69
Text	38	51	75
List of sentences	42	59	71
Long sentence	28	41	68
Words	20	35	57
Nonsense syllables	15	33	42

TABLE 3.4

Objects of memorization	Absolute indices (in %) involuntary memorization	voluntary memorization	Relative indices (ratio of involuntary to voluntary memorization, %)
Directly related to goal of activity	93	100	93
Indirectly related to goal of activity	78	94	83
Unrelated to goal of activity	43	62	69
Unrelated to goal of activity and of no interest to the subjects	1.6	27	6

mental involvement, as is common in experiments with material that is difficult to memorize.

Indicative also are the data characterizing memorization (for the "shopping trip") of what was connected with the main purpose of the activity of the subjects, on the one hand, and, on the other hand, of what did not have such a connection. The data concerning this question cited in the book (and the relative indexes calculated by us on their basis) are presented in Table 3.4.

From the table it is clear that the more connected some facts are with the purpose of the activity of the subjects, the less is the difference between involuntary and voluntary memorizing, i.e., the more productive is involuntary memorizing. This fully agrees with what was found by us and by Zinchenko. In Szewczuk's experiments no predominance of involuntary memorizing over voluntary was noted because his experiments were conducted with adults, in whom voluntary memorizing predominates over involuntary (as compared with children); the tasks put before the subjects when involuntary memorizing was carried out did not stimulate them to intensive thinking activity.

3. ON THE CORRELATION OF VOLUNTARY AND INVOLUNTARY MEMORIZATION IN EVERYDAY PRACTICE

The great significance of mental participation in the activity in which memorizing is included shows up very clearly in everyday practice. If we work at something actively and thoroughly, we memorize quickly and stably, even if we have no intention of memorizing.

One can point to the memorization of a role by an actor as a concrete example of such memorizing. It would seem that in these cases not only is a clearly-expressed mnemonic orientation necessary, but also a corresponding special activity. Undoubtedly, in a number of cases the role is memorized precisely in this manner, i.e., the actor really memorizes the text of the role, pursuing just this mnemonic goal, carrying out his memorizing as a special activity, quite aside from the general work on the character.

There are, however, other ways of memorizing a role, when memorizing is not distinguished as a special activity but is carried out in the process of performing a different activity, working at creating an image. Then memorizing does not need a special task demanding special actions directed towards it.

True, there is undoubtedly orientation towards memorizing, but it is an organic component of the general task before the actor working at his role. He "has it in mind" when he works on the image, it is necessarily assumed as one of the results of this work, but is carried out not by way of special memorizing, but as the result of *the whole work on the image*. In trying to find the embodiment of the image, intonation, mimicry, gestures, motions, the actor is repeatedly involved with the content which he has to memorize, and he memorizes it without giving himself the mnemonic task.

This is precisely how actors characterized their memorizing when we talked with them. The distinguished actress, Yu., with whom we spoke said:

> I do not specifically work on memorizing my role. It is remembered gradually as I work at creating an image. One cannot memorize a role. Cramming makes clichéed delivery. One cannot memorize only words. That would be mere mechanical memorizing even though I'd understand the sense of what I memorize. One must memorize *creatively*, live *inwardly* with it, come to the text, to its memorizing with *one's whole inner life*. Therefore, if the line of psychological motivations is clear, then everything is memorized by itself. Of great importance is the search for the proper delivery. The search sometimes takes a long time. You walk along the street and say out loud sections of your role, search for how they must be said. Once in the Europa Hotel in Leningrad I did not let my neighbors sleep all night. I recited out loud, not to commit the text to memory, but to find the correct delivery. Usually, one tries it with separate pieces.... One must not begin too soon to memorize exactly and fully. Otherwise the learned text "dangles." Therefore, I avoid learning by heart too soon. A gradual memorization facilitates committing to memory. At first one remembers only generally, not so much the words as the actions. In working on a role one breaks it up into pieces, although in order to remember one must not only divide into pieces, but see the whole. What is the basis for a segment? A volitional principle. In other words, *what* precisely I *want* to achieve in this segment: to deceive, express anger, pity, gain consent. Each time I ask myself: what *do* I do here? And I answer this question in each segment, determine my action and my whole attitude. *This action serves as basis for memorization*. Through these segments passes the "psychological thread," and knowing the psychology of the segment it is easier to remember. The words are matched to the action, to feeling. One takes them, of course, from the text of the role, but tries not to memorize them at once exactly. At the beginning much is expressed in one's own words. Here much depends on the sentence itself. There are sentences which are memorized at once and there are ones that are mastered with difficulty. Of great significance is enthusiasm for the role. The more I am carried away by it, the more

> unnoticeably I memorize it.... Action is very important for memorizing. Therefore, "declamation" material is more difficult for me to memorize. When you are on the stage you are doing something, walking, but a reader stands in one place, does, in essence, nothing, he is in a worse position.... Very important is the rhythm of the action. It plays a very great role. You know that this scene goes in such a rhythm and that one in another, and this helps memorization. You remember somehow musically.... At present, visual images of the text itself do not play any role for me, although formerly, when the roles had to be copied by hand, these images were there. The handwriting had an individual character, there was some kind of expressiveness in it. Often I directly saw the page of the role, then it was committed to memory by itself. Typewritten copies neutralize the text. It no longer has the expressiveness which helped to memorize it visually. Therefore I do not see the pages any more.... At a premiere you always know the text well and yet before you appear on the stage it often seems that everything has been forgotten. You are "at the threshold of hell," but once you get out on the stage, begin to *do what must be done,* the text comes by itself and nothing needs to be remembered.

It is not difficult to see that these statements quite definitely underscore that although memorizing the role is undoubtedly one of the tasks toward which the work on the role is oriented, the accomplishment of this task is reached not by means specially directed toward it. It is not a special activity of memorizing, not a learning of the role by heart, but is in the background and occurs while solving another problem, the process of creating an image.

The most important part in creating an image is played by the *actions* and *conduct* which the actor must perform on the stage and which are connected inseparably with the feelings of the character. The words of the role are a component of his actions and conduct, most closely connected with his feelings, and are determined by his actions and feelings and therefore their mastering is supported precisely by performing the actions, by embodying certain feelings.

The same is expressed in the report of other actors we interviewed. Actress K., in response to our questions, describes the process thusly:

> How does one memorize a role? But that is a prolonged process and it merges with the entire work on the role. You turn to the text many times, not to memorize it, but because this must be done in order to create an image, to seed the role and make it grow. How do I work on my role in general? At first I visualize the image of the person, her childhood, her experiences. I try to visualize how she looks, the way she walks, how she squints her eyes, her movements and facial expressions. You develop keenness of observation, turn to memory, make a choice of what you see around you, what you remember. But in order to select, to visualize the outer appearance, one must begin from inside, one must understand the inner world of the person, what her life is. It is here that one has to turn to the text, and not only once, but at various stages of the work on the image and from various points of view. One has to review, think deeply, immerse oneself in it, check oneself, and check one's assumptions, one's image. Then once more you turn to the text, this time still closer, more closely you work at it, but again not to commit it to memory, but to clarify the role in all its details. I search for the logic of the role. I discover what is im-

> portant in each segment, in each sentence, what must be emphasized in it. I do not worry about the words themselves, how to memorize them, but I try to understand what is *being done* in each segment, to understand the condition of the character at the moment. This is the kernel of a segment. And it is these kernels that help one to remember the role. Of great significance also is the emotional background: the mood, the emotional state of the character, her encounters and conflicts with others. One must plot in one's mind the curve of her mood. Often I do not verbalize the role at first, but act without words, although the sense of what is spoken is, of course, in my consciousness. In all this work it also occurs that today I memorize one thing, tomorrow another, but I do not have to study especially. Although not everything, much is memorized by itself. Of course, you always know that the role must be memorized and this always has an influence on memorizing, but first of all you turn to the text with other aims and other tasks.

Analogous is the testimony of the actor Shch.

> Everything depends on the theatrical material. If the role is kindred, inspires, makes it possible to get in deeply, organically merge with the image which must be embodied, the technical aspects disappear. When this is absent, then it is difficult to memorize, "blocks" appear in the memory. One has to study and yet at the end one does not know as one should. One role I have played 137 times and still do not know it really. It does not fit me. The barrenness of the content of the play does not satisfy me. On what do I base memorization of a role? *On actions, twists of actions.* Simultaneously, actions are connected with inward experiences. One notices that the action hinges on such and such a phrase and the phrase merges organically with the actions, the feelings. If the role is "empty," one has to memorize where to say the phrase. But when work goes well the actions are directing, one orients himself by them. The text is not memorized all at once. At first you try to get a clear idea of the segment, the scene, the monologue, and then you forget the text, get away from it, to say it in your own words. Only then do you go back again to the text and probe every word, try to feel it, not especially for memorizing (although this always is present as a task), but to better penetrate the role, to feel it, to take everything that is in the role. It is the actions that help to recall the role during acting. Once there was a time when I forgot what to say in one place, but remembered that in saying it I stroked the curtain; I began to stroke it and at once remembered.

Our fourth interview, with folk actor T., expressed very clearly the significance of action in memorizing.

> You know, of course, that there is visual, auditory, and speech motor memory. It must be said that not one of them serves as support in memorizing a role. Not one of them serves me as support in my work. *Actions serve as support for memorizing.* Needed are neither visual, nor auditory, nor motor memory. *Memory of actions is necessary.* I memorize the role by the actions which I perform. I do not take the words exactly, but learn only what I *do* and how I *manipulate*. What, for example, do I do? I greet someone. In what manner? This is the support for memorizing. Rehearsals begin—at first I do not know the words exactly, I mark only the actions and then think: "It seems these words are spoken." When a monologue must be mastered you discover what thoughts must be expressed, how a thought develops, in what stages it proceeds, what feelings evoke these thoughts. Only then does one go over to exact words. One does not have to cram. One is no longer afraid to mix up the words. One must only know what to do; the words are remembered by themselves. The brain must not be forced. Through rehearsals the text is put into

memory by itself. Here and there the prompter helps at rehearsals and in the meantime you work at the role and return to the text, not to memorize, but in order to understand better what must be expressed. And here you notice where you have messed up the text, notice the shading which must be conveyed, and thereby the needed words are better memorized. *One cannot memorize apart from action,* and later it is difficult to remember, but as soon as the words are connected with action it is easily committed and as soon as you come onto the stage everything is in its place. To review the role before a performance, especially when this role has not been played for some time, is of course necessary, but here, too, you review by actions: "at first I do this, then that," etc. I consider memorizing the text out loud very harmful. If you memorize a text out loud in order simply to remember what words there are, you will develop a bad delivery and make the development of a good delivery more difficult. On the contrary, one must work on the delivery, and then the text itself will be remembered. When you memorize something for reading ("declamatory" material), you lean on the development of the thought, the images, the feelings which they evoke. Again, at first the words are in the background. Only gradually do you make them exact, you do not memorize them so much as you make exact what must be conveyed.

It is not difficult to see that the actors are in agreement with one another. This is all the more important as these were actors of different theaters: the first two actresses were from the Leningrad Pushkin Theater of Drama, the other two actors, from the Moscow Art Theater. Different also were their ages and lengths of service on the stage. In spite of these differences, the content of their reports was basically identical. All emphasized that memorizing a role is not an ordinary voluntary memorizing as observed in schoolwork. It is an activity not especially directed toward memorizing. However, it is not quite involuntary memorizing either (i.e., memorizing carried out when we have no orientation toward memorizing). The actor knows that he has to memorize the role and that work on the role, at creating an image, will result in accomplishing memorization. But his work pursues other goals and has therefore a quite different character.

The most important place is taken by the creating of an image. It demands thought, sympathy for the image, embodiment of the image, work at mimicry, gestures, movements, intense searching for the correct delivery, and this necessitates attention to the text, thinking it through, making it clear. This compels the actor to return many times to the text, to analyze it, but not for the purpose of memorizing, but to clear up the role in order to picture the character in mind, his actions, his behavior. All this necessarily leads to retention of the text, to its memorization, although without special effort.

The actors are also in full agreement concerning the characteristics of *what* serves as support for memorization of the role—the *actions* which must be performed on the stage, the sense of these actions, the feelings connected with them and causing them, the line of actions, their twists, the emotional background for the actions. Such is the basis of memorizing which makes a specific learning of the role, if not completely, then at least to a great extent, unnecessary.

Consequently, this case does not demand an activity especially directed toward memorizing, but it undoubtedly is supported by the degree of active participation of those who are memorizing. It is expressed first of all in an activity which is performed mainly for other purposes but serves simultaneously as support for memorizing and is necessary for memorization to be accomplished. The text of the role is memorized not by itself, but connected with definite actions and organically incorporated into the scene. Were it not for these actions, the text would demand that one work specifically at memorizing.

Thus the activeness in this case is expressed in two ways: on the one hand, memorizing is carried out in the process of performing a complex, diverse, and many-faceted activity (i.e., the work on a role); on the other hand, support for memorization is the action on the stage, what the actor must *do* on the stage, and into what the text of the role is incorporated as an organic component. Active participation in the process of work on the role and involvement in the playing of the role itself, in its very content, is the twofold activeness which takes place and which serves as basis for memorizing, makes memorization possible without special orientation toward memorizing, without special efforts, without special work at memorizing.

All this indicates the correctness of the premise introduced above, i.e., the intimate dependence of memorizing upon active involvement in the activity in which it is carried out.

* * *

The dependence of memorizing on the activity as a result of which it is achieved characterizes, as was said, one of the aspects of the problem of the activeness of memorization. Closely linked with it is another aspect of the same problem: understanding memorization itself to be a special kind of activity, *mnemonic activity*. This aspect merges to a certain extent with the problem of *comprehension* in memorization, because the thinking process occupies a central place in the activity of memorizing. In Part Two we proceed to the examination of this problem.

Part II: Comprehension in Memorization

Chapter 4

THE ROLE OF UNDERSTANDING IN MEMORIZATION

1. INTRODUCTION

The outstanding role of understanding in memorization is well known. The difficulty of remembering what is insufficiently understood is also known.

In our experiments, in which texts of various degrees of difficulty of understanding were learned by heart, the subjects themselves many times emphasized the great difficulty in memorizing caused by the difficulty in understanding. Let us present some of these statements: "It was very difficult to memorize what I could not understand on account of its unclear exposition, its incomprehensibility"; "It was awfully difficult to memorize what I could not understand as I should."

It is therefore quite a natural requirement for everyone attempting to memorize something that he understand the content of what he reads, comprehend it, discern it, for here begins the process of memorizing.

The subjective difficulty of memorizing without depending on understanding is expressed in the objectively sharp difference between the productivity of this type of memorizing and that based on understanding. An intelligent memorizing is more productive than a mechanical one. This is well known from everyday practice, and has been confirmed by many experimental investigations.

In some of them the role of understanding was revealed by comparing memorization of various types of material, some more, some less meaningful. In particular, the speed of memorizing was compared. Ebbinghaus (1885) established (on himself) that to memorize 36 nonsense syllables he needed an average of 55 repetitions, while 36–40 words independent of each other (i.e., not counting words without independent meaning, such as prepositions, conjunctions, etc.) taken from Schiller's translation of the Aeneid he remembered after only 6–7 repetitions (a ratio of approximately 9:1). Other investigators obtained similar results. According to the data of Lyon (1914), for example, 200 nonsense words were memorized, on the average, in 93 min, 200 numbers in 85 min, 200 words from prose texts in 24 min, and 200 words from poems in 10 min. Here, too, the ratio of the speed of the memorization of meaningful material (taken from poetry) to that of nonsense syllables was 9:1.

Great differences were noted also in the *stability* of memorized meaningful and nonsense material. Well known is the "classic" curve of retention of nonsense syllables (learned to perfect reproduction) found by Ebbinghaus. The curve drops sharply in the first hours after memorizing (Fig. 4.1). The curves of reproduction of meaningful material have quite a different shape, e.g., those obtained by Williams (1926) in his experiments with monosyllabic words and by Dietze and Johnson (1931) in their investigations with reproduction of prose texts after a single reading (Figs. 4.2 and 4.3). Analogous results in experiments with memorizing poems were obtained by Whitely and McGeoch (1928). Even the forgetting of numbers, according to data by Piéron (1913), does not accelerate as fast as that of nonsense syllables as found by Ebbinghaus. After one month Ebbinghaus retained 21%, while after two months Piéron retained 40%.

Of Soviet works, Leont'ev's investigation (1931) from which there are comparative data on memorization of nonsense syllables and meaningful words which were memorized either directly or with the help of pictures must be mentioned. Rubinshtein (1946) obtained analogous data. In one work by Gurevich done under Rubinshtein's guidance the final learning trial of memorized meaningful text, performed six days after the first memo-

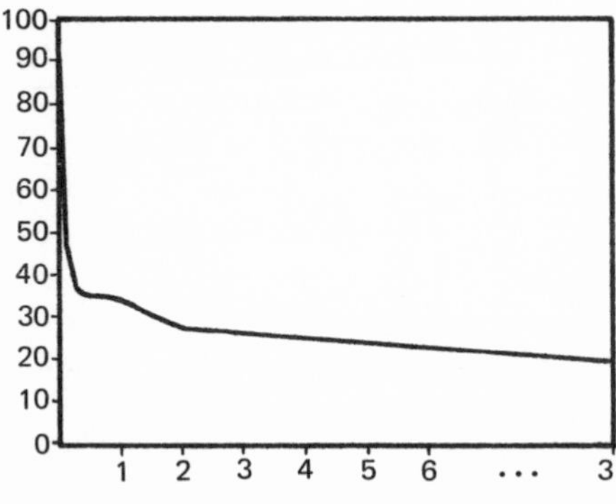

Fig. 4.1. Retention of nonsense syllables. Abscissa: days; ordinate: percent retention.

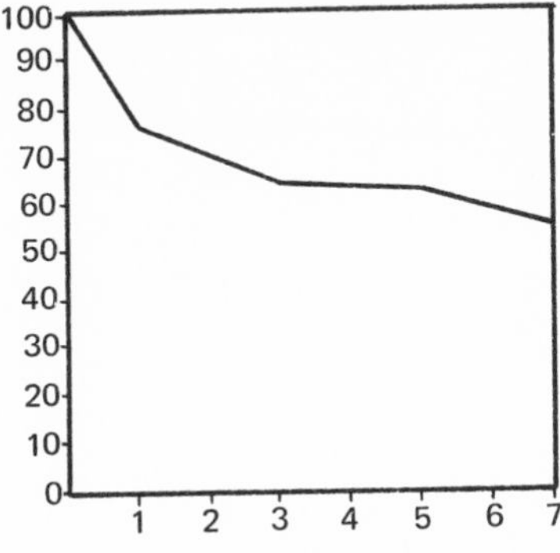

Fig. 4.2. Retention of monosyllabic words. Abscissa: days; ordinate: percent retention.

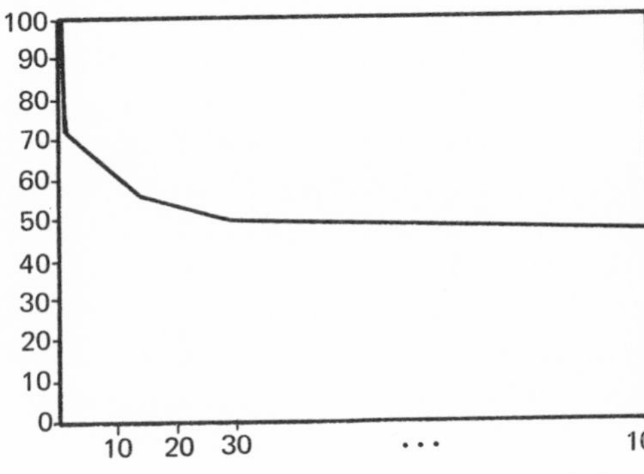

Fig. 4.3. Retention of prose texts. Abscissa: days; ordinate: percent retention.

rization yielded a 71% retention rate, while for Ebbinghaus the corresponding index of retention for nonsense syllables was only 28%.

In some investigations the advantage of meaningful memorization was revealed on the same material, but with the application of various *methods* of memorizing. In some cases memorizing had to be done meaningfully, in others as mechanically as possible, without paying attention to the meaning. Meaningful words were usually used. In some series of experiments they were memorized without establishing any relations between them. In parallel series it was required to make at least an indirect connection between each following pair of words. Such a method was used by Balaban (1910) and Rybnikov (1923).

In an analogous manner, meaningful texts were also used. In some cases they had to be memorized sensibly by scrutinizing the content, in others, without paying attention to the meaning. It is quite obvious that it is hardly possible to become detached from the meaning in mastering meaningful texts (just as one cannot achieve mechanical memorization of individual isolated words). However, varying degrees of comprehension in memorizing could still be achieved in these experiments.

In a number of investigations the retention of various types of school material, memorized under school conditions, was studied. Of the investigations by Soviet psychologists who studied this problem those of Zinchenko (1939*b*, 1961), Shardakov (1940), and Lipkina (1941, 1958) should also be mentioned.

As a result of the large number of studies differing in material and method of investigation, the advantage of memorizing based on understanding has been clearly demonstrated in all facets of memorizing: completeness, speed, accuracy, and stability.

We shall not cite numerical data which characterize this, since it would not be correct to ascribe special significance to the absolute value of these coefficients or search for a single mathematical expression of this advantage. We point out only that the quantitative difference between the two types of memorizing was not identical in the various investigations. This result can be explained by the differences in the material and the different level of understanding which was demanded by experimental conditions. An important role is also played by the differences in the indexes chosen by the investigators for the comparison of the two types of memorizing.

How great the significance of this factor is can be judged from the following example. Binet and Henri (1895*a*, 1895*b*) in comparing the memorizing of sentences and single words came to the conclusion that the productivity of memorizing was in the first case 25 as great as in the second. They base it on the fact that such is the correlation between the quantity of the forgotten material in the two cases. Almost the same coefficient is pointed out in the investigation of memorizing words conducted by Rybnikov.

It is clear, however, that one can judge success of memorization not only by the amount of the *forgotten,* but also the amount of the *retained* material. Moreover, one can consider that this index reflects even better the real picture of *stability* of memorizing. And yet, taking retention as the basis we obtain completely different quantitative correlations between memorization with or without comprehension.

Our calculations of the data in the publications of Binet and Henri showed that if one proceeds from the amount of the reproduced material, then memorizing sentences exceeds memorizing of words not 25 times as Binet and Henri point out, but only 1.5 times. This is explained by the fact that the indexes of the reproduced material were much higher than the indexes of the forgotten material. Therefore, the relative difference between the indexes of the reproduced material was considerably smaller than that between the indexes of the forgotten material.

What has been said does not at all alter the main postulate pointed out above: *memorization based on understanding is in all cases, unconditionally, more productive than memorization not supported by understanding.*

2. COMPREHENSION IN THE MNEMONIC ACTIVITY OF CHILDREN

While in adults the advantage of intelligent memorizing over mechanical is not denied by even the representatives of extreme mechanistic doctrines, it is different with the question of logical memory in a child.

In psychology literature it has been repeatedly asserted that younger children, including elementary-school children, memorize mechanically. This was clearly expressed by Meumann (1912), who asserted that the beginning of the predominance of logical memory must be at age 13–14. Stern (1922) expressed it similarly when he referred to the small value of the comprehension of meaning and to the fact that up to the age of six teaching has predominantly a "sensorimotor nature." Is this really so?

Investigations quite clearly show that mechanical learning in children as in adults has less effect than meaningful memorizing. This position has been proven by many investigations and it pertains to children of school age as well as the preschool children of whom Stern speaks.

But is not the *degree* of this advantage unequal in adults and children? Is it not less in children than in adults? Should one not in this sense understand the mechanical nature of memorizing in children?

This is the premise put forward by Meumann. Concerning the development of memory in connection with age and referring to his own experiments, he asserts that with age the progress of memorizing nonsense material decreases. At the same time the progress of memorizing meaningful material increases. Hence it is clear that in the course of time the advantage of meaningful memorizing increases and at an older age must be more pronounced than at a younger age.

In order to check this we conducted special calculations proceeding from the data in which the changes connected with age were traced on the same material for various ages. The material consisted of nonsense syllables and single words. We calculated two kinds of indexes: indexes of the increase of each type of memorizing, separately, and indexes of correlation between meaningful and nonsense memorization for each age group.

In the first case, fixing the productivity of memorizing for the younger age group (in each experiment) at 100, we calculated the relative value of all other age-group indexes for each type of memorization separately, i.e., for meaningful and for mechanical learning.

In the second case we calculated for each age group the percent ratio of the productivity of meaningful memorization to the indexes of memorizing nonsense material. In these cases we utilized absolute values.

In calculating all these indexes we purposely used not only the data of Soviet investigators (Leont'ev, 1931) but also those of a number of foreign investigators: Lobsien (1911), Pohlmann (1906), and Brunswick, Goldscheider, and Pileck (1932), since it is the non-Soviet authors who speak about the predominantly mechanical memorizing in younger children (Table 4.1). The indexes in the fourth column of Table 4.1 are calculated by comparing not the relative indexes given in the second and third columns, but the absolute indexes obtained for each age group.

The results of calculations in Tables 4.1 show how meaningful and

TABLE 4.1

Age of subjects in years	Productivity of memorization of meaningful material	Productivity of memorization of meaningless material	Advantage of memorization of meaningful material
	Leont'ev (1931)		
4–5	100	100	139
6–7	213	630	216
7–12	284	783	232
10–14	328	813	258
12–16	357	1387	164
Adults	458	1926	152
	Pohlmann (1906)		
9	100	100	268
10	135	138	240
11	161	211	200
12	176	222	209
13	181	281	173
14	191	282	180
	Lobsien (1911)		
9–10	100	100	558
10–11	123	172	400
11–12	156	277	314
12–13	165	255	177
13–14	192	562	191
	Brunswick, Goldscheider, and Pileck (1932)		
6	100	100	167
7	126	157	133
8	106	143	123
9	120	162	124
10	126	190	110
11	137	181	126
12	143	210	114
13	149	205	121

nonsense material is memorized by children of various ages. This table shows that all data express the same principle: the productivity of memorizing meaningful material increases with age more slowly than the productivity of memorizing nonsense material. Therefore, the advantage of memorizing meaningful material at an older age is smaller than at a younger age.

This principle sharply contradicts the thesis of Meumann. His position is decisively refuted by the data in the above investigations.

How must this principle be understood? What is the explanation of the fact that with age the advantage of memorizing meaningful material not only fails to increase but, on the contrary, considerably decreases?

This fact seems paradoxical and demands a careful examination. First, attention must be drawn to the fact that in the investigations utilized by us the difference between meaningful and nonsense memorizing was studied by way of variation of the *material*. In some cases the subjects memorized nonsense syllables, in others, words. This is of significance to an understanding of the conclusions drawn from these investigations.

Indeed, the need to comprehend what is being memorized is very great. We meet with it in memorizing not only meaningful, but also nonsense material, the memorization of which therefore is usually not mechanical. In many cases it includes some factors of giving meaning. Even when memorizing nonsense material, we indirectly, partially, and conditionally give meaning to it. To attempt to completely identify the difference between memorizing nonsense and meaningful material on the one hand and between mechanical and meaningful memorizing on the other, is not correct. The material has an important influence on the nature of memorizing, but does not fully predetermine the *method* of memorizing. Is this assignment of meaning to nonsense material identical in adults and children?

As experimental investigations have demonstrated particularly those of Leont'ev and others, adults show a considerably greater tendency and ability to give meaning to nonsense material than children. More often and with greater ease they connect this material with something meaningful. Therefore, for them the degree of difference in the meaningfulness of memorizing of the two types of material must be lower than for children, and this means that the productivity of memorizing both kinds of material must differ less in adults than in children. This is confirmed by the data above.

Of great significance also is the fact that memorizing nonsense material demands more intensive volitional efforts than memorizing meaningful material. In the latter case a considerable part of the material is retained even when memorization is not intended. It is quite different with the memorizing of nonsense material: involuntary memorizing is insignificant and the material is memorized mainly as the result of active volitional efforts.

It is clear that to children such efforts come with greater difficulty and with less success than to adults. Therefore, the difference between memorizing nonsense and meaningful material must be greater for them than for adults. Do not these experimental data obtained under laboratory conditions differ from what is observed in life?

There are three groups of facts which seemingly do not conform to the premise made and which must be examined for its justification:

1. the easy memorizing by children of what they do not understand and even of nonsense material;
2. the tendency to memorize without considering the meaning of what is memorized;
3. literal memorization.

Let us examine the first finding. One often has the occasion to observe that younger children memorize with great ease what they do not understand, sometimes even what is nonsense; moreover, such material is stably retained. One need only remember how preschool children memorize songs, some beyond their understanding, which they hear from adults, how they memorize unfamiliar and unintelligible words and expressions used by adults. A clear example of with what ease the younger children sometimes memorize material completely devoid of sense is the memorizing of counting-out rhymes. Some of them are a set of artificial nonsense words without any meaningful content. Here is one of them which we heard from children at play:

Ene, due, rabe,
Enchik, penchik, zhabe,
Ene, due, resh,
Enchik, penchik, zhesh.

It would seem there could not be anything more nonsensical than this "poem," and yet it was memorized by the children with great enthusiasm and ease and used as a counting-out rhyme. How can this be understood? Does this contradict the assertion that memorizing of nonsense material in children is more difficult than at a mature age?

In order to answer this one must understand why children often easily memorize material which they do not understand or which is completely nonsensical.

We must regard as a cause of this memorization not the characteristics of the material, not its unintelligibility and meaninglessness, but the special *attitude* which this unintelligibility and meaninglessness can sometimes evoke in children. What is this attitude?

We examine, first, cases in which children perceive material not understandable to them but which is objectively *meaningful*. In these cases they often know perfectly well that such material has a quite specific meaning, though unknown to them. This is very important, since the fact that the child understands that there is a meaning behind the material not understandable to him sometimes makes this incomprehensible material especially important to the child, attracts increased attention, arouses curiosity, prompts searching for the meaning of what he hears, and, consequently, he memorizes it, involuntarily, unnoticed, in spite of the complete incomprehensibility of what he is memorizing.

As one of the many examples of this is a tale told by the poet Mayakovskii from his childhood recollections. One night he heard through the wall "incessant whispering by papa and mama." "About a piano." He did not sleep all night. The same sentence kept bothering him. In the morning he ran to his father: "Papa, what is an installment plan?" The frequently repeated expression "installment plan" which Mayakovskii had heard all night was, of course, significant for the stability of memorization. But it was not only this phrase that played an essential role. More important was what place the strange, troubling expression had in the "incessant whispering of papa and mama." This was what attracted special attention to the expression. The frequency of repetition was of importance not only in itself but as an index of the significance which "papa and mama" gave to the puzzling "installment plan."

An infinite number of analogous examples could be cited. It is well known that preschool children ask adults what a particular word or expression means which they have heard from adults. Sometimes the expressions were heard rather long ago and only once, when they were, literally, dropped by the adults, said in passing, unnoticed by the speakers themselves, and without any emphasis.

The fact that such words or expressions, as yet completely beyond the understanding of the child, are retained rather stably and in spite of the seemingly very unfavorable conditions for their retention (a single perception) can be explained by the child's realization that this word or expression has some kind of specific meaning, which realization prompts him to search for its explanation. It is also very important that the word or expression not understood by the child usually stands out against a background of what is known, accessible, and fully understandable to the child and attracts his special interest. All this is absent when the children under experimental conditions have to memorize nonsense material for the investigation of memory.

What is the attitude of children to *objectively* meaningless material when they for some reason encounter it in life and not under experimental conditions?

Characteristic of this attitude and facilitating memorization of nonsense material in these cases is the fact that sometimes such material attracts the child by its *sound*: a peculiar combination of sounds or pronounced rhythm which in itself facilitates memorizing considerably. In many cases such material evokes a feeling of the ridiculous in a child or some other emotional attitude. All this assists memorizing even more.

It is very important that often such material is *woven into the play activity* of the children; this creates an especially favorable atmosphere for its memorization and makes it a distinctive meaningful act necessary for the carrying out of the game.

It must be noted that the ease of memorizing nonsense material observed in children is not a unique, age-bound property of a child's memory. Similar observations are made in adults. Often adults quickly and stably memorize nonsense precisely because it easily stands out from all else, strikes them with its unusualness and strangeness, causes a special emotional attitude, is sometimes liked for its humorousness, and attracts by its sound.

Under experimental conditions, easy memorizing of nonsense material was often noted, for example, in the use of pair-associations. In these cases it often happens that better memorized (against an overall background of meaningful combinations of words) are those pairs in which the logical connection between concepts is completely absent, where the two concepts express something incompatible. Thus, from among such pairs as "fire—lamp," "stylus—pen holder," "drum—toy," "school—book," "gun—shot," "cat—meat," "feet—cap," best memorized, as the data of our experiments show, was the last pair, although we did not read it as the last pair but in the middle of the other word groups. The basis for this, as the subjects themselves noted, was precisely the "presence of nonsense" in this combination of words, the fact that "this combination was too absurd."

There is no doubt that in adults we encounter less frequently the ease of memorizing nonsense material than in children and that the actual facts under discussion are in maturity less striking than during childhood. But how can this be explained? By the peculiarity of memory in adults and children?

The difference in the ease of memorizing nonsense material between adults and children can be completely explained by the effect of causes not in the memory itself of either the adults or children. This is not to say that memorizing this material in itself is more accessible to children. The only thing that can be asserted with regard to this difference is that in life the nonsense material evokes in children more often than in adults a certain special attitude which considerably increases the facility of its memorization. Under artificial laboratory conditions such an attitude is usually absent in children and hence it is natural that memorizing nonsense material under these conditions is less productive for them than for adults.

Let us examine the second finding pointed out as evidence of the ease of mechanical memorizing in childhood: children sometimes memorize mechanically what seems to be comprehensible to them. Schoolchildren often cram an assignment, not penetrating into its meaning, although they are quite capable of understanding what they memorize.

Some investigators see as the basis for this that the productivity of memorizing nonsense material in childhood is, supposedly, very great and that the difference between mechanical and meaningful memorizing in children is, supposedly, insignificant. Therefore, utilization of mechanical memorizing presents for a schoolchild no difficulties. It seems that precisely for this reason he begins to memorize mechanically what is for some reason not immediately comprehended by him. Is this indeed so?

Observing the work of schoolchildren, how they prepare their lessons, shows that this explanation is incorrect.

First of all, the transition to mechanical memorizing is usually observed not immediately, but only after insistent and repeated attempts to understand what is being memorized. The schoolchild takes recourse to it after his attempts to understand give no results, the explanations of the teacher are forgotten, and there is no outside help. Since he has to learn his lesson, "answer" his assignment, under these conditions he begins to learn mechanically.

But even when the schoolchild does not make attempts to understand the material, he is not prompted to this by the characteristics of his memory but by other causes, primarily by the difficulty of understanding itself. From experience he knows that he often succeeds in understanding only after considerable effort and time. This evokes in him a negative attitude. Therefore, the next time he does not understand at once, he takes a different, mechanical, approach to memorizing. The question of the suitability of this approach is decided not by its correlation with meaningful memorizing, but by comparison with the difficulties of comprehension.

If the effort and time necessary for understanding are considerable and exceed what is needed for mechanical mastery, then it is natural that the latter way is chosen, although by itself it may be rather difficult. No "measurements," no exact comparisons are performed here. The problem is by no means solved consciously, but on the basis of a certain "general feeling" and, most of all, on the strength of the emotional attitude which is evoked by the effort needed for understanding on the one hand and for mechanical memorizing on the other.

Individual differences are here very great. Mechanical memorizing is naturally chosen more often by schoolchildren who are intellectually less active, not trained for intellectual efforts, and not interested in independent search for the solution or the success of the search.

An important role is also played by the *interest in understanding* the material, which is related to the general interest in the subject, in the field of knowledge.

All this emphasizes the fact that here we are dealing with the individual characteristics of the *personalities* of schoolchildren and not with *age-bound properties of memory*.

The *habit* of memorizing mechanically is one of the reasons for mechanical memorizing. If difficulties of understanding are frequent and the schoolchild has to turn to mechanical memorizing many times, he sometimes gets into the habit of not attempting to understand the material, but immediately learns it mechanically. Mechanical memorizing is more and more often substituted for understanding. As the habit becomes fixed, it is also observed when difficulties to understanding are insignificant and could easily be overcome. The child makes no efforts to understand the material even if this could be successful. Learning now means only *memorizing* and not *understanding and memorizing*. The substitution of memorization for understanding characterizes the habitual way of working by such a schoolchild.

Does that mean that mechanical memorization, having become a habit, approaches in facility meaningful memorizing or becomes equal to it?

Undoubtedly, habit does facilitate the performance of an action. Therefore, mechanical memorizing, having become a habit, may become easier than it was before this habit developed. However, this does not mean that it has come close to the facility of meaningful memorizing. What is most important is that, even if a "gain" is observed, it is not an index of an age-bound feature of memory, but again is the result of individual features of the work of individual children who have acquired such a habit.

We turn to the third group of findings which are cited as evidence of the facility of mechanical memorizing in children: literal reproduction.

In life we often meet with the literal delivery by children of what they remember. Even schoolchildren often reproduce literally, or at least close to the original, what they have memorized, although such a reproduction has not only not been demanded but, on occasion, forbidden. Sometimes they cannot tell "in their own words" what they have studied, though just such an account is demanded of them.

The ease with which children achieve literalness in memorizing is striking. How exactly they notice sometimes the smallest deviations from the original when other people retell in a distorted form! Preschool children, for example, often "correct" adults when they are repeating something but do not tell it as it was told the first time. Moreover, preschoolers sometimes notice deviations from the original of which the adult storyteller is not even aware. Is this an indicator of the predominance of mechanical memorizing in children?

In recent non-Soviet literature one can often see attempts at linking literalness of memorizing with mechanical memorizing. Whipple (1914), for example, says that a characteristic feature of logical and intelligent memory is that "in these cases the reproduction of ideas is demanded first of all and not the exact, literal transmission." Thus, literalness is considered to be an indication of mechanical memorizing.

It is characteristic that in the American literature intelligent memorizing is often contrasted with learning by heart. Evidently the latter is said to be close to mechanical memorizing. Is this approach justified?

Undoubtedly, every rendering "in one's own words" demands understanding of what is expressed in new verbal forms. Only under this condition will these forms correspond to the meaning of what has been perceived, and the material learned be rendered correctly. In mechanical memorizing, understanding is absent, and to select other verbal forms which would correspond in meaning to what is being memorized is not possible. Therefore, one has to keep as close to the original as possible. Hence, the more mechanical the memorizing, the more it is, naturally, literal.

To a certain extent the opposite is also true: literal memorizing can serve as an index of mechanical memorizing. In order to reproduce literally, one must lean not only on the meaning, but also on the mechanical connections, the connections in proximity. The easier they are formed, the sooner literalness of memorizing is achieved.

However, the level of literalness depends not only on these connections, on the speed and ease of their emergence. Both are only *premises* of literal memorizing, the condition for its *possibility*. But the realization of this possibility depends on other causes.

Three conditions stand out here clearly: the material, the attitude toward memorizing, and the verbal resources of the one who memorizes.

In speaking of the influence of the *material,* one must distinguish the significance of the *accessibility* of what is being memorized. Inaccessible material causes, naturally, a greater tendency to memorize literally. Children, more often than adults, cannot comprehend what they memorize and therefore the tendency to literal reproduction is more often observed in them. This tendency, a result of insufficient possibility of understanding, is, however, not at all an indicator of the distinctiveness of children's *memory.*

An important role is played by characteristics of the material which determine a particular *set* to memorization. Some material itself demands to be memorized in a definite manner, in particular completely and accurately. It is natural that literal memorizing of such material does not say anything about the general tendency to memorize literally.

Also of great significance are such properties of the material which make a *variation* in reproduction possible. Sometimes the material is such that the possibility of conveying it "in one's own words" is limited. School material which the children must often learn is just such material. Its compactness, saturation, and accuracy often demand much effort in order to express it differently from what it is in the original. It is clear that in these cases literalness of reproduction again does not mean that memorizing is mechanical. It is not an expression of a general tendency toward literal memorization.

Most important among the sources of literal memorizing is the *attitude toward memorizing*. Here also there are great differences between adults and children.

For an adult memorizing something means absorption of the meaningful content, the essence of what is perceived. For a small child memorizing something means to impress it in all its concreteness, with all its individual properties. Therefore, deviations from the original, not changing the meaning of what was perceived but formally leading away from the original, are often considered by children as erroneous reproduction ("it really wasn't so"). Hence their frequent "correction" of adults, as was mentioned. For this same reason children pay great attention to *details* and their memorization. Very clearly the tendency to memorize by copying is seen in children when they must memorize something unusual, expressive, or emotional. They show a special pleasure in repeating such material in an exact, unchanged form. They repeat it themselves many times and make especially "rigid" demands on adult story tellers.

In schoolchildren such an attitude towards memorizing as literal memorizing may be caused by incorrectly understood demands by the school. Demands for accuracy of memorizing are sometimes understood by the schoolchildren as the necessity to keep maximally close to the original, to learn by heart or almost by heart.

What is the relation between literalness of reproduction and the development of speech in children? The child does not yet have a sufficient mastery of speech. His vocabulary is poorer than an adult's. This refers especially to his active speech, to what he really uses. Therefore in his speech there are fewer synonyms and, consequently, fewer possibilities of word substitution. Still more difficult for him is the exchange of expressions. The necessity of expressing his thought in a complete, finished, clearly-expressed form causes him great difficulty. In his speech there are many contractions, inferences, and fragments and yet much that is superfluous, unnecessary, and repetitious. He often does not succeed in finding words and expressions, or constructing sentences. The needed words "do not come," sentences are constructed incorrectly and speech coherence suffers.

Under these conditions the children must adhere closely to what is given them in ready form: to a story they have heard, a text they have read. Here they find ready-made what they themselves achieve with such difficulty.

From this source they can draw what they need without fear of distortion, without trying, sometimes quite unsuccessfully, to express independently, but ultimately still inaccurately, what must be formulated clearly, preserving a specific meaning without any digressions. In this manner the tendency to literal reproduction often occurs.

Literalness of reproduction, insufficiency in conveying "in one's own words" is, to a great extent, explained by the fact that the child does not have "his own words." Literal reproduction gives him the necessary means to give an account and "insures" him against possible distortions. To a certain extent this is caused, even if involuntarily, by an unrealized fear of distorting the meaning of the original. All this does not at all mean that the child does not understand what is reproduced literally.

The cause of literalness is not mechanical memorization, but the limited speech capabilities of the child, his as yet insufficient mastery of active speech. Therefore, it is natural that the need for literal memorizing will decrease as he grows older. The child will proceed to telling "in his own words."

And so, the attempt to derive mechanical memorizing from its literalness must be rejected as must all other attempts to prove a higher degree of mechanical memorizing in children.

We examined three arguments usually cited to prove that mechanical memorizing in children predominates over intelligent memorizing or, in any case, plays an important role in childhood which differs greatly from what is observed in adults.

None of these arguments do in fact decrease the role of understanding in childhood. They all prove only one thing, that the most important role among the conditions determining the success of memorizing is played by the orientation of those who memorize, their tendencies, volitional qualities, sets, and habits. In childhood these factors are such that under some conditions they considerably increase the facility of memorization of senseless, incomprehensible material, evoke the tendency to "mechanize" memorization, weaken the search for meaning or the tendency to understand, and lead to literalness of reproduction. But all this does not mean that in childhood understanding in the interest of memorizing is less necessary and that there is no need to achieve it in every possible way.

The attempts by some psychologists to justify mechanical memorization by schoolchildren must be decisively refuted. Meumann's point of view, according to which one need at first not try to understand in memorizing since, as he says, it will come later to a considerable extent on the basis of memorizing, is also false.

On the contrary, the classical educators were correct in their discovery and emphasis of the role of understanding in the processes of memorization.

Komenskii said that "the minds of children are disturbed when the schoolchildren are coerced to memorize or do something without preliminary and sufficient examination, explanation, and instruction. . . . Nothing must be compelled to be memorized except what is well understood. . . . Everything that the schoolchildren must memorize must be presented to them so clearly that they will have it before them as their five fingers" (1939, pp. 170–171).

All leading Russian psychologists and educators expressed themselves similarly. Tatishchev (1686–1750) in giving a characteristic of memory strongly emphasized the most important significance of "sense" or "surmise" for memorization (1887). Comprehension in memory was given a most important place by Galich, who proceeded, however, in the solution of this problem, as in all his conceptions of psychology, from clearly expressed idealistic positions. Memory, says Galich (1834), is distinguished by "the vastness of its domain to which it draws also abstract fancies of sense and the very ideas of reason." This is why, he points out "it joins thinking where it makes comparisons." The reflective activity must be, according to Galich, the basis in the exercise of memory. "He who is zealous," says Galich in this connection, "in cultivating other forces of his mind, who often deals with an interesting object and intentionally devotes his attention to it, who maintains a logical order and adheres to a reasoning method in the movement of thought...by natural, reasonable, strictly human means, will perfect his memory sooner than by devices of petty and suffocating *training* which we have inherited from antiquity under the name of *mnemonics*" (1834, p. 233). "What has been forced on our pedagogy," he continues, "by sophists, by actors, or by preachers, *the art of memorizing the role,* is just as limited in its goal as it is meager in means."

Galich decisively rejects cramming as memorizing without understanding. He sees in it harm for the memory itself as well as for the development of other facets of mental life. "Where a child is compelled to learn by heart only lessons...where life itself with its relations, supports, and excitations is too trivial and insignificant...there the predominance of memory condemned to take note of everything must necessarily hamper other tendencies of spiritual life" (1834, p. 237).

The importance of the role of meaningful memorization was especially emphasized by representatives of Russian materialistic philosophy and psychology of the nineteenth century.

"A page of some chronological table or an unconnected enumeration of proper names," says Chernyshevskii (1828–1889) "requires more time from the schoolchild than twenty pages of connected, logically developing story which relates events in lifelike images, not encumbered with dozens of unnecessary names" (1940, p. 63). These words clearly disclose what an important role Chernyshevskii ascribed to comprehending what was memorized, understanding its content, and how clearly he saw the difference between logical and mechanical memorizing, anticipating with his conclusion the results of the many experimental investigations which much later were to prove precisely this position.

Chernyshevskii considered it important to understand the *meaning* of what was being memorized. From just this point of view he approaches the evaluation of cases in which some people retain innumerable trivia. In referring to one such case he states: "The names of all popes can be remembered by a person who either specializes in the history of the papacy and then only while he is writing his works concerning the papacy, or by a person who does not know how to distinguish important from unimportant and necessary from unnecessary knowledge and who continuously reads much that is useless" (1940, p. 145).

Dobrolyubov (1836–1861) pointed just as definitely to the significance of meaningful memorizing. "To compel a child in his first stage of development to learn proper names, numbers, tables, general definitions the essence of which he does not understand, means forever to spoil the normal development of capabilities of the child, to dull in him feeling, imagination, and the strength of reason" (1939, p. 368).

Dobrolyubov condemns the teachers of the old school who did not care whether "the schoolchildren understood what they learned by heart or not" (1939, p. 205).

He speaks out categorically against the author of a textbook who declared that he did not at all dare to think that a manual for schoolchildren had to be composed in such a manner that each sentence was completely understood by the pupil. "How can he," exclaims Dobrolyubov, "in compiling a manual allow that not each sentence need be understood by the students? What kind of medieval cabalism is Mr. Pavlovskii [author of the textbook] preaching? To be understandable *in everything and for everybody* is the ideal of any textbook" (1939, p. 315).

Dobrolyubov rejects any kind of artificial mnemonics which leads to senseless memorizing of "whole groups of names not interconnected in the thought of the student." Very clearly he speaks against such artificial, mnemonic memorizing, in place of which, he points out, reasonable memorizing must "install itself" (1939, p. 367).

As pointed out above, Ushinskii devoted exceptionally great attention to the problem of meaningfulness of memory.

3. RECONSTRUCTION IN REPRODUCTION AS THE RESULT OF COGNITIVE PROCESSING OF THE PERCEIVED MATERIAL

The influence of understanding on memorizing is not merely limited to a considerable increase in productivity when it is of a meaningful nature.

Along with the *quantitative* changes in memorizing caused by understanding the material to be remembered, *qualitative* reconstruction of what is being memorized becomes important due to comprehension of the material.

Experimental data and practical observations show that when the material is not learned by heart its reproduction is characterized not only by quantitative deviations from the original. We do not simply reproduce less than is in the original, but make various different *qualitative* changes in the original. The scale and nature of these changes are such that the process of reproduction cannot at all be considered as bare reproduction, as a simple restoration of what was perceived. It is sometimes a very important *reconstruction.*

These qualitative changes are all the more important the larger and more difficult the material, the weaker the orientation towards accuracy of memorization, the longer the period between impression and reproduction, and the lower the level of memorization that has been achieved.

Bartlett (1932) has gathered considerable material on this problem. Among Soviet psychologists the following have worked a great deal on the study of reconstruction of material in reproduction: Blonskii (1935), Rubinshtein (1946), Komm (1940), Shardakov (1940), Zankov (1944), Mayants (1941), Dul'nev (1939, 1940), and also Enikeev (1944), Lipkina (1958), Borodulina (1944), Korman (1945), Komissarchik (1958), and Shul'gin (1958).

Without dwelling in detail on the problem of reproduction as a whole, let us focus on what is most important and of interest to us—on the role of comprehension in the process of memorization.

We first examine the main types of deviation from the original (aside from omissions) observed in reproduction:

1. *generalization* or "condensation" of what is given in the original in a specific, developed, and detailed form;
2. *concretization and detailization* of what is given in a more general or compact form;
3. *substitution* of one content for another equivalent in meaning and also in degree of likeness and detail;
4. *displacement and transfer* of parts of the original;
5. *unification* of what is given separately and *dissociation* of what in the original is connected;
6. *additions* that go beyond the original;
7. *distortion* of the meaning of the original as a whole, as well as of its individual parts.

In examining these forms of deviations from the original it is not difficult to see that only one of them, the last, is in its essence a *distortion* of the original. There *can* be but *must* not necessarily be distortions in additions, displacements, and transfers and also in the unification and dissociation of the material. Concerning the first three deviations from the original, these cannot at all be considered as *distortions* of the original. In making these deviations, we do not distort the content of what we reproduce. The main sense of the original remains unchanged. In contrast to distortions, all these digressions from the text are logically justified. They reflect what in fact is in the material, although they are not its exact reproduction.

Displacements and transfers, additions, and, also, unification and dissociation are of the same nature, i.e., they *may* but *do not necessarily* distort the meaning of the original.

Thus, as a whole the qualitative changes in reproduction are not at all *distortions* of what is reproduced or, rather, do not have to be distortions. Whoever deals with a reconstructed reproduction can obtain rather extensive and, more importantly, correct information about the content of the original. But, naturally, a reconstructed reproduction cannot provide complete and accurate information about the original. This reveals the dual, inherently contradictory nature of such reproduction. It is simultaneously both a *preservation* of what occurred and its *change*. What causes this duality?

Its basis must be sought in the psychological nature of reproduction, in its complexity. Reproduction is not a manifestation of mnemonic function *per se,* which is "conservative" in nature. Likewise, the changes observed in reproduction are not the result of its simple weakening, an insufficiency of "traces" left from former impressions and actualized at the moment. They are the result of a complex *mental activity* in which the mnemonic function is only one of the factors which are a condition for the preservation of "the old."

What is the *source of "the new,"* that is, of the reconstruction of the original in reproduction? Undoubtedly, it is the result of an *active* attitude toward what is reproduced, the result of various manifestations of our activeness among which our needs and interests are of great importance. They determine to a great extent the direction of reconstruction, the content and nature of the changes to which the original is subjected. However, by themselves they do not completely reveal the psychological nature of the changes in reproduction. They point only to some *motives* of reconstruction, to what inclines us to reconstruct. But they say nothing of the *mental processes as a result of which reconstruction is accomplished.*

What are these processes? An analysis of the changes observed in reproduction shows that all of them, with the exception of the distortion of the original, are the result of *reflective* reconstruction of the perceived material proceeding in *regular* ways. In their totality they are the result of a complex reflective activity, including generalization, isolating the particular and unique, unification of the similar, dissociation of the diverse, singling out the most important and essential. It is this *reflective activity in its most diverse and complex manifestations that comprises the psychological core of reproduction.* It is its basic link, the main "psychological mechanism," the action of which results in "reconstruction" of the material. Rubinshtein (1946) in touching on this question, correctly remarks that in its psychological nature this reconstruction is "primarily the result of unintentional but, undoubtedly, directed work of the thought within reproduction." It is just this reflective nature of reproduction that is the basis of the duality, the inner contradiction inherent in reproduction.

Any reflective activity proceeding on correct tracks does not distort reality but, on the contrary, reflects it more correctly. It reveals more profoundly and more truly what is given in reality itself.

"Even the simplest *generalization,* the first and simplest formation of *concepts* (opinions, conclusions, etc.) means the cognition by man of an ever deeper *objective* coherence of the world" (Lenin, Vol. 29, p. 161).

No matter how profound and correct the reflection of objective reality may be in the processes of thinking, it is also always a certain "departure" from it.

"For, in the simplest generalization, in the most elementary general idea (e.g., "table") there *is* a certain bit of *fantasy*" (Lenin, Vol. 29, p. 330). It is all the more necessary to take this into account when the "simplest generalization" is included in the process of recalling. When does this cogitative processing of the perceived material occur which then changes it in reproducing it?

On the one hand it undoubtedly can take place during reproduction, since it often itself includes processes of thinking. As is known, reproduction proceeds not uniformly: along with direct, automatic reproduction there is observed also "reasoning" reproduction, which approaches thinking (Blonskii).

In Soviet psychology the work by Zal'tsman (1949) deals with an extensive description of the processes of thinking in reproduction.

In "reasoning" reproduction we do not as much *recall* as we *infer* what happened in our experience. The presence of these inferences can lead to various kinds of divergences from the original. In inferring, we cannot always restore the past in the form in which it was in reality. Some change in the perceived material can always occur.

It would, however, be incorrect to attribute reconstruction in reproduction only to reproduction itself. This would mean ignoring other forms of reproduction, especially automatic remembrance, which is also connected with deviations from the original, as well as "reasoning" recollection, and yet we have at the moment of remembrance no reflection which would serve as basis for changes. Changes observed in these cases evidently occur before reproduction. When precisely?

In all probability, changes occur during the time between memorizing and reproducing. This time is the period of forgetting and during just this period many of the changes occur which are later revealed during reproduction.

How are these changes accomplished during the period of forgetting? To say simply that they are the result of forgetting is to say nothing. The changes observed in reproduction are changes of a special order. They cannot be considered as the simple disappearance of something from memory, as a result of "weakened traces" remaining from former impressions. They are a completely unique *processing* of what was perceived earlier, requiring special explanation.

These considerations confront us, however, with the following question: what kind of processes of thinking, having as their object precisely what is later reproduced, can occur during the period of forgetting? During this period we do not reproduce what later proves to be reconstructed, and this, it would seem, must mean that during this period we do not think of what we later reconstruct. Is this really so?

In fact, the traces left from the perceived material do not remain in the state of "anabiosis." They "live" also in the period of forgetting. Moreover, the source of their "life" is precisely the reflective activity carried out at this time.

Without reproducing the perceived material as a whole, we can deal many times with separate parts of what we memorized. Moreover, these parts come in a new context in such cases, on a different plane than they were given earlier. To speak under these conditions of *reproducing* what was perceived earlier is hardly proper. The new context of each part of what we have memorized, the new thinking processes connected with this context, the new knowledge acquired influence each of the parts of the "old," change it, and in this form it then enters into the former context, into the whole that was perceived earlier and which we will subsequently reproduce. Having read, e.g., something in a book, we cannot then remember what was read, cannot reproduce it in the exact sense of the word, but we can think about it on another occasion, in connection with other questions, other thoughts, other knowledge, and this new reflective activity becomes the source of the changes to which what has been read earlier is subjected.

The same must be said when the "old" perceived earlier does not at all appear in our consciousness, is not an object of reflective activity, even if in separate parts.

Even in this case one cannot at all negate the possibility of change of the "old" under the influence of reflective activity during the period of forgetting. The new thinking processes occurring in this period directed towards the "new" can be in some, even if indirect, connection with the "old" and thereby influence it, serve as a source of its changes. As a result of the "new," for example, the general level of our development rises, the knowledge we have expands and deepens, new habits of reflective activity are acquired and the old ones change, and all this, naturally, evokes considerable changes in the "old," in what at some time was perceived by us. These changes appear further on as reconstruction of the "old."

Thus, the possibility of qualitative changes of the original during the period of forgetting, which have the nature of reflective processing of the "old," is quite real.

In accepting the correctness of these positions it would, however, be wrong to go to the other extreme and consider that *all* qualitative changes of the original arising before reproduction belong *only* to the period of forgetting.

Reconstruction of the perceived material is also observed when the period of forgetting is so short that there is no need to speak of any kind of reflective activity which could serve as a source of changes in that which is perceived. Under normal experimental conditions, for example, reproduction often follows immediately after perception, and nevertheless changes, even extensive ones, occur in the original.

What causes the changes in these cases? What can be their basis aside from the processes of recalling? What occurs during the period of forgetting?

Evidently only one possibility remains: these changes can also occur *during memorizing*.

In proposing this it is, however, necessary to immediately make the reservation that deviations from the original occur, of course, not at the actual moment of its perception, but later. However, these deviations are based on processes occurring during the time of memorization. How can this be interpreted?

In order to explain, let us examine such a change as, e.g., the reproduction of something in a more general form. It appears as deviation from the original at the moment of *reproduction,* but its basis is the discerning of the "general," which occurs during *memorizing*. This discerning of the general proceeds simultaneously with the perception of the material in all its specific, "unique" peculiarity and seemingly coexisting with it. The original is perceived in both its *specific, unique* expression in which it is in fact given and in a more *general* sense. On a psychological level this is one of the positions of dialectical logic: "The general exists only in the individual, through the individual. Anything individual is (in one way or another) general. Anything general is a particle, a facet, an essence of the general" (Lenin, Vol. 29, p. 318).

The same can be said of any other form of change observed in reproduction. The reflective processes causing them at the moment of memorizing coexist with the perception of the original in its true, unchanged form. We perceive, for example, what we memorize in its full, developed content and at the same time "compress" it, make it shorter than it is in reality. Perceiving what is in the original we at the same time add to it from data of past experience which go beyond the limits of what we at the moment are perceiving. In perceiving the original in a definite sequence, we note it and often inwardly rearrange the order in which we are given the material, we connect what is given separately, dissociate what is given together.

Consequently, perception of the original proceeds seemingly on *two* levels. On the one hand, on the level of permanent features of what is given to us, and on the other, on the level of some changes inseparably connected with the processes of *comprehending* what we memorize. This duality of perception plays a positive as well as a negative role.

Its positive effect is that the probability of forgetting, due to the second level (the level of "processing"), decreases considerably. If in the course of time what was perceived on the level of the original will be forgotten, what became apparent on the other level may be preserved.

Let us assume, for example, that the specific "unique" content of the original will be forgotten. If, at the moment of memorizing, the "general" in it was discerned, then this general can be retained in memory even after forgetting the unique—it can replace it. Therefore, even in a changed form we still reproduce in those cases what we perceived.

A negative effect of the duality of perception is also possible. It consists of a subsequent mixing of the two levels or of a displacement of one level by the other, the level of the original by the level of "processing."

In the first case we remember both levels and which of them is the "original" we cannot say. In the second case we forget the level of actual features of the original and remember only what was on the level of reflective processing which replaces the first level.

4. CASES OF ILLUSORY MEMORIZATION WHEN IT IS COMPLETELY REPLACED BY COMPREHENSION

Noting the very important role of understanding in memorization, it must be emphasized just as much that, no matter how great the significance of understanding, the latter does not exhaust all the complex and multifaceted mental activity which memorizing is. Therefore, its presence does not guarantee complete success in memorizing and can serve as a source of the false impression that we have already memorized what we have understood. Immediately upon acquaintance with material we often have a peculiar *feeling of mastering* the material, that everything has been mastered and there is no need for additional memorizing.

In reality, this is not always so. Often we need only to start reproducing what we have understood and we find that in fact we have not yet mastered the *entirety of the material.* Something, and sometimes much, has been forgotten, although during perception or after it we had the clear impression that no difficulties would be met with in reproduction. The feeling of "mastery" is false. In reality we have in such cases only the *illusion of remembering.*

What favors the emergence of this illusion? The characteristics of the *material* to be memorized must be pointed out. Most often the illusion of memorizing is observed when explanatory material is memorized which presents a certain chain of reasoning and few factual data which would demand special efforts in memorizing. Such material especially stimulates the desire to limit oneself to an understanding and do nothing that requires memorizing.

On the contrary, if the material contains many factual data, which are new and unknown and the mastery of which is not achieved by understanding only, the possibility of emergence of an illusion of memorizing is much less. Such material itself "pushes" the performance of certain additional actions directed towards memorizing, rather than being satisfied with understanding.

Of great importance also are the *personal qualities of those who memorize.* The general set toward understanding or memorizing, the presence or absence of the habit of checking one's work without relying on the immediate experience of mastery, great or little confidence in oneself, the degree of mnemonic experience, and, in particular, previous cases of divergence between the apparent and the actually achieved levels of memorizing, all this is of great significance for the rapidity and ease with which this illusion arises.

The harmful influence caused by this illusion and the fact that its emergence is often explained by the already achieved *understanding* of the material demand from us that, while completely relying on *understanding,* we do not dissolve memorizing in it and do not replace learning by heart by it. *No matter how great and positive the role of understanding may be, it would, of course, be incorrect to identify memorization with it.* Understanding is the most important component of memorization, its main condition for productivity, but memorizing is a more complex activity and is not exhausted by understanding alone. It has its own inherent peculiarity. Therefore, a full mnemonic effect can be achieved only if this activity is carried out in full measure, in all its uniqueness, without any replacement of it—even by its most important component, understanding.

In the practice of memorizing, such a substitution is observed rather often. In our experiments and the experiments of our collaborators the subjects often remarked that for them the whole process of memorization became exclusively or almost completely comprehension. Here are some of their statements:

> There was no actual process of memorizing. I did not so much memorize as think and comprehend the material.
>
> Understanding absorbed memorizing. The sequence of thoughts, logic—that is enough.
>
> The process proceeded by means of understanding. Reading and parallel thinking through. Nothing more.
>
> Efforts only at understanding. Memorizing was incidental and came by itself.
>
> I did not set myself the task of memorizing. I tried to understand what was discussed.
>
> The whole work was reduced to just comprehension.

There are very many such statements. At the same time, the actual productivity of memorizing in the above cases, as well as in others similar to them, does not at all correspond to what could be expected, proceeding from the subjective feeling of the subjects. Thus, the danger of substituting comprehension for memorizing is quite real. Its harm is doubtless. The necessity to combat it is evident.

Chapter 5

THE EFFECT OF MEMORIZING ON COMPREHENSION

1. THE POSITIVE EFFECT OF MNEMONIC ORIENTATION ON COMPREHENSION. THE BASIC REFLECTIVE PROCESSES IN MNEMONIC ACTIVITY

Analogously to the influence of understanding on memorizing, one can speak of the opposite: *the influence of memorization on comprehension.* This means that, being included in memorizing as in a special form of activity, understanding is determined by the peculiarity of this activity, by its characteristics.

Here the greatest role is played by the *task* which confronts the one who memorizes. The presence of a mnemonic task is a condition which determines the peculiarity of understanding when it is included in memorizing.

Before examining the influence exerted by a mnemonic task on understanding, it is necessary, however briefly, to give a very general description of understanding and, based on this, to make clear what changes can occur in understanding under the influence of memorizing.

What does it mean "to understand something" and how is understanding accomplished? To understand something means to discover the essence of an object or phenomenon. Comprehension is the reflection of general and essential properties of objects or phenomena of the real world. However, the cognition of the essence of objects and phenomena is not accomplished at once.

In speaking about the "elements of dialectics," Lenin notes "the infinite process of the deepening cognition by man of things, phenomena, processes, etc., from phenomena to essence and from a less deep to a deeper essence" (Lenin,, Vol. 29, p. 203).

"The thought of man infinitely deepens from phenomenon to essence, from the essence of the first, so to speak, order to the essence of the second order, etc., *without end*" (Lenin, Vol. 29, p. 227).

Hence the question arises of how one must interpret the various stages of understanding, its different levels. The main difference is the *depth* of understanding. It is characterized by "to what order of essence" our thought penetrates in the process of understanding.

A direct expression of this is the completeness, versatility, and, most important, the *significance* of connections disclosed in the process of cognition.

The wider the range of objects or phenomena with which we connect what we perceive at a given moment, the more varied the facets of objects or phenomena disclosed, the more significant they are, i.e., the better they characterize the very essence of the objects, the more they disclose "the objective regularity of the world," the deeper is comprehension, the higher its achieved level.

The number of possible stages here is infinite. From the first stage, in which we distinguish one facet of an object, an incidental, nonessential one and on the basis of this refer the object to some very general and extensive, indefinite category of objects, we progress to higher stages of understanding, discovering different facets of the object, which are more significant for it, showing more diverse connections with other objects or phenomena of the real world. We establish similarity, difference, causal dependence, temporal, spatial, and logical relations. On the strength of this the object is perceived by us as one occupying a definite place in the general system of objects, but maintaining all its peculiarity as something concrete and definite.

The depth of understanding, however, does not exhaust all differences which can be established between its various levels. There are also the differences in *distinctness* of understanding, in *how* we recognize the connections and relations discovered in the process of cognition. Here again we have an infinite number of stages, beginning with a diffuse catching of the sense not yet expressible in a concept, and ending with a precise, clear recognition of the essence of the object expressed in the form of a concept with a strictly defined content.

As an example we will characterize some stages of distinctness of understanding in order to show, at least partially, the diversity of possible levels.

The first, or one of the first, stages is an understanding which it would be correct to regard as an *anticipation of understanding* rather than a real understanding. We have not yet comprehended what has been perceived, but we feel that in a moment something will be comprehended by us. Something seems to loom before us: some indistinct hints of comprehension.

We are in a similar state when we want to remember something and for a long time cannot do so. In this case there comes a moment when the needed name or designation has not yet risen to the surface of consciousness, but we feel that in a moment we will reproduce it. We seem to have something in view, groped for, but not as yet grasped.

At this stage, the stage of "genesis" of comprehension, understanding is experienced in the form of a special feeling which can be characterized as a sensation of something incipient that soon will become understanding.

Close to this stage, but higher, is the next stage in which there is comprehension, but in a most general, undeveloped, and indefinite form; moreover, it is again in the form of a peculiar feeling which, however, is already a feeling of a started and developing comprehension. At this stage, the stage of *dim comprehension,* we have seemingly grasped something, but have not as yet "examined" what precisely we have grasped. Sometimes this is only a dim recognition of the area to which what we have perceived belongs. Sometimes it is a feeling of familiarity, quite indefinite, without any reference to something from past experience. All this is often accompanied by a feeling of transience, elusiveness, and the possibility of immediately losing what was found. The necessity is felt to hold on to it, not to let it go. There is a desire to remove everything that can be in the way. All actions and movements are arrested in the seeming expectation that in a moment the dimly grasped concept will clear up, develop, achieve a clearer comprehension.

From among the successively higher stages must be distinguished the one in which *comprehension is subjectively experienced as already achieved, although we cannot yet express it.* There is as yet no adequate verbal formulation for it. We as yet cannot give an account of the meaning of the perceived.

The impossibility of expressing in words what we have comprehended, which is characteristic of this stage, does not at all imply an erroneous understanding. It indicates only an insufficient clearness of comprehension. In some cases it can be accompanied by incorrect comprehension. The subjective certainty of understanding in these cases is unjustified. It only seems to us that we have understood all. In reality, however, as soon as we begin to give an account of what we have "understood" to another person there arise errors, the illusory comprehension is revealed, as is the necessity of additional thinking-through of what seemed to have been understood. The subjective experience of comprehension is illusory.

The next stage of clearness of understanding is characterized by the fact that we can give an account of the perceived material to another person, but under one condition: by keeping a definite, unchanged formulation, if possible given in the form at hand. For the comprehension of verbal material this stage is characterized thusly: *we simply reproduce the perceived material, moreover, maximally in the words of the original.*

This does not mean that understanding in such cases is absent and that we reproduce mechanically. Not at all. There is understanding, it is even higher than at the preceding stage where we were not able to tell about the perceived material even by using ready formulations. But it is still insufficient. To use our own words at this stage is difficult, sometimes impossible. Even when we succeed in finding our own formulation, i.e., in conveying the perceived material in our own words, we do it as a stereotype and vary our account little when we have to repeat what we have said. We are seemingly bound by our own formulation, the one in which we first expressed what we had understood. At this stage there is as yet insufficient mastery of the material.

Transition to a higher stage of comprehension is characterized by *liberation from the restrained verbal formulation.* We can digress from the original, change the formulation and sequence of our account, generalize the material, tell it in a more "developed" form. Telling "in one's own words" loses its stereotypy, the possibility arises of varying it. Indeed, there occurs a *mastery* of what we have perceived. It literally becomes "our own," is translated into "our language," is subjected to a certain creative reconstruction.

What is the relation of all these stages to the stages of depth of comprehension? They are partially independent of each other. We can understand not deeply, but clearly. Also possible are the opposite cases: by deepening understanding, we grasp the deeper sense, but at first very vaguely, we rather suspect it, anticipate it, are at a low stage of clear understanding.

All this indicates a great variety of levels of understanding and their considerable complexity. This complexity is intensified if one takes into account that, together with depth and clearness, *completeness* of understanding also varies since we usually perceive a complex whole which we have to comprehend not only as a whole but also in all its components.

Such a great variance in comprehension, the possibility of the most diverse levels which it can achieve, naturally confronts us with the question of the nature of comprehension when it is included in memorizing as into a complex activity. What influence does the *mnemonic* task which directs the process of memorizing have on the differences described in comprehension? Experimental data show that the influence of the mnemonic task in this respect can be positive as well as negative.

The positive effect of mnemonic orientation was clearly manifested in experiments in which for some experimental reason it is suggested to memorize either meaningless material or material that is meaningful, but not internally connected: single words, numbers, pictures.

Those who memorize the meaningless material most often attempt to add some kind of sense anyway. For this purpose they connect it with something meaningful which permits, however indirectly, a kind of sensible connection. They attempt, for example, to detect some kind of similarity of the meaningless words with the meaningful ones and in this way at least somehow to give meaning to them.

Analogous observations are made in memorizing disconnected "meaningful" material. In memorizing individual meaningful words, numbers, sentences, or pictures, we also try to include them in some comprehensible whole in order to make them more meaningful.

The nature of the whole into which the unconnected material is incorporated is not uniform. Sometimes it involves images uniting the content of the words or sentences, sometimes word combinations formed from separate words, sometimes meaningful relations which are revealed especially to facilitate the material to be memorized. Whatever the nature of the whole in which we include the material to be memorized, this whole is always something more meaningful and connected than what is actually presented for memorizing.

It is characteristic that the inclination to understand sometimes arises despite a direct prohibition against establishing meaningful connections. Rybnikov (1923), for example, suggested that his subjects learn a number of words without meaningful connections; nevertheless, it turned out that very often these connections were established anyway. It is quite probable that in reality the number of these connections was even greater than indicated by the subjects since they often failed to notice these connections.

Is such an effect observed when meaningfully connected material is memorized, i.e., material which can be understood without the task of memorizing, in the process of simple familiarization with it? To solve this problem we utilized two kinds of data. First, we used reports of adult subjects in ordinary experiments involving memorization of meaningful texts. Each time the same task was given, i.e., to memorize the text and reproduce it subsequently. Besides our own experiments (Smirnov, 1945*c*), we utilized here the results of the unpublished investigation by Dodonova (1941), conducted under our direction. The reports of the subjects in her investigation are marked with "D." The second group of data consists of the reports of subjects in experiments especially aimed at finding the effect of the mnemonic task.

In these experiments some texts were presented with the task of memorizing and other texts without this task. The experiments were conducted in this manner: the subjects were told that they would be given two texts which had to be read carefully, comprehended well, and that they were then to determine which was the more difficult to comprehend. After this, the first text was presented. It was read with the set for comprehending, but without the task of memorizing (mnemonic orientation could occur only to the extent necessary for subsequent evaluation of the text, while there was no conscious orientation towards memorizing and reproducing). After reading the first text, a new instruction was given: they were to read the second text so as to be able to reproduce it later. This time there was a mnemonic task and it was basic to the reading of the second text. At the end of the experiment the subjects had to tell what distinguished the two processes of reading. The question concerning the characteristics of comprehension was at first not asked directly, but if the subjects did not elucidate them in their reports, it was always asked later.

The subjects in this series were 12 adults (scientists and college students). In order to avoid possible influence of the material, the texts were interchanged: what one group was given to read without memorizing, the other was given to memorize and *vice versa.*

The positive influence of the mnemonic task on comprehension was clearly apparent in all experiments. Especially indicative were the data of the second series of experiments. In spite of the fact that the first text in these experiments was read with a set for comprehension, the level of comprehension was usually lower than when the additional task of memorizing was present.

Below we cite several reports of subjects from both series of experiments. We begin with the first series:

> When one has to memorize, not an ordinary, but an intensified comprehension is demanded.
>
> Memorizing was connected with intensifying the logic of thoughts.
>
> Simple comprehension does not cause memorization. But attentive comprehension, the combination of these two factors, comprehension and attention, somehow guarantees memorizing (D).
>
> When the assignment is memorizing, comprehension is carried out more intensively.
>
> Comprehension is itself more profound during memorization (D).
>
> I decided to memorize beginning with the first reading. Therefore I paused while reading. I did not remember immediately. In order to remember one must think, analyze to the end what is being said. Therefore, I read slowly (D).

One of the subjects remarks that the factual data which had to be memorized had stimulated her to a more intensive, reflective work (usually, as will be indicated later, the situation is the opposite).

"The necessity of memorizing dates or a sequence of events compelled me to think more" (D).

The reports from the second series of experiments characterize similarly the influence of a mnemonic task:

> In the first case [in the absence of a memorizing task], I thought over the matter to a lesser degree.
>
> The first text I read faster, here I thought more.
>
> The reading of the second text proceeded more intently. This was undoubtedly because the goal was to memorize, while the first text was read only to understand. Comprehension in the second case was better than in the first.

> Comprehending of the second text differed from the first. I had to understand much better in order to be able to retell it.

These examples suffice to show that the level of comprehension involved in memorizing is experienced by the subjects as a higher one. *Comprehension subjected to a mnemonic task is better than the normal comprehension observed in the simple reading of texts.* What are these changes?

First, it must be pointed out, in the presence of a mnemonic orientation a greater *fullness* of comprehension is reached. The subjects attempt to comprehend not only the text as a whole, but each part of it separately:

> When I read for myself [that is, only to understand], I grasp the general sense, I read in greater chunks. In this case [in memorizing] I penetrate almost every word.
>
> In this case [during memorization] we tried to bring every sentence up to consciousness.
>
> In memorizing I tried to understand each sentence.
>
> I read [in experiments with memorizing] trying to penetrate the content of each sentence (D).
>
> In the second case I comprehended everything in turn, in the first, only what was most important.

A greater fullness of understanding demands, naturally, greater intensity and special volitional efforts:

> In memorizing, one has to read more diligently.
>
> You exert yourself more in reading when you set yourself the goal to remember.
>
> In reading for myself [without a mnemonic task], readiness for a large segment develops. I read a large segment at one time, but when I try to remember each time there is a new charging up, so that reading proceeds by jerks, as if each sentence were nailed down. Here is a more detailed reading, a reading of short breath and volitional effort, and there you glide as if on glass until you come to an incomprehensible place.
>
> When you read for yourself, there is a tendency to leave out some thoughts, especially during the first reading. In reading, one generalizes partially and sometimes due to this some thoughts are overlooked, one does not perceive them fully, one makes a choice in attention, underestimates the individual thoughts which can be omitted, without which one can understand the content in a more general form. In order that this not happen, in order to memorize, in order that everything get into consciousness, special efforts must be applied (D).

The second thing that characterizes comprehension under conditions of memorization is its greater *depth* as the sum total of great reflective work. What do the subjects do to reach this depth of comprehension?

First should be distinguished the *breaking up of the material into parts,* which at the same time is also a *grouping* of the material. In trying to memorize, the subjects divide the text into more or less independent "sections," each of which is at the same time a group of thoughts. This mode is used very extensively and this is what distinguishes reading for memorizing from ordinary reading. Let us present some subjects' reports:

> In the second reading [for memorization], I tried to break up the text into parts. To each part I added what pertained to it. I distinguished separate, main questions, into which I broke up the whole text. In the first reading [without a mnemonic task], I did not do that.
>
> In the second text I grouped the thoughts. I broke up the text into parts. In the first text this hardly happened. Even if I did the same thing, it was evidently done mechanically.
>
> The second text I broke up according to topics, into topical pieces, not so in the first case.
>
> The second text I memorized disjointedly. If there was disjunction in the first, it was after reading, while here it was during the process of reading.
>
> During the second reading [with the task of memorizing], there was a more active tendency to disjoin. I explain it by the fact that you warned me that I would have to relate the content.

As can be seen, the breaking up into parts is sometimes done in ordinary reading when there is no task of memorizing. However, in these cases it is less distinct, less conscious, and occurs sometimes after reading, as a result of attempts to recall what was read. More often it was observed only in reading the second text, i.e., in reading with the task of memorizing.

Arising as the result of a mnemonic task, under its effect, and being, undoubtedly, a means of memorizing, the breaking up of the material also serves as a means of deepening comprehension.

The disjunction of the text is based not on its external features, but on its *meaning*. The material is broken up in such a manner that each part is a relatively independent unit of content. Into it enters what is, or seems to be, related in meaning. The subjects themselves speak about it, remarking that they "grouped the thoughts," "broke up into pieces according to topics." This is confirmed by an analysis of the parts into which the material was broken up. This is *meaningful grouping of the material.*

In a division into meaningful sections based on the unity of the meaning of each section, every part of the text is a certain "meaningful point," in which the whole content of the part is concentrated. The subjects many times noted this fact in speaking of a peculiar "dotting" of the material:

> When you read and comprehend with the aim of memorizing, a certain dotting is created (D).
>
> During reading, the attention is concentrated on points which are carriers of the meaning. Thus, point after point there occurs a special conscious fixation of these points. This is the mode of both comprehending and memorizing (D).
>
> In the process of reading I gather the material around several points, which absorb the content of each part.
>
> From the very beginning I noted the points to which I referred the whole content. This helped understanding and memorizing better.
>
> I gathered the material around points.

> How did I work? As always, I wanted to find some core, or rather not one core, but several meaningful points (D).
>
> In marking points I combined several sentences into a whole.

As can be seen, these meaningful points have a dual function. They are the "carriers of meaning," to them pertains the content of each part and this enhances *comprehension*. And on account of it they facilitate *memorizing*. Therefore, the subjects characterize them as *supporting* points, as *markers* of meaning by which there occur orientations in the content of the text and its subsequent reproduction.

"These are milestones," says one of the subjects. "They mark the comprehension of the text, they also help in memorizing it."

"When I retell now, I recall the points of reference which I marked for an understanding of the text."

This distinction of meaningful points of reference is sometimes accompanied by a visual imagining of them as dots, small blots, X's, situated in place of the part of the text which they replace.

One subject characterizes, for example, the visual image of the meaningful points of reference he isolated as follows:

"I saw a page before me and on it something like traces from printed or written words, possibly from the titles of the sections. They were scattered approximately as the sections themselves were situated."

Another subject says:

"Purely visually, I imagined the breaking up into parts and the points of reference I had isolated. In my head were pegs with whitish silk threads. They were situated in rows and the threads were wrapped around them. The pegs are the points which have been isolated during reading."

What are the meaningful points of reference with respect to the sections into which the text is broken up? As the subjects themselves point out, a meaningful point of reference is a distinctive "extract" of a section.

Such a description means that the meaningful points of reference arise as the result of *the isolation of what is essential, basic, and most characteristic*. Only under this condition can they really be "carriers of meaning" of the section as a whole. But the distinction of what is basic and essential, as was pointed out, is a deepening of understanding. To understand something means to find what is essential in it. Therefore, the creation of meaningful points of reference is undoubtedly one of the means of deepening understanding. It leads to a deeper comprehension of the text.

The subjects often note the searching for what is essential and relate it to the isolation of meaningful points of reference:

> I had to return several times to what I had read in order to emphasize what was essential for understanding and thereby mark the main points.
>
> In the process of reading I often stopped in order to think through what was basic in this section (D).

> I tried to find what was most important in each part.
>
> During reading I marked the main points (D).

The isolation of what is essential is not limited to this "dotting." The isolated points in turn are distinguished by the degree of importance. Again, among them are isolated the main ones and the less important ones.

"In my mind I saw which points were imporatnt, which of secondary importance," says one of the subjects.

"In marking the points I emphasized those which seemed especially important and essential."

The subjects speak also of a "hierarchy" of points, of a distinctive meaningful "relief map" of the text, of "protruding dots" in its content.

Thus, being a product of comprehending what is essential, the meaningful points of reference serve as basis for further work in finding what is essential, no longer in each part individually, but in the text as a whole. This increases their significance for the depth of understanding still more.

What are the described processes of dissection of the text into parts, the isolation in it of meaningful points of reference, the isolation of main and secondary ones among them, their subordination and coordination to each other? It is not difficult to see that they all are individual components of a single process, the *composition of a plan*. The subjects usually characterize them in this manner:

> The isolation of points is a method of composing a plan (D).
>
> In marking points I tried to put everything into a system, to clarify what belongs to what (D).
>
> I plan, single out individual thoughts, and establish their connection as components of a single whole (D).
>
> In marking the main points I attempted to find the principles according to which the plan is constructed (D).

Such indications of the composition of a plan (in the mind, proceeding in a special, peculiar form) are very often found in the statements of the subjects. In a number of cases the composing of a plan is a *conscious* task with the help of which the subjects want to facilitate memorization:

"I thought much about a plan and I memorized with its help," says one subject.

"At the second reading my aim was to compose a plan."

"Before reading I gave myself the task of finding the plan of the text."

In Soviet psychology literature, Sokolov (1941) noted the great significance of dividing the material into parts and isolating meaningful points of reference in memorizing.

Investigating the correlation of internal speech and understanding, he suggested to his subjects that they recite aloud a poem they knew well and at the same time he read to them a text, which they later had to reproduce to the experimenter to check whether they had understood the text. The difficult conditions for understanding and memorizing of the text lead the subjects to divide the text into parts in their minds and to isolate points of reference by means of which they could memorize it.

During first reading of "difficult" texts, the author points out, there was much indefinite, "diffuse" understanding, "understanding in general." However, on second perception of the text there began a breaking up of it into parts and isolation of what was essential. The isolation of points of reference played an especially important part. This was of great significance not only for understanding, but also for memorizing the text.

Referring to reports received from his subjects, the author says: "In trying to fix in their minds the material they heard, the subjects, as they said, 'repeated mentally,' or 'noted mentally' the content of the text. They pointed out that mental repetition was very abbreviated: the content of the text was fixed 'in the mind' with the help of a few 'supporting' or 'generalizing' words; these few words were not pronounced by them, said the subjects, but were 'kept in mind,' 'implied' or 'thought.' In some cases they arose in the form of auditory images" (Sokolov, 1941, p. 131).

To confirm this, the author cites statements by two subjects similar to those by our subjects. Subject B. says that she "tried to label everything with meaningful marks, include it in some meaningful connection, in one meaningful context, meaningful scheme," and that to do this everything had to be somehow "comprehended to the end," "concentrated," "tied into one point," which then made it possible to develop the thought easily. Subject M. notes that during listening to the text she created "in her mind" a "scheme of the material," with the help of which she fixed the order of the material: "first this, then that, etc."

These "mental guideposts" played an important role in memorizing the text. "What was not included in the logical scheme of the material," states the author, "what was not marked by 'mental guideposts,' was usually soon forgotten" (Sokolov, 1941, p. 133). In these cases there appeared a peculiar "sudden amnesia," an instant forgetting of what had just been heard.

It is characteristic that the "sudden amnesia" came when the subjects did not reproduce in their internal speech the general sense of what was read to them, but tried to reproduce only separate parts of the text without tying them in with the whole, without "condensing" the sense or generalizing the content of the fragment, which was necessary for understanding the text.

The author of the work especially emphasizes the fact that the "inner word" which the subjects used as a point of reference for memorization usually was not a full word, but was shortened to one or two letters. The "inner word," he says in this regard, "ceases here to be a word in its grammatical sense, although it not only retains, but still further intensifies its function of generalizing, often becoming the carrier of the overall meaning of the text" (Sokolov, 1941, p. 135).

In works by Rybnikov (1930), Dul'nev (1940), and Favorin (1946) we also find indications of the positive role of the mental breaking up of material into parts.

An analysis of other data from our experiments shows that, in addition to having a plan, *correlation of the new material* with previous knowledge is of great importance as a means of understanding and thereby achieving better memorization. To some extent, any process of comprehension includes correlation with what we already know. But in its concrete expression this association occurs differently. Three differences are especially important here.

The first is the difference in the *wealth* of knowledge which rises to the surface of consciousness during the association of the new with the already known. Sometimes this knowledge is not represented in consciousness at all. In other words, we do not recall from our past experience something definite that could be connected with the material which we perceive at the moment. We are conscious only of the most general range of phenomena to which what we at the moment perceive belongs, their most general "category." We understand the material, we can say what it means, but concrete knowledge on which comprehension actually rests is absent from consciousness. It is the unconscious basis for comprehension. Objectively, what is perceived is correlated with this knowledge; subjectively, however, it is not in our consciousness. In reading about some historical events and understanding what we read, we, of course, lean on the knowledge we have, but we can remember nothing concrete from our previous experience which would go beyond the limits of what is reported in the given material.

In contrast to this, in other cases recall does take place—we recall something definite which somehow or other is connected with what is being perceived at the moment. In reading historical material, for example, we recall other historical facts connected with these events, or something similar to them. In these cases we go beyond the limits of what there is in the material, we augment and expand it.

The second, no less important, difference in the processes of correlation is the *essence* of the connections on which we lean during association. Sometimes what we perceive and what we recall from past experience in connection with it are connected only outwardly, by chance. In reading of an historical event, we may remember the circumstances under which we received information about it for the first time. In reading a date in the text we may remember another event not vitally connected with it, but which occurred at the same time. However, we can also remember what we know of the causes of the event, the results to which it led, and so forth. These recollections are determined by important, meaningful connections. Due to them, the new is included not simply into the totality of what is known, but into our *system* of knowledge.

The third difference observed in the correlation of the new with what is already known is the difference of the degree of *recognition* of relations disclosed when associating.

Sometimes we only recall something from past experience and do not correlate it with something newly perceived, although objectively both are in a definite relation to each other. In other cases we recognize these objective relations. We compare and contrast various relations. Strictly, only in these cases do we correlate in the true sense of the word—as a conscious reflection of relations existing in objective reality between objects of the real world.

From what has been said above concerning the essence of comprehension, it is clear that these differences cause the considerable variety in the depth of comprehension. The greater the knowledge with which the new is correlated, the more it is connected with it, and the more recognized are their connections, the deeper is comprehension. Hence, it is natural that in speaking of the influence which mnemonic orientation has on the depth of comprehension we must elucidate to what extent it influences all the above-mentioned peculiarities of association.

The data of our experiments show that in this respect, too, the mnemonic task has considerable positive effect. This was clearly manifested in a comparative series of experiments. In those cases in which the subject had to memorize as well as understand the material, knowledge acquired from previous experience rose up in greater quantity, was better connected with the content of the text, and the interrelations between the content and what caused them were better perceived. The subjects did not simply recall, but compared, contrasted, and correlated the material.

Let us cite some of their statements:

> In the second case [with the task of memorizing] I looked for modes of mastering a chronological and logical sequence. I correlated with what I know of Portugal. In the previous text [without the task of memorizing] I did not pay attention to this [both texts were of historical and geographical content: the first on Mexico, the second on Portugal].
>
> In the second reading, there were more and diverse associations [the subject uses the term "association" in a broad sense, having in mind all types of connections]. I remembered, for example, how it was with the roads in other countries, in the Urals. I noted the difference and similarity.
>
> In reading the second text I tried to connect with something more simple, more familiar. I remembered what I knew from history. I usually do this when I have to memorize. In the first case I did not do this.
>
> In reading this text [given to memorize] I thought more about what I was reading. I tried to understand "why." This is comprehension. I tried to correlate with a familiar text. This also is comprehension.

> In the second case I more often went beyond the limits of the text. I explained it to myself. I relied on what I already know of microorganisms [both texts were of biological content].
>
> The second text I read more slowly, often lingered, in order to understand better. At these moments there came various thoughts in connection with the text. Reading, for example, about the mass death of progeny [the text was on propagation in animals], I recalled the high mortality rate of peasant children in prerevolutionary times. When I read of the scale of propagation I recalled someone's thought that if there were no obstacles to propagation, then any species of living things would in a short time fill the whole earth.

These examples illustrate sufficiently that the *mnemonic task has a considerable positive effect on the correlation of what is perceived with existing knowledge*. They also reveal that correlation under the influence of mnemonic orientation is often *intentional*. The subjects intentionally take recourse to it as a means of simultaneously deepening comprehension and to better memorization. Here again is the characteristic of correlation under conditions of memorizing.

Different recollections and previous knowledge rise up in the subjects, of course, even when the mnemonic orientation is absent. But in these cases they more often just "rise up," arise involuntarily, without special intention on the part of the subjects. In contrast, the mnemonic orientation stimulates *voluntary* correlation. Under its influence the subjects themselves try to correlate the new with the known, to *consciously* include it in the old. This is fully analogous to how a plan is composed in memorizing. Both methods of deepening comprehension are often used quite consciously.

What is the influence exerted by the mnemonic task on the *clearness* of comprehension? The ways of comprehending a text just examined (composing a plan of the text and correlating its content with previous knowledge) are means not only of deepening comprehension, but of making it clearer. In both cases the material seemingly is fitted into a definite system, but relating something within a system means achieving a clearer comprehension of it.

Several other methods of deeper understanding arising under the influence of a mnemonic task are of this type. One of them is another type of correlation, not with previously acquired knowledge but with what is in the text itself. Reading about something, the subjects correlate it with what has just been read in the same material.

In a broad sense *correlation of various parts of the text* occurs all the time since without it there could be no comprehension of the text as a whole. However, we now have in mind correlation of another kind. On the one hand, relations are revealed which may or may not be observed when general comprehension is sufficient, and on the other hand, these relations are especially emphasized and are especially clearly recognized by the subjects:

> I emphasized that it is the vertebrae that move and not the ribs, which were discussed earlier (D).

> An adder. Ah, this is an adder and there was a cobra. I clearly recognized that it concerned two different snakes (D).
>
> In reading the text I constantly noted what the similarities and differences between the snakes are. I said to myself: now here is a similarity, here a difference (D).
>
> While reading I often stopped in order to emphasize in my mind what had been read, comparing it with what had been said earlier about bacteria.
>
> One had to scrutinize and clearly understand how one thought differs from another [philosophical text].

Such a comparison of some parts with others differs from what happens in composing a plan. In the latter case the *structural relations* between the *parts of the text* are revealed. The subject notes, for example, that "this part is a subdivision of such a part, which also includes such and such thoughts," or says in his mind: "this is a development of the preceding." But in this case we have in mind *content, object relations* revealed between the *objects* themselves which are dealt with in the text.

Revealing these relations, bringing them to a clear awareness, the subjects try thereby to achieve simultaneously a greater depth and distinctness of understanding, as well as better memorization.

"I had to return in order to emphasize the difference between the snakes. I needed this for memorization" (D).

Sometimes a direct connection is noted between the comparison of parts of the text and the mnemonic task:

"If there were no set for memorizing, it would not be necessary to emphasize, compare, and correlate so strenuously, since in general outline I understood the material at once."

Therefore, in the comparative series of experiments reading with mnemonic orientation was accompanied by comparisons more often than was ordinary reading. Moreover, the correlations occurred in a more precise form and were utilized as a conscious mode directed toward memorizing.

The next very important way to strengthen the preciseness of comprehension is the *utilization of visual concepts*. Images of what the subjects read arise in them, of course, both in the presence and in the absence of a mnemonic task. However, there is a difference between these cases, and it is of no small importance: under the influence of mnemonic orientation the visual concepts arise more often than in its absence. In reading with the aim of memorizing, these images illustrate the content of the text itself more often and are not only secondary, as is often the case in ordinary reading.

In experiments without mnemonic orientation there are often statements such as:

"In reading about the Red Sea there arose the image of my grandfather who had told me in childhood about the Israelites walking through the Red Sea."

"Where it spoke of propagation I remembered a cottage where I lived in the summer. It is possible that this was caused by the fact that in summer I often had to pass by a dense grove of propagated trees."

In contrast, in the experiments with a mnemonic task more often there are statements of this kind:

> When the color of plankton and the form of microorganisms was discussed I imagined both. The form is more difficult to imagine than the color. I imagined microscopic organisms as large. There were visual images of the color of the water. I visualized duckweed.
>
> In reading about protozoa the image of an amoeba arose as pictured in a book. Where it spoke of the naturalists there appeared the image of a man with a hand net.
>
> When I read of blast furnaces I pictured a huge one to myself and beside it another one several meters high.
>
> There arose the image of bacilli against a circular background as it is when one looks through a microscope.

In all these cases the images arising in the subjects were appropriate to the content of what was said in the text.

Under a mnemonic orientation, the images are more often evoked by the subjects themselves.

"In reading I tried to picture, evoke visual concepts"—such statements are characteristic of experiments in which memorizing has been assigned.

In reading without this task there is an intentional, volitional evoking of images. However, usually it is observed only when comprehension meets with difficulties. In these cases the subjects attempt to lean on visual concepts in order to understand what is said in the text. But if there is mnemonic orientation, the images come voluntarily even when the content of the text is basically understood. The visual concepts serve mainly as support for greater clarity of comprehension.

The subjects themselves often note the connection of intentional evoking of visual concepts with the task of memorizing:

> I tried to picture how the mockingbird [text taken from Darwin] feeds on meat. There were poles with meat on them to dry: in my mind I saw other birds coming, but the mockingbird drove them away. These are guidelines for memorizing.
>
> In memorizing the first paragraph I tried to give the content a concrete concept in order that it be easier to memorize, to create a chain of visual concepts.
>
> I evoked images on purpose. It seemed that when I had to tell about the composition of plankton, it would be easier to enumerate the forms of the organisms by visualizing.
>
> In order to memorize easier I tried to picture seas, islands, the mainland [the text was on history and geography of Korea].
>
> An additional mode of memorizing is the utilization of mental pictures. In this case they are a support for memory and the concretization of the thought. They do not play an independent role, but are wholly included in the work of memorization and understanding (D).

> Images were needed for the concretization of understanding, in order to remember better.
>
> What does the activity of memorizing consist of? To picture descriptively to oneself what one reads.

In the experiments in which the subjects had to memorize what they had read there are often statements like this:

"There were, I think, no images. Evidently because I did not try to memorize. If images did arise, I did not try to fix them."

Along with the voluntary evoking of images, the mnemonic orientation causes an intentional holding of those notions that arose involuntarily. The subjects use them consciously for memorization. "The image was involuntary, but I used it for memorization." Such statements are found quite often.

In some cases the opposite is observed. The voluntariness is expressed not in retaining the image but, on the contrary, in the inclination to "extinguish" it, or "digress from it." This happens when the image is secondary, not essentially connected with the content of the text, leads away from it, and does not contribute to better understanding.

"There arose the image of an electric tower and images of some kind of buildings [the text was about oil drilling]. They hindered, were incidental. I tried not to give them freedom."

"In reading about ore the image was a deep forest and there was a boxcar with ore. It was not needed for anything, I drove it out of my mind."

The last mode used for greater clearness of understanding is "translation of the text into one's own language."

We noted already that an insufficiently clear comprehension is usually characterized by being bound by the text, lack of dexterity in relating "in one's own words." On the contrary, where comprehension is distinct, the possibility of digressing from the text, to tell "in one's own words" is wider. Hence it is natural that the inclination to achieve greater clarity in comprehension is often expressed by trying to relate to ourselves, i.e., we translate into "our own language" what we have perceived. This is just what our subjects related:

> I tried to translate into definitions more understandable for me.
>
> When I began to read for the third time, I had the desire to say each sentence more simply than it was said in the text.
>
> This text does not lead to interpretation. There is no need to think about it. There is no special need to transpose it into other ideas.
>
> In reading I tried to retell mentally in my own words. When we relate something that we understand in our own words, we adapt the interpretation to the whole system of our mental life. We contribute, perhaps, some criteria, more detail, and this is most important. This assists in understanding, enhances its clarity and distinctness (D).

Such statements occurred only in experiments with mnemonic orientation and were absent when a mnemonic task was not given. The subjects themselves, noting the significance of retelling "in their own words" for *comprehension,* consider it as a way to better *memorization:*

"The desire to say each sentence differently than given arose because this would facilitate later recall. For me, the sentences would be simpler, would better fit my way of thinking, and this would make it possible to retain them better."

Here, as in the preceding statement, the role of translation into one's own language is not only stated, but also explained. In telling in "our own words" we adapt the perceived material to ourselves, "to the whole system of our mental life," to our "way of thinking." Indeed, we assimilate the text.

We have examined a number of ways and means which the subjects use to achieve better understanding with the aim of memorizing the material. The main ones are the following:

1. composition of a plan, including *breaking up of the material into parts, the grouping of thoughts, and isolation of meaningful points of reference* containing what is basic and essential;
2. *correlation of the content of the text with existing knowledge,* incorporation of the new information into a system of knowledge;
3. *correlation of the content* of *various parts* of the text;
4. utilization of *images* and visual notions;
5. *translation* of the content of the text *into "one's own language."*

These processes are also observed when a mnemonic orientation is absent, but the mnemonic orientation makes them more frequent, distinct, conscious, and intentional. Therefore, the material is comprehended more fully, deeply, and clearly under these conditions.

This is the most important positive effect of the task of memorizing. These are the essential changes of the processes of understanding when they are included in memorization.

2. THE NEGATIVE EFFECT OF MNEMONIC ORIENTATION ON COMPREHENSION

In our experiments the subjects often pointed out that the necessity of memorizing reflected harmfully on their understanding, hindered the comprehension of the text:

"The fact that it had to be memorized inhibited understanding."

"I tried to memorize, but this harmed understanding."

Sometimes the subjects also note the *conditions* which cause a negative effect of mnemonic orientation. It arises when the mnemonic task, according to the subjects, "is too dominant," "occupies their whole consciousness."

"From experience I know," says one subject, "if the task of memorizing is too distinct one may lose the capacity to reason" (D).

Why is the "dominance" of the mnemonic task harmful? The subjects themselves give the answer:

"When you memorize without thinking that you have to memorize, you grasp the sequence of thoughts, distinguish the general bases of the logical scheme, but the details evaporate. But if there is a set for remembering details, you lose the basic meaning. These are two different things."

"When you try very hard to memorize," says another subject, "you attempt to memorize everything at once, not excluding particulars and factual data, and this harms understanding."

Thus, the harmful "dominance" of the mnemonic task leads or, more exactly, can lead to premature attempts to memorize everything at once, including details, and a premature memorizing of details can be the source of many difficulties in understanding. This has been widely noted in our materials:

> I began to memorize in detail and lost the thread of the exposition.
>
> In memorizing figures I lost the general meaning.
>
> There are too many factual data. You try to memorize them and as a result the meaning suffers.
>
> When I tried to memorize the years, they took so much of my attention that I stopped following the content (D).
>
> My consciousness was so absorbed in data that the content was not memorized at all.

It is clear that this can occur only when the process of understanding itself is only developing, is in a stage of becoming.

In some cases such a breakup of the whole is even reflected in the visual perception of the text: the visual compactness of the material is disturbed. One of the subjects characterizes what he experienced due to the logical breakup of the text:

"I considered the meaning of each sentence and did not comprehend the whole. The connection with what preceded was broken abruptly. Some kind of emptiness appeared between the sentences. It seemed that not one space on the typewriter was missed, but ten. This is a great fragmentation of the text" (D).

This fragmentation occurs because memorizing details demands special modes not connected with understanding the text as a whole. The single activity directed toward understanding the text as a whole is disturbed. Each detail acquires an independence, goes beyond the limits of the text with all that is superimposed on it, with its own "associations." The unity of the whole disintegrates.

"When you begin to memorize particulars, you try to connect them with something and often connect them with something quite foreign to the text. The detail drops out of the text."

"In memorizing the details, numbers, dates you take them out of the whole, they become independent, begin to live their own lives, make their own associations, you repeat them several times."

The negative effect of the mnemonic task is also caused by the attempts to prematurely memorize exact formulations of the text. Difficulties in understanding arising in these cases are sometimes so great that the subjects reproduce the text with great, even absurd, distortions. As illustration we cite several examples from a group of experiments where definitions of some concepts were memorized, and not connected texts. The subjects were adults with college and partial college educations. Each definition was read until reproduction was faultless. After each reading, reproduction followed.

Example 1: "Detonation is a special form of combustion characterized by an exceptionally high velocity of flame propagation." Reproduced: "Detonation is a special form of combustion characterized by exceptionally high combustion of the flame "(subject T. after second reading). "Detonation is a special form of combustion characterized by a high velocity of the flame of combustion" (the same subject after fourth reading). "Detonation is a special form of combustion characterized by a special increase of the flame" (subject Sh. after third reading).

Example 2: "Rotting is a process of decomposition of plant and animal organisms which are in a moist medium and are deprived of a constant supply of dry air." Reproduced: "Rotting is a process of decomposition of animal organisms which are in a dry medium" (subject Sh. after second reading).

Example 3: "A carburetor is a special device which insures a correct correlation of air and fuel in a working mixture used for internal combustion engines." Reproduced: "A carburetor is a special device which insures a mixture of fuel with a working force for internal combustion engines" (subject Sh. after second reading). "A carburetor is a special device used for the working force in internal combustion engines" (same subject after third reading). "A carburetor is a special device using fuel and something else in its working mixture for internal combustion engines" (the same subject after fourth reading). "A carburetor is a special device which controls the access of air and fuel in a stove" (subject T. after first reading).

Example 4: "A mechanism is the totality of bodies connected so that upon movement of one or several of them each of the remaining bodies has a definite movement relative to any other." Reproduced: "A mechanism is the totality of bodies having a relation relative to each other.... Some kind of nonsense. I can't remember at all" (subject Sh. after second reading). "A mechanism is the totality of bodies having movement relative to each other.... No, that's not it" (the same subject after fourth reading). "A mechanism is a connection of bodies which somehow or other influence each other" (subject T. after the first reading).

Example 5: "A level is a device used in geodetic surveying to determine the elevation of one point of terrain over another in a horizontal line of vision." Reproduced: "A level is a device used...in what.... Ah! in geodetic surveying for increasing...for the determination of the terrain in a horizontal line of vision" (subject A. after second reading). "A level is a device used in geodetic surveying at an elevation of one point over the other.... What has the terrain to do with this? In the elevation of the terrain....In the elevation of one point of the terrain over another in a horizontal line of vision" (the same subject after third reading). "A level is a device to determine the terrain by means of a point above the horizon" (subject N. after first reading).

Let us elaborate on these statements. The first clarification concerns the method of the experiments. The subjects themselves read and after reading each definition immediately reproduced it. The reading speed was not predetermined. Usually the subjects read slowly and considered the content carefully. Some read out loud, emphasizing certain places of a sentence with their voices.

The second clarification concerns the material. It caused difficulties since the subjects knew little of the fields from which the definitions were drawn. However, our task was to find out how memorization of such material proceeds.

Third, we studied how the subjects themselves evaluated their reproduction. In most cases they clearly recognized its absurdity, but were unable to reproduce it differently.

Finally, it should be noted that while reading, the subjects usually thought they *understood* a definition. There were no cases where they did not. The difficulties arose as soon as they had to reproduce the sentences.

Yet the reproduction often was absurd in spite of the fact that the subjects read the material themselves without hurrying, pondering over the content and assuming that they understood it. Distortions were observed not only upon the first reading, but also upon following readings, although the subjects realized well that in their reproducing they allowed gross errors and therefore read the material especially carefully. The material was difficult, but accessible to understanding. Why then was it so poorly reproduced?

There can be only one answer: because it was poorly understood. Otherwise the subjects would have been able to transmit it, if only in their own words; with few exceptions, they were not able to do this. There is no reason to question their statements that they understood the material, but, nevertheless, they had no clear comprehension. The impossibility of transmitting in one's own words despite feeling that the material has been understood is just what attests to insufficient understanding.

What caused this vagueness of understanding? It was the difficulty of the material. But it was not such that under different conditions it would not have been clearly understood. Even after the fourth reading, the subjects, as we saw, made gross distortions.

The source of the errors was, consequently, not the difficulty of the material itself, but that it was combined with the demand of memorizing and reproducing it. This was the basis of the low level of understanding and poor memorization. The subjects themselves speak about it, often remarking that the necessity of memorizing makes it difficult. Here is the cause for their having "lost their mind," "ceased to reason," as one of the subjects from other experiments expressed it.

In order to understand this correctly, one must take into account that as a rule the subjects were told not simply to memorize the definitions, but to memorize at once as exactly as possible. Such a *premature* orientation toward accuracy was caused not by the task which we presented, since we did not suggest that they memorize exactly, but by the nature of the material, by the compactness of the definitions.

"In definitions everything is important," says one of the subjects. "They must be memorized exactly. This I strove for, although I did not think about it especially. This is the reason why for so long I could not repeat correctly."

"Definitions are a cluster of what is essential in what must be said about an object. Any changes can easily distort the meaning of what is said in the definition. To select other words, to express differently and yet retain the exact meaning is very difficult. I tried to memorize as it was said. Rather, I did not try, but it happened by itself. And this was very disturbing. It was even difficult to understand it properly."

Thus, in spite of the instruction, the subjects had a set towards accuracy of memorization. Moreover, they had this *premature* disposition even before they arrived at a clear understanding. And this is what made it so difficult for them, according to their statements. Why is this so?

In order to answer this, let us see what is characteristic of their reproductions. One thing noticed is that they contain many words from the definitions and lack the meaning of the definitions. This means that, just as in memorizing details, the material as a whole was not perceived. It disintegrated into separate, more or less independent parts. In order to memorize a sentence exactly, the subjects distinguished each part and lost the general thread of the whole.

Undoubtedly, sometimes there is a negative effect to mnemonic orientation. It is caused by dominance, too great a "projection" of the task of memorizing at a time when understanding has not as yet been accomplished, but is still developing. One of the most important causes of this is the orientation toward completeness and accuracy of memorizing. The necessity to memorize everything or to memorize as exactly as possible prematurely emphasizes the mnemonic task, compels one to experience it very intensively. If such emphasis of the mnemonic task takes place before understanding is complete, it has a negative influence on understanding. Under these conditions, trying to memorize everything, i.e., not only what is most essential but also the details, and attempting to memorize the exact formulations, we take recourse to special modes not connected with understanding, not included in the understanding of the text as a whole. And this leads to the destruction of the unity of meaning of the material, to the breaking up of the whole. The understanding of the text has been disrupted.

Among the conditions on which the possibility of a negative influence of the mnemonic orientation depends, an important place is occupied by the *characteristics of the material.*

Any material must be understood *as a whole*. It is especially necessary if the material contains a single logical core, a single chain of thought. If there is no such core, complete comprehension is demanded to a lesser extent. The danger of a negative effect of the mnemonic orientation is greater in the first case.

On the other hand, it should be noted that material which must be understood as a whole evokes of itself a set towards its understanding, not towards memorizing. On the contrary, material that demands less-than-whole comprehension evokes rather a set towards memorizing and not towards understanding as a whole.

Thus, if for the material which must be understood as a whole the dominance of mnemonic orientation is more dangerous, then the material itself evokes dominance of such orientation to a lesser extent.

The second characteristic of material influencing a possibly negative effect of mnemonic orientation is the *degree of difficulty of understanding*. If the difficulty of comprehension is great, then the dominance of the mnemonic orientation increases it and can make the material quite incomprehensible. On the contrary, if the material as a whole is easily understood, the difficulties caused by "emphasizing" the mnemonic task may prove to be insignificant, and understanding is accomplished in spite of the harmful, hampering influence of a mnemonic orientation.

The abundance of factual data in the text also plays an important role. If there are many factual data, this in itself can hamper understanding. Yet this is a favorable condition for strengthening the set for memorization.

How must one evaluate the main types of material, descriptive, explanatory, and narrative, from these points of view?

Let us consider the first. What are its characteristics? The separate parts of *descriptions* are often connected in a unifying scheme, typical for descriptions of a definite type. However, the logical core connecting all parts in such a manner that one follows from the other as a development of a general thought is usually absent in descriptions. And descriptions are usually full of factual data which, moreover, are not so insignificant as to be ignored, even if temporarily (or memorized only approximately or inaccurately). Therefore, descriptions favor the emergence of a set to complete, detailed, and exact memorizing and this can contribute to the *dominance* of mnemonic orientation. However, its harmful influence is rather weak. That descriptions lack a single, logical core has as its consequence an understanding of them that is of a special nature. It involves the perception of a scheme, which is often concrete and "objectified," rather than of the logic of thoughts that are internally connected and constitute the development of a general idea. Such a comprehension is easier and is less affected by the dominance of mnemonic orientation.

Explanatory material is the exact opposite of descriptions. It is characterized by a single logical core which runs, if not through all, then through a considerable part of the content. This material usually has fewer details than do descriptions, and they need to be memorized with less exactness, since in this case they play a lesser role and are often necessary not of themselves, but only as illustrations of general propositions. Explanatory material is connected less with the possible dominance of a mnemonic orientation and more with the set for *understanding*.

That explanations demand an especially exact understanding makes mnemonic orientation, if for some reason it begins to dominate, especially dangerous. If the material is difficult, this danger is greater.

Narrative material occupies a special place as compared to descriptions and explanations. The form of the single logical core present in the explanatory material is absent in narration. But the connection between the events must be comprehended very well. Therefore, the set for understanding must be very clearly expressed, sometimes approaching that for explanations.

As for factual data, their number varies with the form of narration. In artistic narration it is insignificant. In a scientific or, especially, an historical text, it can be very high. Therefore, the strength of the set for memorizing varies with the form of narration.

This characteristic of the various types of material agrees fully with the statements made by subjects.

Let us begin with a *descriptive* text: "The text [on morphology of snakes] is not pleasant and terribly descriptive. In another text I can exchange one word for another, but here the text is descriptive. Instead of 'scales' I said 'skin.' That is not exact. Therefore, now I say 'scales,' because I want to be exact. Literalness is involuntary. The text is very limited, it does not lead to interpretation. There is nothing to think about it. There is no need to memorize in terms of other concepts" (D).

The main effort in this experiment is concentrated on memorizing. The mnemonic orientation clearly dominates. Upon second reading, the subject carefully notes the errors committed in the first reading, she emphasizes the exactness of formulations. All this does not hamper understanding, however. The meaning of the text is transmitted correctly and the mastery of it, as can be seen from the self-observation, causes no difficulty.

"Right now," says another subject, "there is no material in need of understanding [the same text]. This is all for memorizing. This is descriptive material. The only place where one has to understand something is where it speaks of the ribs, the rest need only be memorized" (D).

Before reading for the second time, the subject immediately tries to note and remember the omitted details. The mnemonic orientation clearly dominates, but causes no harm. The reason is the same, i.e., the material presents no difficulties of understanding.

How do the subjects characterize the *explanatory* text? "The material immediately seems to be something single, sequentially developing [a text on the topic "Why is there a draft from a closed window?"]. While reading, everything was noted in logical sequence. Here is the main point around which everything is grouped, the main question which dictates the logic of retelling. And if the logic is not disturbed during memorization, does it matter with what words it is told? There is nothing to forget here. Only numbers had to be remembered" (D).

The necessity of clearly understanding prevails in this case over the need to memorize. The material does not pose special difficulties in understanding. It is all the more significant that in this experiment the subject notes that the numbers caused the meaning to be lost (although there were few numerical data). This means that as soon as there arose the need of memorizing the numbers before complete understanding of the text, and the mnemonic orientation became something independent, understanidng was immediately disturbed.

Let us cite other statements: "I tried to understand what it said [a text about religion]. I did not set myself the task of memorizing. In reading I tried to penetrate the correlation of the thoughts, to find the main thought and how it develops. Upon the second reading I was about to memorize the verbal formulations, but I had a feeling that they stand in the way of the content. I thought: 'I shall reproduce worse, it's better if I master the formulations later.' I got tired" (D).

This time the main set of the subject is directed toward understanding. The task of remembering is not posed, but as soon as it emerges its effect is negative. The meaning of the text is blocked. Moreover, it is characteristic that this occurs even upon a second reading, when the subject is basically familiar with the text.

What do the subjects say about narrative texts? Let us cite statements on memorizing historical texts: "I read not to memorize but to understand, in order to find the essence" (D).

"There was no less to reflect upon in this text than in the other [the explanatory text "Why is there a draft from a closed window?"]. I thought about the plan a lot and memorized with its help" (D).

"I tried to put it into a system, to establish what referred to what" (D).

These statements show that the set for understanding is in the subjects rather pronounced. However, the mnemonic orientation too is considerable in these cases.

> I had to study this text like a schoolchild studies his lesson (D).
> I had to specially memorize as if for an examination (D).
> This is a text in which one has to either mechanically memorize or utilize some special ways in order to associate somehow (D).
> Mechanical memorizing was often needed for connecting the thoughts (D).
> In this text there are few connected thoughts. Much must be memorized mechanically. One can freely combine thoughts (D).

Thus, memorization proceeded under the effect of two sets: memorizing (sometimes even mechanical) and understanding. This made it more complex and hampered the process of memorization. One of the subjects describes it thus:

"I read in pieces, stopping in the middle of sentences, repeated, retold, memorized numbers, compared, returned once more, sometimes looked through again from the beginning, and only then continued. I stopped in order to think through, established a connection of events, once more reread, underlined mentally some places three or four times, sometimes more" (D).

How did the task of remembering influence understanding of the material? In these experiments the *negative effect of the mnemonic task on comprehension of the text* is often mentioned.

"I was surprised," says one of the subjects, "that the years took such a hold on my attention that the content was not at all assimilated. I decided to pay special attention to it. I began to read anew. I read as if for the first time" (D).

"Without the dates," remarks another subject, "I would have remembered much more. The dates distracted from the content" (D).

Such statements are a frequent phenomenon. They all disclose that in memorizing an historical text with factual data (names, dates) the danger of "conflict" between the two sets is quite real. Therefore, in these cases a pronounced mnemonic orientation can have a harmful, inhibiting influence on understanding.

In summing up one can state the following:

1. Description causes a more pronounced memorization set, which,

however, does not hinder understanding greatly, since it usually does not present special difficulties.

2. Explanatory material, on the contrary, does not entail an expressed and premature mnemonic set, but if for some reason it arises prematurely, then its harmful influence on understanding can be considerable.

3. Narrative material of historical or scientific content evokes both sets to an equal extent. Sometimes they can enter into "conflict" with each other and this can cause a negative influence of the mnemonic orientation. The possibility of a "conflict" depends on the difficulty of understanding the text on the one hand, and on the amount of factual data in it on the other.

The characteristics of the material are only one of the conditions determining the possibility of a harmful effect of the mnemonic task. The other no less important condition is the sum of the *individual psychological features of the personality* of the person memorizing.

What must be kept in mind here? First of all, a certain stable, relatively constant set to understand or only to memorize, evoked by preceding practice or by the conditions of development and connected with other features of an individual's personality: his interests, experience, habits, and general mental development. When such a set has arisen as a feature of personality, it determines memorization, sometimes in spite of the task posed at the moment and in spite of the characteristics of the material. Therefore, if there is a relatively stable *strictly mnemonic set,* it can harmfully influence understanding even if there are no other premises for this.

Mnemonic orientation, just as the orientation toward understanding, changes in the process of development. Therefore, at various periods of development one or the other can prevail. This means that the possibility of a negative effect of the mnemonic task is not the same at various ages. In children, as we have pointed out, it is greater than in adults.

Chapter 6

REFLECTIVE ACTIVITY IN MEMORIZING

In the previous chapter those processes of thinking which serve under conditions of memorizing as means of achieving deeper and clearer understanding were pointed out. The task of the present chapter is to give a more detailed description of these processes.

We begin with their first group—with the meaningful grouping of the material which is also its categorization by meaning.

1. GROUPING ACCORDING TO MEANING

In psychology literature, grouping of material in memorizing and its positive importance have been noted by one of the outstanding representatives of associative psychology, Müller, who in his three-volume work on memory (1911–1915) devoted a special chapter to the so-called "complexes" and their role in the process of memorizing.

Representatives of Gestalt psychology, in particular Köhler (1933) and Koffka (1935), speak much of the unification and the breakdown of material. However, neither the associationists nor the Gestalt psychologists considered or could consider the problem of discovering the concrete content of thinking activity which takes place in the grouping of material in the process of memorization, and primarily in memorizing connected, meaningful material. This is the most important problem in studying the meaningfulness of memorizing. What have our experiments contributed toward its solution?

Let us examine experiments conducted with adults. As was pointed out, the main characteristic of grouping material observed in our subjects was that it was a *meaningful* grouping of the text. The material was broken up into parts not according to outward indications but by the *meaning* of the content. The basis for unification was the unity of the "microtopics" which connected the individual thoughts of the text. How were these microtopics distinguished?

Basically they were distinguished in two ways. In some cases the separation of the microtopics and grouping of thoughts corresponding to them proceeded as a separate process. This was a *separate action* occupying a special place among the other processes. Such cases were noted usually when the subjects faced *difficulties* in unifying the thoughts, in determining the microtopic in a given part of the text. This is how the subjects themselves explain it:

"The beginning and the middle were broken up easily, but in the last part I had to focus my attention and make special efforts in order to unify the thoughts into groups. I did not unite them immediately. There were several short sentences and each of them dealt with a different topic. It was difficult to unify them."

"It was very difficult to break up into parts. Here each sentence arouses so many thoughts [the text was on philosophy] that the transition to the next one, the connection with it, was difficult. I had to specially think through how to group the thoughts."

In most cases the process was, however, different: not separated from reading as some superstructure above it, but continuously, merging with it as its *distinctive "accompaniment."*

"The dividing into parts occurred during the process of reading itself, not as a separate process, but as an 'accompaniment' of what had been read."

"The breaking up into parts occurred during reading. These processes are very difficult to separate. In essence the process of reading and dividing into groups, into sections, is the same."

"The main sections are marked during reading itself. This process merges with reading itself."

The close connection between separating the microtopics and reading of the text has as a result that the breaking up into parts occurs in these cases involuntarily, sometimes even in spite of the intention of the subjects not to break up the text:

"I did not think of any plan but the parts separated anyway."

"I thought of breaking it up into parts but decided it was not worth it, since we did not have to retell but answer questions which facilitate reproduction of what has been read. But in reading the text it suddenly divided by itself."

"From the second paragraph on, there was the desire to break the text into parts, but I decided to restrain myself since I wanted to read everything in order to familiarize myself at first with the content. I decided to divide later, but some part or another always separated."

The involuntary breaking up into parts was sometimes observed during first reading of the text, at first familiarization with it.

What did this process of breaking up involve? Usually the subjects note that the division into parts amounted to a direct perception of the transition from one topic to another. In reading the text they "suddenly," sometimes quite unexpectedly, noticed that a new topic had appeared and the old one had ended:

> You read and suddenly you notice, or rather feel, that the thought has ended and something new has begun.
>
> During reading, somehow all by itself I noticed the transition from one thought to the other. From time to time I encountered some kind of logical leap and then fixated it. This was the breaking up into sections.
>
> How was the content broken up into parts? Simply. You feel immediately that now something else is being discussed. You feel that you begin to make a qualitatively different mental effort in reading new parts of the text.
>
> It was easy to break up into parts. One thought ends and you immediately feel that you are switching to something else.
>
> You read and involuntarily encounter a breaking point as if a new scene in a film has appeared.

In close connection with this the subjects sometimes speak about the *intuitive nature of the breaking up,* which they closely connect with a certain indefiniteness and indistinctness:

"There was breaking up but it occurred somehow intuitively; you grasp immediately, without any reasoning; during reading, this understanding was sketched in broad outline, and now as I speak of the sections I fill in the details."

"I divided intuitively, directly: did not think specially. The content was given in general outline and did not reach consciousness clearly. In order to tell you now I have to make it more clear."

Not always, however, are these "breaking points" or "logical leaps" noticed when they occur, at the very moment of transition from one topic to the other. In a number of cases the subjects "catch on" only when the new topic is already "developing," when part of the new section, sometimes a considerable part of one, has been read. The realization of the transition falls behind, lags in time from the transition itself. However, the nature of the process does not change. The subjects, although with a delay, with a less clear experience of the "leap," notice that something new has appeared and the former topic has disappeared.

The *characteristics* of the material naturally play an important role in these cases, and most important is the presence of sharp and clear transitions in the text. Of considerable support is the external design of the text, especially its paragraphing. Each passage to a new paragraph causes some reading lag, and this in itself is favorable for noticing the transitions. It also causes the expectation of a "break," since paragraphs are usually connected with such breaks.

The *set for breaking up* the content has an important place as a condition for a timely and clear realization of the transitions. When before reading, the subjects are tasked with breaking up the material into parts, the "breaking" points are noticed with less delay and more clearly, although in the process of reading itself this task is no longer present in consciousness.

Aside from the set for breaking up there was often observed an *expectation of a definite transition*, an anticipation of a definite content of the next part. The basis for this was the concrete content of the preceding parts which prompted the reader to assume what would be said further. This assumption often arose not as a conscious act but, as the subjects said, was only "kept in mind" in the process of reading the preceding parts. Often it was realized only when, in fact, in the later parts of the text there was a different content than what was expected:

> I remember that during the reading of the end of the first page I was perplexed. Before the sentence about the hand net, I expected a detailed description of something (I have forgotten what precisely) and suddenly they began to speak about a hand net. A feeling of disappointment appeared. What should have been said, in my opinion, I do not remember. Then too, I did not specially think about it, but there was some kind of direction, because I noticed very clearly the difference from what I expected. Sometimes I was perplexed at the jump in thoughts. In one place, evidently, I definitely expected something else because I was very much surprised when they spoke of nets. I did not expect such an end. I thought an exposition of factual material would follow and it proved to be a discussion. It at once fitted into a definite section.

In some cases it was noted that a *scheme* typical of texts of a given type, in particular of descriptive texts, was a basis for expectation:

"The material was easy to break up into parts. It is always constructed, approximately, on such a scheme, containing such headings. There was nothing unexpected. Each time I felt: 'Well, that was to be expected.' I did not say that, of course, but had such a recognition, as if I'd met whom I expected; or rather, whom I could expect to see under these conditions."

Having read the text and mentally isolated separate parts in it, the subjects could always tell immediately of what sections it consisted, what the content of each section was, what its topic was, but they were often unable to point out exactly the limits of the sections, i.e., point out where each begins and ends. For this they had to familiarize themselves with the text once more, think it through and then give an answer. This occurred especially often when the limits between the sections were not noticed in time and the new microtopic was established only when the subjects were in the very "thick" of the new section.

In summing up, the following can be stated:

1. When the breaking up into parts and grouping of thoughts are

united in reading, then the task of breaking up the material does not appear in consciousness. If such a task is posed before reading, then it acts as a "set," i.e., during reading it does not arise any more in consciousness.

2. In the process of breaking up, the subjects immediately notice transitions from one microtopic to another while reading. Seemingly, in some cases they come across them as some unexpected obstacle to the trend of thoughts which was developing before this. Such transitions are connected with a sudden switching of consciousness, with a strange change of "mental effort" "sensed" by the subjects, as one of them expressed it. In other cases the transition to the new is anticipated, expected by the subjects. This expectation is the result of the preceding reading. It is considerably facilitated by the existence of the conventional forms which are characteristic of some kinds of material.

3. In characterizing the breaking up into parts, the subjects speak of an instantaneousness, immediacy, intuitiveness, and, often, of an indefiniteness, or vagueness. Therefore, they regard their following report as a "logicalization" and "completion of the awareness" of what earlier was noted only on most general features and was not sufficiently realized.

4. The limits of the sections are often only approximately marked. In order to point them out after breaking up, a special additional analysis of the text is sometimes necessary.

In accordance with these peculiarities, the type of grouping just examined can be designated as *involuntary–intuitive*. How does the grouping proceed when it is a *special action* not included in the process of reading?

Basically it is characterized by the opposite features.

1. While in the preceding cases the task of breaking up the material was absent from consciousness during reading, in the present instance the microtopics stand out due to the presence of such a task. The task rises into consciousness either in the process of remembering what was noted earlier, or, for the first time, during reading.

2. While in the preceding cases the "breaking points" in the text "stood out" by themselves and the subjects either came upon them involuntarily or anticipated them beforehand, this time the new microtopics become apparent as the result of searching. The new microtopic has to be found.

3. While in the former cases the realization of the "changes" proceeds in the form of an instantaneous act, even if sometimes with a lag as compared to when it should have been, when the "transitions" are established as the result of special searching, their separation takes a noticeable segment of time. This is a more or less lengthy process.

4. While the preceding cases are characterized as intuitive breaking up, now the process has a pronouncedly discoursive nature. The subjects think over the breaking up, compare and correlate the separate parts, consciously mark what is common and what is different in them, sometimes attempt to

regroup the material, and evaluate the text from the point of view of logical sequence, or systematic exposition.

5. In accordance with this, the limits of the sections, which formerly were marked only approximately in the process of reading, now are given special attention.

All these characteristics make it legitimate to regard this form of breaking into parts and grouping by sense as *voluntary–discoursive.*

As illustration of this type we cite some statements of the subjects:

> During reading I consciously tried to notice some kind of scheme, separate sections of the text.
>
> The material is difficult since it contains many thoughts. It was difficult to break it into parts. In the process of reading there appeared the fear that I would not be able to break up this text at all. In order to separate the sections I had to see into the content, return, repeat, clear up where the difference in the thoughts was and which ones pertained to the same thing.
>
> At first everything went favorably. The text broke up by itself. I only marked each new section. And then repetition began. Perplexity. A question arose: "How to break up here?" I began to look for differences and whether it would be possible to break it up somehow, otherwise I should have to condense everything or memorize mechanically almost every sentence.
>
> During reading I purposely tried to divide the text into separate chapters so that it would be easier to remember. I did that because there were many small pieces in the text. It was not easy to do. The whole process of dividing took much time. One had to purposely unify some pieces, find the thought which would unify them.
>
> I consciously tried to group the thoughts. In some places the text seemed illogical. I had to rearrange the sentences in my mind.
>
> In reading I noted: this is repetition and this is new. I tried to define the limits of the sections. The absence of clearness, the general complexity of the text hampered the process.
>
> I wanted to add what Lamarck said about the tuco-tuco [name of a South American rodent] and what was said later to the preceding.
>
> I saw that there were many different things and it would be difficult to remember all of them if I did not break it up into sections. But then I might omit much. I intentionally began to unify thoughts, looked for ways to connect them, with what they all dealt.
>
> I tried to break it up into pieces. I marked separate questions and broke up the whole text according to them. To each part I added what referred to it. When I had read the first page I returned to the beginning and followed the development of the thought. When I finished, I made a plan, once more returned to the beginning, and looked for what related to it [the plan].
>
> During reading I tried to create a scheme for memorizing the text, thought over the separate sections according to content. The scheme was short. In composing it I changed the places of some sentences for convenience. For example, where it speaks of oil being used in factories and as fuel for locomotives I inserted the sentence about its significance in aviation because it was close in content.
>
> There were some sentences which I wanted to rearrange in order to get a more coherent narrative. Therefore, as early as the first reading I returned to preceding sentences in order to combine them differently, to make sections.

All these statements not only confirm our characteristic of voluntary–discoursive grouping, but reveal also the conditions which compel the subjects to use this type of breaking up. Such conditions are:

a. insufficiently distinct differences in the microtopics of the text, its logical complexity, repetitions, return to preceding microtopics;
b. a large number of small "pieces" difficult to unite;
c. very long sections difficult to break into smaller sections.

The last two points must be especially emphasized. They show that in breaking up into parts the subjects are guided not only by the content of the text, but to a certain extent also by the *number* and *volume* of the sections into which the text can be broken up.

In a number of statements this factor shows clearly.

"The last paragraph was small in comparison to the others. Therefore, it somehow attracted me less. In order to remember it one had to combine it with others."

"If there had been one sentence about a machine it would not comprise a part, but there was much about machines."

"In the middle there was a long paragraph about blindness. I had to divide everything into parts."

Similar statements also occurred in a special series of experiments in which we examined the peculiarities of the breaking up into parts by having the subjects evaluate a parcelled text. We broke up the material ourselves beforehand and asked the subjects to tell us whether they agreed with our parcelling or not. On the one hand we intentionally marked several small "pieces" and on the other, one large section. The majority of the subjects (7 out of 10) rejected such a breaking up, although it in no way contradicted a meaningful segmentation of the material. They based their rejection on the volume and number of "pieces":

> The first sentences must not be broken up [in our parcelling they were separate "pieces"]. Here everything is broken up sentence by sentence, but one sentence is not a section.
>
> The parcelling is unacceptable, because the first three sentences are separate parts in it. It is tiring to memorize in this manner. There are too many parts. You cannot keep them in memory. They must be combined somehow.
>
> It is difficult to memorize if the text is divided in detail in the beginning and later not divided at all.
>
> Here is a very long paragraph. It must be divided or else it will become monotonous.
>
> At the end one more part should have been made, the section is too large. If it is not broken up, it will be difficult to remember everything in it.

What makes the subjects object to *pieces too small,* although different in content? There may be too many sections and it will be impossible to memorize them directly. They exceed the volume of immediate memorization and they have to be specially "studied," perhaps even mechanically. What causes the objections to a *section too long* although it corresponds to a single topic?

Because the material of such a section is, subjectively, tedious, it will be "compressed" and memorizing its content in a developed form will be difficult. It will either have to be kept in memory in a compressed form or, to avoid that, memorized in a maximally developed form, i.e., again, specially "studied," perhaps mechanically.

Thus, divisions too small or too large are not acceptable to the subjects. Both can "overload" the memory, demand special "learning by heart," even mechanical memorization. Therefore, divisions of these kinds will not fulfill the function for which the breaking was intended. They will not help understanding, meaningful mastering. In order to more easily, "more conveniently" memorize, there must be *sections of intermediate volume*. It is these that make it possible to memorize most meaningfully.

Thus, the attention which the subjects give to the volume and number of sections has in the final analysis as its basis the orientation towards the most meaningful possible memorization, towards the avoidance of mechanical memorizing. The attention is completely subordinated to this basic orientation of the subjects.

The choice of groups "intermediate" in volume coincides with one of the results in the work by Müller. Memorizing complexes too large or too small was less productive than memorizing complexes intermediate in size. Müller's explanation for this differs, however, greatly from ours.

To memorize in large complexes is, according to Müller, inefficient because with increasing volume the attention which is given to each member of the complex decreases. Therefore, all members of such a complex are perceived unclearly. Memorizing in small complexes does not have an effect because localization of each complex is hampered.

We do not mean to deny either the significance of attention or the role of localization but, as our data show, the basis for the unfavorable influence of groups too large or too small which are formed in memorizing connected meaningful material is something else: the necessity of recourse to mechanical memorization. It is for this reason that the subjects try to operate with intermediate-sized complexes. Why does the breaking up into sense groups too small or too large demand a large share of mechanical memorizing?

Each group of thoughts united by the microtopic is memorized logically, on the basis of understanding. The topics themselves are often not at all strictly logically connected and memorizing them, especially their sequence, must be accomplished mechanically. It is clear that if there are many topics the scale of mechanical memorizing is larger and this is the case when the sense groups are too small. The same thing is needed when the groups are so large that their logical unity is disturbed and they seemingly break down into parts and each part becomes an independent topic. This again increases the number of microtopics of the text and demands their mechanical memorization. On the contrary, the intermediate-sized groups decrease the number of independent logically unconnected topics and in these cases the relative singificance of meaningful memorization becomes greater.

The desire to break up the material into intermediate-sized groups cannot always be fully realized. In some cases the text includes such separate sections, insignificant in volume and yet so different in content from all the rest that to unify them with other sections is almost impossible. On the other hand, sometimes there are in the texts such sections which, while being quite considerable in volume, are at the same time so united in content that they do not permit further parcelling.

What do the subjects do in such cases? When they meet with difficulties of the first kind they separate the smaller parts from the total system of the sections and memorize them separately. Sometimes they have to do this with separate sentences which do not fit into the total system. They are memorized as a quite special part of the text not belonging to the total "scheme."

"This sentence perplexed me," says one of the subjects. "It did not fit anywhere. I had to remember it separately as one that did not belong in the overall plan of the text."

"There are sentences quite close in meaning. Those you unite and it turns out in such a way that you cannot conceive of one without the other. But the sentence which said that biology is broken up into two fields (morphology and physiology) I had to remember separately, since it could not be united with anything. Such sentences you learn as you learn theorems and axioms in school, by heart."

On the contrary, if difficulties are caused by the large volume of the section, the subjects divide them into subtopics, as is usually done in drawing up plans. Together with the main sections there are formed *more particular* or *partial* sections entering into the composition of one of the main sections. The subjects resort to such a detailed breaking up, however, only after memorizing the main sections. As they themselves note, this is done in order to avoid the necessity of memorizing a large number of sections immediately.

The significance attached to the volume of sense groups or sections is determined not only by the difficulty or ease of memorization, but also by the needs of *reproduction.*

In recalling, the subjects, as they themselves say, often orient on the *"feeling of volume," "how much must be reproduced."* This refers to the whole material as well as to its separate parts, to the volume of each section. In reproducing, the subjects often compare the volume of what they say with "how much is said about it in the text." The differences noticed between the two serve as a basis for further attempts to recall.

"I want," says one of the subjects, "to recall more, since I feel that I have not said all. In this part of the text more was said."

Such statements are quite frequent. They reveal that the volume of the section is one of the essential criteria in evaluating the completeness of reproduction and the source of additional attempts to achieve fuller recalling.

Taking into account the "feeling of volume" in *reproduction,* the subjects naturally pay great attention to the volume of the section in *memorizing* also.

Considerations pertaining to the volume of the groups, while playing an important role in the sense grouping are, of course, not the only and decisive ones in parcelling the material. Basic and determining, as is clear from the very essence of the sense groups, is the *content* of the text. What must be especially noted here?

First of all, the presence of pronounced *breaks in meaning,* which we often noted as an essential factor determining the separation of the group and its limits.

Very important, too, is the *significance of the various parts of the text.* A part, for example, which is small but important in meaning is often separated as a special section in spite of the general orientation toward forming sense groups of intermediate size.

Differences in the familiarity with the text also have considerable influence. If a certain part of the text is familiar while the text as a whole is little known, or if, on the contrary, something stands out as unfamiliar against the familiar background, then such a part often forms an independent section although there are no other reasons for it.

Of similar influence is *interest.* That which stands out as interesting or, on the contrary, differs from all the rest in its "uninterestingness," sometimes forms a special section. It should be noted that, separating something significant, familiar, or interesting as a special part, the subjects remember such sections by emphasizing their characteristics ("important," "familiar," "new," "interesting," "boring"). These designations play an essential role in later reproduction. In recalling the text, the subjects lean or, at least, often try to lean on these characteristics ("and then came something long drawn out and boring," "I can't remember the next part: there was something well known in it").

Examples and illustrations are often separated into separate sense groups, especially when they are developed and given in a vivid, clear, and descriptive form. Most important among the conditions which determine sense grouping are the tasks confronting the subjects. If the aim is to memorize only what is basic in the text without going into details, the subjects operate with larger groups. On the contrary, if the aim is to "make an effort to memorize as much as possible at once," the breaking up into parts is done in more detail.

The difference between the influence of memorizing for *coherent retelling* and memorizing for *answers to questions* is very noticeable. In the latter case, the volume of the sections decreases considerably, but their number increases. The subjects take into account the possibility of detailed questions and, therefore, naturally try for better memorizing. The large number of sections formed in this case is, however, no hindrance, since there is no need to remember their sequence, the order of transition from one to the other, since they do not need to be reproduced consecutively.

Up to this point, we have spoken about the *general* principles in forming sense groups. Their presence, however, does not lead to full similarity in the breaking up of the same material by the different subjects. True, all subjects say that they proceed only from an "objective" breaking up of the material and that this material, in their opinion, "breaks up by itself in this manner." Their breaking up of the material seems "natural" to them, "the only possible way," "excluding all other variants." In fact, however, the sense groups formed by the various subjects vary, often within wide limits. *This pertains both to the size and to the specific content of each section. The individual differences in the formation of sense groups or sections are very great.*

As an illustration, we shall show how two texts, which were given to the same group of subjects (students), were broken up. All the students were given special assignments: in the process of memorizing, they were to break up the text into sections, to give them headings ("mentally"), and then at the end of memorizing to give the experimenter the resulting plan, having the text before them.

The texts were taken from a series which was conducted for comparison with adults and schoolchildren. For the adults they were very easy, and the content quite familiar. For this reason, it would seem, one should expect uniformity in the plans. What actually did happen? We cite the text and several plans:

The Wolf

The wolf resembles a large dog. Its body is lean, the legs thin, the tail hangs down and is covered with long hair. The muzzle of the wolf is elongated and pointed. The forehead is wide and slopes sharply downward. Its eyes are slanting, the ears are always erect. The wolf has a thick, long, tough coat. The color of the coat is usually grayish-yellow with some black. The length of the wolf's body is 1 1/2 m. Wolves live in dense forests, in ravines, and, sometimes, on the steppes. When the wolf has no young, it seldom lives in one place. In spring and summer wolves live alone or in pairs. In the autumn they live in families and in winter they sometimes gather in large packs. In winter in deep snow the wolves of one pack go in single file. Each of them steps into the tracks of the wolf in front of it. Therefore, it is sometimes difficult even for the experienced hunter to know how many wolves have passed. The wolf is a predator. It attacks large domestic animals and certain wild animals. It also feeds on small animals, and even eats insects. In summer it is less harmful than in winter because in summer it finds much food in the forest: it catches foxes, hedgehogs, mice, lizards, grass snakes, frogs, and it even eats some plants. Therefore, it attacks domestic animals less often in summer. But at the beginning of winter it comes ever nearer to the villages, sometimes gets into the village itself, runs into the cattle-sheds and kills the animals. We organize brigades of hunters to fight the wolves. They arrange raids on wolves, set traps and snares, and scatter poisoned meat in places where wolves come. The wolves captured are killed.

How was this text broken up? Let us cite two plans:

Subject G. 1) Characteristics of the wolf. 2) The struggle with wolves.

Subject L. 1) The appearance of the wolf. 2) Color of coat. 3) Length of body. 4) Abode. 5) How it lives in spring and summer. 6) How it lives in autumn. 7) How it lives in winter. 8) Food of the wolf; domestic and wild animals, sometimes insects. 9) In summer fewer attacks on domestic animals, finds food in the forest. 10) In winter comes to animal-shed and kills animals. 11) Measures to control wolves.

The contrast between the plans is striking. Subject L. breaks up the material in detail, into many points, sometimes formulating them as propositions. Subject G. broke the text up into only two parts, very different in volume and content.

These two plans are the extremes, the rest fall somewhere in between. These other cases, however, also differ noticeably from each other. As an example, let us cite two samples from this group of plans, which to a considerable extent are typical of a number of others:

Subject K. 1) Appearance of the wolf. 2) Way of life. 3) Struggle with wolves.

Subject V. 1) General appearance of the wolf. 2) Its characteristic features. 3) Nature of place where wolves live. 4) Way of life of single wolves. 5) Running in packs. 6) Food of the wolf. 7) The wolf, a pest to agriculture. 8) Methods of struggle with wolves.

It is not difficult to see that the degree of detail and the number of points differ greatly this time also. Let us cite another text:

Iron

Iron is found in nature much more often than other metals. Its use is very extensive. At the present time it is difficult to picture human life without iron. It is a soft metal which easily combines with other substances. Therefore in nature iron is found in the form of ore. Sometimes the ore is deep in the earth and then mines are built to get it. If, however, the deposits are not deep, the ore is mined directly, in open pits. From the mined ore, pig iron is extracted. The extraction is done in special ovens. They are called blast furnaces. These are huge ovens, several meters high. The largest blast furnaces in the world are in our Soviet Union. Coal and ore, brought in gondolas, are loaded into the blast furnace from the top. The furnace is fired from below and from the top coal and ore are continually poured in. Once the blast furnace has been fired it works sometimes for years, until it breaks down. From the intense heat the ore melts and the ready pig iron slowly flows out of the furnace and into molds. In the smelting of pig iron from the ore there are many tailings. Pig iron is used to cast various objects. However, they break easily, since cast

> iron is very brittle. Therefore, great quantities of cast iron go to plants for further processing. Here it is roasted in special furnaces and steel and common light iron are produced. From iron many household objects are made. It is impractical to transport the ore long distances for producing cast iron and steel from it. It is much more convenient to transport the finished articles. Therefore plants are now built where the ore is found. Our industry uses many millions of tons of steel and iron yearly. Therefore, we have built new large plants where pig iron, iron, and steel are produced.

How was this text broken up? Here are some examples:

Subject S. 1) Iron in nature. 2) Smelting of pig iron. 3) Smelting of steel and iron. 4) Conditions for profitable production of steel and iron.

Subject P. 1) Significance of iron. 2) Mining of iron ore. 3) Blast furnaces, their construction and action. 4) The properties of pig iron. 5) Plants for iron and steel. 6) The uses of iron and steel.

Subject R. 1) Properties of iron. 2) Treatment of ore. 3) Specifics of plants for the processing of metal. 4) The building of new plants in our country.

Subject V. 1) Iron and its mining. 2) Uses of iron.

This time too, the plans were different. Subject S. includes in the section "Iron in nature" not only the first sentence, but everything said about the ore. Similarly, R. also refers to the section "Properties of iron" everything said about iron ore. In contrast to this, P. as the first point takes the significances of iron, while he makes what pertains to the mining of ore into a separate section. Further, while P. separates the properties of pig iron from the uses of iron and steel, two other subjects do not do this. Subject R. marks as a special point the statement about plants built in our country. The other subjects do not separate this point.

In contrast to these plans, that of subject V. has only two points: 1) Iron and its mining (to which he refers everything concerning the mining of ore, the smelting of pig iron, the smelting of iron and steel, and the building of plants) and 2) Uses of iron (to which he referred everything said about the utilization of pig iron, iron, and steel). In composing such a plan, V. partially changed the actual plan of the text.

The diversity of sense groupings, evident from the cited examples, clearly shows that, although the subjects themselves consider it as "it goes without saying," "following from the text itself," "a simple statement of what is in the material itself," nevertheless, actually it is not at all as it is pictured. Only for the case of sharp "breaks," in which the subject of exposition really changes radically, does the breaking up into groups by the subjects coincide. Where there are no such breaks the subjects differ, sometimes very considerably.

Thus, in reality the breaking up into groups is not at all a passive statement of "what there is," not a "mirror reflection of an objective breaking up" of the material, but a very active process proceeding differently for different people. *This is a complex, thinking activity, evoked by the mnemonic orientation of the memorizers.*

2. MEANINGFUL POINTS OF SUPPORT AND THEIR SEPARATION

The breaking up of the material into parts, its sense grouping, as was said, is inseparably connected with the other process already mentioned, i.e., the separation of meaningful points of support which deepen understanding and facilitate memorization of material.

In a broad sense, everything with which we connect what we memorize or what of itself "floats up" as connected with it is support for memorizing. Any association can in this sense be a support for memorization. Meaningful points of support are, however, not just any support in memorizing. A meaningful point of support is just that, a point, a kind of "dot," as the subjects sometimes say, i.e., something brief, condensed, by itself, in size insignificant but serving as support of a wider content, which it replaces. It is by this substitution for a larger and greater content that the meaningful points of support differ from those associative "supports" ("*Hilfe*" in Müller's terminology) which usually are noted by the associationists.

The most important positive role of the points of support in this sense has been often noted in psychology. Bergson (1902) in particular attached great significance to them; he also relied on other authors who noted the great role of points of support as conditions of memorizing.

"The talent of a mnemonist," says one of these authors (Audebert) "involves grasping in a section of prose these outstanding ideas, these short sentences, these simple words which lead whole pages."

"To reduce to short and essential formulas... to note in each formula the word central in meaning... to associate these words and form in this way a logical chain of ideas." Thus André, another of the authors cited by Bergson, formulates the rule of memorization.

Bergson himself characterizes memorization in the following manner: "To learn by heart," he says, "means to focus on one point where a multitude of more or less significant images seem to be concentrated in a simple idea which is memorized." The basis for progress in memorizing is, therefore, the "increasing capability of reducing all ideas, all images, all words to one point." In Bergson's opinion, "it becomes, as it were, one coin and all the rest would be small change for it."

This concept of separating points of support is factually incorrect. For Bergson, as an intuitionist, the "compression" of everything being memorized into one point had especially great significance since it could easily be correlated with his main views on understanding as an intuitive "grasping" of the material. It is no accident, therefore, when he speaks about just *one* point, in which in unified, undivided form the whole content of the material is supposed to be included. This is really not so. In fact we usually have to deal with a "logical chain of ideas," i.e., with a *number* of logically connected points of support. Nor is it accidental that, in speaking of the concentration of the whole of the material in one point. Bergson does not mention anything about dividing the material, about breaking it up into meaningful parts, although it is this process which is the basis for understanding the logic of the material.

Clearly idealistic (intuitivistic) also is Bergson's interpretation of points of support as "dynamic schemes" which in his opinion "are difficult to define but are felt by every one of us." It is with such schemes that chess players operate, he says, when, blindfolded, they play several games simultaneously. Bergson considers it erroneous to say that purely visual memorizing plays the major role here, that the player sees in front of him, as in an "inner" mirror, the chess board with the figures. In his opinion, the blindfolded chess players keep in mind not the figures themselves but their "strength," "their value," their "function." "In the memory of the player," he says, "there is a combination of forces or, rather, a certain correlation between the allied and the hostile forces...."

It is not difficult to see that the concept of points of support as peculiar "forces" affecting our memory has a very idealistic nature. These are the notorious "idea-forces" of which the idealists usually speak. And yet this "intuitivistic" nature of the points of support is not in a position to reveal the content aspect of their separation, i.e., the content of our own activity in these cases, or, in still other words, the reflective activity which we carry out when we separate them.

We turn now to the characteristics of the points of support as revealed in our experiments. We note first the great variety of what appears as points of support.

The most developed but least characteristic form of meaningful points of support are a kind of "postulate" which the subjects compose as a brief expression of the main thought of each section. Such points of support are observed comparatively rarely, and usually, as much as can be judged from our materials, under two conditions: first, when there are briefly-formulated postulates in the text itself which sum up the meaning of what has been said, and the subject can take them in a ready form, and second, when the comprehension of the text faces considerable difficulties and, therefore, demands prolonged reflection. The result of reflections which is fixed in the form of a certain judgement, or postulate, is the point of support for the memorization of a given section.

We cite some statements by the subjects which characterize the first case:

"When there are sentences in the text which express the whole section at once, you emphasize them especially and try to memorize them first of all, and all the rest adheres to them by itself."

"It was easy to memorize here. The main thoughts stood out sharply and one did not need to think about their formulation. I leaned directly on the ready sentences. This was not possible everywhere, but where I could, I did it."

It must be noted that not all sentences taken from the text are postulates in the full sense of the word. Objectively they did not always represent a résumé of the whole content of the section. In some cases the subjects separated sentences which, although connected with what the section contained, did not characterize it completely, did not include the whole content of the section, even in a "curtailed" form.

Here are, for example, sentences used as points of support separated by one of the subjects from "The Wolf."

1. "The wolf resembles a dog."
2. "The wolf seldom lives in one place."
3. "The wolf does less harm in summer."

The first sentence, as the subject herself notes, was the "carrier" of the meaning of the whole part of the story where it spoke of the appearance of the wolf. Objectively, however, the content of this part is by no means covered by the sentence chosen by the subject.

The second sentence replaces, according to the subject, the whole part of the text which speaks of the way of life of the wolf. The content of this part, however, again goes beyond the particular case which is pointed out in the chosen sentence (in the text, nowhere is it expressly stated that as a general rule the wolf "seldom lives in one place," as one may think proceeding from what the subject has isolated; rather, it is pointed out that the wolf seldom lives in one place *when there are no cubs;* in accordance with this, there is more information about the life of the wolf in the text).

The third sentence was the support for the whole part of the text referring to the feeding of the wolf, i.e., again, it did not reflect the whole content of this section.

Why did the subject separate these sentences and not attempt to find other points of support? In her words, "this was sufficient to remember the whole content" of the sections. The sentences separated by her meant more to her than their content, as it is objectively revealed outside the trend of thoughts of the subject. These were "notes" which she made "in mind," mentally "pulling toward" them the whole content of the sections. Being individual in their *objective* content, they *subjectively,* i.e., to the subject herself, acquired a generalizing meaning. "In separating these sentences I implied everything that it says here," as the subject herself characterizes the generalized meaning of these sentences.

Similar observations were made in other subjects. This is how the subjects describe the independent composition of postulates:

> I did not understand the text immediately [text on philosophy]. In order to make it clearer, I tried to formulate the main thoughts in the form of brief propositions. This helped my memorizing very much. Actually, one had to memorize only these propositions. Everything else was already in them, was implied by me. It is easy to memorize the text when one recalls such a sentence.
>
> Very difficult text [the same text]. You understand what you read, but precisely what has been said one must consider, find out. You read a certain part, feel that it speaks about something else, you return to what has been read, try to think it through. You understand and fix it in the form of a small sentence, like a short postulate, and go on. Sometimes one has to think for a long time. But when you understand and formulate the essence, you feel that you have found good support for memorizing. So I memorized by means of postulates. They served as good guide lights.

But the subjects did not always formulate their propositions clearly. Occasionally they spoke of the fragmentation and the vagueness of their formulations:

"I read the material and composed postulates. Not real ones, but fragments. I did not even think much about their formulation, but the thoughts themselves were clearly recognized. I felt that I understood what it was about and went on reading."

"I compressed into a small sentence the content of each part. I did not worry about formulating. Fragments, and not very clear ones at that, were generated. I realized that, if need be, I could express myself exactly. For myself I did not need it. I understood well what the essence was without it."

The postulate-type point of support, as was said, is a comparatively rare phenomenon. Much more often *headings of sections* stood out as points of support. According to our data, this is the most prevalent kind of point of support.

Outwardly this kind of point of support differs, of course, greatly from the preceding one. While the postulate is a confirmation or negation of something, a heading does not contain any confirmation. It is only a designation of the subject it concerns.

In reality, however, as our data show, the difference between postulates and headings, when they are used as points of support for memorizing, is not at all so great. In giving a heading to a certain part of the text, the subjects always connect concrete aspects which are in the corresponding section of the material with each heading. The heading designates not only what is discussed in a given section, but also what is reported about the subject, phenomenon, or event. It is not contained in the heading itself, but is implied, as the subjects themselves point out. This is why they call the headings "carriers of meaning," "substitutes" of the content of the section. In speaking of the separation of main thoughts, they note that the content of these thoughts was often "compressed" by them in the heading of the part. The thought and the heading were to a certain extent identified. The heading "bore in mind" a more developed content, some confirmations or negations, often a whole complex of them.

Just as the postulates, the headings were either taken in ready form from the text or were "invented" by the subjects. In the first case the words which acquired the significance of a heading were separated in the process of reading, mentally underscored as characterizing everything or, in any case, the main content of the section. They acquired the function of points of support due to a special inner stress which the subjects put on them. Their role as headings was realized by the subjects, and was usually experienced in approximately the following manner: "Ah! Here it speaks about this" (i.e., about what was named with the given word).

No attention was usually given to the nature of the words or, in particular, to their correspondence to a common type of heading (accepted in scientific literature or the textbooks from which we usually took our reading samples). Therefore, verbs in the third person (the predicate of the sentences) frequently were used as headings, without other explanatory words. In "The Wolf" some subjects, as the heading for the part of the text describing the way of life of the wolf, used the phrase "they live," taken from the text, meaning, specifically, the "way of life of wolves." The part of the story describing the food of wolves is given the heading "attacks" or "feeds." Sometimes adverbs are used as headings, again without the words to which they refer. In the story "Iron" the word "deep" is used to designate the heading of the part in which are described two main cases of iron ore deposits.

Thus, if one takes the headings noted by the subjects by themselves, in such an "isolated" form, separated from what the subjects "have in mind," they sometimes express nothing essential. Out of the context of the subjects' thoughts they can be devoid of meaning, incomprehensible to outsiders. They may mean nothing outside the story.

The "headings" given by the subjects in the text itself sometimes not only do not correspond to the common headings *in form,* but differ from them in their *content* and in the relation of the objective meaning of the words of the heading to the content of the text. Usually the "meaning" of the heading is more or less adequate to what is in the text itself. In a "curtailed," generalized form it includes the main content of the text. A different relation between the heading and the material to which the given heading belongs has been observed in a number of our experiments. The words which the subjects used as headings sometimes had a more restricted meaning objectively than the one demanded by the content of the text.

In "The Wolf" one of the subjects used, for example, the word "packs" for the heading of the whole section on the way of life of wolves, which by no means conveys the meaning of all that is in this section. In this respect the use of words proceeds sometimes just as the use of sentences. Words more restricted in their meaning are felt by the subjects themselves in a more general meaning, are carriers of a wider content. One can say that in this respect the headings arising in the subjects resembled more the headings of fiction than of the scientific literature and textbooks which in fact were given to be memorized.

In some cases, taking the heading from the text, the subjects do not stop at some one word but inwardly underscore and separate several words as headings as they are found in the text; each time, however vaguely, the subjects realize that they all are carriers of the same meaning: "all this is about the same thing." But the "same thing" is not at all exactly formulated.

So, in "The Wolf," reading the description of the wolf some subjects separate as support-point headings the words: "body," "legs," "muzzle," knowing that "all this belongs to the same thing," but the generalizing heading "the appearance of the wolf" (absent from the text) does not appear (in contrast to a number of other subjects).

Thus, even when the "headings" are taken from the texts, they are not clearly crystallized, finished, or strictly defined at all. Often they are rather "notes" on headings, "approximate headlines," as the subjects themselves characterize them. Therefore, the subjects sometimes find it difficult to point out exactly what precisely served as a point of support. They note a number of words and say that "all this was one and the same." And yet they emphasize that "the meaning of the headline was recognized sufficiently clearly."

Still less clear and finished were the headings which the subjects invented themselves. Often these were only "fragments of words," "hints of words," "an orientation toward a word," "beginnings of words," "not so much a word as a feeling," as the subjects characterize them. Often the words themselves did not appear at all in a clear and finished form, though the meaning of the heading, as the subjects said, was sufficiently clear. This is their explanation as to why an exact formulation often didn't interest them. They were not worried about its "crystallization" since for them, subjectively, the heading had already been found.

A special kind of verbally expressed point of support are the *questions* which the subjects sometimes ask concerning the content of the part read. Nothing new, as compared to what was said about the postulates and headings, can be noted relative to this kind of point. It can only be emphasized that, just as were the headings, the questions posed by the subjects are in the consciousness of the subject always present together with certain postulates, with answers to the questions. Such answers are usually not formulated in a developed, clearly expressed verbal form but are to a considerable extent only implied. But their presence even in such a compressed, "implied" form is sufficient reason not to make an essential differentiation between this kind of support point and the two others considered above.

The next kind of point of support are *images* of what is said in the text. In their content the images even more rarely than the postulates, headings, or questions covered the content of the whole part of the text to which they referred. Nevertheless, they served as a point of support for the content of the section as a whole. In spite of their restricted nature, they, just as the sentences, words, and questions, acquired in the consciousness of the subjects a more general meaning, were "carriers" of the meaning of the whole. An individual image arising in the subject in a "compressed" form included a wider content than what was implied in it.

The same must be said about everything concrete, which, even if not embodied in the image, nevertheless illustrated some positions of the text which were more general in their meaning. *Examples,* vivid *numerical data, comparisons,* all this was often used by the subjects as points of support and given a certain more general meaning, was a support of a wider content. Here belong also *titles, names, special terms,* some especially striking and characteristic *epithets,* sometimes simply *unfamiliar* words, or individual *distinctive expressions.*

The last kind of point of support which must be mentioned, although it did not occupy an important place among the others, is the *emotion* arising in the subjects in connection with the reading of some part of the text. Above, when speaking of the breaking up of the material, we noted that it was sometimes based on the attitude which some parts of the text evoked in the subjects. The latter marked some parts as "boring" or, on the contrary, "interesting," as "pleasant" or "unpleasant." Any such distinction was accompanied by some emotion which sometimes becomes a point of support for memorization. It colored the whole content of the section, characterized it, and therefore was also a "carrier" of its meaning.

From what has been said it follows that in their nature and content the points of support for memorization vary greatly. Even the same kind appears in different forms. And yet, in the concrete process of memorization the subject rarely used only one kind of point. In the great majority of cases memorization of the same text was carried out with the help of several kinds of "supports": some parts were represented by some kinds of points, others by different ones. "I leaned on what was easiest to distinguish, I did not expecially think about points; now it was a heading, now a question, sometimes images helped," states one of the subjects.

What has been said makes it possible to characterize more precisely the points of support as *points of the plan of the text.* In their essence the points of support undoubtedly comprise in their totality the plan of the material. But in their formal characteristics they often differ from it. Incompleteness, insufficient external exactness, fragmentary verbal formulations, the purely imaginary or even emotional nature of some points, the diversity of points, all this distinguishes in *form* the "plan" created in the process of memorization from the ordinary "traditional" plans customary for the subjects themselves. Therefore, the subjects often characterized their "plans" as "rough drafts," "plan for myself," "notes" or "hints," a "likeness of a plan." Sometimes they even refuse to recognize what they have noted as a plan. "It was far from a plan," said one of the subjects, although she nevertheless had marked out points of support.

Thus, "plans" created as supports in memorizing are, undoubtedly, of a special nature. Outwardly, they are very peculiar and do not resemble ordinary rationalized plans. But according to the role which their component points of support play, the relation in which each such point is to the material "replaced" by it, these "plans" are, nevertheless, similar to the usual ones.

In spite of all reservations, they must be regarded as plans. Each point of such a plan replaces a certain content, a certain part of the text, designates it, points to it, even if purely subjectively and in a manner understandable only to the subject. And that is after all a basic characteristic of a plan.

The compressed, condensed, unified, and generalized nature of points of support is the basis for differentiating them from the various "props" which often arise in the process of memorizing. The support point is not a simple member of an associative connection, united with its other equal members. Its relation to what "rests" on it is quite special. It is the expressor of a certain general meaning; it unites within itself everything that refers to it on a *meaningful* basis. Everything that rests on it, that does not confront it as an equal member of an association, as each of the links of a chain, but is in a special way already contained in it itself. Both have a single content, in one case (the support point) given in an undeveloped, compressed, generalized form, in the other (the content of the section) presented as something developed, expanded, and made specific.

The important role of support points in *memorizing* does not exclude questions about the extent to which these support points are represented in *reproduction*. Being closely connected with memorization, reproduction is nevertheless not fully determined by it What stands out in the consciousness of the memorizer at the moment of impression, as essentially important for this process, can be absent from the consciousness during subsequent recall. How do our data answer this question?

We have already pointed out that in a number of cases the subjects state quite definitely that they use support points not only in memorizing, but also in the process of reproduction. "Recalling goes by support point." Desiring to remember the text, the subject remembers what he marked as support for memorizing: sentences, headings, or images. Doubtlessly, support points are present in the consciousness of those who reproduce the material.

Such a recalling of support points is, however, not at all a general rule. Usually it is observed only when the text is reproduced immediately after memorizing, i.e., almost at once after marking the points themselves. A different picture is revealed for *delayed* reproduction. When we suggested to the subjects that they remember material which they had memorized some 5–10 days ago, in most cases they remarked that the points they had then separated were now not at all represented in their consciousness. As the subjects said, these points did not "play any role" in the actual recalling. Let us cite some statements to this effect:

"I pictured a page mentally. In my mind I divided it into large pieces, but there were no support points on the page. Therefore, I pictured only the top, bottom, and very end. This helped reproduction, but did not play a great role. Names for the parts did not appear."

"I tried to remember the names of the parts, picture them visually, in a column, written on a wall in large letters [in remembering, the subject looks at the wall]. I saw with horror that there were no names. I began to remember without them, and tried to remember what was said in the text."

It is hardly necessary to emphasize that forgetting the support points did not result in forgetting the text itself. The delay in our experiments was comparatively short: it varied from 5 to 10 days. In the course of this time much of what had been memorized by them was retained in the memory of the subjects. However, a considerable number, though not all, of the support points were forgotten.

One would think that the basis for their being so quickly forgotten was the absence of a "design" in memorizing, in particular an incomplete verbal formulation. One of the subjects expresses it thus:

"There were no titles for the parts. If I had indeed composed a real plan, I would have remembered them. I had separated them, but I did not always formulate them exactly. Therefore I forgot them soon [reproduction occurred 5 days after memorization]."

Is such an explanation justified? In order to answer this and also to check carefully the retaining and forgetting of the supporting points and their role in reproduction, we conducted a special series of experiments in which it was suggested to the subjects that they mark without fail a plan of the text in the process of memorizing and fix it then in written form. All points of the plan in these experiments were to have a distinct verbal formulation (regardless of form: as headings, postulates, or questions).

How did reproduction proceed in these cases? What role did the support points play? The data of the questionnaire show that this time, too, the points of the plan composed in memorizing did not as a rule participate in reproduction. The subjects operated with them only in rare cases. Let us cite several of these statements:

> I did not recall the plan. I don't even remember exactly what points there were in the plan. I have a visual memory, I remember the arrangement of the material.
>
> I did not remember the plan. It did not play any role. Only the text remained in my memory.
>
> I attempted to recall my previously composed plan. Nothing came of it. Only when I began to tell that oil is transferred to oil tanks through pipes did I remember that there was such a point in the plan, that is, the transportation of oil. So it was also with the other parts. In retelling the text I remembered after retelling that such a point was in the plan. It turned out that I did not remember the text from the plan, but restored the plan from my story. I restored the plan, not completely, of course, but only certain points.
>
> I did not remember the plan composed. It played no role in reproduction. I tried to remember what I read.
>
> I even forgot about the existence of the plan.
>
> I don't know whether I narrated according to the plan or not. I do not remember the plan itself, but the logical order of the thoughts has been retained.
>
> First I remembered the text, and then the plan. The plan, of itself, simply could not be remembered.

Such statements were obtained from all 14 subjects who participated in this series of experiments. The subjects were students; the delayed reproduction occurred nine days after memorization.

Thus, in recalling the text the subjects do not remember the support points (sentences and headings) even when they were clearly formulated and had obtained a definite verbal formulation fixed in writing. And yet the reproduction of the text proceeds normally; the subjects remember a considerable part of the material.

Very characteristic are those statements in which the opposite relation between the plan and the text is noted, which does not coincide with what should be expected: the plan is not the basis for the recalling of the text but, on the contrary, only the recalling of the text makes it possible to restore the previously composed plan.

All this, naturally, confronts us with the question: did the plan really play a positive role in memorizing, or was it some kind of superfluous "load," indifferent for the results of memorization? Did we not have here what Foucault called a "parasitic intellectual tendency" which according to his data is revealed by some "auxiliary means of memorization," which do not at all participate later in the reproduction and are of no real help?

Such an assumption would be incorrect. It would contradict the statements of the subjects as well as the objective data.

In memorizing one of the texts, some subjects said:

> I broke it up by points, will forget them very likely before I forget the text, but they help to memorize.

> I did not recall the plan I had composed [in delayed reproduction]. But in the perception of the text it played an important role. It facilitated memorizing. But in retelling I tried to remember the text itself.

> In reading the text I had a great need to mark the main places, to clear up the sequence of the material, to make some sort of a plan. So I did. I broke it up into pieces, gave them headings, but not exact ones. Now [in delayed reproduction] I have forgotten them, but I do not feel a great need of them. They have done their duty, I recalled without them. Little by little, it came by itself.

> Right now I do not remember my support points, although I might be able to recall them. Not all of them, but some, in any case. I did not retell proceeding from them, but earlier I did separate some of them in order to memorize better. Then it seemed to be very much necessary and that it would stay better in memory.

Thus, the subjects themselves feel a definite need to separate support points and consider this to be a means of facilitating memorizing. But having done so they later make no use of it, do not rely on the "support points," but recall the text independently of these points. What helps *memorization* is consequently not utilized at all in *reproduction* (in any case in *delayed* reproduction).

Let us turn to our data. They were obtained in the following manner: parallel to the series of experiments in which a plan had to be drawn up, we conducted, with the same subjects, a control series in which no instructions were given to draw up a plan and fix it in written form. The subjects could memorize the text as they wished. The material for memorization was the same as in the first series, but this time it was assigned by "crossing over," i.e., those who in the first series memorized text "A" now had to memorize text "B," and *vice versa*. Thus, in composition of subjects as well as material both groups were approximately equal. How were the texts in the control series of experiments memorized?

The majority of subjects (9 out of 14) memorized by breaking them up into parts and separating support points. True, these points were not as distinct in their external formulation as in the first series. In particular, they often lacked a final verbal formulation. Nevertheless, individual parts of the text and support points were marked.

As for the other five subjects, according to them, no breaking up of the material into parts and no separation of support points was done. What was the result of reproduction in the two series of experiments? The quantitative indexes are presented in Table 6.1.

In examining Table 6.1 it is striking that immediate reproduction in the series in which the composition of a plan was not stimulated by a special instruction was not worse; on the contrary, it was somewhat better than in the basic series of experiments in which the subjects had to compose a plan.

At first glance this may seem to confirm the doubts of the positive role of a plan. This is really not so. The texts which were given in both series of experiments were very easy, i.e., they dealt with things quite familiar to our

TABLE 6.1

Type of activity	Percentage of reproduced meaningful units of text	
	with plan	without plan*
Immediate reproduction	70.6	73.1
Delayed reproduction	53.1	41.6
Difference between immediate and delayed reproduction (forgetting during delay of reproduction)	17.5	31.5
Difference between immediate and delayed reproduction expressed as % of immediate reproduction	24.8	43.2

*The designation of the experiments "without plan" is arbitrary. As has been pointed out, in reality most subjects broke up the text into parts and singled out points of reference, thus making a kind of plan. By this designation we merely want to emphasize that in these experiments the experimenter did not require a plan, as a result of which not all subjects made a plan and those who did, did not define it precisely.

subjects. This explains the fact that of 14 subjects 5 did not break up the material into parts and separate support points. "I did not break the text into parts, since the material is quite familiar and is memorized by itself." This statement by one of the subjects (two more of the five who had not broken up the material expressed themselves similarly) clearly indicates the special nature of the material utilized in these experiments, the great ease of the text for this group of subjects. Therefore, it is not surprising that the memorization of such material was not determined by the presence or absence of a plan. Both texts were memorized so easily that they yielded approximately the same high indexes independent of the use of any kind of special modes of memorizing, in particular, without the composition of a plan. It is not possible, therefore, to judge from the results obtained the real influence of a plan on *immediate reproduction*. The absence of differences in these indexes does not rule out the possibility of great influence of the plan under other conditions, e.g., in memorizing more difficult material.

Different indexes characterize *delayed* reproduction. The productivity of recalling in the series "without a plan" is this time lower than in the main series "with a plan." The difference between the two series is clearly manifested in the indexes of forgetting. In the experiments without a plan the amount forgotten (due to a nine-day delay) is almost twice as large as in the experiments with a plan (43.2% and 24.8%).

Thus, without solving the problem about the influence of a plan in *immediate* reproduction, without excluding the possibility of this influence in memorizing difficult material, our experiments definitely reveal that the positive effect of a plan on *delayed* reproduction is quite clear, moreover, it is observed even in memorization of easy material. *With increasing delay of reproduction the positive role of a plan, consequently, increases or even becomes apparent for the first time.*

What have our experiments shown? On the one hand, they have revealed that *recalling* proceeds in many cases without the appearance in consciousness of support points which were separated during memorizing. While the subjects often still rely on these points in immediate reproduction (although not always and not on all points), in delayed reproduction (five–ten days) the use of support points sharply decreases. In particular, the "headings" of sections specially marked in composing the plan (during memorization), were absent altogether in delayed reproduction.

On the other hand, from our data it follows that the subjects themselves attach great significance to the support points. They consider them essential to *memorizing*. The objective data also show that the productivity of reproduction, in any case delayed reproduction, is higher in the experiments in which the support points were specially separated during memorization. The delay in reproduction, as is clear from our data, leads to an increase in the effect of support points in the sense of their influence on the productivity of recalling. *The material was forgotten less when the support points were separated in the process of memorization.*

The contradiction in these data is evident. The subjects intentionally mark the support points (thereby trying to facilitate memorization), use them in immediate reproduction, but do not use them when reproduction is more difficult or when it is delayed. Furthermore, although in a number of cases the support points are not present in consciousness during reproduction, the fact that they had been separated during memorization has, nevertheless, a positive effect, i.e., it increases recalling. Finally, while the use of support points, i.e., recalling them in the process of reproduction, decreases as reproduction is delayed, the positive effect of the previously separated points, their influence on the productivity of reproduction, increases.

From all this it follows that the absence of support points from the consciousness of the subjects during reproduction does not exclude the possibility of their positive influence on the actual productivity of recalling.

How is all this to be understood? Let us first of all discuss the following. To a certain extent the elimination of the support points can be described as the transformation of an indirect connection into a direct one. Such a description would make it possible to see in this fact something similar to some other already sufficiently known facts, but it would contribute nothing to its explanation. The basis for the transition of indirect connections into direct ones can differ greatly. Therefore, in characterizing the data as one of the cases of such a transition, we still do not reveal anything as to the *sources* or *bases* for such a transition in a specific case.

What is the transformation of an indirect connection into a direct one? Factually it means that if something (*A*) was connected with something else

(*B*) by means of still something else, intermediate (*M*), then, further on, both these links (*A* and *B*) evoke each other directly, bypassing the intermediate link (*M*) which connected them. At the moment of transition from *A* to *B*, the intermediate link *M* does not arise at all in consciousness. Nevertheless, the transition from *A* to *B* is accomplished by the fact that the intermediate link previously assisted in this transition.

How must one interpret this transformation of an indirect connection into a direct one? Associative psychology attempted to explain it as follows. When an indirect connection arises in our consciousness, there arise consecutively the three components of association *A*, *M*, and *B*. As is known, if we have a series of ideas, associations are formed not only between the two directly adjacent members of the series, but also between remote members. When such associations are repeated, they become more stable and can finally be sufficient for a direct transition from *A* to *B*. If the necessity of the presence in consciousness of the intermediate link *M* for some reason or other becomes superfluous, then the indirect transition ceases and is replaced by a direct connection *A—B*.

This explanation is quite unacceptable. It is not difficult to see that an important place in this explanation is occupied by the repetition of two connections (*A—M* and *M—B*). But in our experiments the repetition of the connections was of little significance. Usually the subjects read the text two or three times, or, very rarely, four or five times.

Something else must be emphasized even more: the support points cannot be considered as "mediating" components of connection in the sense of intermediate components of an ordinary *association,* i.e., as something in its content *outside* of both its main components. As was said, the support point contains the whole content of the section in a "curtailed" form. For this reason, it is easily replaced by this content itself. It can easily happen that not the support point rises up, as if it were something independent and only outwardly connected with the corresponding text, but that the actual content of this section, to which the support point relates, does. In separating support points during memorizing, we have in mind not the points themselves, but the *meaning* which they represent, the *meaning of the whole* which they replace. Therefore, the fact that the absence of support points from the consciousness of the subjects is most noticeable in delayed reproduction is not at all surprising from this point of view. The *meaning of the whole* which we have in mind in the marking of support points is retained better than its specific, to a certain extent chance, carrier, i.e., the very support point which was separated in the process of memorizing. Therefore, the support point can be forgotten, but what it replaces is reproduced by us.

The relationships which are established between the support points and the content of the text are to a considerable extent similar to how thoughts and their external expression, their verbal formulation, are connected. In reproducing thoughts we recall the meaning of certain propositions and not their verbal formulation. The latter is not, of course, immaterial for reproduction but, in recalling, it still can be subject to considerable changes (replacements of words and expressions) without disturbing the meaning. An exact verbal formulation will be forgotten, but the meaning of what was expressed by it will be retained.

What has been said confronts us with a new question: if the true object of reproduction is the "meaning" of the section and not the support point in itself, and if the recalling of the meaning is not necessarily connected with the reproduction of the support points, why then do these points play a considerable positive role in *memorizing*?

In order to answer this, let us see what is achieved by separating support points. First, due to the separation something of the content of the text (postulates, headings, images) is emphasized in mind and thereby acquires a greater chance of being reproduced. But more important is the fact that the necessity to mark postulates and headings or to separate images which would be the carriers of the content of the section compels us to penetrate deeper into the meaning of the text, aiming at a deeper understanding. It is this that is the main role of separating support points, and herein lies their distinction from the intermediate components of association. The intermediate component of association is usually more familiar to us than both its other components and therefore it makes possible a stronger connection between the other two. The strength of the support point, though, lies not in this, but in how deeply and thoroughly we comprehend the content of a section because of it, i.e., how much it assists the reflective activity carried out in memorizing. The meaningful point of support is the support point for *understanding*.

From this point of view it becomes clear why the support points increase the productivity of reproduction, though absent from our consciousness at the moment of recall. Deepening understanding during memorization, they create a firmer basis for the following reproduction, but *by themselves, in their concrete expression* they have no especially important significance and are not firmly retained in memory. For us it is not the *product* of our activity which is important, i.e., not the support points themselves, but the reflective *activity* necessary for their separation, the broader and deeper understanding of the text which is achieved by separating them.

The separation of support points is a *recoding* of the material, just as its subsequent reproduction is a *decoding,* the restoration of what has been learned with the help of a code created in the process of memorization. All forms of mediation which are used in memorizing are, in essence, codes. Their creation (recoding of the material) greatly facilitates memorization and subsequent reproduction. However, in order that the code composed works best and will be sufficiently reliable, an especially close meaningful connection is needed with that for which it serves as a code. Necessary also are various paths from it to the reproduced material which could be used in decoding. This is achieved to the greatest extent (for memorizing coherent, meaningful material) by those reflective operations which are discussed in this book: by separating meaningful points of support as well as by another, previously mentioned, operation, correlation of what is being memorized with what is already known. These operations are the conditions for a successful recoding and decoding of the memorized material, the real basis for its impression and subsequent reproduction.

The significance of the activity carried out in memorizing, its influence on the effect of memorization, is thus revealed sufficiently. Precisely in this activity, in its characteristics, the true support of memorization must be seen.

3. CONDITIONS FOR MEANINGFUL GROUPING AND FOR THE SEPARATION OF MEANINGFUL POINTS OF SUPPORT

The description of meaningful grouping and of the separation of meaningful support points is only one of the problems in the study of these processes. Other, no less important questions are: how prevalent are these processes, to what extent are they a necessary component of memorizing, are they always observed in those who memorize, and what conditions favor or impede them.

Our data show that even in adults memorization does not always include the formation of meaningful groups and the separation of meaningful points of support. In a number of cases both processes are absent:

> In contrast to all other texts, this time a plan for the text did not arise. There was no breaking up into large, meaningful pieces this time.
>
> I did not apply any methods now. I simply read attentively. Only more slowly than I usually read, when it is not necessary to remember. I did not make a plan.
>
> Today I did not break up the text, although I usually do. I read and immediately memorized.
>
> I read the text simply without any subdivision.
>
> I read attentively three times and did nothing more. I did not divide the text into parts as I usually do.
>
> I did nothing special to memorize. I read once attentively and twice fast. No need to break up this text, to divide it into parts.

Thus, memorization accompanied by breaking up of the text into meaningful groups and separation of meaningful support points is only one of the forms of memorizing. It is often very conspicuous, the result of orientation toward a deeper understanding of the material, which in turn is caused by the presence of a pronounced mnemonic task, but this is, nevertheless, not the only way to memorize. Along with *grouping* memorization, our data reveal two other types of memorizing which, according to statements of the subjects themselves, can be designated as *whole-core* and *mosaic-link* memorizing.

Negatively, both are characterized by an *absence* of breaking up of the text into parts. Positively, the first type (whole-core) is characterized by the fact that the whole material is memorized as a whole, as if "connected by a single thread," as "penetrated by a single core":

> Here everything was welded together. In essence, only one thought was developed, all the rest was only branching and detailing. Therefore, I did not divide the text into any parts but memorized it as a general whole.
>
> It was very easy to memorize, since the whole text was logically strung on one core. Everything connected with the core is memorized by itself. No effort or special methods were needed. I did not break up the text. It was not necessary. I simply read attentively and that was sufficient for memorization.
>
> This time only the main thought had to be understood. It ran through the whole text like a thread. Everything was retained on it. I felt no need to break up the text. The need for points was eliminated.

Exactly the opposite characterizes *mosaic-link memorization*:

> The whole material seemed to disintegrate into parts, even into tiny pieces. Some kind of mosaic came out. I had to memorize each part separately. There was no real connection between them, but then I did not attempt to find one. In order to memorize better I sometimes repeated certain sentences several times. Sometimes I did this in my mind. Sometimes I really reread them. I repeated not only one sentence like this, but several at once "in my mind," and reproduced them one after the other, and sometimes I reread them fleetingly, looked them over quickly.
>
> This text was difficult to memorize. The individual thoughts are not connected with each other. They cannot be grouped at all. Each thought had to be filed separately in memory. And that was not easily achieved. You read a thought and sent it somewhere farther into the brain to have it better impressed there. On account of this one had to linger, stop at separate thoughts, think through their content better. I tried to picture them more clearly, distinctly, and consciously. And so I proceeded from one thought to the other.
>
> Here the thoughts were not unified. One could not form groups so that the whole group of thoughts would unite around one point. Almost every sentence was an independent thought. Logically, however, they were connected like links on a chain. One link went into the other, one held the other. Therefore, the material was logically memorized. This is how I reproduced it: I would express one thought and would remember the following by its meaning.

As can be seen from the statements, the mosaic-link type includes in essence two different forms. In some cases (the first two statements) the text "disintegrated into parts," "very small ones," not at all connected. Therefore, they have to be memorized either by repetition or by a special lingering over each one of them in order to picture their content "more clearly, distinctly, and consciously" and "impress them better on the brain." In other cases (the last of the cited statements) the text also fell into pieces, again very small ones, but connected, logically forming a continuous chain. In the first case the material as a whole resembles a mosaic, in the second, links of a single chain. In both cases, however, no grouping of thoughts which would unite them into larger "pieces" or "parts" can be carried out. In fact, such a unification is in any case not done. This is what is common to the two different forms and what compels us to classify them as the same type.

Under what conditions are these types of memorization observed? When do the subjects resort to forming meaningful groups and separating meaningful support points and when do they use other ways to memorize?

The greatest role among the conditions determining the means of memorization is played by the *characteristics of the material* on the one hand, and by the *task* confronting the subjects on the other.

As for the characteristics of the *material*, proceeding from our data one must distinguish as most significant, first of all, the presence in the text itself of distinct segmentation into more or less extensive meaningful "pieces" with an easily recognizable theme uniting a number of thoughts, grouping them into a relatively independent whole. In those cases in which there are such "pieces" they do not demand special efforts for their formation, no "strains" to replan the material, and the meaningful grouping and separation of meaningful support points is observed more often.

On the contrary, if the text by itself is a single, monolithic, whole, all parts of which are so logically "welded" together that each of them easily pulls the other along, to a certain extent already marks it, and, therefore, makes it unnecessary to memorize each one of them separately, memorization oftener proceeds as whole-core memorization. The subjects easily separate the "core" of the text and without special efforts can connect with it all of the rest of the material.

Finally, if the text by itself, in its content and its structure "disintegrates" easily into small parts which either cannot be grouped at all or, if so, only with difficulty, memorization more often proceeds according to the mosaic-link type.

In what cases are these characteristics of the material observed? Our subjects most often spoke of a monolithic whole, of the presence of a single core on which all the rest is strung, when they had to memorize *explanatory* or *narrative* texts.

Such explanatory texts were those in which only one thought is developed and in which its development does not demand a complex system of proofs, but has easily understandable and logically closely connected postulates.

Those narrative texts were characterized as monolithic-whole in which one event, or rather, individual stages of the same event, were discussed. An historical text encompassing events occurring over a number of years (or, especially, decades or centuries) naturally did not belong to this group. On the contrary, if facts were given referring to one historical event, revealing a certain inherent logic of their own which was easily noticed by the subjects, the whole text was perceived and understood as a single whole which did not demand a further division into parts in order to be memorized. This group includes mostly narrative fiction. In contrast to the above types of texts, some of the *descriptive* texts were most often "disintegrating."

One of the subjects says that in many of them "all thoughts are full-fledged citizens" and "one must memorize almost each one of them separately."

"Here in each sentence you dig out a special thought," says another subject. Here "all thoughts are connected, but to unify them into broader groups is difficult, sometimes completely impossible."

Not all descriptive texts were characterized in this manner. In some of them the possibility of grouping thoughts was not excluded, and sometimes it even relied on ready and customary schemes of description. Nevertheless, this material most often stimulated mosaic-link memorization.

The second feature which essentially determines the type of memorization is the *volume* of the material. The following general principle applies here: *the smaller the volume of the text, the greater the possibility that meaningful grouping will be absent and memorizing will proceed as whole-core or mosaic-link memorizing.*

The *degree of difficulty of the text is an important condition determining the type of memorization*: the more difficult the text, the more often the meaningful grouping and separation of meaningful support points occur:

> After the first reading I wanted to break it up into parts, but immediately abandoned the thought. I thought: What for? Everything is easily memorized without it. It only makes extra work.
>
> The text is very difficult. I would not be able to memorize it without breaking it up into parts. I tried to find a heading for each section. Some of it I formulated into postulates.
>
> I felt that if I did not separate parts I would not be able to memorize anything. This text is very complex. I am not used to such texts [the text was taken from Locke]. I marked a plan of the text. I made a brief summary of the content of each part.
>
> The text is easy, as a whole quite familiar. I received only a little new information. I fixed it separately and the rest did not demand any effort. I simply took into account that here it speaks "about this." I knew that as soon as I would begin to retell I would remember everything. A plan was not needed. This time I did not compose one.

Along with the features of the material, an essential condition for the type of memorization is the *task* confronting the subjects. The following must be noted in reference to it. As our data reveal, of considerable influence on the type of memorizing is whether the subjects are requested either to reproduce the material in a *coherent form* or only to *answer questions* which will be posed by the experimenter. In one series of our experiments we presented both tasks to the subjects: one text was given with the instruction to memorize it in order to retell it in the form of a continuous story; the other was given after telling the subjects, beforehand, that a coherent retelling would not be demanded, but a number of questions would be asked which would have to be answered. In order to weaken the influence of the differences in the material, two texts were used (A and B) and each of them was given for memorizing in both types of tasks: the subjects memorizing text A for coherent retelling received text B for answers to the questions and *vice versa,* those memorizing text A for answers to the questions received text B for coherent retelling. The subjects were twenty college students.

Of the 20 subjects, 14 grouped the text according to meaning in the case of memorization for the purpose of retelling, and 4 in the case of memorization for the purpose of answering questions. The difference is rather significant. Let us cite some of the statements of the subjects:

> If I had known that I would have to retell coherently, I would have composed a plan [after memorizing, all subjects had to give a coherent story independent of what instruction was given before the experiment]. I did not make a plan. Maybe the sequence was remembered involuntarily, but in any case I did not try to separate parts, nor to memorize them consecutively.
>
> Usually I divide the text into pieces and give a heading to each, I separate a definite theme. This time I posed individual questions to myself, in much more detail than the usual pieces. I thought over how to answer these questions. There were many questions, but if I were to break the text up into pieces, then there would be fewer section headings, so that in breaking up into pieces I can retell less, now I do it in more detail. Last time I told in whole pieces, but I think I told less. Now I prepared with questions, posed more questions and, I think, memorized more.
>
> This time I studied separate propositions, even separate sentences, since I thought I would really have to answer questions. There can be many questions and you cannot know beforehand about what they will be. That means you have to be ready for anything and not worry about sequence. Order is needed only for a coherent story, therefore it was not necessary to break the text into large sections. But when one has to memorize the sequence of thoughts, one cannot do without such pieces.

It must be noted that even subjects who did break up the text into parts (with assignment to study so as to be able to answer questions) state that there was a difference in how they broke up the text when assigned to study for coherent retelling.

> At first reading I noticed that the text broke up into several main parts. I marked them, but then I thought: "If I limit myself to only this, it will not be enough; I must go deeper into detail or I will not be able to answer when questions will be asked." Therefore, I did not think at all about these sections when reading for the second time, but transferred all my attention to the details.
>
> It was not so much I that broke up the text into groups as the text itself broke up in the process of reading. But I did not attach great significance to this. If I had known that I would have to retell coherently, I would have given it more attention, would have done it more consciously, would have brought it, so to speak, to the end.

Thus, with the assignment to answer questions, the breaking up of the text is characterized by less activeness, less consciousness, and, in the eyes of the subjects, it no longer has the significance which is given when memorizing with the aim of retelling coherently. Qualitatively it proceeds differently and this deepens still more the difference revealed by quantitative indexes.

The next condition influencing the type of memorization is the *period* for which the material is memorized. In some cases the subjects are given the task to reproduce immediately upon memorizing, in others they are told that they will have to reproduce the text after a more or less protracted period and it should, therefore, be memorized as *firmly* as possible. In the series of experiments in which the subjects (another group of 20 students) were given both tasks (using two different texts and applying the cross-over method) we received the following data: with the assignment of memorizing the text and reproducing it immediately after memorization, meaningful grouping was observed in 13 cases, with the assignment of memorizing for a protracted period, in 17 cases. The increase is not great this time, but it must be taken into account that the number of subjects who broke up the material into parts upon the first instruction was already considerable and, therefore, the possibilities of its growth were considerably narrowed.

Characteristic are the statements of the subjects given when memorizing for a protracted period. From them it follows that even if nothing changed externally in the subjects' breaking up into parts, since they grouped the material in both tasks, nevertheless, the grouping proceeded qualitatively differently: in memorizing for a protracted period, the meaningful groups were more sharply defined and the separation of meaningful support points was done more thoroughly. Let us cite several of the statements.

> What did I do to memorize more firmly [the subject repeats the experimenter's question]? First of all, I broke up the text much more clearly; I thought over the content of each part better and formulated the headings more precisely. This time they did not flicker somehow, as is usually the case, but were quite definite. I selected them specially and checked whether they really fitted the sections.

> I broke up the text in both cases, but today [in memorizing for a protracted period] I did it more consciously. I composed a real plan of the text, even tried to picture it mentally. I felt the need to write it down in order to remember it better.

> Last time [in memorizing with the first instruction] I marked a plan as I always do. Today I gave it more attention. I can say I composed it more efficiently. I clearly comprehended the essence of each section, the main thoughts, and I gave headings to the sections. I repeated these headings to myself. After the last reading I once more repeated the whole plan in my mind, that is, not the plan, but the points which I had marked during reading. It was as if I was going deeper from the headings, as if I developed them more.

Thus, while with respect to quantity the influence of the set towards firmness was comparatively weak, in the *qualitative* sense it was considerable, and this compensated to some extent for the insufficiency of quantitative differences.

The presence or absence of a demand to memorize the material *as fully and as exactly as possible* quite definitely affects meaningful grouping. In those cases in which this demand was presented, that is, the subjects were given the task to achieve maximum fullness and exactness of memorization and to reproduce the material as close to the text as possible, although not necessarily verbatim, meaningful grouping was either not observed at all or was carried out involuntarily and did not have the significance it usually had for the subjects, according to their statements.

Of the 22 subjects participating in the series of experiments in which we demanded memorization of a prose text as close as possible to the original (the experiments were conducted with cross-over of the same material which was memorized without this instruction), only 7 marked a meaningful grouping. Five of them stated that it was a peculiar process as compared to what happens in "ordinary" memorizing. Here are some of these statements.

> In reading, I of course noticed what parts the material consisted of, but this time it was something extraneous, seemingly unrelated to memorizing. I felt that the focus, the main difficulty of memorizing, would not be here.

> In the process of reading, the main sections stood out rather clearly. I did not apply any effort to it. Everything went by itself. In contrast to the preceding experiment [in which the material was memorized without instruction to memorize as close to the original as possible] I did not feel the breaking up as a main support for memorization. Everything was of a preliminary nature. In essence this was only a familiarizing with the material. Later, I had to memorize almost every sentence separately. Therefore, this time it made no sense to divide into large parts. Of course, it helped, but little, and this was not the main thing.

Thus, while the set for firmness of memorization positively influences meaningful grouping, stimulates it, makes it clearer, systematic, and conscious, an assignment to memorize the material fully and exactly has an entirely different effect on the grouping. The frequency of forming meaningful groups decreases considerably in this case, and the actual process of breaking the text into groups (where it is observed) occurs in a changed form and, as in memorizing with the aim of answering questions, no longer plays the role which is so characteristic of it in ordinary memorization.

It is important to note the substantial characteristics of the plans composed to facilitate memorization, as compared with the plans composed without a mnemonic task. This problem was especially investigated by Zinchenko (1948). The experiments designated for the comparison of both plans (the subjects were students) consisted of the following: it was suggested that the subjects compose plans for two texts and tell for which of them it was more difficult. However, after composing the first plan (for the first text), the instruction was changed and it was demanded of the subjects that they compose for the second text a plan which would help to memorize the content of this (second) text, as fully and exactly as possible. Consequently, the second plan was composed with a mnemonic aim. Four texts were used, for each of which different subjects composed two different plans.

As the experiments showed, the two plans differed greatly each time. In the cognitive plans there were many more headings of parts of the text, while in the mnemonic type, many separate propositions and factual data appeared. In the cognitive plans, headings noticeably predominated, while, in the mnemonic types, propositions as well as questions (more than for the cognitive plans) were widely represented. All this indicates that, along with generalization of the content of individual meaningful parts into which the text is mentally broken up for memorization, in the process of mentally composing a plan some special elements of the content are separated which must then by themselves be reproduced, or help to reproduce other elements of the text. All this points to the substantially greater complexity and diversity of activity which is necessary for the composition of mnemonic, as compared to cognitive, plans.

What has been said clearly reveals the dependence of meaningful grouping on many conditions, partly contained in the material itself, partly in the task given to the memorizers. While in some cases the breaking up into groups occupies an important place, is, in fact, used most frequently, is cognitive and serves as a most important support for memorizing, in others it yields predominance to whole-core and mosaic-link memorizing, is observed only occasionally, is carried out involuntarily, and does not play an essential role.

These data made it possible to explain a number of conditions increasing or decreasing the significance of meaningful grouping. These conditions must not be considered to be the only ones or that they fully specify everything that determines the frequency and nature of the formation of sense groups.

4. MEANINGFUL GROUPING AND MEANINGFUL SUPPORT POINTS IN CHILDREN

In order to clarify the part played by meaningful grouping in the memorizing by children, in particular schoolchildren, we used two types of text: Some were easily broken into several subtopics, since the thoughts of each subtopic followed directly one after the other *(meaningfully grouped texts)*. In each text there were 16 thoughts divided into four meaningful groups, four thoughts in each. The other texts were structured so that meaningful grouping was difficult. For this purpose the thoughts of these texts were arranged randomly: after a thought of the first subtopic there came at once a thought of the second group, then of the third, the fourth group and then again the first, then the third, then the second, etc. *(random texts)*. Breaking up into meaningful groups in these texts demanded a mental reconstruction of the text. The total number of thoughts in the text and the number of thoughts in each subtopic were the same here as in the meaningfully grouped texts. All texts were descriptive. Therefore, the disconnected thoughts in the texts of the second type did not make them absurd. They were confused, inconsistent, without system, but not senseless.

The choice of these types of texts was determined by the following considerations. The meaningfully grouped texts had to make it possible to determine the presence or absence of meaningful grouping under conditions of maximally easy realization. The random texts were presented because of the following considerations. As the experiments with adults have shown, more stimulating to grouping (although not always successful) are the difficult, i.e., more confused and, consequently, random texts. Attempts to group the thoughts in these cases occur more often and are more intense. Random texts also make it easier to notice the very process of grouping since, proceeding with greater difficulty, it is less likely to escape the attention of the subjects. Their statements in these cases are more reliable. All this made it necessary to use texts not only of the first, but also of the second type.

In order to avoid the influence of some other differences in the material, we proceeded in the following manner: the text presented to some subjects in a meaningfully grouped form was given to others randomly and *vice versa*. The order of the texts was changed: some subjects were given the meaningfully grouped text first and others the random text first.

The Wolf
(Meaningfully grouped text)

The wolf resembles a large dog. Its coat is long and stiff. Its eyes slant. Its tail hangs down. Wolves live in forests, ravines, and, sometimes, on the steppes. In spring and summer they roam alone or in pairs. In the autumn they live in families. In winter they often run in large packs. The wolf attacks large domestic animals and some wild animals. It also feeds on small animals, even on insects. In summer the wolf finds much food in the forest. In winter it sometimes comes into the villages and kills cattle. Hunting parties struggle with the wolves. They make raids on wolves. Traps and snares are made for catching wolves .The captured wolves are killed.

The Wolf
(Random text)

The wolf resembles a large dog. Wolves live in forests, ravines, and, sometimes, on the steppes. Hunting parties struggle with the wolves. In summer the wolf finds much food in the forest. Its coat is long and stiff. In spring and summer wolves roam alone or in pairs. Traps and snares are made to catch wolves. The wolf attacks large domestic animals and some wild animals. The wolf's eyes slant. In winter the wolves often run in large packs. The wolf also feeds on small animals, even on insects. The captured wolves are killed. In the fall the wolves live in families. The wolf's tail hangs down. The hunters make raids on wolves. In winter wolves sometimes come into the villages and kill cattle.

The Fox
(Meaningfully grouped text)

The fox is the size of a small dog. It has a pointed muzzle. Its tail is long and fluffy. The fox's fur is heavy and red. It lives in the forest. It seldom makes its own burrow. It often lives in the empty burrows of other animals. Sometimes the fox lives in a tree hollow, in piles of stones, or in holes among bushes. The fox feeds on small animals. Sometimes it attacks domestic fowl. The fox knows how to catch fish. It loves to eat pears, plums, or berries. The litter is born at the end of April or the beginning of May. The first four to six weeks after birth they stay in the burrow. The mother brings them their food. When the vixen scents an enemy she carries the young in her mouth to another burrow.

The Fox
(Random text)

The fox is the size of a small dog. The fox feeds on small animals. The young are born at the end of April or the beginning of May. The fox's muzzle is pointed. The fox seldom makes its own burrow. The fox knows how to catch fish. When the vixen scents an enemy she carries the young in her mouth to another place. The fox's tail is long and fluffy. Often the fox lives in the empty burrows of other animals. Sometimes the fox attacks domestic fowl. The first four to six weeks after birth, the young do not leave the burrow. The fox's fur is thick and red. Sometimes the fox lives in a tree hollow, in piles of stones, or in a hole among bushes. The fox loves to eat pears, plums, or berries. The mother brings food to the young in the burrow.

The subjects were schoolchildren of the second, fourth, and sixth grades, 24 each. The experimenter read the text to the second graders, the other children read the material out loud. The texts were read twice with a warning that after each reading they would have to be reproduced. After two reproductions a conversation was conducted with the subjects to clear up a number of questions referring to how the meaningful grouping had proceeded, after which several special assignments were given: to break up the text into groups immediately from memory and after an additional reading of the text.

What were the results of the experiments? The first thing to be established is how often the meaningful grouping was used by schoolchildren in memorizing.

The data of the experiments show a negligible percentage of breaking up into groups in the memorization of both meaningfully grouped and random texts. In the second grade there was not a single case of grouping, in the fourth it was observed in only 17%, in the sixth in 25% of the children. The second graders often expressed complete surprise at the question: "Did you mentally divide the text into parts?" They failed to understand what was asked of them. They often answered with a question: "How does one do that, how do I break it up in my mind? What does that mean?"

The attitude of the fourth graders towards this question was different: they understood it, it caused no difficulties, but the answer to it most often was negative.

The sixth graders, just as the fourth graders, rarely used breaking up, but in contrast to the fourth graders they noted that on other occasions they made use of breaking up. When precisely? When they had to study, "do homework."

Asked why they had not broken up the text in our experiments, they usually answered: "Well, here it is different. We're not studying a lesson. This is a small text, in school they are larger. In order to memorize for school, one has to break up into small sections and the book itself is often broken up like this. It begins with a new line or even separate headings. When it is not there, you yourself often break up the text into parts and then you study each part separately."

It is not difficult to see that such answers signify first of all that the method of memorization used by schoolchildren in learning the school material is not yet considered by them to be a method which it is expedient to apply under other conditions too, when it is not necessary "to do homework." In their consciousness it has a limited use.

A possible explanation is that usually the teachers instructing them in the methods for better memorization point to the significance of breaking up the material. They most often acquaint their pupils with the positive role of breaking up texts. The pupils themselves speak of it ("the teacher said it was better to do it this way"). But such directions are given by the teachers in regard to *study material* and evidently the pupils use them only under these conditions.

The second reason why the pupils did not break up the text is attributed by them to the insignificant volume of the text. For them this is closely connected with another circumstance: by breaking into parts they study each part separately. The breaking up plays, consequently, a special role and stands out in a different way than for the adults. Adults use it to separate in each part what is basic, what characterizes it, to deepen thereby *understanding,* to achieve its greater clarity, to systematize the material, and on this basis to facilitate memorization. Therefore, in adults the breaking up into parts proceeds "in the mind," and is marked only *mentally*. In contrast, in schoolchildren it serves as a means to decrease the volume of what must be memorized in each period of time. Therefore, for them it is a *real* breaking up into parts connected with the memorization of each part separately. While the adults by breaking up into parts do not let slip from consciousness each preceding part already separated by them and try maximally to connect "in the mind" the support points of all separated parts, the schoolchildren, on the contrary, maximally digress from all other parts of the text except the one which they are studying at any given segment of time.

The fact that, as the schoolchildren themselves note, this breaking up of the text relies to a considerable extent on such characteristics of the text as the presence of paragraphs and, most important, headings for each "little section" is also explained by its realness.

It is important to add that in our experiments the breaking up into parts (in the fourth and sixth grades) occurred more often when meaningfully grouped texts were memorized.

Again, this noticeably distinguishes the schoolchildren from the adults. The latter, of course, also readily use grouping if it "suggests itself" due to the characteristics of the material. But the formation of sense groups is often also caused by the difficulty of the material, its inconsistency, and confusion. In these cases the adults pay special attention to meaningful grouping, trying by all means to put the text in order, to break it into sensible parts, even if by way of reconstruction. The determining factor for the adults is the *significance* of meaningful grouping and not its ease. This is not observed in schoolchildren.

The basis for this difference is that the formation of meaningful groups is less intentional in schoolchildren than in adults. The adults break up the text into parts as the result of a consciously set aim, which they often achieve after considerable persistence. The schoolchildren most often do not set such a conscious aim for themselves and grouping for them proceeds more passively, as the result of the characteristics of the material itself. Therefore, if the characteristics of the text are such that it easily falls into parts, sense groups are formed.

It should also be noted that in our experiments in the majority of cases (70% of those who broke up the text) the schoolchildren marked the sections of the text not during memorizing (reading) but before beginning to reproduce. This was done to facilitate reproduction. The breaking up which was done in these cases ("in the mind") was a means of *recalling* what had been read rather than of *memorizing* it.

This indicates one of the essential characteristics of the development of memory, the fact that the change in and development of new and more perfect methods of memorizing often begin with recalling. *The method of memorizing is at first a means of reproduction.* Here it arises for the first time and only later is it used as a means of memorizing the material.

Recalling is, to a much greater extent than memorization, connected with evaluation, with the possibility of control, with the consciousness of success or failure. In memorizing we often cannot determine how successfully we have memorized, since checking will come after a more or less protracted period. But in recalling we see at once the result of reproduction, directly experience the difficulties of recalling. Therefore, to a much greater extent we seek ways to facilitate the execution of our task in recalling than in memorizing. Here new methods originate. Since much of what facilitates *recalling* is especially effective if it is carried out during *memorizing*, it is natural that a number of methods developed during reproduction are transferred to memorization.

In order to recall more fully and make reproduction more consistent, before retelling, the pupils remember the basic sections of the text "from memory." Such breaking up, however, is not always successful. It is not always possible to accomplish it completely. Its very realization sometimes demands considerable effort because the material which has to be broken up has already been removed. Naturally, the necessity of breaking up the text arises when it is seen, at the moment of *memorization. The method induced by the need to reproduce becomes the means for memorizing the material.*

Let us further describe the characteristics of sense grouping in schoolchildren.

The insignificance of sense grouping in schoolchildren raises the question: *did they notice the difference between the texts given them to memorize*? Did they notice the sequence in one and the confusion in the other?

Our experiments show that among second graders not a single one noticed, during reading, that the texts differed in the sequence of exposition. When asked if they noticed any difference between the stories, they usually answered positively but mentioned other differences, not in their construction but in *content:* "There the story is about a fox and here about a wolf." "There it says when the fox's young are born and this is not said about wolves." "In the first it says that the wolf resembles a large dog, and the fox is like a small dog." "The fox's tail is thick, while the wolf's tail hangs down."

The differences in the structure of the texts were mentioned either not at all or only insufficiently, even when we asked direct, sometimes leading questions: "Were the stories constructed alike? Didn't everything go in order in one story while it was broken up, mixed, and confused in the other?"

The second graders most often answered without hesitation: "Everything was in order. It was the same in both cases."

In two cases the answer was: "In both cases it was broken up." Asked to point out what was broken up, the students' answers were unclear. One of the subjects answered: "You must say that wolves go in large packs and then you must say something else about that." This subject had received the random version of the wolf text and he possibly noted the inconsistency in the text. The second subject gave this answer about the same text: "The statement about the struggle of hunting parties with wolves was broken up." His answer to the question of what was broken up was: "I don't remember any more." Something inconsistent was caught but the inconsistency was not clearly realized.

One of the subjects considered the meaningfully grouped text "mixed up." To the question: "What was mixed up?" he gave a quite senseless answer: "The hunters hunt wolves, they set up traps and snares. They catch the wolves and then kill them. The wolves attack wild animals and domestic animals, they even eat insects. The wolf goes alone or in pairs. In winter they live as a family." To the second question: "Then what is mixed up?" the subject replied in a similar manner: "How the hunters hunt the wolves." It is quite clear that the subject actually had not caught any disconnectedness.

While not noticing the inconsistency of the text in the process of *memorizing,* 14 out of 24 second graders noticed it later when assigned to break up the texts into parts. This assignment was especially difficult when random texts were used. The pupils often were completely unable to solve the problem and completed it only with considerable help from the experimenter. On his part, a number of leading questions and pointers had to be given, which after a while and with great difficulty made it possible for the pupils to unite into separate groups what was scattered in the text.

The result of this complex and difficult work was that the pupils realized the inconsistency of the exposition in the ungrouped text and understood its differences from the grouped text. When asked after breaking up both texts whether they noticed now how the stories differed, the majority of the second graders this time gave a correct answer either immediately or after a leading question. Thus, only after overcoming considerable difficulties in the grouping of scattered sentences did the pupils for the first time discover that the text was scattered.

The realization of the inconsistency came in the process of activity directed towards an ordering of the text, as a result of active attempts to mark a plan of the material.

It should be noted in passing that a considerable number of second graders, even after such attempts, could not give an account of the differences between the texts. These pupils repeated their former answer, i.e., continued to maintain that both texts were identical, or refused to answer the question, saying only: "I don't know."

In contrast to the second graders, in some cases the fourth graders noticed the difference in the texts in the process of memorization, that is, before breaking up the text. In contrast to the second graders, 25% of the fouth graders noticed differences between the texts. Most of these used meaningful grouping as a means for memorizing. In a few cases, however, the inconsistency of the "scattered" text was noted even by those pupils who did not use grouping.

As for the other fourth graders, again, the majority noticed the difference in the texts only when they realized the difficulty of breaking up the random text. Realization of its inconsistency came only as the result of extensive work on the text.

Of all the fourth graders two could not notice the differences between the texts at all and continued to maintain that both texts were equally "in order."

Half of the sixth graders noticed the inconsistency of the "scattered" text at once. The other half were able to notice the difference between the texts only in the process of working at them, although in contrast to the fourth graders, here the realization of the difference usually came earlier, when they attempted to mark the first division.

Although the difference between the texts *in the sequence of exposition* was insufficiently noticed by the schoolchildren, a considerable number of pupils of all grades recognized it by the *difficulty of memorizing* it which, undoubtedly, was connected with the differences in the structure of the texts. The answers to our question: "Was it equally difficult or easy to memorize both texts, or was one of them more difficult to memorize?" are presented in Table 6.2.

As can be seen from these data, most often the ungrouped text seemed more difficult. The difference between the number of cases in which it was evaluated as being more difficult and the cases of the opposite evaluation was considerable. It must be noted that these evaluations were given by the subjects immediately after reproduction of the texts, before the discussion about breaking up the material into parts.

What was the cause of the difference in the difficulty of memorizing? In only a very few cases did the subjects themselves point to the difference in the structure of the texts:

> It is more difficult about the wolf because it talks about one thing and then about another. For example, they catch them in snares and then several sentences later that raids are made. They picture the appearance and then much later that the tail hangs down, and somewhere before this that the eyes are slanting, and somewhere else about the fur [sixth grader].
>
> About the wolf it is easier. Here [about the fox] it is very scattered; at first a description and then it comes again at the end [sixth grader].
>
> About the fox it is easier. About the wolf first what he feeds on, then about something else, then again what he feeds on. In fall, spring, summer—everything is also broken up [sixth grader].

TABLE 6.2. Evaluation of the Relative Difficulty of Meaningfully Arranged and Random Texts by Schoolchildren (in percent of children in each grade)

Subjects	Meaningfully arranged text is more difficult	Random text is more difficult	Both texts are of equal difficulty
2nd graders	17	50	33
4th graders	25	58	17
6th graders	17	58	25

Such answers were given only by 25% of the sixth graders. But in the great majority of cases, other bases for the differences in difficulty were given. Some referred to the content of the texts. Here are some of these answers.

> About the fox it is more difficult. It tells where it lives, and how it lives [second grader].
>
> It is easier about the fox. Because it tells about the young, how the fox lives and, there, how the wolves are killed [fourth grader].
>
> It is easier about the wolf. There it says only where it lives, what it does, and here [about the fox] how she takes care of the young, how upon approach of an enemy she carries away the young for protection [fourth grader].
>
> It is more difficult about the wolf. Because you forget what is in spring, what in summer, when they go alone and when they go in pairs [fourth grader].
>
> It is easier about the wolf. Less description of the wolf: what kind of tail, what kind of eyes [sixth grader].
>
> It is more difficult about the fox, because there it tells also about the young [sixth grader].

To the question why "this" (as pointed out by the subjects) was more difficult to memorize, usually no explanation was given. In a few cases, the basis for the differences in the difficulty of memorization was said to be the difference in the amount of material, although actually both texts were completely identical in this respect. Sometimes it was noted that in one text "the words were simpler," "it is more simply told," "all sentences were easy." In many cases the subjects could not explain at all why one or the other text seemed more difficult for them to memorize. Usually they either said simply: "I don't know," or gave explanations such as:

"It is more difficult about the wolf because I have not memorized it well" [second grader].

"It is harder to memorize" [fourth grader].

"It is more quickly forgotten" [sixth grader].

Instead of giving *reasons,* they referred to the *result* of the difficulty of the text. From these statements it is clear that, not being capable of realizing the cause of the difficulty of memorizing a random text, many schoolchildren, nevertheless, felt a difference between the texts and experienced difficulties in memorizing the random texts.

TABLE 6.3. Percentage of Reproduced Meaningful Units of Text

	After first reading		After second reading		Ratio of meaningfully arranged to random text	
Subjects	meaningfully arranged text	random text	meaningfully arranged text	random text	after first reading	after second reading
2nd graders	51.0	51.6	67.7	59.4	98.8	114.0
4th graders	58.3	57.3	78.6	70.3	101.7	111.8
6th graders	59.9	59.4	76.0	76.5	100.8	99.3

To what extent did objective differences in memorizing correspond to these subjective difficulties? The answer is presented in Table 6.3.

From the table it can be seen that after the first reading there was no difference in the reproduction of meaningfully grouped and random texts. The reproduction indexes are in both cases almost identical.

A somewhat different result is observed after the second reading. In this case, the pupils of the second and fourth grades recalled the random texts somewhat less well than the meaningfully grouped one; for the sixth grade the results were, however, again identical.

Thus, the objective difference in memorization corresponded to the subjective difficulty only for the younger schoolchildren and then only after the second reading.

We turn now to other questions important for the characterization of meaningful grouping: to what extent did the difference in the construction of the texts affect *reproduction*? How did grouping and scattering influence the sequence of thought reproduction? In other words, to what extent was a *factual grouping* observed in the recalling of the texts? But if the meaningful groups in the text were not noticed, were not the thoughts of the same groups united in reproduction, unnoticed by the subjects themselves?

In order to answer this we turn to a description of the transitions from one reproduced thought to another. In a most general form all these transitions can be divided into two categories: those based on sense relations (*coherent*) and those not based on sense connections (*incoherent*). In the first case, we are dealing with transitions within the same sense group and in the second case, with transitions going beyond the limits of one sense group (the transition from a thought of one group to a thought of another group).

For an answer to these questions it is important to find the number of coherent transitions, especially in the reproduction of random texts. Then we will find out to what extent the pupils, in reproducing the random texts, put them in order and made them more sequential. The data characterizing the percentage of coherent transitions in the reproduction of random texts are presented in Table 6.4.

From the table it can be seen that the percentage of coherent transitions is quite large. With fourth and sixth graders it increases; from youngest to oldest schoolchildren there is a great difference in the ratio of the percentages

TABLE 6.4. Percentage of Coherent Transitions in the Reproduction of Random Texts

Subjects	After first reading	After second reading
2nd graders	33.3	25.7
4th graders	35.4	30.7
6th graders	45.1	44.8

of transitions after one or two readings. The pupils of the second and fourth grades discovered after the second reading a smaller number of their transitions than after initial familiarization with the text. Most probably a considerable role in this case was played by the set for a more exact reproduction, which became stronger after the first familiarization with the text. As for the sixth-grade pupils, no decrease in the percent of coherent transitions is observed. The influence of the set for exactness was compensated by a marked tendency to group the material, and to order the sequence of the exposition. This tendency, we think, compensated for the difference in memorizing which was noticed above; it made it possible for the older pupils, in contrast to the second and fourth graders, to memorize the texts with equal productivity after both readings in spite of the difference in the subjectively experienced difficulty of these texts.

It is important to note that the relatively large number of coherent transitions for the sixth graders, as compared to the younger pupils, was found in pupils who noticed the breaking up into parts as well as in those who did not notice it. *Thus, in spite of the fact that a conscious unification of sentences related in meaning was not made in memorizing, it was done during reproduction.* The sixth-grade pupils did this more often, the fourth- and, especially, the second-grade pupils less often. For all categories of subjects, however, the break between the actions in memorizing and in reproducing is characteristic. During memorizing many subjects do not make sense groups, while in reproduction, although in a hidden, unrealized form, it is done to a considerable extent. This is fully confirmed by the data on the transitions in reproducing grouped texts. The percentage of coherent transitions in reproducing these texts is shown in Table 6.5.

This time the difference between the grades is less pronounced than in the reproduction of random texts. But the total number of coherent transitions is quite large, especially if one takes into account that almost 20% of all transitions inevitably had to be incoherent, since the subjects had to proceed from one sense group to the other (after finishing each of them). If the appropriate correction is introduced, then these percentages will be still higher (Table 6.6).

One would think that such a high percentage of coherent transitions in reproducing grouped texts is explained simply by the effect of proximity,

TABLE 6.5. Percentage of Coherent Transitions in the Reproduction of Meaningfully Arranged Texts

Subjects	After first reading	After second reading
2nd graders	55.6	65.8
4th graders	60.0	69.7
6th graders	59.2	69.2

since all thoughts connected by sense relations and entering the same sense group are adjacent to each other in these texts. Such an assumption would be incorrect. Without denying the role of proximity, it must be admitted that in this case it had no substantial significance. This is shown by the role of proximity in random texts, in which it should be especially great.

The data on the percentage of transitions based on *immediate* proximity in reproducing random texts are in Table 6.7.

As can be seen from these data, transitions based on immediate proximity comprise a very limited percentage of the total number of transitions, which does not increase even after second reading, in spite of the fact that the subjects themselves notice in this reading the set for a more exact memorizing of the text.

Within the framework of the above questions it is very important to compare Table 6.7 with the percentage of transitions in proximity during reproduction of grouped texts (Table 6.8).

The values obtained in these cases considerably exceed the preceding ones. The increase of transitions due to proximity observed in the older pupils is also characteristic. Both findings can only be explained by the fact that in the grouped texts the proximity was combined with the closeness of

TABLE 6.6. Percentage of Coherent Transitions in the Reproduction of Meaningfully Arranged Texts, Corrected for Transitions between Meaningful Groups

Subjects	After first reading	After second reading
2nd graders	74.4	87.7
4th graders	80.0	92.9
6th graders	78.1	92.3

TABLE 6.7. Percentage of Adjacent Transitions in the Reproduction of Random Texts

Subjects	After first reading	After second reading
2nd graders	14.8	15.8
4th graders	16.3	14.5
6th graders	13.9	12.7

TABLE 6.8. Percentage of Adjacent Transitions in the Reproduction of Meaningfully Arranged Texts

Subjects	After first reading	After second reading
2nd graders	33.7	42.7
4th graders	33.0	62.6
6th graders	48.5	63.2

meaning and found in it its support. This support was so great that it sharply raised the percent of transitions due to proximity. This was especially noticeable in the older pupils, in whom sense relations were the basis for reproduction more than in the lower grades. Consequently, *not the proximity itself* was the basis for the transition from one of the adjacent thoughts to the other, but the *sense connection between adjacent thoughts.* Proximity acted only to the extent that this connection was present. Where such a connection was absent (in random texts), the percentage of transitions due to proximity was negligible. Where sense connections (between adjacent thoughts) were present, proximity came into its own and the number of transitions from one of the adjacent thoughts to the other increased greatly.

What has been said once more confirms that *in the process of reproduction* a sense grouping, although partial, not encompassing all thoughts of each group, was in fact made, although often the subjects themselves did not realize it at all. When asked how they recalled the text, whether they tried to recall everything in the order of the text or whether they tried to say sentences in meaningful order, a majority of the subjects gave one of the following answers: "I spoke as it was remembered," or "I tried to recall in the order in which the sentence came in the story." In only a few cases did the subjects reproduce using the sense proximity of the sentences.

A partial and unconscious grouping of thoughts in reproduction confronts us with a very important question: *to what extent were our subjects able to break up the text into parts when it was specially asked of them?*

As was mentioned above, this assignment was usually made after a conversation which was aimed at finding out how memorization and reproduction proceeded. At first we suggested breaking up the material *from memory* without looking at the text and then, whether they had been able to complete this assignment or not, the same assignment was given *working with the text* and, consequently, reading it again. We usually began with the text already grouped as the easier one for grouping.

What were the results of these assignments? Basically, one can note here the following stages. The *initial,* or zero, stage is the complete inability to break up the text into parts, not only from memory but also with the text present. Almost all these cases were observed among second graders. Let us cite some examples:

Subject L. after being asked to break up the story "The Wolf" into parts read the whole text in sequence. After the first part had been read, i.e., the first four sentences, he calmly read the second part without any pause. The experimenter stopped him and said:

> "Was everything you read about the same thing?"
> "No, about different things, but all about the wolf."
> "Is it possible to break up what you have read into some parts to show that in one it speaks about one thing and in the other about something else?"

[The subject is silent.]

"Here everything that you read can be divided into two parts. Read once more and tell me into what parts."

[He reads but cannot point out how to break up the text.]

[The experimenter himself reads the first four sentences and says:]

"This is the first part. Here it speaks about one thing. What about?"

[The subject reproduces all sentences in order.]

"Well, can one somehow unite them, make it shorter, think up a general heading for them?"

"Yes, one can."

"How?"

"The wolf has slanting eyes."

"But that does not fit the other sentences where it says what the wolf resembles, what fur it has. Could one name the part: what does the wolf look like?"

"One can. The wolf is gray (?)."

It is evident that the subject cannot understand what is demanded of him. The same thing is repeated with the following part. At first the subject strenuously tries to reproduce the whole of this part, and to the question of how to make it shorter or what heading to think up for all the sentences he answers: "I don't know."

Similarly, asked how one can break up the text ("The Fox"), i.e., of what parts it consists, subject S. says: "The foxes go into the burrows of others." There follows a new explanation of the task, but the subject remains silent. The experimenter then reads the first part and says:

"Now this is the first part. Here it does not speak about what is told later about the fox. How can one name this part, what heading can one give all these sentences?"

"The fox resembles a small dog (!)."

"But that does not fit the other sentences. What heading can one give that would fit all four sentences?"

"The fox goes into the burrows of others and does not let anyone in."

It is evident that the subject cannot form a single sense group, and asked to think of a heading he answers with a sentence that does not refer to the first part, and, like subject L., who added that "the wolf is gray," S. lets his imagination work: "it does not let anyone in."

Such a complete lack of understanding when asked to break up the text into parts and inability to give a heading to the part marked by the experimenter was observed in 17% of the second-grade pupils. Among fourth graders this occurred in only one out of 24 (4%) and in the sixth grade in none of the pupils.

The *next stage* in solving the problem of breaking the text into parts has the following characteristics: the subjects can now point out the borders of the sections, although not always correctly, but they cannot unify the sentences of the same section with a single generalizing heading. In reading the text with the aim of breaking it up, they stop after each section, saying:

"It ends here," but asked to tell what heading this part can be given, they answer: "I don't know." The result of this inability to think up a heading is that the task of pointing out the parts of the text is fulfilled only if the text is reread. However, at this stage the subjects are unable to point out parts of the text *from memory*. Therefore, the subjects usually refuse to break up the text from memory.

It is not possible to tell with assurance whether this refusal is explained by the fact that the pupils cannot denote each part, although they separate the parts themselves, or whether breaking up into parts is altogether absent here. It would be incorrect to rely fully on the statements of the schoolchildren. It must be noted, however, that these statements mainly confirm the second assumption, i.e., they indicate that breaking up from memory is not accomplished at all.

How does breaking up proceed when the text is before them? Is it done at the moment of transition from each finished part to the next, or do both factors, the breaking up and the transition to the next part, fail to coincide?

Our data show that most often the subjects "jump" over the transition without noticing it. That the preceding part has ended is usually realized by them belatedly, when they have read not only the first, but also subsequent sentences of the following part. Here they realize, stop, sometimes look over what had been read again, and only then, most often with joyful amazement, say: "No, here it is about something else."

In what direction do *further changes in the breaking up into parts* proceed during its transition to the following, *higher* stages?

These changes are:

1. The breaking up becomes more correct.
2. There appears and develops the capability of giving a heading to each part.
3. Breaking up is accomplished not only in the presence of but also in the absence of the text, i.e., it is accomplished from memory.
4. The moment of breaking up, of the separating of a part, comes ever closer to the transition to the new part: the subjects notice the transition at once, in reading the first sentence of the next part.

Let us discuss the first two changes. What deviations from the correct breaking up are observed at the beginning and what does the subsequent transition to a more correct breaking up involve?

The main question here is: is the first breaking up a *larger one,* as a result of which in one part is included what really belongs to different parts or, on the contrary, is it *more detailed,* dividing what belongs to the same part?

The experimental data give reason to accept the second possibility. As a general rule, the incorrect breaking up by the schoolchildren consisted of uniting only some sentences of the same section; in some cases individual sentences became an independent section.

Subject K. (fourth grade), for example, breaks up "The Wolf" in the following manner: 1) how it looks (K. has in mind the first four sentences speaking of the appearance of the wolf); 2) the home of the wolf (5th sentence); 3) where it roams (6th–8th sentences); 4) food of the wolf (9th–11th sentences); 5) what it does in winter (12th sentence); 6) who struggles with the wolves (13th sentence); 7) what they are doing (14th–15th sentences); 8) what do hunters do to the wolves (16th sentence).

Some sentence (5, 12, 13, 16) are marked here as independent sections in spite of the fact that in content they are very close to the other adjacent sentences, e.g., the 16th sentence, which received a special heading, is similar to sentences 14 and 15.

The fourth grader V. breaks up the same text in this manner: 1) of what shape is the wolf (1st sentence); 2) what kind of appearance and eyes does it have (2nd–4th sentences); 3) where does it live (5th sentence); 4) how does it live in summer, spring, fall, and winter (6th–8th sentences); 5) whom does it attack (9th sentence); 6) on what does it feed in summer and winter (10th and 11th sentences); 7) what does it do in the village (12th sentence); 8) what is done with wolves (13th–16th sentences).

Again in this breaking up some sentences (1, 5, 9, 12) are considered as independent sections, as a result of which the number of sections increases.

The second grader Ch. breaks up the same text in the following manner: 1) outer appearance of the wolf (1st–4th); 2) where the wolves live (5th); 3) when do they roam and where (6th); 4) where do they live in the fall (7th); 5) what do they do in winter (8th); 6) whom does it attack (9th); 7) food of the wolf (10th–11th); 8) where does it go in winter (12th); 9) who struggles with wolves (13th); 10) what do the hunters do (14th–15th); 11) how do they kill wolves (16th).

Here half of all sentences were placed in independent sections and instead of four, eleven sections are named.

Similar observations were made in the breaking up of "The Fox". It is characteristic that the tendency toward a detailed division, although not in such a clear form, was also seen in some sixth graders. Subject B., for example, breaks up "The Wolf" in this manner: 1) what appearance does it have (1st, 2nd, and 4th); 2) where does it live (5th); 3) what is it like in spring, summer, and fall (6th–7th); 4) what does it do in winter (8th); 5) what does it eat (9th–12th); 6) what struggle is carried on with wolves (13th–16th).

Again, two sentences (5th and 8th) become independent sections. The same was observed in the other sixth graders.

Thus, great fragmentation of sections, which sometimes include only one sentence, is characteristic of the initial breaking up of the text into parts by schoolchildren. Their main difficulty is not the *breaking up* of the text but the *uniting* of its parts, the grouping of them. They are often not capable of seeing the general. Sentences similar in content seem different to them, appear not to be united. Even to a direct question of whether or not it is possible to unite some sentences they very often answer negatively.

The second grader Ch., for example, to the question: "Can't one unite the 6th, 7th, and 8th sentences of 'The Wolf'?" ("In spring and summer the wolves roam alone or in pairs. In fall they live as a family. In winter they run in great packs.") answered: "No, it can't be done." Subject S. (same grade) negates the possibility of uniting sentences 11 and 12 ("The wolf feeds on small animals, even insects. In summer it finds much food in the forest."): "They can't be united since they are not similar." Similar cases were observed among fourth graders.

The second question for special consideration concerns the *ability to think up a heading* for a part. How does this ability develop?

The *initial* (zero) stage, when the ability is absent, is characterized by the pupils' feeling the similarity of some sentences of the text to each other, but inability to think up a common heading for them. To the question of whether these sentences can be united they answer affirmatively. But asked to think of a heading they are silent for a long time and then more or less decisively refuse to do so.

This inability to find a heading was observed either with respect to *all* similar sentences, or only with respect to *some* of them (other sentences in these cases were combined more or less satisfactorily). Cases of the first kind were observed only in second graders (2 out of 24), those of the second kind even in the fourth graders.

What were the typical errors in the *choice of headings* when they were obtained? Our data revealed two kinds of errors. In some cases the heading was taken from only one sentence of the section, but was referred by the pupils to the whole section (*narrowed heading*). The second grader M., for example, gave the first four sentences of "The Wolf" the heading "What does the wolf resemble," although earlier he himself had correctly pointed out the borders of the first section and had said that "here it is about one thing." When the experimenter remarked that in the 2nd, 3rd, and 4th sentences it did not speak about "what the wolf resembled," M. was silent at first then, after being prompted by "Well, what do you think, does your heading fit or not?" he said "It fits."

These cases were comparatively rare. More often the second kind of error was observed, *summation headings*. In these cases the subjects tried to include in the heading everything in the section and did not point out what was *common* for all sentences, but simply enumarated what was in each sentence separately. The second grader T., for example, gave the last four sentences of "The Wolf" the heading: "Who is fighting the wolves, what do they do, and how do they kill wolves."

Very often this type of heading was observed in the grouping of thoughts in *random* text. Usually it was done in this manner: the subject read the text and noted which sentences could be united into one section with those read earlier and with which ones; and then he was asked to give a heading for these sentences. As an example of the summarizing headings observed in these cases we cite the data from the experiment with the second grader Shch.

After reading the 5th sentence (The wolf's coat is long and stiff."), Shch. answers the experimenter's question "Can one unite this with some sentences already read?" correctly with "Yes, one can, with the first one."

"What heading can you think up for both of them?"

"What the wolf resembles and what coat it has."

"Can it be made shorter?"

"No, it can't."

Reading on and coming to the 8th sentence ("The wolf's eyes are slanting.") the subject stops by himself and says: "This goes there to the preceding sentences, what it resembles and what kind of coat it has."

"What heading can one give then to all three sentences together?"

"What the wolf resembles, what coat it has and what eyes?"

The same happens when the subject reads the last sentence of the section ("The wolf's tail hangs down."). The heading which he gives the whole section is: "What the wolf resembles, what coat it has, what kind of eyes and tail."

The experimenter's comment that this is a long heading has no effect. The subject is not able to find a *generalized* heading.

Thus, while in the first case the content of only one sentence is used as a heading for a section and only part of the whole substitutes for it, in the second case, the general is replaced by a simple sum of its parts; a mechanical "sticking together" of sentences is produced.

Both types of errors were observed not only among second graders, but also (though to a lesser extent) among fourth graders. The great majority of pupils in whom these errors were observed gladly accepted the heading given by the experimenter. A few second graders, however, did not accept our suggested headings.

Let us summarize what was obtained in the experiment with the schoolchildren:

1. Conscious grouping of the text or its breaking up into parts was not observed at all in second graders and rather rarely in fourth and sixth graders.

2. However, in memorizing homework the pupils of the higher grades *do* break it up into parts. But they do not use it as a general method also useful for other cases of memorization.

3. The breaking up into parts used in memorizing school material is not

a *mental* separation of parts with the aim of marking the logical core of the text. It is a means of organizing what is to be memorized and consists of separating sections which have to be memorized sequentially. Its main task is to mark the order of memorizing individual parts and to establish the volume of what must be memorized at one time.

4. When mental breaking up does occur it is most often observed in the memorization of structured (grouped) texts, where it is more easily done. This is connected with the direct, unpremeditated, and more passive nature of grouping in schoolchildren than in adults.

5. *Recalling* is more often accompanied by meaningful grouping than *memorizing,* because the necessity of recalling to a greater extent induces an active searching for a method that will facilitate this process. The basis for this is the direct perception of the results of recalling while the productivity of memorizing is not always immediately established.

6. The result of insufficient utilization of sense grouping is that the difference between texts differently structured is unsatisfactorily perceived by the pupils: only a small number of pupils notice it independently; it is mainly noticed in carrying out a special assignment, e.g., when asked to break up the text into parts.

7. Though they do not notice structural differences between the texts, the pupils do notice the different degrees of difficulty of these texts: the structured texts are more often evaluated as being easier. The cause of the ease or difficulty of the texts is not realized by the schoolchildren.

8. While not grouping the material consciously, the pupils of all grades reproduce a considerable percentage of coherent transitions between thoughts, proceeding from one to the other on the basis of *meaning, topical proximity*. Proximity as a condition of reproduction plays an insignificant role here. More significant is its role only where it is combined with similarity in meaning. Thus, while not grouping the material consciously, the pupils of all grades do group it, even if only partially, unawares.

9. An intentional process carried out in response to a special assignment, breaking up into parts, is not accomplished by some second graders at all. In the fourth grade a complete inability to group the material is noticed in only a few cases; in the sixth grade it is not observed at all.

10. Breaking up of text by memory proceeds with considerably greater difficulty than when the material is before them.

11. In the early stages of the development of the ability to group, transitions are not noticed by the pupils during reading but, usually, only later.

12. Breaking up into parts is at first characterized by a great deal of detail; even some individual sentences are separated as independent parts.

For sentences similar in content the pupils often do not see anything in common.

13. At the early stages of development of this ability, typical errors are made in the use of a part instead of the whole (narrowed heading) and with the use of simple summing up of the parts (summarizing heading).

14. Not being able to find a heading independently, the pupils at once and with great joy accept the correct headings proposed by the experimenter.

What does all this mean? First of all there is a *considerable divergence between what is given in a conscious form and what is accomplished unconsciously.* As a conscious process, meaningful grouping was altogether absent in second graders and in the higher (4th and 6th) grades it was observed in only a small number of pupils. More often, and then only in the fourth and sixth grades, structural differences between the texts are realized. Independently, in the process of reading, they are noticed only by half of the sixth graders and not at all by the second graders. The relative difficulties of the texts (structured and random) are perceived by a considerable number of pupils of all grades, but the cause of the differences in difficulty (presence or absence of structure) is not realized. Thus, on a *conscious* level sense grouping itself as well as structural differences between the texts are not sufficiently represented. At the same time in an *unconscious* form, grouping by content, even if not encompassing all sentences of a section, is rather widespread: coherent, meaningful transitions from one thought to another are observed in a considerable number of cases—even in memorizing random texts; mere proximity plays an insignificant role. The pupil does not see the lack of structure of the text though in reproducing a text he in fact reconstructs it. *Before becoming a conscious process, the meaningful grouping, even if partially, proceeds, consequently, in an unconscious form.* The pupils group the thoughts before they notice the absence of a structure in the texts.

The second result of our data is that *the divergence is no less between what pupils do and what they can accomplish.* In a conscious form the grouping of thoughts, as was said, is insufficiently represented. However, when asked *specifically* to break up the material into parts, the grouping is accomplished by a large number of pupils, including second graders. In memorizing random texts, it is done less often than when memorizing a grouped text, but the special assignment to break up the text is performed in both cases equally well.

The same divergence between the possible and the actual is indicated by the fact that in starting to *reproduce* the pupils often carry out a meaningful grouping; but in *memorizing* the text they do not consciously form sense groups.

In the same manner, *in the process of school work* the breaking up into parts is done in the higher grades, but in our experiments the schoolchildren did not use it. The same must be said about the selection of headings: as a special assignment selection is carried out in some way even by many second graders, during free memorization; however, it is absent even from a considerable number of sixth graders. Thus, *the possibilities of sense grouping* are considerably wider than their *actual realization.* This means that, *though accessible to the schoolchildren, sense grouping has not as yet become a mode of memorization. It is accomplished as a special action, rather than as a part of some other, more complex intellectual activity.* It is not included in another activity but represents an *independent,* relatively complete action. It is not an aim *in itself* but a means of accomplishing the task of breaking up the material into sense groups. It is not yet the *means* of accomplishing another task—that of memorizing the material. Therefore, a mnemonic orientation alone is not sufficient for its accomplishment. To be accomplished, special conditions are needed, first of all, an *assignment* corresponding to it and *directed towards it.*

This means that sense grouping has not yet become a *habit,* a *firmly established action.* Not only second graders, but also the fourth and sixth graders do not accomplish it at once but, as our observations show, they think over the breaking up into parts, sometimes for a long time. The sense grouping of a random text is accomplished with especially great difficulty and demands the help of the experimenter, even for many of the older schoolchildren.

The results of the breaking up into parts are often inadequate. The number of sections is considerable; some sentences are considered to be independent sections. Therefore, there are no clear boundaries of meaning or direct transitions from one to the other sense group.

All this considerably decreases the value of breaking up into parts as a means of facilitating memorization. In such a form it cannot be an effective mode of memorization. Under these conditions it does not fulfill its basic functions: it does not decrease the amount of what has to be directly kept in memory, it does not separate for immediate retention the basic, outstanding support points which would draw all the rest to it.

The fulfillment of these functions is rendered still more difficult because of the insufficiently developed ability to state concisely the content of a section, to give it an easily remembered heading. What the pupils mark as a heading is often either a particular aspect which does not reveal the content of the section as a whole and therefore does not help to recall the whole section, or it is a sum of the separate parts of a sense group, each of which must be memorized by itself, and not by what is common that refers to all parts simultaneously. The headings noted by the schoolchildren are in many cases not support points in the sense in which we defined them previously, i.e., a generalized content of the whole section. Under these conditions they cannot fulfill their mnemonic role.

The breaking up of homework for memorization does not give sufficient help to the pupils. In the form in which it is practiced it differs sharply from the sense grouping pointed out in the analysis of memorization by adults. In schoolchildren this is not a *mental* breaking up, accompanied by the separation of what is basic and essential. This is a purely *technical* division of the text into parts with the aim of a sequential memorization of each of these parts individually.

It would be incorrect to negate the significance of such breaking up as a certain *preparatory* stage to a sense grouping, having as its aim the deepening of the understanding of the text. By separating individual parts, even with the aim of sequential memorization, the pupils are often oriented towards a new subdivision in the textbook: they learn the material by separate "little sections," each of which sometimes has its own heading; they learn it, even if by separate paragraphs which represent a single meaningful whole, more or less distinct in content from adjacent paragraphs. To a certain degree, all this "pushes" the schoolchild towards comprehension of the content of the section as a whole, to a comparison and contrasting of it with other sections, to an elucidation of the thematics of each section. Such "pushes" are, doubtless, essential for subsequent independent breaking up of the material into parts. However, this whole preparatory stage is as yet insufficient for sense grouping proceeding *mentally* and applicable as a *means of deepening understanding*.

It goes without saying that in a number of cases schoolchildren divide homework purely mechanically, externally, by volume, without orientation towards the meaning of each part. Even if this is not the case, i.e., if the material is broken up by meaning, their attitude towards breaking up the text is, nevertheless, different than when it serves the task of helping to retain the essence of each section, to show the most important thing in it, and make this the basis for memorizing the whole section as a unit.

Characteristic for sense grouping in adults is the tendency to keep the defined sense groups in memory. When schoolchildren break up material into parts (with the aim of decreasing the volume of what they will memorize at one time) this tendency is absent. Therefore, in schoolchildren the breaking up into parts is not a *mode of memorizing* in the sense of which we spoke earlier and as memorization is characterized in adults.

Not having developed the habit of sense grouping to a sufficient extent, pupils do not use it consciously and intentionally as a *means for memorization*. In order for this to happen it is necessary that the formation of sense groups become to a considerable degree an automatic process which is accomplished seemingly by itself. Special stimulation is needed for it, someone's direction, or the pupil's own experience. Reproduction, as was pointed out, impels the pupil to sense grouping, but these "pushes" are insignificant. They let themselves be known only gradually. Therefore, the main thing necessary for sense grouping to become a real mode of memorizing is a better possession of the habit of forming sense groups on the one hand, and instruction on the significance of grouping for memorization on the other. It is these directions which the pupils need in order to achieve a greater productivity for their memorization.

5. PROCESSES OF ASSOCIATION

One of the basic means of *deepening understanding* with the aim of achieving better memorization is to *associate* what is being memorized with something known. Association is used also in the case of adequate understanding, but then it is a *means* which must directly help *memorization* itself, since as a result of it connections are formed which are necessary for memorization.

For all the significance of the association processes, their frequencies are not identical in various cases. Hence, naturally, the question arises, under what conditions are these processes observed more often and what, consequently, evokes them to a greater extent.

Our experiments with adults have shown that the main conditions under which the association frequency depends on what is known are the *task* confronting the subject and the *material* which has to be memorized.

Most stimulating to association are tasks which demand careful mastery of the material, a complete, exact, and stable memorizing. This is clearly indicated by the data in Table 6.9 obtained in experiments with the same meaningful texts but with different memorization tasks.

From Table 6.9 it can be seen that tasks demanding a high level of memorizing and, therefore, more difficult to fulfill stimulate association more than a simple memorization task.

TABLE 6.9. Dependence of the Percentage of Associations on the Level of Memorization Required

Objective	Number of experiments	Percentage of associations	
		range of variation	mean
Simple memorization	32	3–18	5
Complete and accurate memorization..	27	5–15	12
Maximally stable memorization	24	4–18	14

The same difficulty principle determines the dependence of association on the *material* which must be memorized. Difficult material evokes more associations than easy material. This is clear from the following indexes found in experiments with memorization of material of different degrees of difficulty with the task of simply memorizing (Table 6.10).

The difference between the cases is rather pronounced. Speaking of the difficulty of the material, one has to keep in view two cases: the difficulty of *understanding* and the difficulty of *memorizing*.

How do they influence association? In order to answer this, two forms of association, noted above, must be taken into account: association with *previous experience,* with existing knowledge, and comparison with what the *given* material contains. Both forms of association can be distinguished in each process of understanding and memorizing, but the frequency with which they are applied and their significance for overcoming difficulties, arising in comprehending and memorizing, are not the same in different cases.

Let us consider first the difficulties in *understanding* and how they influence the nature of the associations utilized to facilitate understanding.

The difficulties in understanding may be twofold. First, different parts of the text may be obscure. In these cases understanding is most often achieved by associating with something known earlier. Second, the text may be obscure as a whole, although certain parts of it are understandable. In these cases an especially important role is played by the second way of association, the association of individual parts of the material.

In memorizing coherent, meaningful texts fully corresponding to the preparation of the person who memorizes them, understanding of individual parts of the text is usually achieved rather easily and the effort is concentrated mainly on the comprehension of the *whole,* on finding the main thoughts of the text, the connection between them, the course of events, the chain of proofs and conclusions. In these cases the second way of association predominates.

Our experiments with explanatory texts which were not especially difficult and corresponded to "normal" textbooks fully confirm this. The number of associations of the first type (with what is known from previous

TABLE 6.10. Dependence of the Percentage of Associations on the Difficulty of the Material in Simple Memorization

Evaluation of difficulty	Number of experiments	Percentage of associations	
		range of variation	mean
Difficult material	29	8–14	12
Easy material	35	4–9	6

experience) was, on the average, 3.6% per text. But the number of associations of the second type was considerably higher, 9.2% per text. The statements of the subjects correspond to this:

> I compared and contrasted with what I had read earlier. I had to find the structure of the text. There were no recollections of something in the past. But then I did not feel the need of them as a support to memorization. Separately everything that I read was understandable. In order to better memorize, I had only to understand the text as a whole, find the sequence of thoughts, the course of reasoning.

> In such texts you rarely turn to former knowledge although, of course, you rely on it. Without it there would be no understanding. However, in consciousness there is nothing concrete of this knowledge. But you pay close attention to the inner logic of the text, to how the thoughts are broken up. This is the main thing for memorizing such texts. Most of all you try to note the association of thoughts, their connection with each other, all the more since you sometimes reorganize the text.

What is the connection between the different types of association and the difficulties that arise in *memorizing* a text? One of the frequent causes of these difficulties is the volume of the material. With its increase, memorization, naturally, becomes more difficult. An insufficient cohesion of the material, the absence of logical sense connections which would make it possible to proceed from one part of the text to another on the basis of an understanding of their correlation, also acts in the same manner.

In order to overcome the difficulties caused by the *volume and insufficient cohesion* of the text, the subjects usually try to systematize the material, which demands association of some of its parts with others. The basis for memorizing in these cases is, consequently, associations of the *second* type.

Considerable difficulties in memorizing may arise because of *the abundance of factual data* in the text. Again these difficulties are overcome by association, but the main role this time is played by associations of the *first* type.

The explanation for this is that the factual data which we memorize are not in so close a logical relation to the rest of the material that in recall one could remember them on the basis of reasoning. In order to reproduce them, it is not so much logical connections with the material that are needed as something that is well known by itself and with which at the same time it would be easy to connect the factual information which is to be memorized. In the new material itself there is usually little with which one could easily connect the factual data of the text, as with something well known. Therefore, it is natural that in the search for support of the memorization of factual data we often have to go beyond the limits of the text, utilizing what we know from previous experience.

The data of our experiments fully confirm this. When the subjects pointed out that the main difficulty for them was the memorization of factual data, the number of associations of the first type increased sharply. When the text was easy to understand, this was accompanied simultaneously by a sharp drop in the number of associations of the second type. This is clearly seen from the data of Table 6.11, in which the figures show the average percent of associations per text.

An important factor in the determination of the associations used by the subjects is the question of the *content* of the relations on which we rely for understanding and memorizing. The nature of these relations can differ widely, especially when they serve as support for *understanding*. This follows clearly from the variety of possibly obscure material in the text. In some cases the causes of the phenomena may be unclear, in others, the logical bases of the propositions which must be mastered, and in still others, classification interrelations, temporal or spatial relations, and relations of similarity or difference.

There is one type of relation that appears more often than others, especially when we seek support for understanding from our previous experience. This is the similarity relation which we establish between what is given and what is known from experience. In order to understand the new we seek in the known what would resonate with the new impression, would make it stronger and clearer. The basis for this is similarity; it serves as support for attempts to comprehend the new and obscure. Similarity is the prevalent type of association carried out for understanding and memorizing.

The data of our experiments confirm this:

"I searched for something similar to the word 'Packche' [the name of one of the three kingdoms during the Silla dynasty, from which Korea was formed]. Strange as it may be, the name 'Chapaev' [Russian historical figure] came to mind. And I connected it with the name of the state."

"The name 'Koguryo' [second Korean kingdom created from China, also during the Silla dynasty, transliterated 'Kokurio' in Russian] was easy to remember, since it resembles 'Kukareku' [Russian rooster-call imitation]. I did not look long for something similar."

"I remembered the duration of the Paris Commune (71 days) by connecting it with the date (1871) by the similarity of figures."

TABLE 6.11. Dependence of Kind of Association on Nature of Text

Text	Percentage of associations: of the first kind	Percentage of associations: of the second kind
Explanatory with few factual data	3.6	9.2
Explanatory with many factual data	7.2	7.8
Narrative (historical) with many factual data	10.6	4.4

There were also statements of a generalizing nature.

"When you memorize factual material, you always look for something similar to what you already know, on which to rely during memorizing."

"As a rule, I look for support in similar material which would draw out the facts or names that I am at the moment memorizing."

"Without a doubt, similarity as support for memorizing plays a positive role."

The processes of association are most significant at a certain stage of memorization. *As the material is mastered, the role of associations and their very nature change considerably*; these changes can be traced in memorization as well as in reproduction.

Our experiments show that in *memorizing,* association takes place at first in a twofold form: *voluntary* as well as *involuntary.*

In *voluntary* association the subjects consciously seek "some support" with a more or less pronounced effort: sometimes the subject cannot at once find what he needs and has to *search* for something useful. Usually the assignment to find something to associate with is almost immediately accomplished: in the consciousness of the subjects there arises immediately something to act as support for memorization. Sometimes a choice is made of the material suitable for association.

In *involuntary* association there is no preliminary assignment of the task to associate what must be remembered with something known that could serve as support in memorizing. It is accomplished "by itself." Without the intention of the subjects, without effort, and at first without any relation to the problems of memorizing, a thought arises from some previous experience. And only after this "something" has appeared is it comprehended as useful for memorization, and then the subjects consciously associate with it what has to be memorized.

How does association change with *repeated perception* of the same material? At first association acquires the nature of simple reproduction. The subjects simply recall with what they associated the material in the preceding reading. There is no searching. Gradually this reproduction loses its definite nature. The subjects do not remember clearly with what they associated some part of the material; in their consciousness arises only a general orientation towards what was the support of memorization, but by itself it is no longer remembered. At the next reproduction even this orientation disappears, and the material is imprinted in memory by itself.

But this does not mean that the intermediate links, the result of association, fully lose their role. When recalling becomes difficult, they can sometimes appear quite definitely. As the material is being mastered, what changes occur in the utilization of associations during *reproduction*?

Gradually, as in memorizing, the reproduction relies less and less on associations to which recourse had to be taken earlier. Thus, as a support for mastering and facilitating it, associations become superfluous. *They are only a scaffold needed while the building is unfinished.* To know something well and thoroughly means to remember directly, under the influence of the task oriented recall. When we have to recall something that we know well we remember at once without searching. Any intermediate links only impede us. We must free ourselves from former connections and associations. The process of connecting a certain *A* with *B* by means of an intermediate link *M* is simultaneously a strengthening of the connection *A—B* and a weakening of the service connection *A—M*. This is a twofold, in a certain sense internally contradictory process: as the complex path *A—M—B* is repeated, part of it, *A—M*, is not strengthened but, on the contrary, disappears. What causes its disappearance?

One cannot explain it by the repetition of the process *A—M—B*. The connection *A—M* should be strengthened rather than weakened by repetition. Evidently, there are other causes for its weakening. This is the *task* of remembering *B* and not just *M* by itself. The latter is only the *means* for recalling *B*. Therefore, we have a *different attitude* towards them and an orientation appears to recall just *B*. This is the reason for the gradual disappearance of *M* as an intermediate link, no longer of interest to us.

Under our direction Raksha (1948) conducted an investigation devoted to memorizing Morse code. In this work the subjects had to memorize the sound of the letters transmitted by various combinations of long and short sounds (the dots and dashes).

At first many subjects used various intermediate links. Sometimes they had visual images of the letters (a schematic picture of the Morse alphabet or the images of the letters of the Russian alphabet). Sometimes the visual representation of the letters was combined with motor images (the subjects imagined that they were writing the letter). Sometimes object, visual, or auditory images served as support for memorization (at the sounding of the letter "u" [pronounced "oo"], for example, one of the subjects saw an image of a locomotive sounding "oo–oo–oo"). Sometimes words and combinations of words which corresponded in rhythm to the signs served as intermediaries (for example, in memorizing the letter "n" (–•) some subjects used the words: *Na*ta, *Ni*na; for the letter "u" (••–) the word ube*gu*, etc.). Sometimes symbolic images of sound served as support (the letter "z" (– –••) was perceived as the double humming of a bumblebee with subsequent double sting) and sometimes a melody was sung mentally.

But as the code was being mastered, all these intermediaries gradually disappeared. The sound of the letters was recognized immediately and only when difficulties arose (for example, when a letter memorized individually began to be "given" with other letters), did the subjects return to their supports.

A *diversity of associations* plays an essential role in the disappearance of intermediate links. When we want to remember something, we connect it not with one but with several known facts and remember it better than when we associate it with *one* thing, and, what is very important, recalling of what is connected with many things is often accomplished *without* the appearance in consciousness of intermediate links. The "freeing" of what is being remembered from what it is associated with then proceeds with greater ease in the process of memorization. We have encountered such facts in our experiments quite often. Here are some statements of the subjects.

> I remembered the name "Koguryo" by connecting it with "Kukareku" [rooster]. And another thought struck me: "Koguryo" resembles "Korea"; and "Korea" comes from the word "Koguryo." Visually the middle part of the word "kur" became distinct and the words "Kurit' " and "Kuritsa" flitted through my mind. But when I reproduced the text I did not make use of these aids. "Koguryo" came as if I had known the word well.

> I had to work a great deal to remember the date "1876." At first the thought came: the numbers go in a descending order—8, 7, 6. Then 18, 36, and 76 appeared in my consciousness. And a hazy localization of some visual scheme of the century, as if I had placed a dot on a line, in the middle of its right half. But in retelling I did not think of it. The date was imprinted in my memory, since I had examined it from various angles while memorizing.

> When I memorized the years 57, 37, and 17, my attention was drawn by the fact that the difference between each of them was 20, that all end in a 7, and that all are uneven numbers. And there were other thoughts: in connection with 37 there came 1837, the year of Pushkin's death, and in connection with 17 a hazy recollection of the October Revolution (1917). I had a pleasant feeling in connection with these numbers: I like uneven numbers, they are sharp and more definite. I experience them subjectively. Another thing: all numbers were perceived as years in human life and mentally I pictured: 17—youth, 37—maturity, 57—old age. And a recollection of a book in which a seven-year rhythm in human life is mentioned. True, here the difference is 20 years, but the recollection appeared in connection with the sharp distinction of the number 7. There was nothing of this when I recalled the dates later. The dates were remembered by themselves, and I thought this quite natural as I had worked on them quite thoroughly.

These examples are only a part of a considerable number of similar cases. In the statements of the subjects there is an indication of where to look for the source of *direct* reproduction of facts which have been memorized by multiple and diverse intermediaries. The words "I examined the date from all sides," and "I worked over the dates thoroughly" show this. It is not difficult to see that all this indicates the duration of those data which were memorized in various ways. The perception is positive when the subjects use only one intermediate link in memorizing. And yet reproduction which then followed was often not accomplished directly and at once but by recalling the intermediate link which was found by the subjects. Thus, of essence is the indication not of the duration of perception but the *diversity and "thoroughness" of the activity* performed by the subjects. What is important is that the subjects examined what they memorized from *various* angles.

This diversity of activity was the source of better memorization of the material and its direct reproduction later. Each connection established by the subjects made it possible to comprehend the material better, clearer, reveal it in its concrete form, made it more familiar, "their own," led indeed to its *mastery,* and this facilitated reproduction, made it direct, and did not demand the recollection of intermediate links.

What has been said also makes it possible to understand the cases when ease, assurance, correctness, and directness of reproduction were achieved as the result of using not diverse connections, but only one association. *Here too the main role was played by the activity which was accomplished in the process of association.*

From the statements of the subjects it could be seen that the process of association occurring during memorization played a positive role, facilitating reproduction and making it more certain. Thus, *it is not the* product *of association itself which facilitates reproduction in these cases, but the* process *of association.* Association widens and deepens the familiarization with what we memorize even when what we associate it with is forgotten and does not participate in the reproduction.

But this does not mean that the role of the auxiliary links themselves is negated or considered insufficient. The process of association can be important of itself even when its product—the connection established by us—does not arise in consciousness during reproduction. Its positive role proves to be broader than one should assume by proceeding from the acceptance of the significance of the connections themselves, quite aside from the influence which association has on the perception of the material and its memorization, i.e., the activity which in these cases is accomplished.

Recognition of the broad significance of the association processes must not lead to ignoring the *negative* role which they can play, e.g., those cases in which we remember that with what we associate what is to be remembered and cannot reproduce the material itself. If we use the scheme of connections *A—M—B*, that means that the connection *A—M* functions but the connection *M—B* is inactive. Cases of this kind are well known from personal experience and have been observed in many experimental investigations. What is the reason for this?

From the point of view of associative psychology it must mean that the transition from *M* to *B* was not fixed by a sufficient number of repetitions in the process of memorizing. The significance of repetitions cannot be denied, but of what the very process of connecting *M* and *B* consists, in the form in which it actually takes place in memorizing, must be revealed. The data of our experiments show that in reality the essence lies not in simple repetition of what is being memorized together with what it is associated with but in the *analysis* of both, in the *comparison* of one with the other. The subjects do not simply *repeat* one thing after another but *compare* what has to be memorized with what is used as means of memorization. This *comparison* serves as the basis for memorization.

Sometimes, while memorizing, the subjects remembered something that could be useful as an intermediate link but did not compare it with what they perceived; in reproducing they recalled only the association itself but not what had been memorized on the basis of this connection.

"I know," says one of the subjects, "that this word [which had to be remembered] made me remember the Black Sea, but what this word was I cannot say." [The sentence "Erosion is the washing out of the shore by the sea" was memorized and a few days later the subject was asked to remember what word meant "the washing out of the shore by the sea."]

Complete absence of comparison of what had to be memorized with what served as a means for memorizing was rare; more often it was only *insufficiently* done. In memorizing, *only the similarity* of what was to be remembered with what served as support for it was noted, and sometimes what was remembered referred only to a *general, broad,* category of things or phenomena. In reproduction only the intermediate link appeared in consciousness, but what had been memorized was not reproduced.

> I remember there was something like ambrosia ["abraziya" was the Russian word used for erosion], but just what, I don't remember. When I memorized I paid attention only to the similarity [the correct definition of the word "erosion" was remembered].
>
> Something similar to "crisis," but what, I can't remember [the sentence was "Lysis is a slow lowering of temperature during illness"]
>
> It sounds like podagra, but I can't remember right now [the sentence was "Gonagra is rheumatism of the knee"].
>
> A year in the second half of the 19th century, I think, in the 60's or 70's, or something. I don't remember exactly [the date 1876 was to be remembered]. I remember that I placed the date in some spatial scheme (in its right half). That was all I did.

Such cases are well known. Chekhov expresses it in his story "A Horse's Name." The difficulty in remembering the name "Ovsov" (Russian for oats) was caused by the too general nature of the "category" to which the name was referred by everyone who recalled it ("something about a horse").

Thus, the success in using something as an auxiliary link for memorization and reproduction depends to a considerable extent on the *nature of the comparison* occurring during memorization. In order that the transition from the auxiliary link to what must be reproduced be accomplished, it is desirable to perceive not only the similarity but also the *differences,* not only the general category to which what must be memorized belongs but also its *specific features*. The significance of the unity of the similar and the dissimilar, the general and the particular, appears here quite clearly. This unity is one of the essential conditions for the productivity of memorization.

Under this condition the auxiliary links serve as support for better familiarization with the specific features of what is to be remembered, and this makes it possible to reproduce it later. If this is not the case, the transition can be accomplished only by many repetitions of both what is to be remembered and the auxiliary link.

It is clear that comparison of the new, that which must be memorized, with something known from previous experience must include the realization of the *similarity* between them and the exposure of their differences, i.e., the specific features of what is being memorized as compared with what is used as support for memorizing. In associating what is to be remembered not with many auxiliary links but with just one of them and utilizing the diverse relations between them, we achieve good results not simply by increasing the number of relations but by revealing the relations and thus making it possible to show more *fully* and *diversely* the unique properties of the material. Not the connections by themselves, but *the connections as basis for extensive, clear, and deep comprehension of the characteristic features of what is to be remembered—this is the real cause of better memorizing with the aid of associations*. This, of course, does not exclude the significance of the connections themselves, nor the positive role of the auxiliary links in reproduction, but it also serves as basis for a more detailed perception and comprehension of the qualities which define the material, and this, naturally, leads to a more successful memorization and a more productive reproduction later.

In practice, association is not at all fully utilized; sometimes it is not used at all. Associations frequently are one-sided, move from what is to be remembered only to something similar. This has as its result that in reproduction the reverse transition from the similar and the general to what must be recalled on their basis is not realized. Any similarity can be the starting point for recalling many things, but only one *specific* possibility must be implemented, but the consciousness of the similar or the general which has been chosen as an auxiliary link cannot point out which one.

If, for example, in memorizing the sentence "Erosion is the washing out of the shore by the sea" the subject fixes only that the word "erosion" ("abraziya" in Russian) is somehow connected with the Black Sea (evidently by the similar word "Abkhasia" [district in the Caucasus]) it is natural that later thinking of the Black Sea may serve as a starting point of very much that is connected with it, but by itself it will not predetermine precisely what must be recalled.

In order to limit the possibilities of transition, it is necessary to fix a number of characteristics of what is being memorized which would distinguish it from what matches them in a general category or is similar to it and so is used as an auxiliary link. But when consciousness is directed only towards the similar, the association with it can only detract from the specific characteristics of what is being remembered. Then the auxiliary link plays not a positive but a negative role.

Of significance is the *realization of differences* when similar material must be memorized and it includes some differences that are essential in some respect and cannot be ignored.

The Soviet psychologists Matlin (1940, 1958) and Shvarts (1947) have shown this in their investigations in which the subjects were asked to memorize texts which were in one respect (or in some parts) similar and in another respect (or other parts) dissimilar. In his investigation Matlin used texts which were close in content but contained some sentences which differed considerably from each other. Shvarts gave his subjects pairs of words to memorize; they were composed in such a manner that some of them were very similar: the first word of one pair was also the first word in another pair (for example, the same Russian word formed a pair in one case with its Spanish equivalent, and in another case with some made-up, experimental, word).

The results of these experiments showed that when the subjects in the process of memorization noticed the similarity as well as the difference in what was to be remembered they later recalled more successfully than when there was no comparison consisting of the realization of the similarity and—very important—the difference.

Shvarts showed the necessity of a *conscious comparison* of similar material in his experiments in which the subjects had to master "orthograms" that were similar and, therefore, interfering: the case endings of nouns (genitive, dative, and prepositional) and of adjectives (instrumental and prepositional cases). Special work with the wide use of *comparison* of similar situations (i.e., with the realization of similarity and *difference* between them) gave very favorable results.

Solov'ev (1940) and Nudel'man (1940) in their investigations showed how difficult sometimes the role of similarity and the necessity of realizing a difference can be: the changing of the visual images of similar objects in forgetting was used as the object of study. Our best teachers and methodologists emphasize the significance of comparison when studying similar material. Ushinskii pointed out that "a new name very similar to one we already remember will not be remembered if we do not pay special attention to the difference that may exist between them" (1950*a*, p. 349).

On a physiological level the significance of contrasting similar stimuli for differentiation in the elaboration of conditioned reflexes was most strongly emphasized by Pavlov. Speaking of the method by means of which differentiation can be achieved in the field of conditioned reflexes he points out:

"One [method] is only a multiple repetition of a definite agent as conditioned stimulus with a constant reinforcement by the unconditioned reflex. The other is an *alternating contrasting* [our italics] of this definite, constantly reinforced conditioned stimulus with an agent close to it but not accompanied by an unconditioned stimulus. At present we are inclined to acknowledge the reality of only the latter method" (1951*a*, pp. 129–130).

6. ASSOCIATION IN CHILDREN

Leont'ev (1931) made a special study of the processes of association in children. Its theoretical basis was the cultural-historical theory of Vygotskii. The author's main conceptual framework is: "The development of memory...does not proceed along the continuous path of gradual quantitative change. It is a deeply dialectical path presuming transitions from some of its forms to qualitatively different, new forms." In the author's opinion one can picture it in the following manner: "The first stage of memory development is its development as the natural activity of imprinting and reproducing. This stage of development ends, under normal conditions, probably before school age. The next stage, typical of early school age, is characterized by a change in the processes of memorization, which become indirect but proceed with external means predominating. In its turn, indirect memorization develops along two lines: the line of development and perfection of the methods of auxiliary means which continue to remain in the form of external stimuli; the line of transition from external means to internal ones (Leont'ev, 1931, pp. 81–82; 1959, pp. 340–341).

The author conducted experiments with adults (students) and children of various ages, using the so-called "functional method of double stimulation."

In the first group of experiments the material to be memorized (nonsense syllables and meaningful words) was given to the subjects without instruction or presentation of something that could be used as *support for memorizing* (as an *auxiliary means*).

In the second group of experiments the words had to be memorized with the *utilization* of an auxiliary means. The subjects were given a selection of pictures and instructed that upon the calling out of a word they were to choose from these pictures the one which would help them to remember the word (Zankov [1940] conducted similar experiments with retarded children).

The author found that "At the very early stages of the development of memorization (children of early preschool age) the introduction of the second series of stimulus symbols [pictures given to the subjects] which, upon entering the operation as the 'means of memorizing,' are capable of changing it into an indirect, signifying one, hardly increases its effectiveness; the operation of memorization still remains direct and natural" (Leont'ev, 1959, p. 351). At this age, the number of words remembered without the pictures or with them is identical.

"At the next stage of the development of memorization (children of early school age), characterized by a preliminary, very great increase in indexes of externally transmitted memorization, the introduction of the second series of stimuli-means is, on the contrary, decisive; this is a moment of great divergence of indexes" (Leont'ev, 1959, p. 351). The presence of pictures at this stage of development has a considerably greater effect on memorization than their absence. The pictures are already a *means of facilitating memorization*; they are used as support for memorization. Further on, the tempo of index changes and, consequently, their relationship, change again: the indexes of externally transmitted memorization (by means of pictures) increase more slowly than the indexes of memorization without pictures. The indexes converge, but this is not on account of the intensive growth of the "natural" untransmitted memorization, but because memorization without pictures now becomes transmitted, but not by external means (pictures) but by internal, verbal means, which at this stage of development make memorization a *logical* memorization. "Verbal connections unifying the separate elements being remembered into a single structural whole change this operation into a *logical* one" (Leont'ev, 1931, p. 221). Logical memory is defined as "an internally transmitted activity relying on the instrumental function of speech" (Leont'ev, 1931, p. 222). It yet remained to clear up the role of verbal supports when just they (and not the pictures) would be offered to facilitate memorization.

Under our direction (much later than Leont'ev's work) by a method similar to that of Leont'ev, Mal'tseva (1958*a*) conducted an investigation of this problem. It showed the great possibilities of using verbal supports by younger schoolchildren. Of special interest was the question of how associations are utilized in memorizing not artificial material, as used by Leont'ev (nonsense syllables and series of separate words), but in work with the ordinary meaningful material with which a schoolchild has to deal in study, i.e., in memorizing coherent, meaningful texts.

To find out how association proceeds, we carried out experiments in which the subjects had to memorize texts of different content but which contained material stimulating association: names, designations, dates, numbers. We used three texts (historical and geographical). The duration of the work and the number of readings were not limited. No instructions on how to memorize were given. The subjects were schoolchildren of the fourth, sixth, and eighth grades (ten from each grade). It was not possible to establish the number of associations in memorizing the text as a whole, since self-observation is unreliable at school age. Therefore, at the end of memorization each subject was interrogated only relative to a limited number of parts of the text—those, as shown from experiments with adults, which most stimulate association. The question was not phrased generally (e.g., point out when you connected what you memorized with previously known material or when you associated one part of the text with another), but with regard to each part of the text separately.

For comparison we conducted similar experiments on ten adults with secondary and college education. The texts were the same for all subjects. The three texts had 15 parts (factual data to be memorized) in all on which the subjects were interrogated.

As can be seen (Table 6.12), the difference between the schoolchildren and the adults is quite considerable. In the fourth and sixth graders association was rare (Dodonova [1941] had similar results in her experiments with fifth graders). Of 15 items, the fourth graders in our experiment only remembered an average of one by means of intermediate links, and the sixth graders remembered an average of two.

It is characteristic that neither group discovered the relations between the dates of historical events: 57, 37, and 17 B.C., and that both memorized each of these dates separately, although in the text they followed directly one after the other and referred to similar events—to the formation of the three states from which Korea was formed. This also determines the nature of the errors in recalling dates. The adults sometimes gave the years 59, 39, and 19 or 53, 33, and 13 instead of the given dates, forgetting only the last digit but retaining the relation between the numbers; the fourth and sixth graders, however, made the most diverse errors, giving such years as 57, 48, and 15 or 57, 37, and 16, i.e., remembering one of the numbers correctly but completely distorting the others. No relation between the numbers was retained.

The name of one of the states of which Korea was formed was often remembered by the fourth and sixth graders directly, without association with any other words, while the adults connected "Koguryo" with various Russian words like *kukareku, pokurila, kok, kuritsa,* or with the name Korea.

Does this difference mean that the schoolchildren do not know how

TABLE 6.12. Percentage of Associations, Calculated on the Basis of the Maximum Possible Number of 150 Associations, in Different Age Groups

Subjects	Percentage of associations
4th graders	8
6th graders	14
8th graders	28
Adults	46

to establish a connection between what is being memorized and knowledge gained earlier? In other words, can the small number of associations observed in schoolchildren be explained by the fact that the very process of association proceeds with greater difficulty in them than in adults, or do the schoolchildren simply not utilize this process as a mode for memorization?

In order to answer this question we did the following: after interrogating the subjects as to whether they had associated the names or dates with something, we asked them to do so *intentionally,* i.e., to point out with what, in their opinion, one could connect what was in the text in order to remember it. This task was assigned separately for every name and figure.

The results of the experiments showed that, while some of the data evoked in the children something that could facilitate memorization immediately, other data did not evoke "supports." Less difficulty arose with words than with numbers. Even if they could easily be associated with something the children did not use them.

The statements needed in these experiments were not difficult for people inexperienced in self-observation as our subjects, schoolchildren, were. Their statements concerned facts the presence or absence of which could easily be noticed. Nevertheless, they cannot be considered sufficiently reliable, since the fourth and sixth graders could simply have forgotten whether there were intermediate links during memorizing and this could lower the number of noticed associations. Therefore, we augmented our experiments with a special one involving children of the second, fourth, and sixth grades (24 from each) and also some adults.

The subjects were given a series of ten sentences selected in such a manner that each two sentences were close in content. For example: "A strong wind blew from the sea" and "In the mountains blew a light wind," or "A lamp was lit in the room" and "It became light in the room," or "We cut down a large tree" and "Now we have much wood." And then there were sentences with similar names (for example: "Manya, Vanya, and Tanya are the best pupils" or "I was in three villages: Volkovo, Medvedevo, Zverevo" [names derived from wild animals], or similar numbers (for example "The school bought 77 spades, 57 rakes, and 37 watering cans"). The pairs of similar sentences were separated by two or three other sentences. In all, four different combinations of sentences were used (two each for each subject). With the first combination no indication was given that the sentences had been selected in pairs. The subjects had to read the whole series of sentences twice and try to memorize them as well as possible. They were allowed to reproduce them in any order.

In memorizing, would the subjects associate the similar sentences and thereby facilitate memorization and, if so, what would the differences between the subjects of the various ages be? So the question was asked:

"Among the sentences were there some similar to each other?" If the answer was positive, the similar sentences had to be pointed out and it also had to be indicated in what the similarity or difference consisted; the subjects also had to indicate when they first noticed the similarity—when the sentences were read or after the question was asked, i.e., "from memory."

The subjects also had to tell whether in memorizing they *utilized* the consciousness of similarity, or whether they just *ascertained* it.

If the answer was negative, the subject was asked to reproduce the sentences in his mind once more and tell whether there were any similar ones. If the subject noticed only part of the sentences he was asked to *reread* the whole material and then answer the question (the same was done if the subject immediately noticed the similarity of sentences but could not reproduce them).

If difficulties arose even after rereading the sentences and the subject could not say whether there were similar sentences, one of the similar sentences was read to him and he was asked whether among the other sentences there was a similar one. The same method was applied with regard to names and numbers. This always followed the discussion about the sentences.

To what extent does the subject who did not notice the pairing of sentences (or names and numbers) during memorization immediately notice it when directly asked? It was necessary to elucidate this in order to establish to what extent the difficulty of actually discerning the similarity in content between sentences is the cause of the insufficient use of connections between sentences during memorization. What were the results of these experiments?

Let us first examine the data referring to *adults*. All adults noticed the "pairing" of sentences immediately, upon first reading. In only a few cases was this not observed. In these few cases, the connection of only one pair was missed. The same held true with regard to names, although to a lesser extent than to numbers. Their similarity was noticed quickly and easily. Of what help was the discerning of these connections in reproduction?

Some of the subjects recalled the sentences in pairs, i.e., made use of the similarity in content, and this was the basis for their reproduction. The majority tried to reproduce in the order in which they had read the sentences because "The number of sentences is small, and that means they must be memorized exactly, that is, not only literally but, if possible, in the same sequence in which they were read." The task the subjects had posed for themselves they could not always successfully fulfill. After reproducing several sentences they experienced difficulty in reproducing the remainder of the sentences in the original sequence. Then they began to utilize the connections noticed during reading and continued to reproduce the rest of the sentences by pairs.

And what did the experiments with *schoolchildren* show? Far from all subjects discerned the connections between sentences *during reading,* as is shown in Table 6.13.

As can be seen, only 25% of the second graders and half of the fourth and sixth graders noticed the similarity of sentences during reading; in fact it may be less since we based the calculation on the statements of the subjects, which may not always have been correct.

If not the number of *subjects* who discerned the connection between the sentences is counted, but rather the number of *sentences,* the pairing of which was noticed, the difference between the adults and the schoolchildren becomes still more noticeable. Not all sentences were recognized as being close in content by the subjects who, generally speaking, noticed a connection between the sentences and were, consequently, among those contained in the data cited above. Most often only two or three pairs of sentences out of four were noticed. Therefore, the total number of sentence pairs noticed by all subjects participating in these experiments was low. The indexes are given in Table 6.14.

The connection between the sentences noticed *after reading,* in the process of direct *questioning,* is shown in Table 6.15.

TABLE 6.13. Percentage of Subjects Who Noticed Relations between Sentences during Reading

Subjects	Percentage who noticed relations between sentences
2nd graders	25
4th graders	46
6th graders	50

TABLE 6.14. Percentage of Sentence Pairs Noticed during Reading

Subjects	Percentage of sentence pairs noticed
2nd graders	10
4th graders	25
6th graders	35

TABLE 6.15. Percentage of Subjects Who Noticed Relations between Sentences Only during Questioning

Subjects	Percentage who noticed relations between sentences
2nd graders	33
4th graders	46
6th graders	42

Adding up the percentages given in Tables 6.13 and 6.15, we get the results shown in Table 6.16.

It can be seen that the connection between sentences was noticed in the process of reading or interrogation by almost all fourth and sixth graders, while only somewhat more than half of the second graders noticed the connection.

The number of *sentence pairs* noticed also increased considerably during interrogation. This held true for subjects who noticed pairs during reading (and who were later asked to find other pairs) as well as for those who discerned "pairing" of sentences only after being asked (Table 6.17).

What about the pupils who could not correctly answer the general question as to whether there were sentences which were similar in content?

With rare exceptions they did notice these sentences, but only when asked a direct question *concerning each sentence separately*. What conclusion must be drawn from this?

Let us examine the data obtained from experiments with second graders. Very seldom did they notice a connection between sentences, but, especially important, they often did not see it even when directly asked about it and the text was given them to be reread. Consequently, the *process of comparison itself, the discerning of common content* in what was being read presented considerable difficulties. This must be considered to be the main reason why the second graders did not use these processes in memorization and reproduction as means to facilitate them. Association was not a *method of memorizing* for them.

The data obtained from experiments with fourth and sixth graders must be interpreted differently. Undoubtedly, during reading for memorization these pupils noticed the connection between sentences considerably less

TABLE 6.16. Total Percentage of Subjects who Noticed Relations between Sentences during Reading or during Questioning

Subjects	Percentage who noticed relations between sentences
2nd graders	58
4th graders	92
6th graders	92

TABLE 6.17. Total Percentage of Sentence Pairs Noticed during Reading and during Questioning

Subjects	Percentage of sentence pairs noticed
2nd graders	48
4th graders	81
6th graders	86

often than adults and this is, of course, one of the reasons that the similarity of the sentences was not sufficiently utilized in memorizing and reproducing. But something else is revealed here: a direct question to point out similar sentences, while reading, was answered by the fourth and sixth graders quite rapidly and easily.

Thus, *in itself the process of comparing and discerning sentences with similar content did not present essential difficulties for these pupils.* But the fact that comparison was carried out by the majority of pupils only after a *direct* question stimulating comparison means that there was no *set toward such a comparison in the process of reading.*

What is the reason for the absence of this set? The main reason is that *the processes of association have not as yet become a method of memorizing for the fourth and sixth graders.* With *direct* stimulation they are accomplished *easily, under conditions of memorization* they are *absent* to a considerable extent. The subjects who noticed the connection in the process of reading speak of this. The question of whether or not they made use of the "closeness" of the sentences to facilitate memorizing and recalling usually elicited a negative answer. According to the subjects, they did not think of the possibility of using it as a basis for memorizing, although they did notice it in recalling and reproducing.

Does this mean that the connection between sentences did not play any role for them? Our data show that sentences were often reproduced on the basis of their similarity in content. The subjects recalled them not in the order in which they had been read, but by their content. It is characteristic that even those subjects who did not discern the similarity in content of the sentences at all sometimes reproduced according to the similarity of sentences. Those pupils who saw this connection during reading later often did not notice that they were reproducing the sentences on the basis of this connection and when reminded of this fact they explained it by saying: "it came out that way by itself" or "I don't know how it happened." *There was no conscious aim to utilize the connections noticed as support for recalling.*

We spoke of association of *sentences,* but to an even greater extent the same might be said about the associations of *names and numbers.* The schoolchildren did not use the connections between them as *means of memorization.* They did not discern the similarity in this material, or, if so, they discerned it after reproduction and during questioning when directly asked to determine whether there were similarities between what was being memorized (the names or numbers).

Most difficult to discern was the similarity between names, in which the meaningful relationship of words determined their closeness, e.g., the names of ships [derived from the Russian words for thunder, lightening, and thunderstorm], Gromov, Molniya, Groznyi or the names of villages, Volkovo,

Medvedevo, Zverevo. Usually a leading question was needed here: "From what words are these names derived?" "What do the words have in common from which these names come?"

Easier to notice was the sound similarity of proper names: Kolya, Volya, Tolya; Manya, Vanya, Tanya. It is characteristic, however, that many pupils noticed the similarity to be of *one* letter, most often the last. Sometimes all three identical letters were noticed ("o," "l," "ya" or "a," "n," "ya"). The endings as a whole (-olya, -anya) were named only by the older pupils, and then rarely. The fact that the words form a rhyme was never noticed.

The similarity between numbers was noticed almost exclusively during interrogations. In memorizing, the identity of only the last digits was discerned and then only by the older pupils (17% of the fourth graders and 33% of the sixth graders). The same relation of the first digits was as a rule noticed even by the upper-grade pupils only upon the asking of leading questions.

To the difficulties in discerning similarity in names and numbers correspond the many errors made in *reproducing* these parts of the material. The *nature* of the errors also corresponds to these difficulties. While the adults said Polya instead of Tolya in their attempt to reproduce the names, i.e., they retained the general structure of the word and the rhyme, the schoolchildren sometimes substituted names which differed sharply from the names given in sound composition.

In summing up the following can be stated. The reason that the connection between sentences, names, and numbers was not utilized as an aid to memorization was, on the one hand, *that the connection itself was not noticed during the reading of the sentences,* and, on the other, that *it had not as yet become a method of memorizing* for the schoolchildren. Thus, *the general course of development of the processes of association as means of memorization* can be characterized as follows.

At first these processes present considerable difficulties in themselves. But the picture changes as the child develops. Associations are made in many cases, but, in contrast to adults, schoolchildren, and not only the younger ones, do not as yet grasp the relations quickly and easily or directly in the process of reading, although they understand them. At this stage association is accesible only as a *special process, not as a means of memorization.* The schoolchildren have as yet no set toward association in memorizing. Association is not as yet a method of *memorization,* an auxiliary operation which serves as an aid to memory. As association is mastered, there begins a new stage—its application in the memorization processes. It stands out more and more as a *conscious method of memorizing,* as a means consciously used to facilitate the task of remembering. Here associations become part of a broader activity—memorization—and are one of the factors of this activity. It is not difficult to see that the development just described coincides with what was said about the development of meaningful grouping.

Part III: Repetition in Memorizing

Chapter 7

SIGNIFICANCE AND FUNCTIONS OF REPETITION

1. THE PROBLEM OF REPETITION IN NON-SOVIET PSYCHOLOGICAL WRITINGS

The positive role of repetition in the processes of memory is well known and yet there are many (and, in many cases, justified) objections raised against overestimating its effect if one regards repetition as a simple, mechanical sequence of impressions or actions without genuinely conscious human activity.

In non-Soviet psychology decisive opponents to acknowledging the leading role of repetition are the representatives of gestalt psychology and other psychologists, including even some behaviorists, in particular Guthrie, Thorndike, and Tolman.

As evidence that the criticism of associationism was valid, Lewin (1922) referred to his many experiments which, in his opinion, reveal that a multiple succession of one notion after another does not by itself create a connection between them. In one of his experiments a subject read a series of syllables up to 300 times (no mnemonic task was assigned). Under these conditions, it seemed to Lewin there would be full freedom for the effect of associative tendencies, i.e., in reading one of the syllables the following one should be recalled, since the transition from syllable to syllable had already occurred 300 times.

The experiments showed that no effect of associative tendencies was revealed. Either nothing appeared in the consciousness of the subjects, or some *meaningful* words occurred. The syllables memorized earlier were with rare exceptions not reproduced. The subjects did not even recognize them when later shown them.

Lewin came to the conclusion that association, by itself, does not evoke the tendency to reproduce a syllable associated with the one presented. Other conditions are needed for association to take place.

As the most important and decisive condition Lewin considers "the readiness for action" arising, in his opinion, from the inclinations and needs of man. He advances the doctrine of needs as the basis for the "movement" of concepts as well as of all human activity and of all mental life as a counterbalance to the doctrine of associations.

But Lewin's doctrine is erroneous since he regards the needs as self-sufficient, having in themselves "mental forces" forming closed "systems" of some "mental tensions" which together with some other "intense mental systems" comprise the "soul of man." These "forces," according to Lewin, interact with "a force field" of man's environment and with equivalent "forces" of the physical and social medium surrounding man, as a result of which man's behavior and the concrete forms of his mental activity are determined by a peculiar mechanics of all such "forces." The "inner," "vital" forces, in Lewin's interpretation, also prove to a certain extent to be external with respect to man: they act independently, are not subject to him, and do not depend on him.

This idealistic and mechanistic conception of needs as self-sufficient forces which together with "the force field of the environment" are the "mover" of human behavior treats quite incorrectly the basis for human behavior and the role and nature of human activity.

The needs, and with them the whole behavior and personality of man, are torn from the *material existence* which determines them and from the *social conditions* of his life. They are deprived of their true basis and torn from the personality of man. They act as some independent forces within man. It is not man that is active, according to this conception, but the inclinations and needs which "reside" in him and which by themselves determine his actions. The role of *comprehension* by man of his needs and the role of *activity* carried out by him are eliminated. Speaking against associative psychology, Lewin is no less an idealist and mechanist than the associationists.

Köhler and Koffka, representatives of gestalt psychology, also criticize the associationistic solution of the problem from false positions. These authors not only reject the positive effect of repetition, but emphasize the *negative influence* of multiple repetitions. "Instead of strengthening the structure," says Koffka, "repetition can lead to its destruction" (1935, p. 147).

When does this occur? In the opinion of the gestaltists, "when the activity becomes *saturated* or *supersaturated* by repetitions." "Then," says Koffka, "a strong resistance arises and the quality of the action being carried out worsens considerably" (1935, p. 147).

Koffka refers for corroboration to the experiments of Karsten (1928) in which the subjects were given a poem to read or recite until the desire arose to stop it. Such an instruction lead to an exceptionally large number of repetitions. However, after a certain time it lead not to improvement but to deterioration of the effects. For example, when the same poem was read repeatedly, at first its content was most apparent. With continuing repetition, only individual expressions stood out. This broke up the unity of the poem, and its external, verbal aspects became paramount. As a result, its meaningful recitation was impaired. With the disintegration of the unity of the poem, mispronunciations, faltering, and stuttering set in and forgetting occurred. After reading a poem many times, subjects were sometimes completely unable to remember it in spite of their best efforts.

There is no doubt that this negative effect of repetition can be observed, but only when the repetitions become mechanical, and this does not lower but, on the contrary, emphasizes the positive role of active, meaningful, and conscious repetition.

Another incorrect position on the problem of repetition is taken by the representatives of American behaviorism.

Some of the behaviorists attach an exceptionally great significance to repetition (Watson and others). Others, on the contrary, limit its role, do not consider it a basic condition for the formation of connections. Such a position is held by the adherents of the so-called "dynamic" conceptions of behaviorism, in particular Woodworth and Tolman.

Thorndike in his early work *The Psychology of Learning* (1914) attributes an important role to repetition, although he treats it mechanistically, i.e., considers it as a simple mechanical sequence of the same action ("reaction") after the stimulus which caused it. In his later works, particularly in *Human Learning* (1931), Thorndike rejects the role of repetitions by themselves as the basis for the formation of connections.

"Our problem" he says "was to find out by experimental investigation whether repetition of the same situation could in itself be the basis of learning. The results of our investigation have given a clear, negative answer" (1931). "Repetitions of the same situations produce just as few changes in the human mind as, for example, the repetition of the same message along a wire changes the nature of that wire." From this position Thorndike maintains that "all pedagogical doctrines which ascribe educational significance to repeated reactions independent of the consequences accompanying them are more than doubtful. Life experience by itself, if it does not interest man, is a poor teacher. It does not teach him anything" (1931). Thorndike refers to data of his experiments which were conducted to solve the problem concerning the role of repetitions. The same procedure was followed in all these experiments: the subjects were asked to perform the same action many times. They were not told whether they did it correctly or not, but it was assumed that, if the "law of repetition" were valid, the performance of the action would gradually become standardized, i.e., that each subsequent performance would be an exact copy of the preceding one.

In one of the series of experiments a subject was asked to close his eyes and draw a 4-in. line with one stroke. The same subject repeated the experiment 3000 times in the course of several days. The results showed that the length of the lines was not identical; in successive experiments the subject did not reproduce what he had done in previous ones. "The same stimulus repeated 3000 times" says Thorndike, "has not taught the individual anything" (1931). He draws the conclusion: "Repetition of the same situation in itself cannot be the basis for learning" (1931). The conviction of "many psychologists" that "multiple repetition of the same reaction under the same circumstances must evoke the tendency towards definite, more-or-less uniform reactions must be rejected" (1931).

In drawing such aconclusion Thorndike does not take into consideration that the basis for mastery of a habit must not be the repetition of the task but the *repetition of the action* which is to be mastered. In his experiments only the task—drawing a line of definite length—was repeated, but this did not guarantee its identical fulfillment, since drawing lines depends on many factors. There could be no repetition of actions and, consequently, they did not have to be fixed. Thorndike thinks that the subjects in each successive experiment should have reproduced their previous actions mechanically. Yet acting consciously, they could solve the problem anew each time. They could introduce corrections into their movements, change them proceeding from purely subjective evaluation of the preceding movements, from a selective and changing notion of the length of the line. No fixing of movements could occur under these conditions.

Just as untenable is Thorndike's second series of experiments in which the subjects were given a number of syllables and to each syllable several letters had to be added to make a word, which, however, was not specified. Some syllables were repeated many times in the list distributed. At the beginning the same letters were added to the same syllable but later were substituted by others. Proceeding from this, Thorndike maintains that repetition of itself does not play a role.

Evidently here too he does not take into consideration the conscious changes by the subjects of the task, i.e., he thinks that the subjects each time had as their aim the writing of any word that came "to mind." In reality it is most probable that they changed the task in the course of experiments and wrote not the first letters that came to mind, but those that made it possible to finish the word quicker. Therefore no fixing of the first written endings occurred.

The main defect of Thorndike's experiments is that, proceeding from clearly expressed mechanistic positions, he assumed that his subjects had to reproduce *mechanically* the preceding actions. Rejecting the significance of repetition, he tries to give his own explanation to the basis of memorization.

As such a basis Thorndike points out first the recognition of the "cobelonging" of what must be connected in the process of memorizing. But he immediately weakens his position by maintaining that "the moment of recognition of the cobelonging, although having some positive results in forming connections between the various experiences, is, however, a comparatively weak factor in the process of learning" (1931).

Thorndike attributes the greatest significance as basis for memorization to the "law of effect," according to which connections accompanied by satisfaction are fixed and those accompanied by dissatisfaction are weakened. He objects decisively to the identification of the *effect of actions with the recognition of their results*. In his opinion the effect of actions helps to master even such connections which are not recognized by us.

Thorndike tries to accept such an unconscious, purely mechanical formation of connections as possible because the bases of the connections, according to him, are movements of neural processes representing the appearance of a special instinct inherent in the neurons and supported by the presence of satisfaction.

The role of repetition is consequently limited by Thorndike not because of some antimechanistic consideration but, on the contrary, to oblige the clearly mechanistic principle of effect, the physiological explanation of which contains nothing but a hypothesis.

What is the principle of effect promoted by Thorndike? It means that a pupil who correctly performed some action is told that he did it correctly and that is all. No explanation of why the action is correct is given. Consequently he cannot comprehend his action and is compelled to assimilate it purely mechanically. Awareness is completely absent. For the pupil only mechanical learning remains, blind imitation of his own actions which have received a positive evaluation without his understanding precisely when and why they are correct and when they must be changed for other actions.

So, neither Thorndike nor the gestaltists have made the role of repetition apparent. For them repetition was only a *mechanical* reproduction of an action already accomplished and not its *conscious* repeated accomplishment with the aim of achieving better results in memorizing. Repetition was set against conscious learning.

2. THE ROLE OF REPETITION IN THE LIGHT OF THE CONCEPT OF MNEMONIC PROCESSES AS ACTIVE THINKING ACTIVITY

How must the problem of repetition be solved proceeding from our concept of memory in the light of acknowledgment of activeness and comprehension in memorization?

The physiological basis for remembering is the mnemonic function of the nervous system expressed in the formation of traces from preceding excitations and in the Bahnung of paths coming from one excited section of the nervous system to another which simultaneously or immediately after it is in a state of excitation. Pavlov's doctrine on the higher nervous system states this position quite clearly. The role of repeated excitations becomes evident. The intensity of the trace and the degree of Bahnung of the paths depend, undoubtedly, to a great extent on how many times a given excitation left a trace and participated in the Bahnung of the neural path.

The acceptance of this position does not set aside the fact that the memorization effect, the consequence of any mental process, most strongly depends on the activity in which such a process is in some way always involved. Therefore, to pose a question concerning the adequacy of traces left in the nervous system and the paths resulting from Bahnung between them without characterizing the concrete activity in which these traces arise and are fixed means to attempt to solve the question of what in fact never occurs, i.e., to avoid that from which one actually cannot digress. The posing of such a question is itself false and, therefore, a solution to it cannot be found. There is always an influence of activity and it can go in various directions, depending on the properties of this activity itself.

In some cases these characteristics are such that the consequence of the processes occurring in carrying out this activity is considerable, the effect of memorizing is pronounced, and each repetition of the process reinforces still more what already has been achieved. The positive effect of repetition is quite distinct in these cases. Repetitions have great influence, although they depend on the activity which we perform. It determines their influence and herein is its most important role, not at all lowering, however, the significance of repetitions.

In contrast to this, there are cases when the characteristics of the activity are such that the consequence of the processes which are incorporated into it is insignificant. Memorization in these cases is weakly manifested or is absent altogether. If such characteristics of the activity are retained even when the same processes are repeated, then the influence of repetition is not at all noticeable. Then repetition does not play a positive role. It can be carried out many times, but since each time it leaves an insignificant effect which very soon completely disappears, the final result of the many repetitions is not concretely revealed.

Thus, the role of repetition is fully determined by the characteristics of the activity under the conditions of which the repeated process is carried out. *The significance of repetition depends on just what man does when he repeats actions.*

Depending on the activity, the repetitions, in their turn, influence it. In repetition, man very often acts differently as time passes. Part of an action is dropped, new actions are carried out, former actions are modified. The direction of the actions, the content of the activity, the nature of execution change. *Repeated executions of actions are not exact copies of the first execution. They are not stereotypes, standardized reproductions of what was done before. Sometimes they are considerable modifications of former actions, important changes of the initial activity.* The action seems to live and develop and is in perpetual motion and change.

These changes can be clearly traced in the repeated performance of thinking activity. Each new comprehension of the same material results in the revelation of new aspects not noticed earlier, leads to a fuller, deeper, and more exact understanding, and reveals new connections and relations. The whole of the material is often comprehended from a new point of view, acquires a new aspect, a new meaning. Sometimes only repetition makes it possible to understand the material as a whole.

If repetition is correctly organized, it not only does not lead to mechanical memorization but, on the contrary, is of great help in avoiding mechanical memorization. The attempt to contrast repetition and understanding is absolutely unjustified.

Chapter 8

THE PROCESS OF REPETITION

1. DIVERSITY OF REPETITION IN THE MNEMONIC ACTIVITY OF ADULTS

Study of repetition in connection with the activeness and comprehension of memorization requires a qualitative description of the content of each repetition carried out in memorization. From the psychological point of view the individual repetitions are not identical and, therefore, one may speak of various stages of memorization.

In non-Soviet psychology, attempts were made to mark stages of memorization by proceeding from the data of experimental investigation. Ebert and Meumann (1904) differentiate five stages or phases of memorization: 1) orientation in the material; 2) fixative reading; 3) rhythmization of the material; 4) anticipatory reading (anticipating what follows from preceding familiarity with the material); 5) reading for control (when we accent what formerly was most difficult).

A similar description of memorization stages is found in the work of Kraemer (1911) conducted under the direction of Meumann. But the results of these works are unsatisfactory. Both point out only the *tasks* in the process of memorization and the most general characteristics of the reading process at the various stages of memorization. These works do not elucidate the question of what repeated reading means from the psychological point of view.

In one of Rybnikov's works (1930) a characteristic of memorization is given. In studying the tempo of reading in memorizing texts, he differentiates three "modifications": a decreasing tempo as the repetitions accumulate, an increasing one, and a rhythmic tempo, that is, one that alternately increases and decreases. The modes of memorizing the text are in these three cases not identical.

In a decreasing tempo the set towards assimilation of the *meaning* of the text is characteristic. For those of this type, as Rybnikov points out, the first reading is for orientation. It gives a general, not altogether clear picture of the meaning. Upon second reading, the meaning of the text begins to be differentiated. Most often this process ends with a third reading and is often accompanied by the composition of an outline or a synopsis of the section. This synopsis serves as a guide for the memorization to come. The attention of the subject is more or less uniformly distributed over the material. In further reading he tries to unite the verbal material around those basic, meaningful groups which he has composed in preceding readings. Due to this, his attention is sequentially concentrated first on one part of the section, then on another; the part mastered is read in a faster tempo; if he has mastered it so that he can reproduce something, he looks away, anticipates something, and checks the correctness of the perceived material.

An increasing tempo of reading is characterized by a set towards words. "Of course," notes the author, "meaning also has significance but seems to be secondary, the subject prefers to rely on especially striking forms and expressions, first words of sentences, similar conjunctions. These 'catches,' as one subject expresses it, serve as a kind of 'landmark' which guides him in the process of memorization."

Finally, the third (rhythmic) type of reading, according to Rybnikov, has no definite set but is "ready to utilize both modes of memorization provided there is a reason for it."

How does asking the subject to memorize with a particular set, corresponding to either the habitual method of memorization or to an unfamiliar method, influence memorization?

Rybnikov's experiments have shown that the "set corresponding to the behavior of the subjects has no important influence on this behavior, but the set contrary to the accustomed form of memorization impedes somewhat, although its influence is not great. Only when subjects had a set for the meaning of memorization did the instruction for a set toward form somewhat impede their work during the first readings. With further reading this difference in behavior was less noticeable because the final aim in all experiments was the textual reproduction of the section. And this demanded attention to form anyway" (1930, p. 88).

In order to elucidate the relation of other aspects of memorization to repeated reading we used the data of our experiments in which the subjects were asked to memorize material without indications of how to memorize it, without limiting the process of memorization. The number of readings was not limited. The task was to memorize in any way the subject wanted to, but well and correctly, not necessarily literally.

The subjects were adults (scientists and students) and schoolchildren (second, fourth, and sixth graders). Texts of different volume and content were used as the memorization material.

The experiments with adults showed considerable variety in the number of readings needed for memorization. The same text, for example, was read by one of our subjects only twice, by others six times, the rest were within these limits. It stands to reason that the rapidity of memorization in the subjects played an important role, and it varied considerably. But it would be incorrect to reduce these facts to only these differences. An important role was also played by the *task* which the subjects set, i.e., the *level* of knowledge which they considered it necessary to achieve. That there was a *consciously set task* is confirmed by the statements of the subjects:

"I wanted to achieve complete recollection, not leaving out any details. I wanted to keep the sequence of the text."

"In the text were so many facts that I immediately decided to memorize only the basic, the general course of the thoughts; the details I would use only for comprehension and better elucidation of the meaning of what I read. The details would be needed to confirm the general thought. Therefore, they need to be known only approximately."

Indirect evidence indicates the presence of a *set* mainly similar to the task but distinguished by lesser dependence on the characteristics of the material and greater stipulation of accustomed orientation of the subjects: reproduction of the material by those who read it two or three times was often inadequate. Yet the subjects themselves were satisfied with their reproduction and considered the text well memorized. They must have had an unrecognized criterion of what had to be achieved, i.e., a *set* for *a definite level of memorization*. And this caused the premature halt to reading.

On the other hand, those subjects who read the text many times often noted that an additional reading was made only "to polish up," to remember details which were often omitted in reproduction by the first group. So the second group, too, had a definite set for the level to be reached.

Often in noting the number of readings the subjects pointed out that they *usually* read that many times. This was most often observed in subjects who read two or three times. The largest number of these cases were students.

The presence of a *set towards a specific number of readings* is further indicated by the fact that this number remained more or less constant for each subject. It is characteristic that the extreme cases (reading twice on the one hand, and 5–6 times on the other) were represented more often than the intermediate (3–4 readings). This shows the effect of two qualitatively different sets for memorization: a) *the set towards general familiarization with the material* without careful study of details and without careful self-testing; b) *the set towards complete memorization of the text* with all particular factors in it and a careful check of the results of memorization.

The following indicates how stable and yet unrecognized the set toward the number of readings can be. Some of the subjects received new instructions every time: to memorize as completely or as stably as possible, to memorize in order to answer questions, etc. It turned out that in spite of the difference in instructions one of the subjects in the course of four experiments read each text twice (the experiments were conducted with intervals of several days) and only in the fifth experiment did she notice that each time she read only twice. "I tried to explain it," she said. She was unable to find an explanation, but reflecting on the question she noticed that "although the reading is performed twice the texts are not read identically each time: for the various experiments reading is done with a different stress, depending on the material and instruction."

In some experiments a conflict was observed between the set customary to the subject and the conscious task which he set for himself:

> In spite of my usual habit of assimilating only the basic information from the text, this time I compelled myself to pay attention to all the details in order to memorize everything, if possible. This demanded great exertion, great willpower on my part, since I can't stand such work.
>
> Usually I do not try to memorize trifles and nonessentials: I don't care for it at all, but this time I made myself do it.
>
> As a rule I read twice but this text I read another time, not because the text was difficult, but I remembered the instruction: "memorize as fully as possible." Under the conditions of this experiment I felt strange and, therefore, showed unusual behavior. In reality, the additional reading was probably unnecessary.
>
> Before starting to read, I thought about having to concentrate on all the trifles since it was asked that we memorize "everything." In reality, however, I worked as usual. It is boring to stop for long on the same thing and I am very unaccustomed to "cramming" like a schoolchild.

Sometimes it was the *attitude* towards the process of memorization that determined the number of readings.

"I can study only as long as the text evokes my interest, as long as I find something new in it, but this is usually not longer than the second reading; therefore I read no more than twice."

"I hate cramming. I can never compel myself to memorize in detail. I especially dislike and can't remember numerical data and dates. It is only interesting to grasp the main thing. Therefore, there is no necessity to memorize a text and no desire. I read it only twice."

All this quite definitely reveals that the difference in the number of readings is not at all due only to the peculiarity of the subjects' memories, or, more exactly, to the mnemonic function in itself, but is the result of the *active attitude* of the subjects towards the task posed by the experimenter. Therefore, the same instruction and, objectively, the same task are refracted in each of the subjects differently and evoke different subjective tasks and unequal sets towards memorization. And it must be noted that each separate reading of the text was not at all a process proceeding in *one* direction, from the preceding parts of the material to the following parts. Often the subjects *returned* to what had already been read before reaching the end of the text, looked it over *once more* as a whole or fixed upon some places. Sometimes this was done in order to understand the material better, sometimes with the aim of *remembering* better. The *first* was observed, naturally, when there were *difficulties in comprehension*:

> The introductory part was very difficult, obscure. I reread it three times and could not comprehend it at all, and due to the unclear exposition it was difficult to fix it in memory. One sentence I read five times.
>
> The first sentences I reread three times since I could not comprehend them immediately.
>
> Some sentences I read several times because I could not grasp their meaning at once.
>
> At first reading it seemed as if a thought had been skipped at the end of the first page. I stopped understanding the text clearly. I returned in order to find the connection with the preceding, in order to understand better what had become hard to understand.
>
> I understood the excerpt with difficulty. Difficult language. I returned to what I had read. At one place I changed the text in my mind.

The main reason for returning to the portion already read in order to *memorize* better was the *nature of the material*:

> There were some sentences which I wanted to rearrange on order to obtain a smooth narration. Even upon first reading I had to return to the preceding sentences in order to better remember their sequence.
>
> I returned to the first paragraph because I was not sure whether I had assimilated everything. Since the text is historical (difficult for me), it seemed to me more expedient to memorize it in parts.
>
> The first part I read three times. This was the most difficult place, especially the first sentence and one other. These two made memorization of the whole paragraph difficult. They impeded memorization.
>
> Sometimes I had to repeat words which I wanted to associate with something known.
>
> I read attentively from beginning to end. I stopped at words which needed fixing in memory, reread them, repeated them to myself.
>
> I repeated definitions in the text several times.
>
> In reading the first time, I repeated the sentences most difficult to remember.

Sometimes the subjects felt that if they continued reading they would forget everything they had read and so first they had to fix what had been read and then continue:

> The material was saturated with facts. When I came to "agriculture" I felt that it would be useless to read on since I would immediately forget what I read. I returned and began to fix what I had read in my memory.
>
> As I continued to read I felt it difficult to keep everything in my memory. The new material kept on impeding the old. I had to discontinue reading temporarily, to note just what I had already found out, fix it in my memory, and then continue reading.
>
> Approximately in the middle of the text I felt I had to stop and look over once more what I had read in order to unhurriedly examine the new material.

This mode of memorizing sometimes has as its result *memorization by parts,* i.e., consecutive, multiple reading of each part separately. Sometimes this is due to distraction and insufficient set toward memorization.

> I began to read. There was no set toward memorization. I was interested in finding out what topic was given, what it was about. I read the heading attentively. A set toward memorization arose only after I had read several lines. I realized that I was simply reading and started all over, looking at the heading.
>
> The return to [an earlier part of] the text was somewhere in the middle of my reading and was caused by my being distracted from what I was reading.
>
> One place I read twice, since I wanted to penetrate its meaning. Another place, somewhere near the end, I read once more, since I was distracted during reading.

The next important fact is *the heterogeneity of perception of the same material during repeated reading*. Each successive reading has its own purpose, performs a function different from the preceding reading of the same text. Two basic cases are most characteristic. Some subjects point out that the first reading is *informative*. They simply get acquainted with the text without any aim of remembering it fully, without trying to analyze it.

> The first time I read it to get acquainted with the material.
>
> I read it the first time to find out what it was about.
>
> The first reading was for acquaintance with the material.
>
> The first time was a relaxed reading.
>
> The first time I read for orientation.
>
> At first I decided to read everything and try to understand what it was about. I did not set myself the task of memorizing. I didn't think about it. I was going to read it again (D).

In an extreme case the first reading is a simple *scanning* of the text.

"I began not by reading, but by scanning the whole text. I grasped the general nature of the material. I saw that it did not contain numbers or details that had to be especially remembered."

Sometimes, even during the first reading, the subjects set themselves the task of *understanding the text more thoroughly*.

"The first time I read through the whole text. This was a general familiarization with the text. I read not to memorize, but to understand, to grasp its essence" (D).

The nature of the first reading determines the characteristics of the subsequent readings. In reading the material for the second time, the subjects who read for the purpose of getting acquainted with the text have now a different task. They try to analyze the text carefully. These attempts have a twofold expression, one of which is the tendency *to attempt to understand* the text as well as possible.

"The second time I read and tried to comprehend how it goes in my own words. I repeated some; thought of how I could tell about it."

"The second time I read for thoughts, trying to analyze the meaning, assimilated, and then went on. For example, the first sentence I understood, I repeated it in order to be able to retell it later. I felt that I knew it and continued. In this manner I proceeded to the end."

The second reading for such subjects is often accompanied by the drawing up of an outline of the text: a meaningful grouping and distinguishing of support points.

"In reading the second time I gave myself the task of breaking the text up into points."

"I usually draw up a plan when I read for the second time" (D).

"At the second reading, breaking up into parts occurred without formulation of names for the parts."

To the same category belong attempts by the subjects to note during the second reading the sequence of the material.

"At the second reading I tried to imagine the sequence of thoughts" (D).

"Reading the second time, I tried to notice the order of the sentences."

The attempt to analyze the meaning of the text during second reading is all the more natural since the first reading in these cases is sometimes insufficient for an understanding of the text.

"In the first reading there were some sentences which I did not understand at all, especially at the end, although I read slowly."

In other cases attempts to analyze the text are expressed in the striving to *remember* the text:

"The second time I read more attentively, I tried to memorize the material."

This striving is, of course, characteristic of the first group of cases in which the subjects try to *understand* the text, since understanding is in these cases the means of memorization and is subordinate to the task of remembering. Therefore, in distinguishing as a special group of cases the orientation of the subjects towards *memorization* itself during second reading, we have in mind cases in which memorization is achieved not only by understanding, but also in other ways. Usually, for the second reading the subjects in these cases set themselves the task of *remembering the details* which were either completely dropped or not sufficiently fixed during the first reading.

"During the second reading I memorized the dates and numbers."

"The task for second reading was mainly to remember numbers and names" (D).

Details were often noticed only during second reading:

> I began reading for the second time and noticed new sentences which had slipped by unnoticed before (D).
>
> When I read the first time I did not remember anything. I usually read in such a manner that the first reading does not count.
>
> Usually, when we read to ourselves, especially for the first time, there is a certain tendency to pass over some thoughts. We read, often generalizing somewhat and, therefore, pass over some thoughts; not that we forget them, but we "do not perceive them fully," that is, in reading we select by means of our attention, underestimate some thoughts which can be omitted, without which one can grasp the content, although [only] in a more general aspect. For this not to happen it is necessary to make an effort, to read once more what has escaped attention (D).
>
> During first reading I did not note all the details. For example, I overlooked the fact that animal organisms also belong to plankton. I noticed it only during second reading.

The attempts to analyze more carefully the meaning of the text by drawing up a plan and the tendency to elucidate and remember the details and note what had been omitted or insufficiently comprehended are sometimes observed even after the second reading. For example, breaking up into parts often is carried out only during the third reading and sometimes even later:

> The first two times I read without any subdivisions and only during third reading did I break up the text into parts.
>
> After the first or second reading I felt the need to break up the text into parts.
>
> When I read the text for the third time I made up an outline and a plan.
>
> During third and fourth reading I broke up the text into parts.

The same must be said with respect to *memorizing details*. This task, too, often comes later.

"When I read for the fourth and fifth time I tried to comprehend and remember the details. During preceding readings not all the details reached my consciousness, I did not pay attention to numbers. At that time I felt that I would mix them up."

All this shows a gradual "getting into" the text by the subjects. The content is only approximately assimilated during first reading, in general outline. The first reading is considered to be only a "beginning" of memorization. However, the real memorization, and the deeper understanding necessary for it, comes only when the material is read for a second, and sometimes even a third or fourth, time. In other cases "entering into" the text was completed during the *first* reading:

> I read so as to be able to remember after reading once (D).
>
> I decided to remember it during first reading. Therefore, I stopped. It did not immediately fall in place in my mind. I had to think. I assimilated everything. That's why I read slowly (D).

In these cases one could observe a breaking up of the text even during first reading:

> During first reading I read every word attentively, kept the thought "in mind"; finishing with a thought, I felt that I was passing over to the next one. A plan was outlined during the first reading (D).

The task of the first reading in these cases determines to a considerable extent the nature of the following readings. Most often, repeated reading here is an examination of the text with the aim of fixing what has already been assimilated as a result of the first reading:

> During the first reading I kept thinking that I had to memorize. There was great tension. During the second reading everything flitted by as in a speeded-up film.
>
> The first time I read attentively, the second time I only scanned.
>
> The first time I read and selected headings, the second time I ran over it with my eyes.

Consequently, characteristic of the second way of memorizing is the fact that the process of assimilation of the text begins with a careful study of the material, achieved during first reading. The following readings serve only to fix what has for the most part already been assimilated.

Aside from these extremes we also observed *intermediate* cases, most often due to the impossibility of accomplishing for some reason or other the mastering of the material during first reading. In some cases this was due to difficulties in understanding the text: the subjects did not always analyze its content and structure immediately. For example, the plan they had made during first reading sometimes proved to be only a draft; therefore, the next reading was directed at making this plan more exact and at a deeper understanding of the text.

In other cases the task of "squeezing out" the maximum possible from the first reading was not accomplished because of the great demands the text made on memorization. This usually happened when the material was overloaded with facts. In these cases, during first reading the subjects had to concentrate mainly on the comprehension of the text and the memorization of a few factual data. The main part of factual material they left for memorizing during subsequent reading:

> During first reading I paid attention to some details but did not memorize them (D).
>
> I didn't need numbers now. I decided to pay attention to them later. First I had to assimilate the thought (D).
>
> I did not want to linger over dates. If I stopped, the text would possibly slip by (D).

Such an attitude towards factual data arises as early as the process of reading and in spite of the adopted decision to master, if possible, everything:

"I read the first paragraph while trying to remember, but when the numbers came I decided that I could not remember them at once and, therefore, should familiarize myself with the text" (D).

The intermediate forms of memorization bring a considerable diversity to the specific ways in which the process of memorization develops, to the nature of the tasks which the subjects set themselves before each successive reading. A still greater diversity in memorization is caused by the fact that the reading of the text is sometimes replaced by other processes. Instead of rereading the material, the subject tries *to mentally retell the text,* only occasionally looking into it. Sometimes he tries to reproduce the material in the process of reading, running ahead mentally and trying to recollect what will be said next:

> Reading the beginning, I tried to reproduce it to myself; it was very difficult to memorize.
>
> After the first reading I read it in parts and immediately retold it to myself.
>
> The first time I read for orientation. After that I retold the text to myself. Since it was not difficult, I hardly looked at the text.
>
> The third time I reread everything and simultaneously retold it to myself.
>
> Reading the sentences, I recollected what would come next. If I recollected correctly, I did not read these parts any more.
>
> During the second reading I tried to comprehend and remember; for this purpose I was trying to tell it to myself, but in my own words.
>
> Reading for the third time, I tried to recollect what followed, but since I was not yet successful I had to look at how the next sentence began. Then I tried once more, hardly looking in the text—and then only to recollect the most important things.

In some cases the attempts to retell mentally were not continued to the end, since such reproduction seemed boring and tiring to the subjects.

> I thought I should reproduce to myself; I began but was too lazy, as it usually happens in life.
>
> I tried to restore the text but became bored and left it.
>
> During fourth reading I tried to retell to myself. I began, but then it seemed boring and I decided I would remember without it.

These attempts to reproduce the text often lead to a *checking of reproduction* during further reading of the text: "I remembered what I had read and then began to read anew, mentally checking my reproduction."

Self-checking is especially clearly seen in experiments in which subjects are asked to make an attempt to reproduce the content of a text after each reading. In some cases, this self-checking had a peculiar accompaniment in all subsequent readings of the text: the subjects constantly referred to gaps noticed in their reproduction.

"I spoke about the scales but not of the molting. I said 'sheath' but left out 'with the tips of their ribs they move their bodies.' I said 'by slithering' and in the text it says with the tips of the ribs and also by slithering. There is another form of movement given. It bites! 'The larger the snake'—this thought I left out. I said 'boa' and there it was 'cobra.' 'In the Transcaspian region.' I ranked the boa with poisonous snakes. Here are mentioned characteristics of boas. Where do they live? In hot countries! I left that out" (D).

Having difficulty in reproducing and realizing that errors may be made, the subjects, after attempts to tell the text to themselves and especially after reproducing it out loud, pose for themselves a special task—by further reading *to find the deficiencies in recalling in order to eliminate them:*

> For the second reading I set myself the task of paying attention to what I had left out (D).
>
> The task for the second reading was to complete what had been left out; in particular, I wanted to find out what was written at the bottom: it spoke of some changes in the state structure. I caught it, understood it in the process of reading, but did not fix it (D).
>
> During the second reading my work proceeded differently: I did not fix what there was in the text but compared what was retained in my memory [reproduced for the experimenter] with what was in the text (D).

All this reveals a large variety of ways used by the subjects for memorization. These ways differ primarily by their dependence on the *personal characteristics of the subjects,* who often emphasize that they "are used to doing it that way," they "usually do it in this manner," "it is more convenient to do it this way."

At the same time these ways vary even in the same subjects since they depend on the *material,* on the difficulty of understanding and memorizing it, on the presence of factual data in it, on the success of its reproduction in the process of memorization, and on the direct experience of the degree of its mastery.

This introduces a great diversity not only into the process of memorization as a whole but also into every separate, repeated reading of the same material. *Each reading does not represent, therefore, a copy of the preceding one, but has its own aim, solves its own problem, has its own characteristic features distinguishing it from the other readings.* The tasks are determined by the concrete conditions of the experiment, the aim set by the subject, the results achieved, and by how memorization proceeded before a particular reading.

Thus, *the total process of memorization is not a sum of homogeneous readings*—separate, stereotypically proceeding repetitions of the same material—*but is a complex activity of those who memorize, carried out in various ways and proceeding quite differently in different cases.* It is not the totality of successive passive processes of imprinting what is being memorized but is *a varied and truly active work upon the material.* This multiplicity and activeness is the cause of the peculiarity in memorizing different material, as well as the cause of the peculiarity of each separate reading of the same material.

Not stereotype and standard repetition, but diversity of action, an active attitude towards each component of the memorizing process—this is what is characteristic of memorization and what really makes it a special, distinctively carried out activity.

2. THE NATURE OF REPETITION IN MEMORIZATION IN CHILDREN

We conducted the experiments with schoolchildren of the second, fourth, and sixth grades (12 each). Immediately after memorizing a text, each of the pupils participating in the experiments was asked how he had memorized it. The aim was to find out how repetitions following one another differed and what operative actions were performed to achieve better memorization.

In studying the answers of the subjects, the great variety of statements observed, even among students in the same age level, was striking. Pupils of the same school year described completely differently how memorization proceeded for them. The individual differences among pupils overlapped to a considerable extent the age differences; this wide range of individual characteristics was observed even in pupils of the same grade and having the same instructors.

What did the statements of the second graders show? Here the individual differences were especially pronounced. The least capable pupils of this grade only read the text in a monotonous fashion. This was because the technique of reading was not satisfactorily mastered as yet and much attention was directed towards reading the text correctly. In answering the question as to whether a reading differed from the one preceding it, these second graders only pointed to a difference in their reading technique.

"The second time I read better" said one of the pupils. "What does 'better' mean?" asked the experimenter. "I pronounced the words and endings better."

They could not point out any other differences in spite of direct questions; one must assume that this corresponded to the real situation, because the attention paid to the technique of reading was so considerable that they could not think of any variations in reading.

It is important to note that at this stage reading is usually carried on out loud. This narrows still more the possibility of variation for each reading of a text.

Mental reproduction, i.e., telling the text to oneself was completely absent from this group.

"I never recite to myself" said one of the pupils. "When the teacher asks, then I recite to her. At home I do not recite to anyone either."

Some of the second graders were even surprised at the question concerning retelling to oneself.

But the most capable second graders, those who had sufficiently mastered the technique of reading, brought some *diversity* to memorization. The task was not the same during first and second reading of the text:

> At first [says a pupil of this group] I read in order to memorize. That was during first and second reading. And then I read in order to review [the text was read 5 times].
>
> The first time I read slowly in order to understand. The second time I read faster in order to remember better. When I read the third time I already knew the story; I read in order to stabilize it properly, so as not to make mistakes later. The fourth time I did not read everything but only what I did not remember well. Maria Alekseevna taught this to us this year and last year. I always read four or five times.

In reading the text differently each time, with a different task, these pupils never returned to what had been read, i.e., they never repeated parts of the text: "I read everything one after another as it is written here; I did not turn back."

In some of the pupils of this group one could clearly observe an *active self-checking during the process of memorization, a telling of the text to themselves with "glancing"* into it (in case something was forgotten or the pupil was not sure of his reproduction). This retelling was not silent as the reading but most often in a whisper.

Between these two groups of second graders were the rest of the children of the same grade. Most characteristic for them was reading without task differentiation for each repeated reading but with sufficient utilization of self-checking after several readings: "I posed no new task before each reading. I read simply to memorize. When I felt I knew it, I began checking myself"—a typical answer of this group.

The only variation was that some pupils read silently, others in a whisper, still others out loud: "The first time I read silently, the second—out loud, the third—in a whisper."

We think this variation must be considered indicative. It undoubtedly attests to the fact that the reading process did not proceed identically even in its inner content. Of course, the pupils did not turn to these different modes of reading by chance.

What compelled them to act in different ways? The various modes of reading were, undoubtedly, connected with some definite achievements in memorization, with a definite stage of learning. Objectively, therefore, they were directed towards solving different problems.

It is quite possible that in the case cited the first reading was done silently because it was needed for a general familiarization with the text as a whole; reading out loud, following the first reading, was dictated by the necessity not simply to *familiarize* oneself with, but really to *memorize* the content of the text; reading in a whisper, observed later, was needed to *fix* the content already assimilated. The requirements of each reading were, of course, not recognized by the pupils and they did not see differences in their perception of the text. Subjectively they did not set any tasks for themselves. The whole memorization process, each of its components, was experienced by them as one task, common to all components, simply that of memorization of the text.

Even in the second grade one can note three stages in the development of diversity in repetition during memorization of a text.

The *first stage* is characterized by the absence of *diversity,* identical perception of the text, and identical work on it in the course of the whole memorization process. The text is read several times, but each repeated reading is the same process as the preceding one.

During the *second stage* a *certain diversity* is noted, but *as yet it is manifested only objectively.* Indeed, the pupil reads differently the second time, but he does not realize the difference. Subjectively, he experiences each repeated reading as performing one and the same task. He realizes only one thing, that he must memorize the material, but what he must do at each stage of memorization, how to differentiate this total task—this he does not realize and does not notice.

A conscious differentiation of the overall task characterizes the *third stage* in the development of diversity of repetition. This stage differs from the preceding one not only objectively, but also subjectively. Repeated reading is in fact carried out differently, and the pupil himself experiences it as the solution to a certain special problem differing from those already solved. The pupil sets himself a special task before each reading. During reading he is oriented towards solving a definite, differentiated, more particular problem and utilizes each new reading for the solution of this problem.

It stands to reason that the range of these problems is not wide at first, and the means to solve them are limited. Our data revealed that none of the second graders, not even the most capable, used the mode of periodic return to what had been read, which was the prevalent mode for adults.

Of the three stages we observed only the last two in the fourth grade. The first, lowest, stage was not observed at all; on the contrary, the third was prominently represented. In a number of cases these pupils quite consciously used diversity in repetition. One of the subjects was quite surprised at the question of whether he read the same way or differently each time. "Of course, differently. The first time I only got acquainted, the second time I studied, and the third time I polished up in order to answer you completely." And then he explained: "As you wash your face, at first you splash water on, then use soap, and then wash off all the dirt. That is how I am used to studying."

Aside from increasing consciousness and diversity in repetition, the fourth graders also revealed a wide range of means by which memorization is achieved. Some of the pupils return more than once to the parts of the text already read, and they mentally recall what has been read even while the reading of the text is in progress.

But it must be mentioned that among the fourth graders, not only the least capable ones but also the most capable ones, one could observe the absence of various tasks in reading. Thus one of our subjects, a very capable fourth grader, told us: "I always read the same way: why read differently? I remember it immediately anyway. I read slowly, I think over every word and remember it."

This pupil indeed memorized very successfully. He also reproduced well after reading once or twice. He read slowly, often lingering at some places, and explained this thus: "I stop in order to understand better." It is evident that good memory in the sense of immediate retention and the conscious comprehension of the material during first reading made superfluous a differention of the tasks, which was characteristic for the other pupils.

This applies in many respects to the sixth graders. Here too, only the second and third stages were observed. But in the sixth graders, more often and clearer than in the fourth graders could be observed a conscious posing of various tasks during repetition. The range of means used for memorization was also wider.

Quantitatively, both stages were represented in the sixth grade almost equally. This reveals that the transition to more complex forms of activity, including diverse processes participating in memorization and consciously utilized as modes of memorization, is accomplished in the course of a protracted time. As far as one can judge from the data obtained, this transition is not yet completed in the sixth grade since many of the sixth graders were as yet at the second stage. As they use various modes of memorization, varying and complicating the content and nature of the mnemonic activity, the sixth graders do not always do this consciously. Herein lies the essential, qualitative difference in memorization observed among many of the pupils as compared to what is characteristic and common in adults having sufficient memorization experience.

CONCLUSION

I. We analyzed the problems of the psychology of memorization which are most important for the understanding of the memory processes.

Emphasized were the study of the *dependence of memorization on the activity of the subject and the characteristics of memorization itself as a special kind of human activity.*

The latter occupied a central place in our work. We not only gave more attention to memorization in our analysis of the problem of activeness itself but subordinated to it the study of the question of the meaningfulness of memorization. *The task in the study of this problem consisted of giving a concrete description of thinking activity under conditions of memorization, revealing thereby the essentials of memorization as a special kind of human activity.*

Similarly analyzed were the problems of *repetition during memorization.* Again, the main attention was on the description of the subject's activity.

All this is in agreement with the basic trends of Soviet psychology and follows from the conception of mental processes as an active reflection of objective reality carried out in man's concrete *activity.*

In studying the dependence of memorization on the activity in which it is carried out, we analyzed this relation in two ways. On the one hand, we attempted to find out how each facet of an activity which characterizes it influences memorization: *its orientation and the nature of its accomplishment*; in the latter case we studied mainly the influence exerted by the *activeness* of our activity. On the other hand, we studied the interrelations of these aspects of activity.

In analyzing the dependence of memorization on the *orientation* of the activity, we dwelt on the problem of the influence of the *mnemonic* orientation and its significance in *learning* activity in the process of assimilating knowledge under school conditions. We stated not only the positive role which the mnemonic orientation plays but also attempted to find out how the various *forms* of mnemonic orientation influence memorization. In contrast to other investigators, we studied not the quantitative relations of the productivity of the individual forms of mnemonic orientation but the *qualitative* changes in memorization under the influence of a certain mnemonic orientation. Of main interest to us was precisely what man *does* in relation to a specific form of his orientation towards memorization.

We traced the influence of various kinds of mnemonic orientation in comparing the characteristics of memorization proceeding under these conditions in *adults and children*.

In addition to the various kinds of mnemonic orientation, we analyzed the characteristics of memorization carried out in the *absence* of a mnemonic orientation, i.e., of so-called *involuntary memorization*. We attempted to determine how it is influenced by the orientation of the activity in which it is carried out. Investigations conducted by us and other authors showed the same clear dependence of memorization on the orientation of the activity during which memorizing proceeds: *what is remembered is mainly that which lies in the main channel of our activity*.

In analyzing the influence of the nature of an activity on memorization, we concentrated on the dependence of memorization on the *activeness* of the activity. We not only stated its positive role but attempted to find differences in the influence exerted by various types of activity included into an actively carried out activity on memorization. As a result of our investigations an important difference was discovered between memorizing what is the object of goal-oriented actions, and what is only the starting point for the activity, what serves as the object of actions which play only a *preparatory role* and do not immediately lead to the achievement of a goal.

We paid special attention to the *interrelation* between the orientation and nature of an activity—the comparative role of each in the total dependence of memorization on the activity in which it is carried out. Investigation of this problem revealed much more complex *interrelations of voluntary and involuntary memorization* than are usually depicted in psychology literature.

Not rejecting the significance of the *orientation towards memorization* and, consequently, the advantages of voluntary memorization, we showed that this advantage can be realized only when the mnemonic activity of the subject is of a specific *nature* and, first of all, under the condition of high activeness of his activity. The absence of this condition can lead to a directly opposite relation between voluntary and involuntary memorization as compared with what is usually considered uniquely characteristic of them. In other words, we have shown that *at high activeness of the activity as a result of which involuntary memorization is achieved it can be much more productive than voluntary memorization if the latter is carried out with less active activity of the subject.*

It was found that memorization of a pronounced voluntary nature and consisting of a very attentive and active perception of the material but limited only to its *perception* is not an activity which guarantees great success in memorization. It is not coupled with the intellectual activeness that is necessary in these cases and is, therefore, less productive than involuntary memorization that is based on precisely such activeness. Only when voluntary memorization incorporates *diverse* and, moreover, *the highest forms of intellectual* activeness does it really become maximally productive and realize all the rich possibilities in it.

By itself, the mnemonic orientation does not have the proper effect. Its presence may or may not lead to successful memorization, and its absence can be compensated for by the *nature* of the activity in which memorization is carried out, *by high forms of intellectual activeness* even if this activity was not directed towards memorization. *Only the combination of orientation towards memorization and high forms of intellectual activeness really creates a stable basis for a maximally successful memorization and makes it most productive.* This is not only of theoretical but also practical significance.

There is no doubt that this orientation must be widely utilized in the practice of teaching. Unsatisfactory memorization in schoolchildren can often be explained by the fact that they sometimes lack the proper orientation when faced with the necessity of memorizing something. While listening to the teacher or reading material in class, the pupil may preceive what is told to him without special orientation towards memorization and this, undoubtedly, lessens the effect of memorization. It is clear that the teacher's task here is, somehow or other, to evoke in the pupils an orientation towards memorization, to awaken a *striving to remember* what they are perceiving. One must keep in mind, however, that in many cases successful memorization, as follows from our experiments, can be achieved without a special orientation.

We do not analyze the problem to what extent the pupils in the process of studying must *always* have a rather pronounced *mnemonic* orientation and to what extent it can be evoked in each case. Important here is that when this orientation has not been evoked or is insufficiently evoked for some reason, the teacher can always organize the activity of the pupil in such a way that as its result memorization will be achieved, although orientation towards it was absent.

The main way which must be utilized in these cases, as is clear from our experiments, consists of evoking in the pupil an active intellectual activity on the material which has to be memorized.

Precisely what activity must be chosen depends upon the particular case. As a general principle, however, the following must be emphasized: *this activity must demand of the pupil a real intellectual activeness and its direct object must be that which is to be memorized.* The material must not be something *secondary* to the given activity and must not be only more or less casually connected with it. *It must lie in the main channel of the given activity, in the very center of its orientation.*

The important role which the nature of an activity plays in memorization demands that special attention be paid to the choice of activity, not only when the mnemonic orientation is absent but also when it is present in the pupils. And yet, in school practice pupils often strive to memorize the material, but their activity is reduced to the repeated *perception* of the material, to simple rereading, and includes no intellectual participation the object of which is that which is to be memorized. As a result, a satisfactory effect of memorization is not reached in spite of the presence of a mnemonic orientation. The pupil must not only *aim* to remember the material but have the real *means* for it. And this means that *even voluntary memorization must be included into an activity which because of the very nature of its implementation (intellectual activeness demanded of it) will lead to successful memorization.*

As one of the clear illustrations of this, the following fact once observed in studying how pupils prepare their homework may be cited. A fifth grader was studying an assignment in botany which had information on the form of plant leaves. There were eight forms of leaves and names of eight trees. Thus, the pupil had to study eight pairs of names associated with each other. Many names, especially those of all trees, were familiar to the pupil and he had only to associate the name of a particular leaf form with the name of each tree.

It would seem that this work should not present any difficulties. In reality, it was revealed that the pupil spent 30 min in studying this material. Though he worked intensely and clearly strived to remember, he could not recite without errors.

Of course, this was not a rule in our observations but an exception. And yet it must be considered indicative of what difficulties pupils experience when they really desire to memorize something and show a pronounced mnemonic orientation, but do not have the *means and modes* to help them and are limited to multiple monotonous repetition.

If the pupil mentioned had been given the task not simply of *memorizing* the eight pairs of names but, instead, had been asked to participate *actively and intellectually* (to point out the differences and similarities of the various forms of leaves, draw a picture of each type, define the leaves of various trees [from memory or pictures], tell himself about a number of trees he knew which had a particular form of leaf, etc.), the work would have been much easier and memorization would have had a greater effect. This was not done and the pupil simply crammed what could have been memorized easily if memorization had been included in an active intellectual activity.

It is quite clear that a *choice* of such an activity is not always within the capabilities of the pupils. *The teacher must organize* this activity. He must know how to organize the assignment in such a manner that it will make full use of the influence of "the orientation towards memorization" and to protect it from an "idle" effect.

One more fact must be pointed out. The orientation towards memorization must not only be reinforced by actions which due to the demand of intellectual activeness would help memorization, but it must itself have a strictly defined nature, be not a mnemonic orientation in general but an orientation towards such memorization which satisfies definite demands of completeness, accuracy, stability, and sequence in reproducing. In order to reach a result satisfying specific demands, it is necessary that this process proceed in a definite manner, and this is achieved by a clearly-assigned concrete task, *orientation not towards memorization in general but memorization corresponding to the demands of each individual case.*

And this poses the problem *of achieving a clear perception by the pupils of the demands presented by memorization, to awaken in them an orientation towards a strictly specific memorization, to point out the ways in which to achieve it, the nature of the process which helps to achieve the result demanded of them.*

The significance of this problem is all the more important since schoolchildren, especially in the lower grades, often do not show a differentiated mnemonic orientation, being satisfied with the most general, indefinite orientation. Also, under the influence of a false understanding of what is required, they sometimes try to memorize all material in the same definite manner, literally, and often where it is not at all needed.

II. In revealing the interrelation of mnemonic orientation on the one hand, and the nature of the activity during memorization on the other, we attempted to find out not only the relative influences of both aspects of activity but also to study the interaction between them. Special attention was paid to the influence which a mnemonic orientation can have on the nature of an activity; we had in mind its influence on understanding what we memorize as well as the effect it has on the very *nature of the intellectual activity* carried out during memorization.

With respect to the first of these factors we found the following: *a mnemonic orientation can have a double effect on the understanding* of what we memorize. In some cases it can impede understanding, and lead to mechanical memorization. In other cases we encounter the opposite phenomenon: the orientation towards memorization, especially the consciously set task of remembering, acts as a stimulus to a fuller, deeper, and more exact comprehension as compared with what is achieved when this task is not set. This is especially important in connection with the often-observed contrasting of memory and thinking which distorts their true interrelation, which in reality has a more complex and contradictory nature.

In our investigations we did not limit ourselves to the study of the effect on the *result* of the thinking activity rendered by the mnemonic orientation, but we also studied the question of how the mnemonic orientation influences the *nature* of the thinking activity which is the support of memorization. This made it possible to characterize memorization as a special kind of activity since the thinking processes represent the essential factors in the content of memorization as a special activity of the subject.

Among the most important processes are: *sense grouping, distinction of meaningful points of support, and sense association or comparison of what is being memorized with something already known.* We showed the exceptionally important role not so much of the *products* of the activity as the *acts* themselves oriented towards memorization, i.e., the active and independent fulfillment of acts carried out with the aim of memorizing the material.

Our experiments showed that not the *plan in itself,* as the *result* of our actions or their most immediate product, so much as the very *process of its composition* is important in memorization and is an important and real support. The same was revealed relative to the significance of intermediate, auxiliary links of the connection to which we take recourse in order to facilitate memorization and which is established in the process of associating what is being memorized with what is already known. In this case not *these components by themselves as a product* of association but the *process of their formation* is the basis of memorization.

For teaching, these propositions are very important. They point to the necessity of maximum stimulation of the pupil's participation in memorizing, of getting an aware, independent execution of the actions serving as supports of memorization: a grouping of the material, independent distinguishing of meaningful groups of support, and independent association of the new with the known.

One cannot reject the significance of all the standard means, in particular the breaking up of texts into paragraphs, headings for sections, emphasizing by use of italics what is important in a text, etc. All this, of course, must be used, especially in textbooks. But it would be a great mistake to use only these *ready means* to facilitate memorization. It is very important that the pupil *himself* perform the operations necessary for a deeper understanding of the text. He *himself* must group and break up the material, separate the support points in it, and compare and associate what he memorizes with what he already knows.

Our experiments have shown that schoolchildren, especially the younger ones, are not able to do this satisfactorily.

Between the mastery of the acts serving as support for memorization and utilizing them as modes of memorization there can exist a considerable gap. The action itself may have been mastered but it is executed only when the pupil is given a special *aim*—the execution of a *given* action. But when such an aim is absent from *memorizing* and the action is only a *means* facilitating memorization, the pupil does not take recourse to it. It has not yet become a *mode* of memorizing. This emphasizes the fact that it is not enough to teach pupils actions which help to memorize *in isolation from the process of memorization,* but that they must be taught to use these actions *when they memorize* as a means facilitating memorization. It is not enough that pupils know how to draw up a plan of material when it is specifically demanded of them, they must be taught to draw up plans in the interest of memorization and as a means, as an action subject to the mnemonic task—the task of memorizing.

III. The study of memorization as a special human activity made it possible to find out not only the general content of the thinking processes occurring during the memorization process as a whole, but also the nature of the subject's activity at each stage of memorization. From this point of view *memorization must be understood not as a monotonous multiple fixing of what is to be remembered, but as a complex and diverse activity,* each separate component of which, each repetition, is directed towards solving a *new* problem which depends on the results already achieved and on a general goal which must be reached. The setting up of such tasks is one of the important indicators of the activeness of memorization and of a conscious approach to the processes of memorization.

Comparative experiments with adults and children have shown that in this respect there are noticeable differences between the two.

At a younger school age memorization proceeds monotonously and consists of stereotyped repetition, subject to only one final, completely undifferentiated task. Differentiation and the diversity connected with it arise only later in repetition as the schoolchildren gain practice in memorizing and depend on instructions given by the teacher. At first the pupils introduce diversity into memorization without noticing it. Only later does it acquire a conscious nature and the conscious differentiation of tasks set at each stage of memorization.

Diversity of repetition is of great significance to the productivity of memorization. It makes it possible to look afresh at material already perceived, distinguish in it what had not been distinguished before, and in accordance with the new tasks which are set before each new repetition to direct memorization each time along a definite path. Therefore, it is natural that a standard fixing of the material has a lesser effect than memorization with a diverse, modifying repetition. This is clearly seen when memorization is done "at a single sitting" as a home assignment and when repetitions are extended in time and are carried out with the aim of renewing and fixing in memory what has been learned earlier.

This imposes a definite obligation on the school: to teach the pupil to vary repetition in the process of independent work in studying school material, to teach him to set concrete differentiated tasks before each rereading, and to note these tasks in accordance with the results already reached and the overall results required.

Repetition of what has been studied must be conducted in school. The role of diversity in repetition is thus enhanced since aside from its direct effect it exerts a considerable influence on the *attitude* of the pupil towards repetition, which in its turn determines the resultant effect.

It is well known that schoolchildren do not like to review what has been learned earlier and underestimate the value of repetition. When they have to review what is fresh in their minds, they consider repetition superfluous and will answer the question of what has been assigned with "Nothing has been assigned." "Assigned for review" seems to be identical with "Nothing has been assigned." On the other hand, it is also known, as Ushinskii correctly noted, that pupils do not like to review what they have forgotten. To restore to memory what has been forgotten means to restore something old, already learned, not to acquire anything new, and that, of course, is not interesting and does not stimulate them to reviewing. In order to overcome the underestimation of the value of repetition by the pupils and their negative attitude towards it, *it is necessary to organize repetition in such a manner that it always contain something new*. Repetition must be built on the basis of *diversity, diversity of the actions* which the pupils perform and, partially, of the material which is being used.

Proceeding from the principles of activeness and meaningfulness of memorization and their importance in awakening the interest of the pupils, it is of great significance to set *new thinking tasks*, for the solution of which the pupils must utilize information obtained earlier and show independence in their work. Then repetition of the old will not be a kind of aim in itself but will be included in a new activity, which can be so chosen as to be of interest to the pupil. Thereby it evokes an interest in the material with which the pupil has to deal and which needs review.

Repetition acquires a new and interesting meaning for the pupil and he realizes that in order to accomplish the new and interesting task he, indeed, has to return to the material already learned and review it. From a boring and underestimated task sometimes carried out only to satisfy the demands of school, repetition changes into a necessary part of a new and absorbing work, the interest in which spreads to repetition itself. This time its significance is recognized and accompanied by a new and higher evaluation.

The positive influence of diversity in repetition is all the greater since the solution of new thinking problems results in *new connections* in which that which was studied before did not originally occur. For the solution of the new problem it is often necessary to change the order in which the material was offered earlier and to include the old in the new connections and relations.

Our best teachers carry out repetition in precisely this manner: they ascribe great significance to the principle of diversity in repetition; toward the realization of this principle is directed a considerable portion of their methodological search; they pay much attention to the selection of new thinking problems, the solutions of which include the review of what was studied earlier. The Soviet psychologists hold the same positions.

What has been said clearly demonstrates that, *without solving the problem of activeness and meaningfulness of memorization, the problem of repetition cannot be correctly solved.* The significance of these problems is apparent and our attention was focused on these problems.

BIBLIOGRAPHY

Aall, A. (1913), "Ein neues Gedächtnisgesetz," *Z. Psychol.*, Vol. 66.

Achilles, E. (1920), "Experimental studies in recall and recognition," *Arch. Psychol.*, Vol. 44.

Alper, T. (1946), "Task-orientation *vs.* ego-orientation in learning and retention," *Amer. J. Psychol.*, Vol. 59.

Anan'ev, B. G. (1960), *Psychology of Sensory Perception*, Moscow, APN RSFSR.

Balaban, A. (1910), "Über den Unterschied des logischen und des mechanischen Gedächtnisses," *Z. Psychol.*, Vol. 56.

Bartlett, F. (1932), *Remembering: A Study in Experimental and Social Psychology*, Cambridge.

Bennett, R. (1916), "The correlation between different memories," *J. Exp. Psychol.*

Bergson, H. (1896), *Matter and Memory*, London, Macmillan.

Bergson, H. (1902), *L'effort intellectuel*.

Bernard, J. and R. Gilbert (1941), "The specifity of the effect of shock for error in maze learning with human subjects," *J. Exp. Psychol.*, Vol. 28.

Binet, A. and V Henri (1895*a*), "La mémoire des mots," *Année psychol.*, Vol. 1.

Binet, A. and V. Henri, (1895*b*), "La mémoire des phrases," *Année psychol.*, Vol. 1.

Blonskii, P. P. (1935), *Memory and Thinking*, Moscow, also in: *Izbrannye Psikhologicheskie Proizvedeniya*, Moscow, Prosveshchenie, 1964.

Borodulina, A. S. (1944), *Methods of Memorization in Independent Work of Children of the II, IV, and VI Grades*, Dissertation, Moscow.

Borodulina, A. S. (1954), "Activity of reproduction in the process of memorization," *Uch. zap. Mosk. gor. pedagog. inst., Kafedra psikhol.*, Vol. 36, No. 2.

Broadbent, D. (1961), "Effects of a subsidiary task on performance involving immediate memory by younger and older men," *Brit. J. Psychol.*, Vol. 52.

Broadbent, D. (1962), "Short term memory," *New Scientist*, **16:** 307.

Brown, G, (1954), "Factors influencing incidental learning," *J. Exp. Psychol.*, Vol. 47.

Brunswick, E., L. Goldscheider, and E. Pileck (1932), "Untersuchungen zur Entwicklung des Gedächtnisses," *Z. angew. Psychol.*, Beiheft, Vol. 64.

Burešová, O. and J. Bureš (1963), "Physiology of direct memory," *Vopr. psikhol.*, No. 6, 63–75.

Chernyshevskii, N. G. (1940), *Selected Pedagogical Opinions*, Moscow, Uchpedgiz.

Claparede, E. (1915), "Expériences sur la mémoire des associations spontanées," *Archives de Psychologie*, Vol. 15.

Denny, M. and W. Greenway (1955), "Recall and intentional *vs.* incidental learning," *J. Percept. Mot. Skill,* **5:** 140.

Dietze, A. and G Jones (1931), "Factual memory of secondary school pupils for a short article which they read a single time," *J. Educ. Psychol.,* Vol. 23.

Dobrolyubov, N. A. (1939), *Selected Pedagogical Opinions,* Moscow, Uchpedgiz.

Dodonova, A. A. (1941), *Dependence of Memorization on the Content of the Material,* Unpublished manuscript.

Dul'nev, G. M. (1939), *Significance of the Intention for Completeness and Exactness in Reproducing a Text,* Dissertation, Moscow.

Dul'nev, G. M. (1940), "Significance of the Intention for Completeness and Exactness in Reproducing a Text," in: *Voprosy psikhologii glukhonemykh i umstvenno otstalykh detei,* I. I. Danyushevskii and L. V. Zankov, eds., Moscow, Uchpedgiz.

Ebbinghaus, H. (1885), *Über das Gedächtnis,* Leipzig.

Ebbinghaus, H. (1912), *Osnovy psikhologii, Fundamentals of Psychology,* St. Petersburg.

Enikeev, Kh. R. (1944), "Reproduction and forgetting in relation to the difficulty of the text and the form of its presentation," in: *Psikhologicheskie ocherki,* I. F. Sluchevskii, ed., Ufa.

Enikeev, Kh. R. (1946), "Additions, Inventions, and Distortions in the Process of Reproduction," in: *Trudy kafedry psikhologii i pedagogiki Bashkirskogo gos. ped. in-ta i Bashkirskoi psikhiatricheskoi b-tsy,* No. 2.

Ebert, E. and E. Meumann (1904), "Über einige Grundfragen der Psychologie der Übungsphänomen im Bereiche des Gedächtnisses," *Arch. ges. Psychol.,* Vol. 4.

Favorin, V. K. (1946), "On structuring memorization," *Uch. zap. Novosibirsk. gos. pedagog. inst.,* Vol. II.

Freud, S. (1898), "Zum psychischen Mechanismus der Vergesslichkeit," *Monatsschr. Psychiat. Neurol.,* Vol. 4.

Galich, A. (1834), *The Picture of Man,* St. Petersburg.

Guthrie, E. (1935), *The Psychology of Learning,* New York.

Guthrie, E. (1940), "Association and the law of effect," *Psychol. Rev.,* Vol. 47.

Hilgard, E. (1956), *Theories of Learning,* New York, Appleton–Century–Crofts.

Hollingworth, N. (1913), "Characteristic differences between recall and recognition," *Amer. J. Psychol.,* Vol. 24.

Hovland, C. (1951), "Human learning and retention," in: *Handbook of Experimental Psychology,* S. S. Stevens, ed., New York—London, Wiley.

Hull, C. (1943), *Principles of Behavior,* New York, Appleton–Century–Crofts.

Hull, C. (1951), *Essentials of Behavior,* New Haven, Yale.

Hull, C. (1952), *A Behavior System,* New Haven, Yale.

Hurlock, E. (1925), "An evaluation of certain incentives used in school work," *J. Educ. Psychol.,* Vol. 16.

Idashkin, Yu. V. (1959), "On involuntary memorization," Vopr. psikhol., No. 2.

Istomina, Z. M. (1947), *Development of Voluntary Memory at Preschool Age,* Dissertation, Moscow.

Istomina, Z. M. (1948), "Development of voluntary memory in children of preschool age," in: *Voprosy psikhologii rebenka doshkol'nogo vozrasta,* Leont'ev, A. N., and Zaporozhets, A. V. (eds.), Moscow, APN RSFSR.

Istomina, Z. M. (1948), "Development of voluntary memory at preschool age," *Izv. APN RSFSR,* No. 14.

Istomina, Z. M. (1948), "Development of voluntary memory at preschool age," *Doshkol'noe vospitanie,* No. 1.

Istomina, Z. M. (1953), "Concerning the development of voluntary memory in children of preschool age," *Doshkol'noe vospitanie,* No. 4, 1953.

Janet, P. (1928), *L'évolution de la mémoire et la notion du temps,* Paris.

Jenkins, J. (1933), "Instruction as a factor in incidental learning," *Amer. J. Psychol.,* Vol. 45.

Karsten, A. (1928), "Psychische Sättigung," *Psychol. Forschung,* Vol. 10.

Key, C. (1926), "Recall as a function of perceived relations," *Arch. Psychol.,* **13**:83.

Kirkpatrick, E. (1894), "An experimental study of memory," *Psychol. Rev.,* Vol. 1.

Kirkpatrick, E. (1914), "An experiment in memorizing *vs.* incidental memory," *J. Educ. Psychol.,* Vol. 5.

Koffka, K. (1934), *The Bases of Mental Development,* Moscow—Leningrad.

Koffka, K. (1935), *Principles of Gestalt Psychology,* New York, Harcourt, Brace.

Köhler, W. (1929), *Gestalt Psychology,* New York, Liveright.

Köhler, W. (1933), *Psychologische Probleme.*

Komenskii, Ya. A. (1939), *Great Didactics,* Izbrannye ped. sochin. Vol. I, Moscow.

Komissarchik, K. A. (1953), *Sequence of Memorization of Various Kinds of Material by Students of Intermediate Schools,* Dissertation, Moscow.

Komissarchik, K. A. (1958), "Sequence of memorizing verbal material by students of intermediate schools," *Izv. APN RSFSR,* No. 98.

Komm, A. G. (1940), Rekonstruktsiya i vosproizvedenie (Reconstruction and reproduction), *Uch. zap. Leningrad. gos. pedagog. inst.,* Vol. 34.

Komm, A. G. (1941*a*), "Reconstruction and reproduction," *Sov. pedagog.,* No. 1.

Komm, A. G. (1941*b*), "Reconstruction and reproduction in schoolchildren," *Sov. pedagog.,* No. 3.

Korman, T. A. (1942), *The Role of Visual Perception and Attention in Memorizing Verbal Material by Preschool Children,* Dissertation, Moscow.

Korman, T. A. (1944), "Dynamics of thinking and reproduction," *Doshkol'noe vospitanie,* No. 3–4.

Korman, T. A. (1945*a*), "Differences of word-sense memory in younger and older preschool children," *Doshkol'noe vospitanie,* No. 7.

Korman, T. A. (1945*b*), "Characteristics of reproduction activeness in preschool children," *Sov. pedagog.,* No. 9.

Korman, T. A. (1954), "On the question of the psychology of reproduction," *Uch. zap. Mosk. gor. pedagog. inst., Kafedra psikhol.,* Vol. 36, No. 2, Moscow.

Kraemer, N. (1911), *Experimentelle Untersuchungen zur Erkenntnis des Lernprozesses.*

Lenin, V. I. *Complete Works,* Vols. 18 and 29.

Leont'ev, A. N. (1928), "Mediated retention in children with insufficient and morbidly changed intellect," *Vopr. defektol.,* No. 4.

Leont'ev, A. N. (1931), *Development of Memory,* Moscow, Uchpedgiz.

Leont'ev, A. N. and T. V. Rozanova (1951), "Dependence of the formation of associative connections on the content of the action," *Sov. pedagog.,* No. 10.

Leont'ev, A. N. (1959), *Developmental Problems of the Mind,* Moscow, APN RSFSR.

Lewin, K. (1922), "Das Problem der Willensmessung und der Assoziation," *Psychol. Forsch.,* Vols. 1–2.

Lewin, K. (1926), *Vorsatz, Wille und Bedürfnis,* Berlin.

Lipkina, A. I. (1941), *Memorization and Reproduction of Geographical Material by Schoolchildren,* Dissertation, Moscow.

Lipkina, A. I. (1958), "Reproduction and forgetting of concrete-vivid and abstract course material," in: *Voprosy psikhologii pamyati,* A. A. Smirnov, ed., Moscow, APN RSFSR.

Lobsien, B. (1901), "Experimentelle Untersuchungen über die Gedächtnisentwicklung bei Schulkindern," *Z. Psychol.,* Vol. 27.

Lobsien, B. (1911), "Zur Entwicklung des akustischen Wortgedächtnisses der Schüler," *Z. pädag. Psychol.,* Vol. 12.

Luriya, A. R. (1962), *Higher Cortical Functions in Man*, Moscow, Moskovsk. Gos. Univ., 432 pp.

Lyon, D. (1914), "The relation of length of material to time taken for learning and the optimum distribution of time," *J. Educ. Psychol.*, Vol. 5.

McGeoch, J. and A. Irion (1961), *The Psychology of Human Learning*, New York, McKay.

Maller, J. (1929), "Cooperation and competition," *Teach. Coll. Educ.*

Mal'tseva, K. P. 1948, *Sense Connections in Schoolchildren during Memorization*, Dissertation, Moscow.

Mal'tseva, K. P. (1958*a*), "Visual and verbal props during memorization in schoolchildren," in: *Voprosy psikhologii pamyati*, A. A. Smirnov, ed., Moscow, APN RSFSR.

Mal'tseva, K. P. (1958*b*), "A plan of the text as sense support for younger schoolchildren in memorizing," in: *Voprosy psikhologii pamyati*, A. A. Smirnov, ed., Moscow, APN RSFSR.

Marx, K. and F. Engels, *Works*, Second Ed., Vol. 3, p. 23.

Matlin, E. K. (1940), *The Influence of Similarity of the Material being Memorized on Its Mastery*, Dissertation, Moscow.

Matlin, E. K. (1958), "The influence of similarity of materials being memorized on their mastery," in: *Voprosy psikhologii pamyati*, A. A. Smirnov, ed., Moscow, APN RSFSR.

Mayants, D. M. (1941), "Retention and reproduction of verbal material by deaf schoolchildren," in: *Voprosy vospitaniya i obucheiya glukhonemykh i umstvenno otstalykh detei*, I. I. Danyushevskii and L. V. Zankov, ed., Moscow.

Mazo, N. (1929), "La valeur de l'activité de l'esprit dans la fixation des idées," *Archives de Psychol.*, Vol. 21.

Meumann, E. (1912), "Beobachtungen über differenzierte Einstellung bei Gedächtnisversuchen," *Z. pädag. Psychol.*, Vol. 13.

Meumann, E. (1913), *The Economy and Technique of Memory*, Moscow.

Muenzinger, K. (1934), "Motivation in learning: II. The function of electric shock for right and wrong responses in human subjects," *J. Exp. Psychol.*, Vol. 17.

Müller, G. (1911–1915), *Zur Analyse der Gedächtnistätigkeit und des Vorstellungsverlaufes.*

Müller, G. and A. Pilzecker (1900), *Experimentelle Beiträge zur Lehre vom Gedächtnis.*

Müller, G. and F. Schumann (1893), *Experimentelle Beiträge zur Untersuchung des Gedächtnisses.*

Myers, A. (1914), "Comparative study of recognition and recall," *Psychol. Rev.*, Vol. 21.

Myers, G. (1913), "A study in incidental memory," *Arch. Psychol.*, **4**:26.

Nudel'man, M. M. (1940), "On the alteration of visual images during forgetting in deaf and mentally retarded children," in: *Voprosy psikhologii glukhonemykh i umstvenno otstalykh detei*, L. V. Zankov and I. I. Danyushevskii, eds., Moscow, Uchpedgiz.

Pavlov, I. P. (1951*a*), *Experience of Twenty Years of Objective Study of the Higher Nervous Activity in Animals*, Works, Second Ed., Vol. III, Books 1 and 2.

Pavlov, I. P. (1951*b*), *Lectures on the Work of the Cerebrum*, Works, Second Ed., Vol. IV.

Piéron, H. (1913), "Recherches expérimentales sur les phénomènes de mémoire," *Année psychol.*, Vol. 19.

Pinskii, B. I. (1948), "Unpreconceived retention in the process of repetition and its peculiarities in mentally retarded children," *Izv. APN RSFSR*, No. 19.

Pinskii, B. I. (1952), "Peculiarities in the process of memorization in children of auxiliary schools," *Uchebno-vospitatel'naya rabota v spetsial'nykh shkolakh*, No. III–IV, Moscow.

Pinskii, P. I. (1954), "The process of reproduction in premeditated memorization and its peculiarities in children of auxiliary schools," *Izv. APN RSFSR*, No. 57.

Pinskii, P. I. (1962), *Psychological Characteristics of the Activity of Mentally Retarded Schoolchildren*, Moscow, APN RSFSR.

Pohlmann, A. (1906), *Experimentelle Beiträge zur Lehre vom Gedächtnis.*

Poppelreuter, W. (1912), "Nachweis der Unzweckmässigkeit der gebräuchlichen Assoziationsexperimente mit sinnlosen Silben nach dem Erlernung und Trefferverfahren zur exakten Gewinnung elementarer Reproduktionsgesetze zu verwenden," *Z. Psychol.*, Vol. 61.

Postman, L. and V. Senders (1946), "Incidental learning and generality of set," *J. Exp. Psychol.*, Vol. 36.

Postman, L., P. Adams, and L. Phillips (1955), "Studies in incidental learning: II. The effects of association value and the method of testing," *J. Exp. Psychol.*, Vol. 49.

Radossawljewitch, P. (1907), "Das Behalten und Vergessen bei Kindern und Erwachsenen nach experimentellen Untersuchungen," *Pädag. Monogr.*, No. 1, Leipzig.

Raksha, E. A. (1948), "The psychology of the formation of sensory habits," *Izv. APN RSFSR*, No. 13.

Rozanova, T. V. (1959), "Involuntary retention of various components of a situation depending on their role in the activity," *Vopr. psikhol.*, No. 4.

Rubinshtein, S. L. (1946), *Foundations of General Psychology*, Moscow, Uchpedgiz.

Russel, W. and Y. Farber (1948), "Retention of verbal material as a function of degree of failure experienced in original learning," *Amer. Psychol.*, Vol. 3.

Rybnikov, N. A. (1923), "On logical and mechanical memory," *Zh. psikhol., nevrol. psikhiatr.*, No. 3.

Rybnikov, N. A. (1930), "Memorization and reproduction of complex material," in: *Problemy Sovremennoi psikhologii*, K. N. Kornilov, ed., Vol. VI, Moscow.

Schellow, S. (1923), "Individual differences in incidental memory," *Arch. Psychol.*, **10**:64.

Schwartz, G. (1961), "Fluctuations in immediate memory," *Percep. and Mot. Skill*, Vol. 13.

Sears, R. (1937), "Initiation of the repression sequence by experienced failure," *J. Exp. Psychol.*, Vol. 20.

Sechenov, I. M. (1947), *Selected Philosophical and Psychological Works*, Moscow, AN SSSR.

Shardakov, M. N. (1938), "Repetition in teaching," *Uch. zap. Leningrad. gos. univ.*, Vol. XIII.

Shardakov, M. N. (1940), "Mastery and retention in training," *Uch. zap. Leningrad. gos. pedagog. inst.*, Vol. 36.

Shardakov, M. N. (1947), "On memorization in the process of training," *Estestvoznanie v shkole*, No. 5.

Shaw, F. (1944), "Two determinants of selective forgetting," *J. Abnorm. Soc. Psychol.*, Vol. 39.

Shaw, J. and A. Spooner (1945), "Selective forgetting when the subject is not egoinvolved," *J. Exp. Psychol.*, Vol. 35.

Shul'gin, A. K. (1958), "Psychological analysis of repeated retelling of a text by schoolchildren of the IV and VI grades," *Izv. APN RSFSR*, No. 98.

Shvarts, L. A. (1947), "The role of comparison in mastering school material," *Izv. APN RSFSR*, No. 12.

Sims, V. (1928), "The relative influence of two types of motivation on improvement," *J. Educ. Psychol.*, Vol. 19.

Skinner, B. F. (1938), *The Behavior of Organisms*, New York, Appleton–Century–Crofts.

Skinner, B. F. (1959), *Science and Human Behavior*, New York, Macmillan.

Skinner, B. F., ed. (1940), *Educational Psychology.*

Smirnov, A. A. (1945*a*), "The influence of effort and the nature of activity on retention," in: *Trudy Inst. psikhol. AN Gruz. SSR*. Tbilisi.

Smirnov, A. A. (1945*b*), "Thinking processes during memorization," *Izv. APN RSFSR*, No. 1.

Smirnov, A. A. (1948), *The Psychology of Memorization,* Moscow, APN RSFSR.
Sokolov, A. N. (1941), "Inner speech and understanding," *Uch. zap. Gos. inst. psikhol.,* Vol. II, Moscow.
Solov'ev, I. M. (1940), "Alteration of concepts depending on similarity and difference of objects," *Uch. zap. Gos. inst. psikhol.* Vol. 1.
Stern, W. (1903–1904), *Beiträge zur Psychologie der Aussage,* B. 1; (1904–1906), B. II.
Stern, W. (1922), *Psychology of Early Childhood,* Moscow.
Stern, W. (1930), "Personalistik der Erinnerung, " *Z. f. Psych.,* Vol. 118.
Szewczuk, W. (1957 and 1965), *Psychologia zapamitywania,* Warszawa.
Tatishchev, V. N. (1887), *Talk on the Use of Learning and Schools,* St. Petersburg.
Thorndike, E. (1914), *The Psychology of Learning,* New York.
Thorndike, E. (1931), *Human Learning,* New York.
Thorndike, E. (1932), *The Fundamentals of Learning,* New York.
Thorndike, E. and G. Forlano (1933), "The influence of increase and decrease of the amount of reward upon the rate of learning," *J. Educ. Psychol.,* Vol. 24.
Tolman, E. (1932), *Purposive Behavior in Animals and Men,* New York.
Ushinskii K. D. (1950*a*), *Man as Object of Upbringing,* Works, Vol. VIII, Moscow, APN RSFSR.
Ushinskii, K. D. (1950*b*), *On the Training of the Memory,* Works, Vol. X, Moscow.
Uznadze, D. N. (1961), *Experimental Bases of the Psychology of Set,* Tbilisi, AN Gruz. SSR.
Vygotskii, L. S. (1960), *Development of Higher Mental Functions,* Moscow, APN RSFSR.
Watson, J. (1924), *Psychology from the Standpoint of a Behaviorist,* Philadelphia.
Wertheimer, M. (1945), *Productive Thinking,* New York, Harper and Brothers.
Whipple, G. (1913), *Handbook for the Investigation of Physical and Mental Activity in Schoolchildren.*
Whitely, P. and J. McGeoch (1928), "The curve of retention for poetry," *J. Educ. Psychol.,* Vol. 19.
Williams, P. (1926), "A study of phenomenon of reminiscence," *J. Exp. Psychol.,* Vol. 9.
Wohlgemuth, A. (1915), "Simultaneous and successive association," *Brit. J. Psychol.,* Vol. 7.
Woodworth, R. (1915), "A revision of imageless thought," *Psychol. Rev.,* Vol. 22.
Woodworth, R. and H. Schlossberg (1954), *Experimental Psychology,* New York, Holt.
Zal'tsman, B. N. (1949), "Thinking processes during recalling," *Nauchnye zapiski In-ta psikhologii Ministerstva Prosveshcheniya Ukr. SSR,* Vol. I, Kiev (in Ukrainian).
Zankov, L. V. (1940*a*), "Mistakes made in reproducing a chronological sequence of historical events," *Sov. pedagog.,* No. 7.
Zankov, L. V. (1940*b*), "On the peculiarity of memory in mentally retarded children," *Byulleten' uchebno-vospitatel'noi raboty v shkolakh dlya glukhonemykh i v vspomogatel'-nykh shkolakh,* No. 8.
Zankov, L. V. (1941), Posledovatel'nost' vosproizvedeniya i ee osobennosti u umstvenno otstalykh shkol'nikov (Sequence of reproduction and its characteristics in mentally retarded schoolchildren), in: *Voprosy vospitaniya i obucheniya glukhonemykh i umstvenno otstalykh detei,* I. I. Danyushevskii and L. V. Zankov, eds., Moscow, Uchpedgiz.
Zankov, L. V. (1944), *A Schoolchild's Memory,* Moscow, Uchpedgiz.
Zankov, L. V. (1949), *Memory,* Moscow, Uchpedgiz.
Zeigarnik, B. (1927), "Das Behalten erledigter und unerledigter Handlungen," *Psych. Forsch.,* Vol. 9.
Zhinkin, N. I. (1958), *Mechanisms of Speech,* Moscow, APN RSFSR.

Zinchenko, P. I. (1939), "Forgetting and reproducing school knowledge," *Nauch. zap. Khar'kov. gos. pedagog. inst. in. yaz.*, Vol. I, Khar'kov.

Zinchenko, P. I. (1939), "Problems of involuntary memorization," *Nauch. zap. Khar'kov. gos. pedagog. inst. in. yaz.*, Vol. I, Khar'kov.

Zinchenko, P. I. (1945), "Involuntary memorization," *Sov. pedagog.*, No. 9.

Zinchenko, P. I. (1948), "Dependence of Involuntary Memorization on the Motives of Activity," *Nauch. zap. Inst. psikhol. Ukr. SSR*, Vol. I (in Ukrainian).

Zinchenko, P. I. (1950), "Involuntary and voluntary memorization of the text by schoolchildren," *Nauch. zap. Inst. psikhol. Ukr. SSR*, Vol. II (in Ukrainian).

Zinchenoko, P. I. (1950), "Psychological characteristics of memorization processes," in: *Tezisy dokladov sessii In-ta psikhologii Ukr. SSR*, Kiev (in Ukrainian).

Zinchenko, P. I. (1954), "On the formation of involuntary and voluntary memorization," *Sov. pedagog.*, No. 4.

Zinchenko, P. I. (1956), "Some questions on the study of memory," *Vopr. psikhol.*, No. 1.

Zinchenko, P. I. (1956), "On the dependence of association formation on the content of actions," *Nauch. zap. Inst. psikhol. Ukr. SSR*, Vol. IV (in Ukrainian).

Zinchenko, P. I. (1956), "On the psychology of memory," *Nauch. zap. Inst. psikhol. Ukr. SSR*, Vol. VI (in Ukrainian).

Zinchenko, P. I. (1958), "Psychology of memory," *Nauch. zap. Inst. psikhol. Ukr. SSR*, Vol. 8 (in Ukrainian).

Zinchenko, P. I. (1961), *Involuntary Memorization*, Moscow, APN RSFSR.

Zinchenko, P. I. and G. V. Repkina (1964), "Formulation of the problem of operative memory," *Vopr. psikhol.* **10** (6): 3–12.

CONDITIONS FOR RETROACTIVE INHIBITION

1. THE CONCEPT AND THE SIGNIFICANCE OF RETROACTIVE INHIBITION

Retroactive inhibition is the negative effect of an activity following memorization on the retention of the material memorized. If memorization is followed by some other activity, recall of the material may not be as complete as when the memorization is followed by rest. This deterioration of recall is due to the "inhibitory" effect of the activity following the memorization. Therefore, the inhibition involved has been designated retroactive inhibition. Obviously, this "retroactive effect" cannot be interpreted literally as an influence on the actual process of memorization. By the time the next activity begins, this process has already been completed, and therefore we are dealing not with an influence on the process itself, but only on the "traces" resulting from the memorization.

The first systematic study of retroactive inhibition dates back to Müller and Pilzecker (1900) who coined the term (rückwirkende Hemmung). Retroactive inhibition became the object of extensive study (printed in a considerable number of publications) in which the effects of the most diverse conditions on this phenomenon of great scientific interest were examined.

Retroactive inhibition is of substantial *theoretical* interest, since it pertains directly to the problem of the causes of forgetting. Some investigators even believe that retroactive inhibition is, if not the only, then at least the main cause of forgetting. In this regard, the French psychologist Foucault (see Britt, 1935) states that "what causes forgetting is not time itself, but how this time is occupied." Störring (1931) holds the same views, asserting that "not time in itself, but the impressions received in the course of time lead quite naturally to the forgetting of old impressions." Analogous views are expressed by the American psychologists Jenkins and Dallenbach (1924), who believe that "forgetting is not so much the result of the destruction of old impressions and associations as the product of interference, inhibition, and changing of the old by the new." The cause of forgetting the old is acquisition of the new.

On this basis, some foreign investigators raise objections to the widely known "law of disuse" proposed by Thorndike (1923) and formulated as follows: "If the connection between a situation and the response to it does not occur for a prolonged period, the stability of this connection decreases." For example, McGeoch (1932) states in regard to this law that "to say that forgetting is caused by mere disuse means to advance a proposition that is too general to be significant." According to this point of view, the lack of repetition of something previously occurring is thus not in itself the cause of forgetting.

While we categorically reject any attempt to reduce forgetting to the influence of subsequent activity alone, i.e., to retroactive inhibition (since retroactive inhibition is an example of *external* inhibition, while forgetting is determined to a considerable extent by *internal* inhibition), we can by no means deny the role of retroactive inhibition as one of the causes of forgetting. Mental processes do not proceed in isolation, but in intimate connection and interaction with each other. Retroactive inhibition is one of the types of this interaction, and its study will undoubtedly advance the investigation of the problem of forgetting in many respects.

The *practical* importance of the problem of retroactive inhibition is also apparent. The study of cases of inhibitory influence of the activity following memorization could lead to suggestions regarding the correct organization of the learning process. If retroactive inhibition is one of the causes of forgetting, obviously the elucidation of the conditions under which it can occur and of the conditions which decrease or altogether eliminate it would aid educators in organizing the sequence of their students' work in such a way as to minimize the effect of this type of inhibition.

2. THEORIES OF RETROACTIVE INHIBITION

Various theories of retroactive inhibition have been proposed in foreign psychology; the theory of perseveration (Müller and Pilzecker, 1900); the theory of transfer (De-Camp, 1935); the theory of transfer and destruction (Webb, 1917, see Britt, 1935); and the theory of Melton (1940).

As its name indicates, the first of these theories is based on perseveration. The essence of this phenomenon is that, upon completion of perception, the physiologic processes on which it is based do not cease immediately, but continue, or persevere, for a certain (rather negligible) time with gradually decreasing intensity. According to Müller and Pilzecker, the existence of perseveration is of great importance in the memorization of what has been perceived, since the associative connections formed during perception continue to become stabilized during perseveration. If after perceiving some material we immediately engage in some new activity, the perseveration is disrupted since work of the brain "in one direction," according to the authors of the theory, "decreases its simultaneous productivity in another direction." Therefore, in such cases the associative connections become stabilized less firmly and memorization deteriorates. Thus, Müller and Pilzecker explain the inhibitory effect of activity following memorization by disruption of the perseveration of the processes occurring during memorization and the resulting impossibility of firm stabilization of the associative connections formed during memorization. Proceeding from this, they assume retroactive inhibition to be the more significant, the shorter the interval between perception (memorization) and the subsequent activity, i.e., the less prolonged the perseveration of what has been perceived. In support of this, the authors of the theory cite the results of their experiments.

Also of substantial importance for the intensity of retroactive inhibition is the level of attention required for the subsequent activity. When this activity requires increased attention, its retroactive effect is greater. On the basis of their data, Müller and Pilzecker claim that *similarity* of the preceding and following activities does not affect the magnitude of retroactive inhibition.

In recent years, a number of hypotheses have been advanced to explain retroactive inhibition as conceptualized by Müller and Pilzecker. Some investigators believe that the activity following memorization results in a disruption of the "delay" (continuation) of biochemical processes, others see the cause of retroactive inhibition in the disruption of the reverberation of the neural currents originating during the preceding memorization by the subsequent activity, and still others discern this cause to be the disruption of inertial processes in the muscles of the vocal motor apparatus. Further study of the problem is needed.

De-Camp's theory of transfer is based on the following propositions. Immediately after memorization, residual discharges, or "afterdischarages," occur in the appropriate neural elements. They are of short duration, but are of great importance for the association of the parts of the memorized material. If during these "discharges" the same neural elements become involved in further activity, the "discharges" cease, the association of what has been memorized is disrupted, and the performance of the subsequent activity impairs the results of the memorization. In these cases, retroactive inhibition occurs. If, on the other hand, neural elements not involved in the preceding memorization participate in the subsequent activity, there is no retroactive inhibition.

De-Camp thus regards retroactive inhibition as a function of the partial identity of the neural elements involved in the preceding and the subsequent activity. Therefore, in his concept the similarity of the two activities is of paramount importance as the basic condition for retroactive inhibition. However, a substantial place must also be accorded to the interval between the activities. This interval is so important because of the very short duration of the afterdischarges. Therefore, when an activity very similar to memorization is carried out not immediately after it, it may fail to have an inhibitory effect on the memorization, since the "discharges" necessary for the stabilization of what has been memorized may already have been completed by the beginning of the new activity.

Upon comparison of the theories of De-Camp and of Müller and Pilzecker, points of similarity and difference between them become readily apparent. Both theories proceed from the recognition that the physiological processes on which perception (memorization) is based do not cease immediately. The continuation of these processes is of great importance for the stabilization of the associative connections formed during memorization. Therefore, the disruption of the aftereffect of these physiological processes, caused by the activity following memorization, impairs the results of memorization. However, this impairment occurs only if the subsequent activity is carried out a rather short time after memorization since the duration of the aftereffect of the physiological processes in question is very short.

While they agree on these premises, the two theories differ sharply in their evaluation of the role of the *content* of the preceding and of the subsequent activity. Starting from the premise that strictly specific neural elements are involved in the implementation of each particular activity, De-Camp maintains that retroactive inhibition occurs only when the subsequent activity is *similar* to the preceding one, since only in this case are the same neural elements involved and, hence, only in this case can the subsequent activity disrupt ("block") the "discharges" that are a continuation of the memorization. In contrast, Müller and Pilzecker, who on the basis of their experiments completely deny any role of the similarity of the activities, attach great significance to the level of attention required for the performance of the subsequent activity, i.e., to the difficulty of this activity, a criterion completely rejected by De-Camp. Thus, the two theories differ fundamentally on the basic questions of what kind of activity leads to retroactive inhibition of the results of preceding memorization and what characteristics of such an activity determine the intensity of the inhibitory effect.

Webb's theory encompasses two hypotheses: the "hypothesis of transfer" and the "hypothesis of destruction." According to the "hypothesis of transfer," retroactive inhibition is explained by the fact that the connections formed during the subsequent activity are subsequently "transferred" to the reproduction of what had been memorized before the performance of this activity, i.e., they are reproduced instead of the connections previously formed. According to the "hypothesis of destruction," retroactive inhibition is explained by the fact that during the performance of the subsequent activity, when new connections are formed, the connections formed during the preceding memorization are destroyed: the subsequent activity "breaks" the previously formed connections.

According to Webb's theory, the most important condition for retroactive inhibition is similarity of the preceding and of the subsequent activity. In the light of the two hypotheses mentioned above, the importance of this proposition is beyond any doubt. In order for new connections to be able to replace old ones (to destroy them in one case and to be reproduced instead of them in the other) it is necessary that both connections have something in common, i.e., that some components of each old connection and the new one replacing it be the same. In other words, it is necessary that, when material *A* and material *B* are memorized, these materials share certain components (*a, b, c, d*), and that each of these components be connected with a different component during the memorization of *A* (with *l, m, n, p*) and during the memorization of *B* (with *x, y, z, t*). Thus, in the first case the connections *al, bm, cn, dp* and in the second case the connections *ax, by, cz, dt* would form. Only under this condition can the two sets of connections compete and really interfere with each other (the same *a*, for example, will evoke *l* in one case and *x* in the other). On the other hand, those connections which have nothing in common cannot inhibit each other in any way. Therefore, the more similar consecutive activities are, the greater is the retroactive inhibition.

The recognition of the similarity of the preceding and of the subsequent activity as a condition for retroactive inhibition closely links the theories of Webb and of De-Camp. However, they differ substantially in what they *base* the importance of similarity on. Also very important is the role attributed in the two theories to the time interval between the preceding and the subsequent activity. De-Camp believes that retroactive inhibition can occur only if the subsequent activity is carried out soon after the preceding one. Webb's theory does not lead to this conclusion, since the destruction of old connections and the transfer of new ones can occur even a long time after the formation of the connections.

Melton's theory, the theory of two factors, explains retroactive inhibition by the following: 1) the transfer of connections from one material being memorized to another; 2) the extinction (or disuse) of the connections formed during the memorization of the first material which sets in during the memorization of the second material. The cause of this extinction is that if during memorization of the second material a connection formed during the memorization of the first material is reproduced, it is not reinforced (one may even say that it is evaluated negatively, as being inappropriate), as a result of which this would-be connection is extinguished.

As much as these theories differ, there are still some common features. Both these similarities and differences place the role of the similarity of the preceding and the subsequent activity and the significance of the difficulty of the subsequent activity among the basic problems requiring further investigation. In other words, we are faced with the problem of the role of the *content* of the two activities that interact and cause the phenomenon of retroactive inhibition.

3. THE DEPENDENCE OF RETROACTIVE INHIBITION ON THE CONTENT OF THE PRECEDING AND THE SUBSEQUENT ACTIVITY

The question of the significance of *similarity* was raised for the first time by Müller and Pilzecker (1900). They used memorization of nonsense syllables as the preceding activity and memorization of either nonsense syllables or pictures as the subsequent activity. Retroactive inhibition was the same in both cases. On the basis of this result, these investigators claim that similarity of the preceding and the subsequent activity has no effect on retoarctive inhibition.

An entirely different result was obtained by the American investigator Robinson (1920), who reported in his first publication on retroactive inhibition that a similar subsequent activity has a stronger inhibitory effect on the retention of memorized material than a dissimilar one. The preceding activity in his experiments was the memorization of numbers (in two series of experiments) and the memorization of the arrangement of chess pieces (in a third series of experiments). In both cases, the subsequent activity was varied: in some experiments it was similar to the preceding memorization (the subjects were asked to memorize a different series of numbers or a different arrangement of chess pieces), while in other experiments memorization was followed by an activity differing from it (mental multiplication or the reading of some text). In the second case retroactive inhibition was less pronounced than in the first. A similar decrease in inhibition was also observed when after the memorization of numbers in the first two series the memorization of some other kind of material (numerals, letters, or poems) was required. Retroactive inhibition was thus greatest when the subsequent activity was similar to the preceding memorization.

A more complex relation between the similarity of the two activities and the extent of retroactive inhibition was observed by Skaggs (1925). He advanced the following propositions: 1. If the subsequent memorization is identical in content and method with the preceding one, there is no inhibition; rather, there is stabilization of what has been memorized. 2. As the material becomes less and less similar, the effect of stabilization decreases; inhibition arises and increases with increasing diversity of the material. 3. This trend continues until at a certain point retroactive inhibition reaches a maximum. 4. This maximum is followed by inversion: as the diversity of the material continues to increase, the inhibitory effect of the subsequent activity decreases, but without ever disappearing completely.

Skaggs derived these principles from his experiments. In these experiments, the preceding activity was memorization of the arrangement of chess pieces. The subsequent activity involved on the one hand different arrangements of the chess pieces and on the other hand multiplication and addition and the memorization of pictures. It turned out that in the first case, in which the subsequent activity was more similar to the preceding one, the retroactive inhibition was greater. However, the use of various arrangements of the pieces as the subsequent activity revealed that retroactive inhibition increased with decreasing similarity between the subsequent and the initial arrangement. Thus, in the first case the following principle applied: the greater the similarity of the preceding and the subsequent activity, the greater is the retroactive inhibition. The opposite was true in the second case: the inhibition is greater when there is less similarity between the two activities.

The propositions advanced by Skaggs were checked in a number of experimental investigations. These studies, however, did not produce unequivocal results. Some investigators believe that the experimental data confirm the principles of Skaggs. This is how, for example, the data obtained by Robinson (1927) in his second investigation and by Harden (1929) are interpreted.

Robinson attempted to establish a quantitative scale of the degree of similarity of the preceding and the subsequent activity. For this purpose he used for both activities the memorization of two sets of consonants, systematically varying the number of letters common to both sets from complete identity to complete difference. The results of the experiments showed that the retroactive inhibition increased with increasing difference between the materials. No inversion was observed. Robinson explains this by the fact that the differences in the material he used were very minor (since only letters were presented) and that he therefore obtained only part of the curve plotted by Skaggs (before inversion). In accordance with this, Robinson expressed the assumption that inversion must occur as the differences in the material increase further.

An attempt to check this assumption was made by Harden. She also chose sets of consonants as her material for the preceding memorization, while for the subsequent memorization she presented material involving not only letters, but also numerals. The number of numerals was varied in order to increase gradually the degree of similarity of the material. Rather than increasing as in Robinson's work, this time the retroactive inhibition decreased with increasing difference. Harden regards this result as an indication of the correctness of Robinson's assumption and thus as a confirmation of the rules observed by Skaggs.

Positive results in the verification of Skaggs' curve were obtained by Cheng (1929), and this, moreover, in an experiment involving only one type of material. Cheng used memorization of three-letter nonsense syllables and, just like Robinson and Harden, he varied the degree of similarity of subsequent and preceding groups of syllables. To this end he presented for the subsequent memorization syllables differing from the *corresponding* syllables of the preceding series in one, two, or all three letters. The results showed that with increasing difference between the initial and the subsequent syllables the retroactive inhibition at first increased and then decreased. When the new syllables differed from those initially memorized in two letters, the inhibition was greater than for a difference in only one letter, but also greater than for a difference in all three letters. With increasing difference between the materials there was thus an inversion of the effect of this difference on the extent of retroactive inhibition.

In contrast with Cheng's data, the later investigation by Dreis (1933) did not reveal any inversion. In his work, the preceding activity was the memorization of a code and the subsequent activity was the memorization of other codes. The result was quite unequivocal: with increasing similarity of the codes the retroactive inhibition increased.

An original approach to the verification of Skaggs' curve was taken by Gengerelli (1934). In order to establish a scale of similarity of the preceding and of the subsequent activity, he determined the correlation coefficient between these activities. In his experiments, the initial activity was the memorization of a code, while the subsequent activity involved the memorization of five other codes, as well as addition, crossing out letters in a text, and the arrangement of dots in circles. The degree of inhibitory action of each subsequent activity was correlated with the correlation coefficient between it and the activity preceding it. It turned out that at first the retroactive inhibition increased with decreasing similarity of the two activities (down to a coefficient of 0.73), then it decreased (within the range of correlations from 0.73 to 0.64), and then it again increased. Thus, the relation observed by Gengerelli was even more complex than that observed by Skaggs (twofold rather than single inversion).

This result obviously differs sharply from the data of Dreis, in whose work the memorization of codes was also used, but no inversion appeared. Admittedly, Dreis used nothing but codes as the subsequent activity, while Genegerelli used quite different types of activity as well. However, in Gengerelli's work inversion was observed even during the use of codes.

Summing up all these attempts to elucidate the problem of the inversion of retroactive inhibition in relation to the degree of similarity of the activities, one may note that, although discrepancies between their results exist, basically they can by no means be regarded as contradictory. All those investigations in which the subsequent activity differed rather negligibly from the preceding one revealed that in this range the retroactive inhibition increased with increasing difference between the activities. On the other hand, where the subsequent activity differed sharply from the preceding one, the retroactive inhibition decreased with increasing difference between the activities. Thus, all the investigations essentially confirmed the principles outlined by Skaggs. However, it must be noted that, as they have just been presented, these results are quite formal. They give as yet no indication of the *content* of those differences between the preceding and the subsequent activity which in some cases cause an increase and in others a decrease in retroactive inhibition. They do not deal at all with the question of whether the different effect of the similarity of the preceding and the subsequent activity is due only to quantitative changes in the degree of this similarity or whether it is caused by qualitative changes in that which makes the two activities similar, and, should the latter be true, what qualitative changes determine the different effect of similarity.

This question can be answered by analyzing the *content* of the activities used in the capacity of similar or different activities in the investigations discussed. This analysis reveals that in the work of Robinson (his second investigation), Skaggs (one series of experiments), and Dreis, what was similar in the subsequent and the preceding activity was first that they both involved *memorization* and second that the material memorized by the subjects was partly the same in both cases. For the subsequent memorization, Robinson presented letters, some of which occurred in the material memorized during the preceding activity (only the number of letters included in both materials was varied). Dreis presented codes (letters and arbitrary symbols representing them) in the subsequent activity, which again partly included the same letters (with their respective symbols) that were presented in the preceding activity. Skaggs used the memorization of the spatial arrangement of the same chess pieces at different locations or of different pieces at the same locations as the subsequent activity. Thus, all experiments were conducted in such a way that the subjects, in performing the subsequent activity, partly *stabilized what they had memorized before* (during the preceding activity). Under these conditions it is quite apparent that, the greater a fraction of the preceding material was incorporated into the subsequent material, the more was the preceding material *stabilized* during the subsequent memorization and the better was this material thus reproduced upon completion of the subsequent activity. Since the degree of retroactive inhibition is characterized specifically by the reproduction of previously memorized material upon completion of the subsequent activity, it follows that if the two materials coincide to a considerable extent, the inhibitory effect of the subsequent memorization is less than if their overlap is negligible.

An entirely different kind of similarity was used in a number of other investigations (or in other series of the same investigations). Harden, Gengerelli, and Skaggs (in another series of his work) presented material *of the same type* as the preceding material for subsequent memorization (rather than partly *identical* with it, as in the first group of investigations). In Harden's work, the subjects, after memorizing letters, memorized material that partly consisted of letters (now, however, different ones), but also of numerals. Gengerelli presented for the subsequent activity codes that were of the same type as the preceding ones but did not share common elements with them (either different letters with different symbols were used or combinations of letters and numerals). Skaggs asked for the memorization of the arrangement of different chess pieces at different locations or even of their arrangement on graph paper rather than on a chessboard. The results of all these investigations have shown that in these cases the inhibitory effect of subsequent memorization becomes greater when the degree of similarity (belonging to the same type) of the subsequent and the preceding material *increases,* rather than when it decreases, as in the first group of investigations.

One should also include in the second group of investigations the work of McGeoch and McDonald (1931), in which the subjects were asked to memorize first one series of adjectives and then other series of adjectives that were either synonyms or antonyms of the first ones or had no meaningful relation to them. In these experiments, retroactive inhibition was also the greater, the more closely related in meaning the preceding and subsequent series of words were. An analogous result was obtained in the work of Johnson (1933), which also involved the memorization of words.

Correlating this result with that obtained in the case of partial identity of the material, we can draw the following conclusion: if the similarity of the subsequent and the preceding lies in their partial *identity,* the degree of retroactive inhibition increases as the number of components identical in the two materials decreases; if, however, the material is similar only in *belonging to the same type,* the retroactive inhibition decreases as the amount of material of the same type (or the degree to which it is of the same type) decreases. Inversion coincides with the transition from partly *identical* material to material *of the same type*. Thus, the *quantitative* changes in the relation between retroactive inhibition and the degree of similarity of the material are based on *qualitative* changes in the similarity of the material.

What happens when something other than memorization is used as the subsequent activity? Such cases occurred in the first work of Robinson, as well as in the investigations of Skaggs (in one of the series) and Gengerelli. Robinson discovered that when memorization is followed by some other activity the resulting retroactive inhibition is the same as that evoked by a subsequent activity similar to the preceding activity but is performed on different material. If, for example, memorization of numbers was followed by multiplication or the reading of a story, the inhibition was the same as when memorization of numbers was followed by memorization of letters or poems (Robinson, 1920). In both these cases, however, the retroactive inhibition was less than when memorization of numbers was followed by memorization of the same type of material, i.e., different numbers.

Skaggs obtained somewhat different results. Using as the preceding activity memorization of the arrangement of chess pieces on a chessboard and as the subsequent activity memorization of the arrangement of chess pieces on paper, addition, and examination of pictures, he discovered that in the first two cases the retroactive inhibition was the same (in agreement with Robinson's data), while in the case of examination of pictures it was less pronounced.

Gengerelli also observed an unequal value of the inhibitory effect of activities not similar to the preceding memorization. In his experiments, memorization of a code was followed by crossing out letters in a text, addition, and the placement of dots in circles. It turned out that retroactive inhibition was not the same in all these cases and that it increased with decreasing similarity of the preceding and the subsequent activity.

Thus, these investigations do not give unequivocal results regarding the degree of inhibitory effect of a subsequent activity differing from the preceding one. This is probably due to the differences between the activities used in the various investigations. Only one of these activities (addition) was common to two investigations. Moreover, only Gengerelli made an attempt to determine the degree of similarity of the subsequent and the preceding activity and to correlate the extent of retroactive inhibition with this similarity. In the other investigations, the interrelation between the activities was not examined from the point of view of their similarity.

All this compels us to admit that the problem of the correlation between retroactive inhibition and the degree of similarity of the preceding and the subsequent activity (where the two activities differ in type) is still not fully solved and requires further study. It should be noted that when we speak of subsequent activities that differ in type from the preceding memorization we must not forget that the difference between activities is relative. For this reason it is legitimate to speak also of the degree of similarity of the activities.

Even less close to a solution is the problem of the role of the *difficulty* of the activity performed after memorization. Müller and Pilzecker emphasized the importance of difficulty, regarding it as the main factor determining the extent of retroactive inhibition. As was mentioned before, other investigators countered this view with theories in which the role of difficulty was denied and everything was attributed to the *similarity* of the two activities. There are, however, no data in the literature that would clearly demonstrate the correctness of one or the other point of view; there have been no experimental attempts to vary the degree of difficulty of the subsequent activity and to trace its effect on the extent of retroactive inhibition. At the same time, the evident theoretical inadequacy of the theories of similarity (of De-Camp and of Webb) raises doubts about the possibility of attributing retroactive inhibition exclusively to the effect of similarity and completely ignoring the difficulty of the subsequent activity.

4. PURPOSE AND METHOD OF INVESTIGATION

On the basis of the above discussion we deemed it necessary to carry out an investigation that would contribute to the solution of the problem of the role of the similarity of the two activities on the one hand and the difficulty of the subsequent activity on the other hand. Our task was thus to determine how the magnitude of retroactive inhibition changes when, along with a decrease in the similarity of the preceding and the subsequent activity, we also increase the difficulty of the subsequent activity: whether an increase in the difficulty will have the opposite effect, i.e., cause an increase in the retroactive inhibition, or whether it will not make any difference.

As the basic, preceding activity we used the memorization of adjectives. All the words in the same series had the same number of syllables and were stressed on the same syllable. The words were read aloud by the experimenter at 2.5-sec intervals. There were 24 words in each series and the total duration of a single reading of each series was 1 min. Each series was read five times in succession. Immediately after the reading, the subjects were asked to perform some activity or were allowed to rest. As the subsequent activity we used memorization of another series of adjectives, memorization of nouns, memorization of numbers, mental multiplication, and solving difficult algebraic problems in writing. We selected these activities on the basis of the following considerations. On the one hand, activities of varying degrees of similarity with the preceding activity were chosen. From this point of view, the activities can be arranged in an order of decreasing similarity to the initial memorization. Quite obviously, the memorization of another series of adjectives is the most similar activity, followed by memorization of nouns and memorization of numbers; mental multiplication should come next, since this activity also involves memory processes to a considerable extent (the memorization of intermediate results), and the written solution of problems last, because here the subjects do not need to memorize anything.

In addition to the similarity, the difficulty of the activity was taken into account. It was very difficult to select activities from this point of view, since it is unlikely that sufficiently definite objective criteria of the degree of difficulty of an activity can be formulated. We therefore had to rely here mainly on information provided by the subjects. It was also difficult to rank *all* the selected activities according to difficulty. For this reason, we compared the difficulty of only the two activities that differed most from the initial memorization, namely, mental multiplication and the solution of problems. The subjects evaluated solving problems as considerably more difficult than mental multiplication; this is borne out by the very small number of algebraic problems solved by the subjects.

For relative rest, the subjects looked through short stories by Chekhov, after being told that they would not be asked any questions about them and that they were given the stories so that they could rest after memorizing the words.

Each subsequent activity, as well as the rest period, lasted 5 min and was thus of the same duration as the preceding memorization. Immediately after the subsequent activity or the rest period, the subjects were asked to reproduce the series of adjectives that they had read before performing the subsequent activity or resting. This was followed in all cases by a 15-min rest period (looking through stories) and then by a second reproduction of the series, which was aimed at determining at least to a small extent the stability of retroactive inhibition.

The subjects were ten students of the College of Mechanical Engineering and Mathematics of Moscow State University. They were divided into two groups of five each. After memorizing the adjectives, one group had to perform a subsequent activity in the first experiment and was allowed to rest in the second. Conversely, the second group was allowed to rest in the first experiment and performed a subsequent activity in the second. Effects of training and of differences in the material were eliminated by this crossover method. The experiments involving memorization (of adjectives, nouns, or numbers) as the subsequent activity were performed twice, with a different sequence being used during the repetition, again in order to eliminate the effect of training.

The extent of retroactive inhibition was determined as follows. The difference between the number of words reproduced after rest and after a subsequent activity was calculated. In those cases in which there was retroactive inhibition, this difference obviously had to be positive, i.e., the number of words reproduced after rest had to exceed the number of words reproduced after a subsequent activity. The percent ratio of this difference to the number of words reproduced after rest served as the index of the extent of inhibition. All calculations were carried out separately for each pair of experiments; in other words, the results of each experiment involving a subsequent activity were compared with the results of *its corresponding* control experiment involving rest.

In addition to the *extent* of retroactive inhibition we also determined its *frequency,* i.e., the number of cases in which the subjects reproduced fewer memorized words after a subsequent activity than after rest.

5. RESULTS OF THE INVESTIGATION

The mean indexes of the extent of retroactive inhibition are presented in Table 1.

As can be seen in Table 1, during the first reproduction retroactive inhibition was greatest in the case of the greatest similarity of the preceding and the subsequent activity, when in both cases adjectives were memorized. It decreased with decreasing similarity of the two activities, becoming negligible (during the first reproduction) for mental multiplication, i.e., a subsequent activity very different from the preceding memorization of adjectives.

However, the data in Table 1 also clearly show that it is not universally

TABLE 1. Mean Indexes of the Extent of Retroactive Inhibition (percent deterioration of reproduction under the influence of a subsequent activity)*

Subsequent activity	Extent of retroactive inhibition			
	during first reproduction		during second reproduction	
		mean		mean
Memorization of adjectives I.	26.6	28.3	23.4	20.9
Memorization of adjectives II.	30.1		18.4	
Memorization of nouns I.	20.5	19.8	14.3	18.9
Memorization of nouns II.	19.1		23.6	
Memorization of numbers I.	7.2	8.2	5.9	7.3
Memorization of numbers II.	9.2		8.8	
Mental multiplication.	4.1	4.1	14.8	14.8
Solving of algebraic problems.	15.9	15.9	15.7	15.7

*Subsequent activities are listed in the order of decreasing similarity with the preceding activity.

TABLE 2. Percentage of Cases of Deterioration, Improvement, and Identity Observed in the Reproduction of Memorized Adjectives After Various Subsequent Activities in Comparison with the Level of Reproduction after Rest

	Deterioration of reproduction				Improvement of reproduction				Identity of reproduction			
Subsequent activity	during first reproduction	mean	during second reproduction	mean	during first reproduction	mean	during second reproduction	mean	during first reproduction	mean	during second reproduction	mean
Memorization of adjectives I	80		80		20		20		0		0	
		80		80		15		15		5		5
Memorization of adjectives II.	80		80		10		10		10		10	
Memorization of nouns I	70		50		20		40		10		10	
		75		55		20		35		5		5
Memorization of nouns II	80		60		20		30		0		0	
Memorization of numbers I	70		60		30		40		0		0	
		60		65		30		35		10		0
Memorization of numbers II	50		70		30		30		20		0	
Mental multiplication	60	60	90	90	30	30	10	10	10	10	0	0
Solving of algebraic problems.	70	70	80	80	20	20	20	20	10	10	0	0

true that retroactive inhibition decreases with decreasing similarity of the activities. When the memorization of adjectives was followed by an activity that differed sharply from it but required very great effort (solving difficult algebraic problems), the retroactive inhibition again increased and was 15.9%, i.e., it considerably exceeded the inhibitory effect of the memorization of numbers, an activity much more analogous to the memorization of adjectives. Thus, the *difficulty* of the subsequent activity is without doubt also a factor, and a very significant one, contributing to increased retroactive inhibition. The principle of similarity, which American psychologists propose as the only, or at least the main, principle of retroactive inhibition (if one has the content of the activity in mind), must by all means be supplemented by the principle of difficulty. The data for the second reproduction (see Table 1) fully confirm this conclusion. Moreover, during the second reproduction there was a considerable increase (in relation to the corresponding control experiment) in the inhibitory effect of mental multiplication, i.e., of an activity that without doubt differs more from the memorization of adjectives than does such a subsequent activity as the memorization of numbers. This is still further evidence that the principle of similarity can by no means be regarded as a universal explanation of retroactive inhibition.

In addition to the extent of retroactive inhibition, calculated as the average of the data for all ten subjects, we used as a further index the frequency of the deterioration of reproduction under the influence of the subsequent activity. This index was used because the subsequent activity did not always lead to deterioration: in a few cases the results of reproduction after rest were the same as or even worse than after a subsequent activity.

We therefore present in Table 2 data on the *frequency* of the deterioration of reproduction after a subsequent activity in percent of the total number of experiments in each series. The table also shows how often reproduction after a subsequent activity was better than or the same as reproduction after rest. As is evident from Table 2, cases of deterioration of reproduction after a subsequent activity considerably exceeded cases of its improvement. The percentage of cases in which the two reproductions were the same was negligible. At the same time it must be noted that the prevalence of cases of deterioration was more pronounced when memorization was followed by the activity most similar to it, the memorization of completely analogous material (another series of adjectives). Under these conditions, deterioration of reproduction occurred in 80% of all experiments in both the first and the second reproduction. Thus, the importance of the similarity of the two activities becomes clearly apparent in the analysis of the indexes of the frequency of the changes as well.

At the same time, the data in Table 2 also fully confirm the importance of the other condition determining retroactive inhibition: the *difficulty* of the

TABLE 3. Extent of Retroactive Inhibition (Percent Deterioration of Reproduction under the Influence of the Subsequent Activity) in Different Subjects

Subjects	Extent of retroactive inhibition		
	during first reproduction	during second reproduction	average
1	27.9	27.3	27.6
2	25.2	26.9	26.1
3	25.9	16.1	21.0
4	22.6	21.8	22.2
5	12.6	22.9	17.8
6	13.7	17.7	15.7
7	9.5	11.2	10.4
8	6.9	14.1	10.5
9	4.5	–1.8	1.4
10	–2.3	–6.3	–4.3

subsequent activity. The number of cases of deterioration of reproduction in those experiments in which the memorization of adjectives was followed by the solution of difficult algebraic problems was as great as that in the experiments in which the subjects were given a more similar subsequent activity (memorization of numbers). This becomes especially apparent if the data of both the first and the second (delayed) reproduction are taken into consideration.

The fact that retroactive inhibition was observed not in all, but only in most of our experiments raises the question as to whether this is not due to individual differences between the subjects or, in other words, whether this finding is not explained by the complete absence of retroactive inhibition in some subjects. This brings us to the overall problem of individual differences in the action of retroactive inhibition, a problem of great importance to an understanding of the conditions of retroactive inhibition. Specifically, it must be determined whether retroactive inhibition occurs in *all* subjects, how its *magnitude* varies, and how often it is observed in individual subjects.

The first two questions are answered in Table 3. Retroactive inhibition occurred in the great majority of the subjects (in eight out of ten). Its extent, however, was not the same (the average indexes ranged from 10% to 27%). In subject 9 during the second reproduction there was on the average not a deterioration of reproduction after the subsequent activity, but a very slight improvement (indicated by a minus sign). In subject 10 an improvement was observed during the first reproduction as well.

The *frequency of occurrence* of retroactive inhibition in different subjects is shown in Table 4, which is patterned after Table 2, except that the data of the first and second reproductions have been combined because of their

TABLE 4. Percentage of Cases of Deterioration, Improvement, and Identity Observed in the Reproduction of Memorized Adjectives after a Subsequent Activity in Different Subjects

Subjects	Deterioration of reproduction	Improvement of reproduction	Identity of reproduction
1	100.0	0.0	0.0
2	81.0	19.0	0.0
3	81.0	12.5	6.0
4	81.0	19.0	0.0
5	75.0	19.0	6.0
6	81.0	12.5	6.0
7	62.5	37.5	0.0
8	62.5	37.5	0.0
9	31.0	44.0	25.0
10	37.5	50.0	12.5

small number. Examination of Table 4 reveals that deterioration of reproduction under the influence of the subsequent activity occurred in only one subject in 100% of the experiments performed with him. In the other subjects there were, in addition to cases of deterioration, also cases in which reproduction improved or remained unchanged. However, the frequency of cases in each category was very uneven in different subjects. In subjects 2, 3, 4, 5, and 6, cases of deterioration are in the great majority, while in subjects 7 and 8 the prevalence of cases of deterioration over cases of improvement is less pronounced (62.5% *vs.* 37.5%). In subjects 9 and 10, the indexes of improvement rather than deterioration of reproduction are the highest; in other words, in these subjects there was virtually no retroactive inhibition (here fluctuations of reproduction in the direction of deterioration must be regarded as incidental rather than characteristic).

The existence of considerable differences between subjects in the extent and frequency of retroactive inhibition has thus been demonstrated beyond doubt. This raises the question of the causes of these differences. Why did retroactive inhibition occur in some subjects and not at all in others?

Our data do not permit us to answer this question definitively, yet some conjectures regarding one of the *possible* causes must be pointed out. We proceed here from an analysis of the characteristics of the memorization process in subject 10, in whom retroactive inhibition did not occur either during the first or during the second reproduction. This subject reported that he memorized the material not as a series of individual words, but as words within a coherent story that he was making up while the experimenter was pronouncing each word. It is very important to note that the subject began to use this method only after several experiments had already been carried out with him. We are therefore able to compare the extent of retroactive inhibition *before* and *during* the use of this method. This comparison shows that during the first part of the experiment, in which the words were memorized individually, the deterioration of reproduction after a subsequent activity was 31 %, i.e., it was exceptionally high. It was higher than in subject 1 (see Table 3), in whom the average value of retroactive inhibition had been greatest. But during the second part of the experiment, in which the words were memorized in the form of a coherent story, there was on the average not a deterioration, but an improvement in the reproduction, which moreover was characterized by the rather high index of −18.4%.

All this compels us to suggest (as yet only as a possibility) that one of the causes of an absence or decrease of retroactive inhibition could be a change in the methods of memorizing.

The problem of retroactive inhibition in the memorization of meaningful coherent material has been studied in two publications (McGeoch and McKinney, 1934*a*, 1934*b*). Retroactive inhibition was studied for the memorization of *poems* in the first publication and for the memorization of *prose* in the second. In both cases the existence of retroactive inhibition was confirmed, but the degree of inhibition (especially for immediate rather than delayed reproduction) was negligible. We therefore believe that further study of retroactive inhibition under conditions of memorization of *coherent* material is necessary.

In analyzing the results of our study of retroactive inhibition, two further problems of interest must be discussed. The first problem concerns the nature of the errors made by the subjects in those cases in which both activities involved memorization of material of the same type (two series of adjectives). Our data show that there were no cases here in which during the reproduction of words of the first series the subjects would erroneously reproduce words from the just-memorized second series. Consequently, none of the "transfer of connections" from one series to another, postulated by the theory of transfer, was observed in our experiments.

The final problem to be discussed is a comparison of the extent and frequency of retroactive inhibition in cases of immediate and delayed (by 15 min) reproduction. The data in Table 1 show that in four out of eight cases the retroactive inhibition during the *second* reproduction was less than during the *first*. This was the case in those experiments in which the subsequent activity was memorization of adjectives (both series), memorization of nouns (series I), and memorization of numbers (series I). In two cases (series II of memorization of numbers and the solving of algebraic problems), retroactive inhibition during the first and the second reproductions was almost identical. Finally, in the remaining two experiments (series II of the memorization of nouns and, especially, mental multiplication), the retroactive inhibition was even greater during the second reproduction than during the first.

As for changes in the frequency of occurrence of retroactive inhibition, we have the following data: in three cases out of eight the frequency of retroactive inhibition increased during the second reproduction, in three cases it decreased, and in two cases it remained unchanged.

On the basis of these findings we can state that in our experiments there were no substantial changes in the extent and frequency of retroactive inhibition between the immediate reproduction and the reproduction delayed by 15 min. During the time interval we used, the effect of subsequent activity on the retention of memorized material continued to remain unchanged. It cannot be predicted on the basis of our work whether this effect remains the same for longer periods. The solution of this problem requires a special investigation.

BIBLIOGRAPHY

Britt (1935), "Retroactive inhibition," *Psychol. Bull.*, Vol. 32.

Cheng, N. (1929), "Retroactive effect and degree of similarity," *J. Exper. Psychol.*, Vol. 12.

De-Camp, J. (1935), "A study of retroactive inhibition," *Psychol. Monog.*, No. 84.

Dreis, T. (1933), "Two studies in retroaction," *J. Gen. Psychol.*, Vol. 8.

Gengerelli (1934), "Similarity and retroaction," *J. Exper. Psychol.*, Vol. 17.

Harden, L. (1929), "A quantitative study of the similarity factor in retroactive inhibition," *J. Gen. Psychol.*, Vol. 2.

Jenkins, J. and K. Dallenbach (1924), "Obliviscence during sleep and waking," *Amer. J. Psychol.*, Vol. 35.

Johnson, L. (1933), "Similarity of meaning as a factor in retroactive inhibition," *J. Gen. Psychol.*, Vol. 9.

McGeoch, J. (1932), "Forgetting and the law of disuse," *Psychol. Rev.*, Vol. 39.

McGeoch, J. and W. McDonald (1931), "Meaningful relation and retroactive inhibition," *Amer. J. Psychol.*, **43:** 579–588.

McGeoch, J. and F. McKinney (1934*a*), "Retroactive inhibition in the learning of poetry," *Amer. J. Psychol.*, **46**:19–33.

McGeoch, J. and F. McKinney (1934*b*), "The susceptibility of prose to retroactive inhibition," *Amer. J. Psychol.*, **46**:429–437.

Müller, G. and A. Pilzecker (1900), *Experimentelle Beiträge zur Lehre von Gedächtnis.*

Robinson, E. (1920), "Some factors determining the degree of retroaction," *Psychol. Monog.*, No. 128.

Robinson, E. (1927), "The similarity factor in retroaction," *Amer. J. Psychol.*, Vol. 39.

Skaggs, E. (1925), "Further studies in retroactive inhibition," *Psychol. Monog.*, No. 34.

Störring (1931), Über den ersten reinen Fall eines Menschen mit völligem isolierten Verlust der Merkfähigkeit," *Arch. f. d. ges. Psychol.*, Vol. 81.

Thorndike, E. (1923), *Educational Psychology*, Vol. 2.

Webb, L. (1917), "Transfer of Training and Retroaction," p. 104, summarized in: Britt (1935), "Retroactive inhibition," *Psychol. Bull.*, Vol. 32.

THE INTERRELATION OF IMAGE AND WORD IN THE DEVELOPMENT OF MEMORY

1. BLONSKII'S CONCEPT OF THE INTERRELATION OF IMAGE MEMORY AND VERBAL MEMORY

The interrelation of image memory and verbal memory during their development was studied extensively for the first time in Soviet psychology by Blonskii (1935, see Blonskii, 1964), who approached the solution of this problem from the point of view of his proposed general concept of the development of memory.

This concept was based on the postulate that the four kinds of memory (motor, emotional, image, and verbal) are *ontogenetic* stages in its development and appear in just this sequence. Image memory is an earlier and lower stage in the development of memory than verbal memory.

The earliest kind of memory, motor memory, is initially manifested in the first conditioned motor reflexes in children, especially in the characteristic conditioned reaction that sets in when an infant is picked up and held in the feeding position. This reaction is observed during the first month after birth. Blonskii believes that emotional or affective memory, which is manifested in the appearance of an affective reaction before the *direct* action of the stimulus evoking it, has its inception during the first half year of the life of the child (during the sixth month or, in his words, "even earlier, it seems"). On the basis of data published by other authors, Blonskii concluded that image memory (which, according to him, it would perhaps be most prudent to associate with the first rudiments of free recollections) originates during the second year of life; but he also cites other data that indicate the possibility of an earlier or later appearance of image memory. Thus, if one assumes the participation of images in the so-called "coherent" memory, in which a child recalls something associated with the stimulus presently acting, then (again on the basis of literature data) the age of six months must be regarded as the beginning of this participation (Blonskii, 1935, p. 23). On the other hand, if one proceeds from the study of dreaming in children and regards the so-called night terror of children as one of the objective indicators of dreaming, one can assume that images, at least in dreams, occur beginning with the age of two years. There is no contradiction between the different periods indicated by Blonskii, because they involve different indicators of the existence of images. Still, the difference between the periods is quite substantial, and it remains unclear which of these indicators is sufficiently reliable. We must therefore admit that Blonskii is, to a certain extent, correct in his assertion that we do not yet know when images appear in children. Under these conditions it is safest to conclude that image memory appears somewhat earlier than verbal memory, but considerably later than motor and affective memory (Blonskii, 1935, p. 162).

The earlier appearance of image memory does not signify its subsequent disappearance and replacement by verbal memory. Blonskii asserts, however, that image memory continues to remain a lower level of memory than verbal memory. This pertains also to the most highly developed—the visual—memory images, which arise most readily when human consciousness is at a lower level than during complete wakefulness (Blonskii, 1935, p. 49). In Blonskii's words, visual memory, "which for the psychologists of antiquity was memory *per se,* since they referred primarily to it when discussing memory, proves to be a very imperfect memory" (Blonskii, 1935, p. 88). Vivid images are characteristic of childhood rather than maturity. Moreover, the images reproduced persist only very rarely; usually, they are transformed and undergo great changes. Visual memory can be regarded only as a lower type of memory. It is not yet "true" memory, i.e., fully developed memory. Under normal conditions, images are only sketches in the memory of the adult (Blonskii, 1935, p. 183). Image memory can be of use only in the exceptional cases in which the image is of extraordinary strength and character. Usually, visual memory is very scanty, and therefore, another, higher kind of memory, narrative memory (meaningful communication), which in its highest forms merges with thinking, is incomparably more useful.

According to Blonskii, narrative memory is true verbal memory, which must be distinguished from the memorization and reproduction of speech movements as, for example, in the memorization of nonsense syllables. In the latter case we are dealing not with verbal memory in the true sense of the term, but with ordinary motor memory, which is the lowest rather than the highest kind of memory.

While it is the highest level of memory, narrative memory is not immediately manifested in its most perfect forms. It undergoes a certain development, which is characterized by the main stages in the development of narration. At first, narration was merely the verbal accompaniment of action, then it was words accompanied by action, and only later did verbal narration begin to function independently as vivid and graphic communication (Blonskii, 1935, p. 104). Moreover, one must distinguish between narration from reproduced images and verbal reproduction of what has been visually perceived, on the one hand, and verbal reproduction of what has been visually perceived and verbal reproduction of verbal material, on the other hand. Each of these kinds of reproduction has its distinguishing features; their detailed description constitutes a substantial part of Blonskii's work.

Human memory (verbal memory in the true sense), which in its highest stages of development is narrative memory (that is, the communication of something to others), is socially conditioned. This social influence is manifested in the fact that, as Blonskii points out, verbal reproduction becomes more and more precise and brief, i.e., a person endeavors to reproduce what is essential. But memory that reproduces only the essential already verges on thinking (Blonskii, 1935, p. 200). At the highest stage of development of memory, memorization and recall become thinking memorization and thinking recall. Concepts, which make it possible to memorize and recall what is most essential while forgetting everything incidental, are of the utmost importance in them. Blonskii points out that "such a memory can be so unliteral that the reproduced text will not contain a single word of the original." And yet this will be a correct rendering of the text. In these cases the process of memorization involves to a considerable extent the replacement of the concepts of the original by higher, equivalent, or lower concepts. "This," says Blonskii, "is the conceptual processing of what is memorized" (Blonskii, 1935, p. 86). At this stage in its development, memory becomes thinking, and recollections become not just recollections, but thoughts of the subject making use of them (Blonskii, 1935, p. 87).

However, verbal memory does not manifest itself immediately as selective, socially conditioned reproduction, as reproduction of what is essential. According to Blonskii, three main stages can be distinguished in the development of verbal memory: simple reproduction, socially conditioned selective reproduction, and "literate" memory, which makes use of writing. The second year of life, during which reproducing verbal memory appears, must be regarded as the beginning of the ontogenetic development of verbal memory. This type of memory (simple reproduction) reaches its highest level by the beginning of puberty, but its fastest development occurs during preschool age, and the reproducing memory of a 7–8-year-old child is not so very different from the maximum. Beginning with adolescence, this type of memory weakens.

While simple reproduction, continues Blonskii, is the starting point of the development of verbal memory in children, subsquently, under the very powerful influence of social demands, this type of memory is very quickly pushed into the background by a higher type: selectively reproducing verbal memory. The development of verbal memory during childhood is primarily the development of this selective and socially conditioned memory. It develops during the preschool years, but is "cultivated" most vigorously in school. This type of memory reaches its maximum during adolescence. Its development is closely linked with the development of thinking and speech.

Finally, memory that makes use of writing develops, of course, last, beginning with school age, and reaches its highest level only during maturity. These are the basic postulates of Blonskii's concept of the interrelation of image memory and verbal memory during their development.

2. EXPERIMENTAL INVESTIGATIONS OF SOVIET PSYCHOLOGISTS ON THE INTERRELATION OF IMAGE AND WORD IN THE DEVELOPMENT OF MEMORY

What data on this problem have been obtained in *experimental* investigations by Soviet psychologists?

A number of publications deal with the comparative study of the memorization of object-image and verbal material. This problem has been extensively studied by Faraponova (1953, 1958). In her experiments, the subjects (schoolchildren of the second, fifth, and seventh grades and college students) were asked to memorize the following types of material: in the first series of experiments, graphic material (depictions of objects); in the second series, verbal material that can be visualized (names of objects); in the third series, graphic material difficult to name (depictions of different kinds of fish and mushrooms); and in the fourth series, abstract verbal material that cannot be visualized (words designating abstract concepts).

It can readily be seen that the relation between the actions of the two signaling systems was changed by means of these variations. As Faraponova correctly points out, one must not assume, of course, that memorization of graphic material (image memory) is an activity of the first signaling system only and that memorization of verbal material (verbal memory) is the exclusive function of the second signaling system. In both cases, both interacting signaling systems are involved. Their interrelation, however, is different. In the memorization of graphic material, the first signaling system dominates, and words (the names of the depicted objects), though present, are not of primary importance. By contrast, in the memorization of verbal material, the second signaling system plays the main role, although visualization (sometimes very faint and fleeting) of what is designated by words can occur. In the third and fourth series of experiments, this predominance of one of the signaling systems was even more definite. In perceiving the pictures of different kinds of fish and mushrooms, the subjects were not always able to name them with different words, as a result of which the role of the second signaling system was even more limited here. In the fourth series, the role of the first signaling system was restricted, since visualization was very difficult when abstract concepts were presented.

In addition to the four series of experiments involving *recognition,* three analogous series (the first, second, and fourth) were conducted involving *reproduction* of the memorized material. In both groups of experiments, both immediate and delayed recognition and reproduction were used.

The results of these experiments revealed the following. 1. In all age groups, the memorization of graphic, easily verbalized material was best; the memorization of similar, but verbal material was also good, yet not quite as good. 2. Under conditions of special restriction of the activity of one of the signaling systems (in the third and fourth series), the indexes were lowest and were different for different age groups: the second graders remembered graphic material better (third series), while the older schoolchildren and the adults did better with words (fourth series). 3. In all series, the memorization of both the graphic and the verbal material increased with age, but the indexes of the recognition and reproduction of *words* increased faster than those of the recognition and reproduction of graphic material. As a result, the difference between these indexes tended to disappear with age. 4. The indexes of the memorization of abstract verbal material increased with age somewhat faster than those of the memorization of concrete verbal material. 5. In the experiments involving reproduction, the indexes of the memorization of different kinds of material increased with age considerably faster than in the experiments involving recognition. 6. Marked age differences were also observed in the qualitative characteristics of memory processes; in particular, meaningful grouping of the material increased with age. 7. In addition to the ontogenetic changes, individual differences in the memorization of graphic and verbal material were also observed, yet the correlations noted above were present in the great majority of subjects of the indicated age groups.

Memorization of object (image) and verbal material in preschool children was compared by Kornienko (1955) by a method very similar to that used by Faraponova (1953). The subjects (preschool children) were asked to memorize and reproduce the following: a number of objects (toys) easy to classify into meaningful groups (first series), the same number of words of concrete meaning (second series), and names of trees and shrubs unfamiliar to the children (third series). In analogous experiments, in which memorization was checked by recognition rather than reproduction, an additional fourth series was introduced, in which the children memorized and then recognized a set of leaves of various trees and shrubs unfamiliar to them.

The results of the experiments were very similar to those obtained by Faraponova and revealed the following. 1. In all age groups (younger, intermediate, and older preschool age) the highest indexes for reproduction and recognition were obtained in experiments involving the memorization of objects. 2. The memorization of words of concrete meaning was second. 3. The memorization of unfamiliar names and of the leaves of unfamiliar trees and shrubs was least productive. 4. The difference between all types of memorization decreased with age. Thus, while 3–4-year-old children reproduced on the average twice as many objects as words of concrete meaning, in 6–7-year-old children the ratio of the indexes of reproduction of these two categories was no longer 2.2:1, but 1.2:1. Even more drastic was the change in the ratio of the reproduction of words with a concrete meaning to that of names of unfamiliar trees and shrubs: the three-year-olds could not memorize the latter at all, in 4–5-year-old children the ratio of the reproduction of concrete words to that of names of trees and shrubs was 12:1, and in 6–7-year-old children this ratio was only 4:1. In the experiments involving recognition, the mean index of memorization of concrete words in three-year-olds was 7.2, their index of recognition of unfamiliar trees and shrubs was 6.6, and their index of recognition of the leaves of unfamiliar trees and shrubs was 6.4; in children 6–7 years old, all these indexes had equalized (8.8, 8.4, and 8.4). 5. The differences between the productivity of memorization of diverse material in the experiments involving reproduction were considerably more pronounced than those in the experiments involving recognition (in which all indexes were naturally considerably higher than those obtained in the experiments involving reproduction).

Age differences in the memorization of concrete (image) and abstract (verbal) material were also studied by Razmyslov (1958). In his investigation, pupils of the sixth, eighth, and tenth grades were given two groups of texts to memorize. One group was saturated with emotional image content of various kinds, while all emotional image factors (examples, illustrations, etc.) were eliminated as much as possible from the other group of texts, the content of which was abstract. Texts of different levels of difficulty were used. The texts were reproduced immediately after familiarization with them and after two weeks.

It was discovered that while with age the number of reproduced thoughts increased for both kinds of text, the increase was greater for the abstract texts. While, for example, in one group of experiments the number of thoughts reproduced from emotional image texts increased by only 6–10% between the sixth and tenth grades, the number of thoughts reproduced from abstract texts increased by 56–72% (in texts of different difficulty).

Substantial differences in the memorization of the two types of text were observed between groups of pupils of different academic achievement. While in the memorization of emotional image material the differences between excellent, average, and failing pupils were small (the difference between the excellent pupils with the highest indexes and the failing pupils who remembered least was 14.5%), in the memorization of abstract texts these differences were marked (62.8%).

Individual differences between pupils were very significant and in a few cases they even overlapped the age differences. They did not always coincide with academic achievement either. At the same time they were rather stable and did not depend on the nature of the material being memorized.

A dependence of the manifestation of age differences on the nature of the texts was also observed in the number of errors (in particular, errors distorting the text) made during reproduction. While the number of distortions of abstract thoughts decreased considerably with age, age differences in the distortion of emotional image texts were either not observed at all or were negligible. Therefore, in the tenth grade the difference between the number of distortions in the reproduction of abstract and emotional image thoughts was almost completely obliterated, while in the sixth grade it was very pronounced.

Important data were also obtained in experiments conducted with a modified method. The subjects were asked to memorize texts containing both abstract and emotional image sections; they were instructed to pay special attention to the memorization of the generalizing thoughts in one case and to that of the examples given in the other. It was found that in the case of the first instruction there was no difference between the memorization of material of different kinds in the sixth grade, but with age a difference appeared and gradually increased; in the case of the second instruction, no definite age differences were observed. Consequently, the memorization of generalizing thoughts increased with age regardless of the instruction given, while the memorization of emotional image factors increased noticeably with age only in the case of the instruction to pay particular attention to the emotional image factors.

The experiments conducted by the method just described have further shown that a connection of the difference between the memorization of the abstract and the emotional image sections of the text and the academic achievement of the pupils was observed only when the instruction was given to pay attention to the generalizing thoughts. Consequently, the memorization of abstract texts (or of abstract factors in mixed texts) is more differentiating with respect to both age and achievement, while the memorization of emotional image factors (at least in the age range studied by Razmyslov) differentiates either slightly or not at all.

A somewhat different approach to the comparative study of the retention of material of differing content was taken by Lipkina (1941, 1958). She determined the productivity of the reproduction of various kinds of study material (on geography) by pupils of both the grade in which this material was studied in school and subsequent grades (up to the tenth). Among her results one must note the following. 1. Different kinds of concrete and abstract material are memorized unequally. 2. Those kinds of concrete material which are part of the basic content of the subject under study and the memorization of which is supported by visual images (for example, cartographic data in a geography course) are retained considerably more stably than concrete material that does not have independent significance in the given subject and is memorized without reliance on distinct visual concepts (such as names not connected with a map and various supplementary descriptions in a geography course). 3. Different kinds of abstract material are also memorized unequally: what is intimately linked with the concrete material (explanations of facts) is memorized more stably than what stands apart from the factual material (definitions). 4. Consequently, the memorization of both kinds of material depends to a large extent on the position occupied by the given material in the subject under study and on the connection between the abstract and the concrete data. 5. The basis for the reproduction of different types of course material changes substantially with age: younger schoolchildren reproduce concrete material on the basis of concrete material, while in older schoolchildren the reproduction of concrete material is also based on general principles.

In all these investigations, the memorization of different types of material (object and verbal material and image and abstract material) was studied, making it possible to compare its retention at different age levels. Mal'tseva (1948, 1958*a*, 1958*b*) formulated the problem of the relation of the roles of object and word in memory processes at different ages differently. In her work, visual and verbal entities were not the *goal,* but the *means* or *support* of memorization. The method of studying indirect memorization proposed by Leont'ev (1931, 1959) was used (see Chapter 6, Subsection 6), but while Leont'ev used only pictures as support for memorization, Mal'tseva utilized both visual (image) and verbal material for this purpose. The purpose was to compare the roles of the two as means facilitating memorization. In addition, the roles of *ready* supports (provided by the experimenter) and supports *devised by the subjects themselves* were compared. This was necessary in order to determine the possibilities of independent use of the two types of supports by schoolchildren of different age. The subjects were pupils of the second, fourth, sixth, and eighth grades of varying academic achievement and adults.

The experiments have shown that for both immediate and delayed reproduction the results of memorization in all groups of subjects were better when visual material (pictures) was used for support. However, the productivity of memorization increased faster with age when words were used for support than when pictures were used. Therefore, the difference between the use of the two kinds of support decreases with age.

The experiments aimed at comparing the effectiveness of ready and independently devised supports have shown that in subjects of all ages the productivity of memorization with independently devised (verbal) supports was greater than that with ready supports. There were no distinct age differences in the interrelation of these two procedures of memorizing. Comparison of memorization supported by ready pictures and by independently devised words revealed that memorization was more successful in the latter case. Thus, independently devised verbal supports were a more effective means of memorization than ready pictures, which, in turn, were more effective than ready words. The comparison of memorization with the aid of independently devised verbal and ready visual supports did not reveal any significant age differences.

Mal'tseva's work further demonstrated substantial age differences in the use of various verbal and visual (in this case in the form of mental representations) supports in the case of "free" memorization, i.e., when the subjects were not specifically prompted to use supports. The voluntary use of various kinds of supports increased considerably with age. While in the second grade supports of some kind were used in 10.6% of all cases, this figure rose to 18% in the fourth grade, to 47.3% in the sixth grade, and to 61.3% in the eighth grade, decreasing to 52% in adults. In all age groups, verbal supports were in the majority, which is natural, since in these particular experiments there was no object material that could have been used as support for memorization.

Thus, all the examined investigations indicate the same thing. With age, the role of the second signaling system, which is manifested in the memorization of verbal and abstract material and in the use of verbal supports, increases; as a result, the difference between the memorization of the two indicated kinds of material and between the use of the two kinds of support gradually decreases. However, even in adults visual material is memorized more productively than verbal abstract material and visual supports are more effective than verbal ones. Optimal memorization is observed when both signaling systems function together.

Two further problems in the study of the interrelation of image and word in memory processes are the role of images in the memorization of verbal material and the role of words in the memorization of image (graphic, object) material.

In a study of visual memorization in the performance of various kinds of school work, Novomeiskii (1950) examined the role of images in the memorization of verbal material. The subjects, fourth and ninth graders, received history texts, from which they were asked to do different assignments: in some cases, just to memorize, in others, to memorize in order to give a written report or to prepare a plan or to enumerate the main ideas in the text, etc. Questioning of the subjects about their methods of memorizing the texts showed that about half of the fourth graders and about one third of the ninth graders relied primarily on images. The images were of different nature; they were mainly images of imagination, memory images occurring much more rarely. The prevalence of images of imagination was especially pronounced in the younger schoolchildren. Whereas in ninth graders about 69% of the images were images of imagination, in fourth graders the proportion of such images was about 89%. The images differed substantially in other respects as well. Whereas in fourth graders a large part of the images were images of specific details discussed in the text, in ninth graders images encompassing the basic content of the entire text or the content of its main parts in sequence predominated. In almost 50% of the fourth graders in whom images did appear, these appeared only occasionally, whereas for ninth graders the corresponding value was only 21%.

Although the frequency of appearance of images did not change when the nature of the assignment was changed, substantial qualitative differences were observed in the images. When the task was most general (to memorize), the images primarily reflected only details of the text. However, when the assignment was to give a written report, to prepare a plan of the text, or to enumerate its individual points (but not when it was to answer questions), the images encompassed the basic content of the entire text or the content of its main parts in sequence. In contrast to images of details and incidental images, such images substantially increased the productivity of memorization. These more specific assignments led to further changes: the images were more often intentionally evoked, they were more distinct, clear, vivid, three-dimensional, colorful, diverse, and dynamic, and they reflected more adequately the content of the text and facilitated its understanding. All these changes in the images under the influence of various tasks were observed to a considerably greater extent in the ninth grade than in the fourth. Consequently, the effect of more specific tasks increased with age.

It is important to note the interrelation of two kinds of set in the subjects. If there was a set for a more exact and literal memorization of the text, this interfered with the appearance of images. If, on the other hand, many images appeared, only the essence of the text was reproduced and there was no literal reproduction (not even of some passages in the text).

Finally, considerable individual differences between subjects were observed, not only in the frequency of utilization of images in memorization, but also in the nature of the images. This made it possible to distinguish several types of subjects.

In another study of the role of images in memorization, Novomeiskii (1958) did not confine himself to asking the subjects what form memorization had taken, but intentionally regulated the process by instructing the subjects (college students only) in some experiments to visualize the content of the text and giving them no such instructions in other experiments.

It turned out that, of the objects described in the text, the number reproduced was considerably greater in the experiments with the task of visualizing them than in the experiments without this task. After attempts to visualize the objects, they were described more fully, graphically, and correctly; considerably more reference was made to the connection between the characteristics of the objects and their purpose; actions performed with the objects were more accurately described; the objects were less often mistaken for each other; and the memorization was considerably more stable.

An attempt to determine how the effect of images on the memorization of verbal material changes with age was made by Golubev (1955). He investigated the memorization of foreign (English) words by third, fifth, seventh, and tenth graders and graduate students. The words were memorized with and without the use of visual material (pictures of the objects designated by the words). The experiments showed that for the third, fifth, and seventh graders the average time required to memorize a word accompanied by a picture was two-thirds to one-half that required when no picture was shown. On the other hand, in the older subjects (tenth graders and adults) the memorization required the same time in both cases or was achieved even faster without the use of pictures. In the younger schoolchildren the memorization was considerably more stable when pictures were used than without the aid of pictures (in the older subjects the stability of memorization was not tested).

Analogous results were obtained when a coherent story was read to the subjects in the native and the foreign language with and without the presentation of a complex composite picture illustrating the story's content, and the subjects were then required to translate words marked in the Russian text into the foreign language. The experiments showed that sixth graders correctly translated 65.1% of the designated words when the picture was shown and only 34.2% without the picture. In the seventh grade (for a different bilingual text and picture) the corresponding figures were 48.6% and 27.3%.

Baranov (1940) compared the memorization of words in a foreign language with and without the use of pictures in seventh graders. In his experiments, during the reading of a story in German, subjects from one section of the seventh grade (section A) were shown pictures illustrating objects and actions discussed in the story, whereas no pictures were shown to subjects from the other section (section B). The testing involved translation from Russian into German of a number of words new to the subjects. The test was repeated after 15 days, and after 50 days the subjects had to rewrite the story in German and were required to use in it the above-mentioned new words.

During the first testing, the pupils from section A reproduced 48% of the words and those from section B, 61%. However, after 15 days section A reproduced 83% and section B only 75%. After 50 days, this difference increased even more: the pupils from section A recalled 92% of the words and those from section B only 76% (the increased reproduction in both sections in the delayed tests was due to the longer time allotted during them for the recall).

Considerable differences between the sections were also observed in the presentation of the story. In section A the presentations were more emotional, dynamic, and detailed, whereas in section B they were more monotonous and less detailed. Upon questioning, most pupils from section A stated that they clearly visualized the pictures shown to them, and that these images served them as support for developing the story. Logical connection was established on the basis of the images and the words were reproduced so as to match the flow of the images.

As indicated, Soviet psychologists have studied the role of words in the memorization of visual material as well. Novomeiskii (1958) showed sets of two color pictures to college students and asked them to determine (by mentally stating) the age and posture of the people depicted in one of the pictures, and to determine in addition (also by mentally stating) the color of the clothing of the people shown in the other picture. Memorization was not required, but then the subjects were unexpectedly asked to reproduce the age, posture, and color of clothing of the people in both pictures. It turned out that the success of reproduction depended on the content of the verbalization: the color of clothing was reproduced considerably better in the experiment in which it had been mentally named.

In another series of these experiments, naming the content of pictures was deliberately made difficult: while they were looking at a picture, the subjects had to listen to instructions for the subsequent solution of a problem in arithmetic. These experiments revealed a great deterioration of the memorization of certain characteristics of the depicted objects (in particular, color of clothing) in comparison with how well these characteristics were reproduced when naming was not impeded during the examination of the pictures.

In the next series of experiments, college students had to do work on a map not very familiar to them in regard to both the shape and the coloration of the depicted countries. They had to arrange these countries in a certain order on the basis of their area and their extension from north to south and from west to east. The naming of the colors was not included in the assignment, but after completing the work the subjects were asked to reproduce them. The success of reproducing the colors was found to depend on the ease of their verbalization.

In all the above series of Novomeiskii's experiments, the subjects themselves named (mentally) what they perceived. In his subsequent series, conducted with fifth graders, the teacher did the naming. While explaining new material (the structure of the stem in plants), the teacher named the colors of all but one of the depicted layers of the stem to one section of the class and only the color of that particular layer to another section. Testing after class showed a clear dependence of the reproduction of these colors on their being named by the teacher. Similar results were obtained when this experiment was repeated on different material (the explanation of the structure of flowers). In ninth graders, these experiments gave similar results. At the same time, however, they revealed considerable individual differences in the role played by the naming of the characteristics of objects, on the one hand, and by active involvement with these characteristics, on the other. Whereas in some pupils the naming resulted in good reproduction even when there was no active involvement with the color, in others, on the contrary, better results were obtained in those cases in which the color was not named but they carried out an activity involving the color. A third group of subjects occupied an intermediate position.

An attempt to determine age differences in the role of words in the memorization of visual material in younger and older schoolchildren was made by Tarabrina and Khokhlacheva (1955). They showed two series of pictures to pupils of the second, fourth, and seventh grades. Only looking at the pictures was required in one series, whereas the objects depicted in the other series also had to be mentally named. In both cases, the subjects had to write down the names of the objects depicted after each picture had been shown. Memorization was found to be more successful when the objects had to be mentally named. However, this advantage decreased with age from 50% in the second grade to 35% in the fourth grade and 20% in the seventh grade. It is quite possible that the cause of this steady decrease was that the older pupils more often mentally named the depicted objects even when they were not specifically asked to do so and that this prompting therefore had little effect on their memorization.

In preschool children the role of words in the memorization of visual material was studied by Zal'tsman (1956*a*, 1956*b*). Colored mosaic figures were shown to children 3–7 years old, after which the subjects had to reconstruct these mosaic figures from memory. In the first series of experiments, the figures were examined without verbal accompaniment, while in the second series the names, number, and arrangement of the colors in the figures had to be stated.

In the first series, the *youngest* preschoolers perceived the figures in silence and then most often took mosaic pieces at random and put together *any* figure, rather than the one they had been shown; only two out of eighteen children reconstructed the figure shown to them completely. In contrast, of the twelve children in the second series none were completely unable to reconstruct the figure and eight reconstructed it faultlessly. In this series there was purposeful searching for the components of the figures rather than the unsystematic putting together of pieces observed in the first series. Words clearly enhanced the analyzing and synthesizing activity in the children.

The preschoolers of *intermediate* age made extensive use of speech (already using their *own* words at this age) even in the first series of experiments, both in examining the figures put together for them and in reconstructing them from memory. They needed no special prompting for this. Therefore in their case the difference between the results of the first and second series was negligible.

In the *oldest* preschoolers the use of speech (again their own words rather than those of the experimenter) was even more extensive. In contrast with the preschoolers of intermediate age, they designated the characteristics of the figures put together in front of them more systematically. They were significantly influenced in this direction by questions from adults (in the second series). It is also of importance that at this age not only external speech, but also internal speech anticipating outward actions began to play a facilitating role in memorization.

Soviet psychologists have given much attention to the study not only of *age,* but also of *individual* differences in the interrelation of image and verbal memory. Dul'nev (1948) observed a clearly manifested image basis of memorization as an individual feature of the memory of some pupils. Such individual differences were extensively studied in B. M. Teplov's laboratory by Borisova (1951, 1956*a*, 1956*b*). In her work, ninth and tenth graders were in some cases shown (for 3 sec) a tree leaf, which they then had to recognize from among ten different leaves shown consecutively. In other cases, the whole set of leaves was shown for 10 sec, and one of them had to be remembered so well that it could later be described in words so completely and exactly that another person could recognize it from this description among the other leaves; the description was then jointly evaluated by the experimenter and the subject.

The experiments have shown that some subjects recognized well and described poorly, others recognized poorly and described well, and still others either described and recognized well or did poorly in both tasks. The first signaling system was dominant in the first group and the second signaling system in the second, whereas in the third group the two signaling systems were in equilibrium.

Turpanov (1953, 1954) studied these individual differences by another method. He introduced fifth graders to geographic entities either by verbally describing them or by showing pictures of them to the pupils and then tested the pupils for the formation of concepts by asking them to describe these entities verbally and to draw pictures of them.

According to the source and method of the formation of concepts, the subjects could be divided into three groups. In some subjects, concepts formed best on a visual basis; they were characterized by concreteness and clarity and by memorization of striking, although superficial, characteristics of the objects, even details, with essential features often being overlooked. In others, concepts formed best on a verbal basis; in these pupils, the concepts usually corresponded only to what was essential in the entities. In still others, concepts formed best on the basis of simultaneous recourse to both visual and verbal materials and were characterized by the fullness, diversity, adequacy, and stability of their content.

With regard to the characteristics of reproduction, there were four groups: 1. Some subjects verbalized visual material easily and accurately, but found it difficult to convey verbal material in visual form; in these subjects, correct concepts were formed on a visual basis. 2. Other subjects easily conveyed verbal material in visual form, but found it difficult to verbalize visual material; in them, more-correct concepts were formed on a verbal basis. 3. Still others performed both tasks with equal ease; correct concepts formed in them upon either visual or verbal familiarization with the entities. 4. Finally, a fourth group had difficulty with both operations and needed simultaneous visual and verbal familiarization with the entities. It can be readily seen that all these groups are types that differ in the interrelation of the two signaling systems.

Among other problems pertaining to the interrelation of image memory and verbal memory, one must note the problem of changes in the images during forgetting and of the influence exerted in this case by verbal fixation of the similarity or difference of perceived objects on subsequent changes in the images of these objects. These problems have been studied by Solov'ev and by his collaborator Nudel'man.

Nudel'man (1940) showed pictures of objects (for 10 sec each) to normal, mentally retarded, and deaf children, after which the children had to make drawings of the objects (immediately and after 6 and 30 days). The experiments revealed that in normal schoolchildren the accuracy of reproduction is higher and decreases considerably less with time than is the case for mentally retarded or deaf children. Normal children make fewer additions and fewer significant changes in the shape of the objects. Most common in mentally retarded children is an "obliteration" of the specific features of the objects shown to them and their alteration in the direction of depicting common objects. In deaf children, on the contrary, stressing of the specific features of the objects was observed more often; this tendency was even more pronounced in normal schoolchildren, among whom obliteration of the distinctiveness of objects was observed only in a negligible number of cases.

In the next series of experiments, Nudel'man specifically examined the role of words in the preservation of images. Mentally retarded and deaf children were shown pictures of objects for memorization. Before the pictures were shown, certain characteristics of the objects were described in some cases, but not in others. In all cases, the subjects had to draw a picture of what they had perceived after being shown the picture of the object. The difference in the productivity of reproduction was very substantial: the amount reproduced increased under the influence of preceding explanation from 1.8% to 11.1% in mentally retarded children and from 9.5% to 33.4% in deaf children.

As has been shown by these and other experiments by the same investigator (Nudel'man, 1940, 1941, 1953), the frequency of likening to common objects (that is, obliteration of the distinctiveness of the given object) decreased considerably in the presence of verbal explanations (descriptions). If, however, the mentally retarded subjects were given only verbal descriptions unaccompanied by showing of the objects, likening to common objects was most intense.

Experiments by the same author, in which the subjects were shown several similar objects (four fish), revealed that, while normal schoolchildren on perceiving similar objects compared them with each other and distinguished what was peculiar and characteristic in each of them, mentally retarded children made no such comparison. It must be assumed that this is an important cause of the prevalence of obliteration (rather than stressing of the specific features of objects) observed when mentally retarded children reproduce objects from memory.

All these data are in good agreement with the results obtained by Solov'ev (1941), who also observed that concepts were altered primarily in the direction of increased emphasis on the distinctiveness of the objects by normal schoolchildren and in the direction of obliteration of this distinctiveness by mentally retarded ones. In another publication this author reported that the specificity of recognition of objects increases with age and is lower not only for small children, but also for mentally retarded children and children with brain damage. In one of his publications, Solov'ev (1940) notes the significance of comparing objects; e.g., in the absence of a thorough verbal description of the differences between objects, the influence of their initially noticed similarity increases. Moreover, the experiments demonstrated the favorable effect of verbal information about the characteristics of the objects (their similarities or the differences between them) given *prior to* memorization on their subsequent retention in memory—pointing out differences had the most favorable effect.

The retention of images of more complex content and the role of speech in such cases have been investigated by Basmanova (1954). She studied changes in the content of pictures of historical subjects shown to fourth, fifth, and sixth graders and later reproduced by them after various periods. Characteristic changes observed included loss of detail, combination, generalization, compression, greater dynamics, and an approach toward the subjects' personal experience. The role of speech in a number of the changes observed is shown.

It is apparent that the results of all the investigations of the interrelation of image memory and verbal memory, of image and word in the processes of memorization and reproduction, point to the indissoluble unity of the two types of memory, to the unity of the sensory (that pertaining to objects, the graphic, the concrete) and the verbal-logical and abstract in memorization and reproduction. This unity follows directly from the fundamental theoretical and cognitive positions of Soviet psychology and in its turn confirms that these premises are fully justified. At the same time, these investigations also reveal those specific interrelations of image memory and verbal memory that are present and are differently manifested in different cases (and at a different age) within this unity of the sensory and the logical. The unity spoken of does not by any means remain static throughout the entire course of development of the mind, but, on the contrary, gradually develops and consolidates with age and finds its expression in changing and diverse forms.

The dominant role of image memory steadily decreases with age and the difference between it and verbal memory lessens considerably in the older age groups without, however, disappearing completely.

BIBLIOGRAPHY

Baranov, T. P. (1940), "Memorization and recall of words in a foreign language," in: *Uchenye zapiski MGPIIYa. Eksperimental'naya fonetika i psikhologiya,* Vol. 1, Moscow.

Basmanova, Z. P. (1954), "Alteration of the visual concept of the meaningful content of a picture about a historical subject in 4th and 6th graders," *Uch. zap. kafedry psikhol. Leningrad. gos. pedagog. inst.,* Vol. 96.

Blonskii, P. P. (1935), *Memory and Thinking,* Moscow; [also in: *Selected Works in Psychology,* Moscow, Prosveshchenie, 1964].

Borisova, M. N. (1951), *On the Problem of Types of Higher Nervous Activity Characterized by the Interrelation of the First and Second Signaling Systems,* Candidate's Diss., Moscow.

Borisova, M. N. (1956*a*), "A method of determining the interrelation of the first and second signaling systems under conditions of visual memorization," in: *Tipologicheskie osobennosti vysshei nervnoi deyatel'nosti cheloveka,* B. M. Teplov, ed., Moscow, APN RSFSR, pp. 307–332.

Borisova, M. N. (1956*b*), "An investigation of phenomena of relative predominance of the first or the second signaling system under conditions of visual memorization," in: *Tipologicheskie osobennosti vysshei nervnoi deyatel'nosti cheloveka,* B. M. Teplov, ed., Moscow, APN RSFSR, pp. 333–347.

Dul'nev, G. M. (1948), "The reproduction of newly acquired words by auxiliary-school pupils," *Izv. Akad. pedagog. nauk RSFSR,* No. 19.

Faraponova, E. A. (1953), *Age Differences in the Recognition and Reproduction of Graphic and Verbal Material,* Candidate's Diss., Moscow.

Faraponova, E. A. (1958), "Age differences in the memorization of graphic and verbal material," in: *Voprosy psikhologii pamyati,* A. A. Smirnov, ed., APN RSFSR, Moscow.

Golubev, Ya. V. (1955), "Problems of the psychology of beginning study of a foreign language," *Uch. zap. Leningrad. gos. pedagog. inst.,* Vol. 112.

Kornienko, N. A. (1955), *Recognition and Reproduction of Graphic and Verbal Material by Preschool Children,* Candidate's Diss., Moscow.

Leont'ev, A. N. (1931), *Development of Memory,* Moscow, Uchpedgiz.

Leont'ev, A. N. (1959), *Developmental Problems of the Mind,* Moscow, APN RSFSR.

Lipkina, A. I. (1941), *Memorization and Reproduction of Geographical Material by Schoolchildren.* Candidate's Diss., Moscow.

Lipkina, A. I. (1958), "Reproduction and forgetting of concrete graphic and abstract course material," in: *Voprosy psikhologii pamyati,* A. A. Smirnov, ed., Moscow, APN RSFSR.

Mal'tseva, K. P. (1948), *Sense Connections in Schoolchildren during Memorization,* Candidate's Diss., Moscow, 1948.

Mal'tseva, K. P. (1958*a*), "Visual and verbal props during memorization in schoolchildren," in: *Voprosy psikhologii pamyati,* A. A. Smirnov, ed., Moscow, APN RSFSR.

Mal'tseva, K. P. (1958*b*), "A plan of the text as sense support for younger schoolchildren in memorizing," in: *Voprosy psikhologii pamyati,* A. A. Smirnov, ed., Moscow, APN RSFSR.

Novomeiskii, A. S. (1950), *Visual Memorization in Various Kinds of School Work,* Candidate's Diss., Moscow.

Novomeiskii, A. S. (1958), "The interrelation of image and word in memorization," in: *Voprosy psikhologii pamyati,* A. A. Smirnov, ed., Moscow, APN RSFSR.

Nudel'man, M. M. (1940), "On the alteration of visual images during forgetting in deaf and mentally retarded children," in: *Voprosy psikhologii glukhonemykh i umstvenno otstalykh detei,* L. V. Zankov and I. I. Danyushevskii, eds., Moscow, Uchpedgiz.

Nudel'man, M. M. (1941), "On the alteration of similar concepts in mentally retarded and deaf schoolchildren," in: *Voprosy vospitaniya i obucheniya glukhonemykh i umstvenno otstalykh detei,* I. I. Danyushevskii and L. V. Zankov, eds., Moscow.

Nudel'man, M. M. (1953), "Some characteristics of the concepts of pupils of auxiliary schools," in: *Osobennosti poznavatel'noi deyatel'nosti uchashchikhsya vspomogatel'noi shkoly,* I. M. Solov'ev, ed., Moscow.

Razmyslov, P. I. (1958), "Age and individual differences in the memorization of emotional image and abstract material," in: *Voprosy psikhologii pamyati,* A. A. Smirnov, ed., Moscow, APN RSFSR.

Solov'ev, I. M. (1940), "Alteration of concepts depending on similarity and difference of objects," *Uch. zap. Gos. inst. psikhol.,* Vol. 1.

Solov'ev, I. M. (1941), "Forgetting and its characteristics in mentally retarded children," in: *Voprosy vospitaniya i obucheniya glukhonemykh i umstvenno otstalykh detei,* I. I. Danyushevskii and L. V. Zankov, eds., Moscow.

Tarabrina, L. and I. Khokhlacheva (1955), "The importance of verbal designation of what is perceived," *Uch. zap. Leningrad. gos. pedagog. inst.*, Vol. 112.

Turpanov, A. N. (1953), *A Psychological Analysis of the Formation of Concepts in Fifth Graders with the Use of Material on Geography,* Candidate's Diss., Moscow.

Turpanov, A. N. (1954), "A psychological analysis of formation in the development of geographic concepts in schoolchildren," in: *Doklady na soveshchanii po psikhologii,* Moscow, APN RSFSR.

Zal'tsman, B. N. (1956*a*), "The role of speech in the development of free memory in children of preschool age," in: *Naukovo-doslidnyi instytut psykholohii, Naukovi zapysky,* Vol. 5 (in Ukrainian).

Zal'tsman, B. N. (1956*b*), "The role of speech in the development of free reconstruction in children of preschool age," in: *Naukovo-doslidnyi instytut psykholohii, Naukovi zapysky,* Vol. 6 (in Ukrainian).

ON SOME CORRELATIONS IN THE FIELD OF MEMORY

1. THE PROBLEM

The interrelation of psychological processes is one of the most important problems of psychology. Its significance is determined by one of the basic concepts of Marxist–Leninist philosophy concerning the general interrelationship of the phenomena of reality. There is no doubt that of greatest importance is the dependence of mental processes on the *external* causes which have evoked them. But there is also no doubt that the very important role of external effects, if correctly understood, presumes an interrelation of the mental processes themselves.

This interrelationship can appear in various forms such as, for instance, the *joint participation* or *presence* of various mental processes in some complex form of mental activity, e.g., participation of the thinking processes in memory or the participation of operative or long-term memory in human thinking activity or in perception. Also of interest is the *influence* which one mental process has on other mental processes, i.e., their *interaction*. Such, for example, is the influence of sensations (auditory, motor) on other sensations (on visual sensitivity) or the interrelation of the mental qualities or properties of the *personality*. The mutual influence of inclinations and talents and of temperament and character is a good example of the latter.

Aside from the two types of interrelation mentioned above, there is yet another, very important, one: the interrelation of the *development* of one facet of mental life with that of its other facets. And, depending on just how this development is examined, it may itself be broken down into several areas:

1. The interrelation of the mental processes with the qualities of the personality in their *ontogenetic development*. Sought after here is an understand-

ing of how the development of one mental process or personality trait is connected in the life of a child or adolescent with the development of some other facets of his mental activity or personality, how it influences them, how it is itself influenced by them, and how it depends on their development; such, for example, is the question of how the development of a child's thinking activity is reflected in the change of his other intellectual processes: perception, memory, or imagination.

2. Interrelations of the *reverse* development (*involution* or *pathological change*) of some mental processes, e.g., of the mental processes with the qualities of personality during mental changes occurring in old age, brain injury, or mental illness.

3. The influence of the *exercise* of some types of mental activity on other types, i.e., the investigation of the phenomena of *co-exercise* or *transfer of exercise*.

4. Finally, a rather special type of connection and a special method of investigation: the *correlation of the already achieved levels of development* of mental processes in the same individuals, finding out to what extent the existing level of development of some facet of mental activity or some mental property of the personality corresponds to the level of development of one of the other facets of the mind or to one of the other qualities of the personality. Such a correspondence is never complete in every respect, i.e., it never happens that everyone in whom a given type of mental activity is developed to a high degree reveals just as high a level of development of the other types of mental activity, and *vice versa*. In other words, it does not happen that *all* those on a relatively low level of development with respect to one type of activity will have the same low level of development of some of the other, comparable, types of mental activity. Here *probabilistic, stochastic* relations, quantitatively characterized by the *correlation coefficients* between the compared processes or qualities of the personality, are valid. *Correlation analysis* represents a special method, based on mathematical statistics, of studying the interrelation of the various types of mental activity and mental qualities of the personality. The investigations described in this section utilized correlation analysis and had as their aim the determination of the correlations valid for the *field of memory*.

In psychology, correlation analysis has been used in the study of the interrelation of a wide circle of processes and qualities of personality. A development of this method is so-called *factor analysis*, aimed at showing the "factors" which form the basis for correlating mental processes and qualities of the personality. There are many such investigations, but their results cause justified dissatisfaction because of the frequently observed psychological indefiniteness of the factors resulting from the analysis. Often these factors have a quite formal, even conventional, character; their specific psychological content is not revealed at all or is characterized in a very superficial and general way. The data of correlation analysis are also not satisfactory, since they usually amount only to the calculation (which often gives contradictory results) of correlation coefficients without any attempts to find out *what* causes these indexes.

As mentioned above, correlations are never total, one hundred percent; even quite reliable, positive ones are always within a rather wide zone, and this indicates that along with the many, often predominant, cases of coincidence of levels of development in the processes compared (showing positive correlation) there are also divergences of these levels. The psychological basis of both coincidence and divergence of the levels of development of the mental processes of correlation have not been extensively investigated. The *quantitative* determination of correlations has not been combined with the *qualitative, psychological* analysis of the processes compared and the qualities of personality. It has not been made clear to what extent the quantitative indexes are determined by the qualitative, meaningful characteristics of the correlated facets of mental life. Whether these quantitative indexes are invariable (or, more correctly, vary within relatively narrow limits), or whether they depend to a greater extent on some specific psychological conditions, on the specific content of the types of mental activity the correlation between which is under study, also has not yet been investigated.

The investigations described in this section were designed to combine quantitative correlation indexes with the qualitative characteristics of the types compared and the components of mental activity carried out by the subjects. Although the experiments conducted were on memory, and dealt with a very narrow area of the field, at that, the use of this procedure can be of a broad, fundamental significance. It is important for the discerning of the meaningful (not merely quantitative) characteristics of the correlations between mental phenomena, for the theoretical understanding of the data of correlation analysis, as well as for the basic methods of their study.

2. SCOPE AND RESULTS OF EXPERIMENTAL INVESTIGATIONS

This section deals with investigations conducted in recent years under our direction at the Institute of Psychology in the Academy of Pedagogic Sciences of the R.S.F.S.R. by Istomina, Samokhvalova, and Barkhatova. Correlations were studied between involuntary and voluntary memorization, between memorization under conditions of carrying out various types of activity (mnemonic and nonmnemonic), between memorizing various types of material, and between two important facets of memory (rapidity and stability). The subjects were adults and children. The first two problems—involuntary and voluntary memorization and memorization by carrying out various types of activity—were studied on preschool children (investigated by Istomina); the third problem—memorization of various types of material—on schoolchildren (second, fifth, and eighth graders) and on college students (investigated by Samokhvalova); the last problem—rapidity and stability of memorization—on preschool children (investigated by Istomina) and schoolchildren (investigated by Barkhatova). Each age group consisted of 30 subjects. The preschool children comprised four age groups, the schoolchildren in each of two studies three age groups, and the adults one group; altogether, there were 11 groups and 330 subjects.

The objects of memorization in the experiments with the schoolchildren and the adults were pictures (depicting single objects), series of individual words (concrete and abstract), series of numbers (two-digit and three-digit), and series of nonsense syllables. In addition, the schoolchildren were given series of single sentences and whole texts. In the experiments with college students, memorizing was brought to a faultless reproduction of each series (words, names, names of pictures, syllables); in the experiments with schoolchildren, the number of presentations of the material was limited, depending on the nature of the material. After each presentation of any material, its reproduction was required. After memorization of a whole series, questions were asked concerning the process of memorization at its various stages.

For preschool children, games, work-games, listening to stories, and experiments of the usual laboratory type were the kinds of activity during which memorization was carried out. During memorizing while playing (at "traveling") one of the children (a different child each time) was asked to remember names of the things which he had to take for his group from the instructor, who was in another room. At work-play (repairing children's toys), too, each of the children was asked to get from the kindergarten director a number of things which the group needed for work. The child had to remember the names of these things. In both cases the children had to immediately reproduce what had been named to them. In the experiments with listening to a story, one of the children was unexpectedly asked to reproduce the names of animals and birds which appeared in the story. In each of these cases the children had to remember ten names. The same number of individual words were used for memorization in the laboratory-type experiments (as above, the words were presented once, and immediate reproduction was demanded).

Before analyzing them, it should be emphasized that in these investigations we were not concerned with the *absolute* productivity of different types of memorization (e.g., involuntary or voluntary) or of the memorization of different types of material, with their comparison, or with finding out which types of memorization are more and which are less productive. This was the previous task (in the work of Zinchenko, in some of my publications, in earlier investigations of Istomina, and also in the work of many Soviet and non-Soviet scientists). Here we are dealing not with the comparative productivity of some types of mnemonic activity, but with the *conformity* or *non-conformity* of the levels of development of various types of memorization in the same individuals. In other words, it was necessary to determine whether a person who involuntarily remembers material well will memorize well similar material voluntarily and *vice versa*. It is quite immaterial which of the two types is more productive; more important is their *relative* level *in a given person as compared to their development in others*. The object of comparison is the place which a given person occupies, according to each type of memorization, in comparison with other persons. Is it approximately the same under various conditions or are there considerable divergences expressed, i.e., do many of those who in one type of memorization give good results (occupy a "good" place) occupy "bad" places in another type of memorization?

The main, most general, and most important result of the investigation is the finding of a great variability, lability, and dynamism of the correlations. The magnitude of correlations between the same types of memorization varied greatly depending on the age of the subject, the stage of memorizing the material, and the differences in the indexes of productivity of memorization (in particular in the indexes of retention).

Let us analyze first the *age* indexes and begin with correlations obtained in preschool children. The correlation coefficients between voluntary and involuntary memorization in the youngest (three and four years of age) were +0.67 and +0.69, respectively; in the older ones (five and six years of age) only +0.41 and +0.52. Consequently, with age (between four and five) there was a noticeable lowering of coefficients. Statistically, all these coefficients were significant.

In experiments with memorizing under conditions of carrying out various types of activity, the coefficients were calculated in pairs (between each two situations of memorization; 6 coefficients for each age group). All coefficients were positive: for the three- and four-year-olds the average magnitudes of the coefficients were +0.44 and +0.46. For the five- and six-year-olds they were, respectively, +0.32 and +0.34, i.e., this time also, the correlation was lower for the older than for the younger children.

Samokhvalova studied the correlation between memorizing various types of material in schoolchildren and adults. Since in these experiments the same material was presented and reproduced several times, the correlation was calculated from various reproductions separately, in particular from the data of the first reproduction (carried out after the first presentation of the material) and from the data of the third reproduction. The average values of the coefficients were +0.40 for the second grade, +0.21 for the fifth grade, and only +0.09 for the eighth grade, i.e., a sharp decrease throughout. According to the data of the third reproduction, the average values were somewhat different, namely: +0.58 for the second grade, +0.28 for the fifth grade, and +0.30 for the eighth grade. Only for the second grade can the coefficients be considered statistically reliable.

In the experiments with college students, the average, according to the data of the first reproduction, was +0.26 (for the eighth grade it was +0.09). According to the data of the third reproduction, the average of all coefficients for adults was +0.27, i.e., the same as for the fifth and the eighth grades (+0.28 and +0.30).

Comparing the data on correlations for schoolchildren with the coefficients obtained for adults, one can state that initially correlation between memorization of various types of material decreases with age, later it either increases somewhat or ceases to decrease. The coefficients obtained for older schoolchildren are statistically unreliable.

What are the results of experiments on the correlation of *rapidity* and *stability* of memorizing (experiments of Barkhatova)? For the description of stability, two kinds of indexes were used: the absolute amount of material reproduced after seven days, and the same amount taken with respect to what was reproduced at the end of memorization (i.e., the *percentage* of the reproduced material). This time, according to absolute data, the average values were +0.70 for the second grade and +0.70 for the fifth grade. Here there was no decrease. It must, however, be noted that in memorizing various types of material, nonidentical results were obtained: for memorizing numbers the correlation increased with age, while for memorizing words, sentences, or texts it decreased. According to relative indexes, the average values were +0.29 for the second grade and +0.25 for the fifth grade (again, essentially no decrease). However, for the eighth grade the correlation was again lower than for the two grades examined above; the average magnitudes of the coefficients were +0.53 and +0.07. Thus, this time also, there was a decrease of the correlation coefficients with age, though in all experiments only during transition from the fifth to the eighth grades, and in the experiments with words, sentences, or texts also in comparing the second and fifth grades.

In summing up the results of all three investigations, one can assert that during the preschool and school ages as a whole there is a decrease of the correlation between the various types and facets of memory; in adults one observes either a rise or, at least, a cessation of the decrease.

What does this conclusion mean? Not at all an increase or decrease with age of individual (interindividual) differences, i.e., not that the older preschoolers or the older schoolchildren differ more from each other than the younger ones; not at all that the older groups are more diverse than the younger ones. The correlation coefficients reveal the extent not of these *interindividual* but of the *intraindividual* differences, i.e., the difference in the degree of development in the same subjects of various facets or types of mental activity, in this case the frequency of coincidence or noncoincidence in *one and the same subject* of a high, average, or low level of development of various types and facets of memory.

How does one explain the age changes of these *intraindividual* differences? Why does the number of coincidences of productivity of various types and facets of memory change with age in the same individuals? Why does it decrease with age?

The answer to this is given by the data of qualitative analysis, i.e., the study of the actual activity of memorization carried out by subjects of various ages. These materials show the following: the higher coefficients were obtained when the mnemonic activity itself was more consistent. Thus, the younger preschoolers (especially the three-year-olds), more often than the older ones, revealed an *identical* behavior in involuntary and voluntary memorization and in both cases none of them used special ways of memorizing. The four-year-olds in voluntary memorization also showed features of behavior reminiscent of behavior in involuntary memorization. In the five- and six-year-olds a greater difference of behavior is noticed in voluntary memorization than was apparent in involuntary memorization and also a greater variety of behavior in the first case; this pertains also to the degree of activity, premeditation of memorization and reproduction, to the degree of development of these processes, and to the tendency to rely on some connections, i.e., to establish, even if only the simplest, logical correlations. It was the same for the six-year-olds. This difference in behavior of older children under various conditions of memorization was what determined the increase in the number of cases of noncoincidence in the productivity of memorization in both these situations. Children showing a *high* level of involuntary memorization when it was not possible to utilize any special mnemonic devices, often had a *low* level of voluntary memorization. This happened when they did not yet have (or had very little of) any of the mnemonic devices necessary for voluntary memorization. Conversely those who occupied in involuntary memorizing "middle" or "poor" places in rank could noticeably better their positions in voluntary memorization if they mastered some mnemonic device.

The same is true of the dynamics of the correlation coefficients for the experiments in which preschool children carried out *activities of various types*. In these experiments the coefficients were also higher, accompanied by a greater monotony of mnemonic activity in the same child in various situations of memorization. This monotony was more often noticed in the younger children, who usually memorized directly, without using any mnemonic methods, and rather passively. In the older preschool children this monotony was disrupted since they had already mastered some mnemonic devices in carrying out the various types of activity. This, then, is the reason for the increase in the number of cases of noncoincidence of places occupied by some of the older preschool children in various situations of memorization.

The same causes underlie the age changes of correlation coefficients noticed in schoolchildren. Second graders memorized varied material, as a rule, rather monotonously: they grouped several of the first members of the series, several of the last, or some consecutive, intermediate ones. Elements of meaningful grouping appeared only as separate little islands. The task of remembering is set, but no special devices for its realization are used. In essence, here, too, direct memorization is evidently caused by the greater volume and difficulty of the material, which demands more complex methods of memorization not yet mastered by the younger schoolchildren.

In the fifth grade, important shifts are noticed in the nature of mnemonic activity. The children make attempts to find more meaningful ways to memorize, going beyond the structure of the material. However, the active *reworking* of the material by fifth graders is as yet insufficient and is often applied only with respect to certain types of material: some children divide the material into those parts which allow the use of mnemonic methods and those which, supposedly, do not, but demand simple "cramming in." It is quite evident that all this serves as favorable ground for the increase in the number of divergences in the memorization levels for various kinds of material (memorized by the same children) and, consequently, for the lowering of the correlation coefficients which characterize their individual differences.

An increase in the diversity of ways of memorizing and an as yet insufficient level of their mastery and consequent limited use (for memorizing only certain kinds of material) was observed in the eighth graders also and causes a further lowering of the correlation coefficients for the memorizing of various types of material, i.e., an increase of intraindividual differences in memory.

A different picture is observed for college students: although the ways to memorize are to a certain extent more diverse than for eighth graders, applicability of mnemonic devices is wider for them (the devices are used over a broader range of materials); the level of mastery of these devices rises considerably, and, as a result, its dependence on the characteristics of the material decreases. This is favorable for the obliteration of the intraindividual differences noted in the subjects, for equalizing (in the same subject) the possibilities of retaining the same rank (among the other subjects) for the memorizing of various types of material, and this causes a certain rise in the correlation coefficients.

Similar relations between the quantitative indexes of correlations and qualitative characteristics of mnemonic processes are observed in the study of the changes of the correlation coefficients *at various stages of memorizing the same material.*

In one of the investigations by Samokhvalova (1962), conducted with college students, a difference was noticed between the correlation coefficients calculated from data on reproductions at different times. A very interesting phenomenon was revealed: during first reproduction all memorized materials fell into two groups: in one there were the materials easier to remember (pictures, words, two-digit numbers), in the other—the more difficult ones (three-digit numbers and nonsense syllables). The correlation coefficients of all materials of the first group, according to the data of the first reproduction, were rather high; but memorization of the second group did not correlate with memorization of the first group; the materials of the second group did not themselves correlate either. Important changes, however, occurred during the third reproduction and even more so in those following (to judge from the coefficients calculated from the total number of repetitions needed for complete memorization of each material). The correlation coefficients for memorizing materials of the second group with all the rest of the materials this time rose considerably (more than the correlation coefficients of the materials of the first group) and in the final analysis (from the data of the total number of repetitions) were of the same order of magnitude as the coefficients of the first group (all were positive and within the limits of the average values—from +0.40 to +0.60).

A rise in the correlation coefficients in subsequent reproductions as compared with the preceding ones was also noticed in schoolchildren.

How do the data of qualitative analysis of mnemonic activity of subjects correlate with these differences in the *quantitative* correlation coefficients? The verbal accounts of the subjects show that in memorizing *easier* material they used various methods facilitating memorization and recall at the first perception and reproduction of the material. But *difficult* material was at first either memorized without the use of any auxiliary modes or by the not-very-successful use of some method or other. However, as the process of memorization progressed, the utilization of these methods became more extensive. The differences in mnemonic activity for memorizing materials diverse in difficulty were, thus, gradually leveled off, causing a rise in the correlation between memorization of various types of material at its subsequent presentations (the more significant, the farther perception and reproduction of the material were removed from the beginning of memorization—from the first presentation). The dependence of the correlation between memorization of various types of material on the nature of the mnemonic activity was here, too, quite definite.

Quantitative correlation coefficients also depend, to an exceptional degree, on the *types of indexes of the productivity of memory* among which the correlation is determined (clearly shown in the experiments of Barkhatova). In studying the ratio of rapidity and stability of memorization, two kinds of indexes were used: the absolute quantity of the material reproduced after a delay and the percentage ratio to what had been memorized (before the delay).

The correlation coefficients between rapidity and stability of memorization calculated from both groups of data differed sharply: for second graders their average values (for all types of materials) were, respectively, 0.70 and 0.29, for fifth graders, 0.70 and 0.25, and for the eighth graders, 0.53 and 0.07.

These quantitative differences are based on definite *meaningful* relations. The comparatively high correlation coefficients calculated from the *absolute* indexes mean that after a delay (one week) those who memorized rapidly retained absolutely more than those who memorized poorly, but this advantage decreased sharply and became quite insignificant (and statistically unreliable) if the comparison was conducted on relative indexes. These relative indexes show that those who memorize well lose during the one-week delay a larger part of what they memorized than those who memorize poorly. And this means that forgetting in the former increases faster than in the latter, and the advantage of those memorizing well according to absolute indexes is due only to the fact that, as a whole, they memorized noticeably more than those memorizing poorly, and had consequently a larger reserve from which they could lose without as yet losing their superiority. But as soon as their forgetting accumulates more rapidly, this superiority can be lost and their reproductions with increase in delay may also by *absolute* indexes become less complete than those of the poorly memorizing subjects.

Depending on the length of the delay, the ratio between those who memorize rapidly and those who memorize slowly (according to the stability of retention in memory of what has been memorized) can "turn around"; the correlation coefficients of rapidity and stability can become negative (even if they are calculated from absolute data). This time they again reveal, consequently, a great variability and lability similar to what had been noted with respect to other facets of memory.

In summing up, the following must be emphasized: the interdependence of the various facets and types of memory, revealed by correlation analysis, is not stable: its quantitative expression changes, depending on the age of the subjects, on the stage of memorization, and on the conditions under which memorization and reproduction are carried out. Here a very important role as the basis of the variability (lability) of the correlations in memory is played by the characteristics of the mnemonic activity carried out by the subjects: the methods and means of memorization and reproduction. The acknowledgment of the whole significance of this does, of course, not at all exclude the role of the memory trace itself, the organic basis of memory, which quite possibly has a differentiated nature, which can also determine some *intra-individual* differences in the level of development of some facets or types of memory. However, the most important role of the content and the nature of the *activity* carried out in solving mnemonic tasks is convincingly and comprehensively demonstrated by the results of these investigations. Thereby one of the basic positions of Soviet psychology in the field of memory is once more confirmed: the dependence of the productivity of memorization on the characteristics of the mnemonic activity itself.

BIBLIOGRAPHY

Barkhatova, S. G. (1963), "On the interrelation of the speed and stability of memorization. Communication I," in: *Novye issledovaniya v pedagogicheskikh naukakh,* No. 1, Moscow.

Barkhatova, S. G. (1965*a*), "On the interrelation of the speed and stability of memorization. Communication II," in: *Novye issledovaniya v pedagogicheskikh naukakh,* No. 3, Moscow.

Barkhatova, S. G. (1965*b*), "On the interrelation of the speed and stability of memorization. Communication IV," in: *Novye issledovaniya v pedagogicheskikh naukakh,* No. 4, Moscow.

Istomina, Z. M. (1964), "Ontogenetic and individual differences in the interrelation of involuntary and voluntary memory in preschool children," in: *Novye issledovaniya v pedagogicheskikh naukakh,* No. 2, Moscow.

Istomina, Z. M. (1965*a*), "Ontogenetic and individual differences in the interrelation of levels of memorization in preschool children during the performance of different kinds of activity. Communication I," in: *Novye issledovaniya v pedagogicheskikh naukakh,* No. 4, Moscow.

Istomina, Z. M. (1965*b*), "Ontogenetic and individual differences in the interrelation of levels of memorization in preschool children during the performance of different kinds of activity. Communication II," in: *Novye issledovaniya v pedagogicheskikh naukakh,* No. 5, Moscow.

Samokhvalova, V. I. (1962) "Individual differences in the memorization of different kinds of material," *Vopr. psikhol.,* Vol. 8, No. 4.

Samokhvalova, V. I. (1965), "On the interrelation of the speed and stability of memorization. Communication III," in: *Novye issledovaniya v pedagogicheskikh naukakh,* No. 3, Moscow.

Smirnov, A. A. (ed.) (1958), *Problems of the Psychology of Memory,* Moscow, APN RSFSR.

SUMMARIES

A. THE PSYCHOLOGY OF MEMORIZATION

1. In this section we describe experiments conducted in our laboratory on the basis of the following propositions: (a) memory processes, as all psychological processes, reflect objective reality; this reflection of the world around us is active in character; people cognize reality while themselves acting upon the world that surrounds them, remaking this world; cognition is always part of some activity; unity of cognition and activity is one of the basic precepts of Soviet psychology; (b) cognition is not only part of the activity, but itself is a complex activity of a special type; we always perform certain work in the process of cognition, though our actions may be only of an internal, intellectual character.

2. Proceeding from this proposition, two major problems are dealt with in this section: (a) the relationship between memorizing and the activity in the course of which it takes place and (b) the characterization of memorizing as a special type of psychological activity.

3. The first problem required us to study the dependence between two kinds of activity: (a) mnemonic activity or memorizing and (b) nonmnemonic activity, i.e., activity which does not require any memorizing effort when one is engaged in some task. The object of study thus was voluntary memorizing in the first case and involuntary (incidental) memorizing in the second. Varieties of both cases have been thoroughly studied.

4. Volutary memorizing was studied when subjects were performing the following tasks: (a) with or without special request, memorizing the material offered (coherent intelligent text) as fully as possible; (b) reproducing it word for word by heart or in their own words (accuracy of memorizing); (c) memorizing the time sequence of the material; (d) memorizing the material in order to preserve it in memory for a long time. The experiments revealed

qualititative differences in the memorizing processes, depending on the above-listed tasks. On this basis, age differences of the quantitative indices (showing the effect these tasks have on the productivity of the process of memorizing) could be explained.

5. Involuntary (incidental) memorizing was also studied in various kinds of activity. Two series of experiments helped to reveal what was memorized in the first place in performing tasks in a natural environment when the subject was not asked to memorize anything connected with these tasks. In one series the subjects were (quite unexpectedly) asked to recall all they had seen, heard, and thought that day on their way from home to their place of work. In the other they were asked to recollect everything they remembered after a meeting at which a scientific report had been presented and discussed. In both cases a sharply defined determining role of the purpose of the activity (practical in the first case, i.e., to arrive at work on time; and cognitive in the second) was revealed in the memorizing process.

We also investigated the relationship between involuntary memorizing and the degree of the subject's intellectual activity in performing a particular task.

6. A series of experiments was devoted to studying the interrelation of voluntary and involuntary memorizing. The first experiment was always conducted under the same conditions: the subject was given material to read in order to memorize it. The second experiment was carried out on analogous material under the pretext of some nonmnemonic activity, i.e., the subject was not asked to memorize the material. These activities included writing down dictated words, free associations, logical associations, pointing out spelling mistakes, and "true or false" evaluation of statements. The subjects were both children and adults. Considerable differences became apparent in the relation between these two kinds of memorizing in various experiments and at various ages, depending on the degree of activity of the subject in performing the given task, which in its turn was determined by the degree of difficulty of the task for the given category of subjects.

7. All experiments with voluntary and involuntary memorizing convincingly proved the determining role of the activity which led to memorizing, and made it possible to explain its influence more concretely.

8. In studying characteristics of memorizing as a special kind of activity, major attention was paid to analyzing thinking processes which take place during voluntary memorizing of verbal material. In this section we discuss problems characterizing the relationship between memorizing and understanding: the positive role of understanding is stressed not only in adults but also in preschool children, a new explanation is presented for the mechanical memorizing often observed in schoolchildren, the qualitative rearrangement of the memorized material conditioned by its comprehension is analyzed,

the "illusion of memorizing," i.e., instances when memorizing is replaced by understanding, is discussed, and the possibility of different influences of the task of memorizing material on its understanding is elucidated.

9. Considerable attention is given to the characteristics of the thinking processes (thinking activity) in memorizing: (a) grouping of memorized material by meaning; (b) determination of meaningful supports; (c) comparison of the material being memorized with already familiar material and comparison of various parts of the new material with each other. Detailed characteristics are given of the variants of all these processes and their dependence on different conditions: on memorizing tasks and on the stages of learning. Individual and age differences and special features of the usage of means and methods of memorizing were studied.

10. In connection with the characteristics of memorizing as a special kind of activity, we paid particular attention to the changes which take place in this activity when the material is given to the subject for the second time to memorize. The experiments have shown considerable age differences in the degree of variations of repetitions in memorizing: stereotyped and patterned at an early age and more consciously and purposefully regulated variations in the older age groups.

B. CONDITIONS FOR RETROACTIVE INHIBITION

1. This section describes the results of research on factors involved in conditions of retroactive inhibition of memory. The significance of these factors is evaluated differently by various theories dealing with this phenomenon: (a) the perserverance theory, attaching particular importance to the difficulty of the activity which immediately follows the memorizing process and produces an inhibiting effect on the retention of the learned material in one's memory, and (b) the transfer theory, according to which the similarity of the preceding and the subsequent activities plays an important role in retroactive inhibition.

2. We compared in our experiments the effects produced by each of these conditions, while varying the degree of similarity of the two activities (the preceding one and the subsequent one) and the difficulty of the subsequent activity. All the experiments were conducted with the same subjects.

3. As a result of our experiments, the following has been revealed: (a) Retroactive inhibition may be caused either by the similarity of the subsequent activity to the preceding activity or by the difficulty of the subsequent activity. (b) There are considerable individual differences between subjects both in regard to the presence or absence of retroactive inhibition and in regard to the degree of inhibition if it took place.

C. THE INTERRELATION OF IMAGE AND WORD IN THE DEVELOPMENT OF MEMORY

1. Comparative studies of memorizing object-image and word material conducted on pupils of various ages and on adults have shown that the capacity for memorizing this material steadily increases with age. With greater age, however, the capacity for memorizing abstract word material increases more rapidly than that for memorizing visual material which is hard to verbalize. In general the ability of memorizing both abstract and concrete word material improves far better with age than the ability of memorizing visual material (whether it can be verbalized easily or with difficulty). The advantage of memorizing visual material better than word material observed at an early school age becomes less prominent with increasing age, and the difference in memorizing the two kinds of material gradually diminishes.

2. Similar changes with age have been noted in comparable memorizing of two kinds of text: emotional and figurative on the one hand and of abstract character on the other. Considerable differences have been noted when the capacities for memorizing these texts by students with various levels of achievement were compared (small differences between good and poor students in memorizing emotional and figurative texts and great differences in memorizing texts of abstract content).

3. Considerable differences have been revealed in memorizing different school study material (particularly, in keeping it in memory for a number of years). Experiments have demonstrated that, as a rule, memorizing of both concrete and abstract school study material depends on the place it occupies in the given subject matter and also on the connection between the two kinds of material (escpecially of abstract propositions and concrete data).

4. Comparable study of visual and word materials as aids for memorizing has revealed that memorizing is more productive both in children and adults when visual aids are used; with increasing age, however, the effectiveness of verbal aids to memorizing increases; therefore, the difference in aid rendered by these two types of support decreases with age. It has also been found that memorizing with the help of aids which were invented by the subjects themselves is far more productive than that with the help of ready-made aids offered by the experimenter.

5. Considerable dependence of the use of images as aids for memorizing word material on the degree of definition of the tasks given to the subject has been determined in one of the experiments. When a very general task was given (for instance, simply to memorize the material), the images reflected mostly details, whereas if the subject was told that he would later have to reproduce the text he had read in written form or to construct an outline of

the text, the images covered the entire content of the text or at least its major sections. When instructed to memorize the text word for word, the subject failed to produce images altogether. Significant age and individual differences have been revealed in the use of images, depending on the mnemonic task set before the subject.

D. ON SOME CORRELATIONS IN THE FIELD OF MEMORY

1. This section presents the results of researches conducted under the guidance of the author on the problem of correlations between various kinds and aspects of memory. Correlations were studied between involuntary and voluntary memorizing, between memorizing in the course of different activities (games, work-games, listening to stories), and between the speed of memorizing and the persistence of memory. The experiments were conducted with preschoolers, schoolchildren, and adults, who were offered word material (word series, isolated sentences, meaningful texts) and also pictures and numbers to memorize.

2. The experiments showed that the interdependence of the various aspects and types of memory, as revealed by correlation analysis, is not stable. Its quantitative expression changes depending on the age of the subject, the stage of memorization, and also the indices used to characterize memory productivity (for instance, absolute or relative indices of memory persistence). It has been shown that with age the correlation coefficients first decrease (in preschool, elementary, and highschool children), but later (beginning with the last years of school and particularly in adults) begin to increase or at least cease to decrease.

3. Qualitative analysis of the processes of memorizing has shown that the characteristics of the mnemonic activity of the subjects, the methods and means of memorization, play a decisive role in the variability of the correlations. When these characteristics are similar, the correlation coefficients are much higher than when they are not. Uniformity of mnemonic activity (in one and the same subject for various mnemonic tasks) is achieved either by steady immediate memorizing or by mastering the use of advanced, intermediary methods of memorizing, which depend on the age of the subject, the stage of memorization, and other conditions which determined the variability of the coefficients. On the whole, the quantitative indices of correlation turned out to be dependent on the qualitative features of the memorizing process and were largely determined by them. One of the basic precepts of Soviet psychology, that of the determining role of human activity in psychological processes, has thus found further confirmation.

INDEX